About the Author

Professor Edmund O'Sullivan is coordinator of the Transformative Learning Centre at the Ontario Institute for Studies on Education (OISE) of the University of Toronto. From 1983 to 1992 he was Professor of Applied Psychology at OISE. He is the author of numerous books including: *Critical Psychology and Pedagogy* (Bergin and Garvey, 1990); *Critical Psychology: An Interpretation of the Personal World* (Plenum Press, 1984) and (with D. P. Ausubel and W. Ives) *Theories and Problems of Child Development* (Grune and Stratton, various editions). He has also contributed a large number of chapters to various volumes, as well articles in scholarly journals.

Critical Reception of this Book

One of the most far-reaching, compelling books on education and educational reform that I have read in a decade. *Henry A. Giroux, Waterbury Chair Professor, Penn State University*

A very powerful book on profoundly important concerns which should be read by all those who are interested in human and planetary survival. *David Purpel, author of The Moral and Spiritual Crisis in Education: A Curriculum for Justice and Compassion in Education*

This ambitious and imaginative book addresses the reform of education in new terms. Where most contemporary 'reforms' are really about how to make education cheaper, O'Sullivan focusses on how to make it more relevant to the tremendous problems of global society and personal change in the new millenium. *Professor R W Connell, University of Sydney; author of Making the Difference*

As an anti-racist educator, I find O'Sullivan's reading of race, difference and power very useful. Transformative Learning requires that we deal with the cancer of racism at its multifarious levels: social, spiritual, environmental, economic and political. *George Sefa Dei, author of Anti-Racist Education: Theory and Practice*

In this visionary book Edmund O'Sullivan poses a major challenge to educators today to acknowledge and support in their work the boundless beauty and creativity of the planet and our place in it. *Angela Miles, author, Integrative Feminisms: Building Global Visions, and co-founder, Woman for a Just and Healthy Planet*

A beautifully written book. What O'Sullivan envisages is a true globalisation — for humanity, and for life itself. *Johan Galtung, Professor of Peace Studies and Director of Transcend: A Peace and Development Network*

Ed O'Sullivan presents, shares, articulates from a heart-formed mind. His book is destined to travel far. People of all races will want to thank him. *Dr Joe Couture, Cree Healer and former Director, Native Studies Programme, Trent University, Canada.*

A deeply felt and thrillingly insightful articulation of a cosmology for educational sustainability. *David Selby, author of Global Teacher/Global Learner and Reconnections: From National to Global Curriculum*

A sweeping, provocative challenge to all citizens and educators. Read it! *Professor Michael R. Welton, author of In the Defense of the Life World: Critical Perspectives on Adult Learning*

A powerful ecological vision for education ... [which] provides a way for it to develop whole human beings in the context of a sustainable planetary environment. *John Miller, author of The Holistic Curriculum*

Edmund O'Sullivan reveals the moral and spiritual atrophies resulting from the current dominant development model. His book will serve as an inspiration and will bring hope to the next generation. *José Zarate, a Quechua from Peru and Canadian Development Coordinator, Primate's World Relief Development Fund, The Anglican Church of Canada*

In this eye-opening book, O'Sullivan presents a new conception of planetary consciousness relevant to education and oriented to community and the natural world. *Professor Ching Miao, Beijing Academy of Social Sciences*

This book has a scope and depth which makes it of value far beyond the confines of educationalists. It is a truly integrative study which challenges us to relocate the roots of many of the critical issues facing humanity today. *Colin Craig, Director, The Corrymeela Community, Northern Ireland*

Professor O'Sullivan transcends a provincial 'northern', perspective and creates a vision of universal application. *Professor Abelardo Brenes, University of Costa Rica and the United Nations University for Peace*

Sullivan's bold imaginings are potentially the generative principles of educational reforms for the next millennium. Against the destructive reality of what he labels the biocide of competitive industrial globalisation, he proffers a rich and imaginative alternative vision for education. *Ciaran Sugrue, Professor of Curriculum, St.Patricks, Dublin*

O'Sullivan moves past the cliches of globalization and consumer culture and draws a graphic picture of a divided globe in ecological and social peril. He then proposes a convincing critical and holistic education as an essential strategy if we are to survive as a species. *Richard Swift, New Internationalist*

An invaluable companion for researchers and practitioners in education. His book brings an integrated approach to social transformation and educational reform. *Thomas Mark Turay, Director, Caritas Makeni, Sierra Leone*

A sweeping analysis of transformative learning on a planetary scale. This book captures the dilemmas, struggles and potential for new educational visions. *Michael Fullen, author of The New Meaning of Educational Change and Change Forces*

A text of rare discernment in a time of turbulent change. His admirable grasp of complexity makes him both a sure guide and an innovative educator. *Stephen G. Dunn, Director, Elliott Allen Institute for Theology and Ecology, Toronto, Canada*

Transformative Learning

Educational Vision for the 21st Century

Edmund O'Sullivan
foreword by Thomas Berry

An OISE/UT book
published in association with
University of Toronto Press
TORONTO

Zed Books
LONDON • NEW YORK

Transformative Learning: Educational Vision for the 21st Century was first published by Zed Books Ltd, 7 Cynthia Street, London N1 9JF, UK and Room 400, 175 Fifth Avenue, New York, NY 10010, USA in 1999.

Published in Canada by the University of Toronto Press Incorporated in 1999.

Distributed exclusively in the USA by St Martin's Press, Inc., 175 Fifth Avenue, New York, NY 10010, USA.

Cover designed by Andrew Corbett
Set in Monotype Dante by Ewan Smith
Printed and bound in Malaysia

A catalogue record for this book is available from the British Library

Library of Congress Cataloging-in-Publication Data
O'Sullivan, Edmund, 1938–
 Transformative learning : educational vision for the 21st century / Edmund O'Sullivan.
  p. cm.
  Includes bibliographical references.
  ISBN 1-85649-698-8. – ISBN 1-85649-699-6 (pbk.)
  1. Critical pedagogy. 2. Environmentalism. 3. Education––Economic aspects. 4. Postmodernism and education. I. Title.
  LC196.07 1999
  370.11'5–dc21   99-17550
                                                              CIP

Canadian Cataloguing in Publication Data
O'Sullivan, Edmund, 1938–
 Transformative learning : educational vision for the 21st century
Includes bibliographical references and index.
ISBN 0-8020-8309-9

1. Critical pedagogy. 2. Environmentalism. 3. Education—Economic aspects. 4. Postmodernism and education. I. Title.
LC196.078 1999   370.11'5   C99-930732-0

ISBN 1 85649 698 8 cased
ISBN 1 85649 699 6 limp
Canadian ISBN 0 8020 8309 9

Contents

Acknowledgements

I would like to acknowledge the following people who have been of both assistance and support in the writing of this manuscript. The book was written over a period of eight years so I have had numerous opportunities to use pre-publication versions of this work in my graduate seminars. I wish to thank the many students who have shared their ideas with me in theses matters over the years.

I would also like to thank my colleague Budd Hall who used my manuscript in one of his seminars and gave me valuable feedback and early encouragement. I thank him also for connecting me to my publisher Robert Molteno at Zed Books, an editor with substance. To my friend Tom Lyons, former Director of the Ontario Teachers' Federation Project on Teaching for a Global Perspective, a note of gratitude for his early work with me on issues around 'globalization'.

To Dorothy Golden Rosenberg for her early reading of the manuscript and encouraging me to tackle head-on issues around gender in a global perspective. To Lisa Lipsett, for her wonderful help on the reorganization of the final chapters and a clarity on what was necessary in the Prologue. Finally, to Luciana Ricciutelli, her final editing of this manuscript was magnificent.

And then there is Thomas Berry. He has been an elder, mentor and close friend. We had numerous personal discussions on this work and he generously shared with me all of his pre-publication manuscripts of *The Universe Story* that he co-authored with Brian Swimme. Their ideas figure prominently in the final chapters of this book. Thomas has been generous to a fault and he has also written the Foreword.

I must also acknowledge the great sadness that enveloped my life in the early development of this manuscript. On Monday 22 August 1993, Thomas Berry came to my wife, Pat's, deathbed and said last prayers with her. She passed away on Tuesday 23 August 1993. I learned in the years of her illness how utterly precious life is and how utterly precious she was to both me and my children Jeremy, Meara, and Damian.

Finally, I would like to express how joy has re-entered my life. I dedicate this book to Eimear O'Neill. Her feminist consciousness and Celtic ways have deeply informed this book

Edmund O'Sullivan, Toronto

Foreword

Thomas Berry

A meaningful vision for education in the twenty-first century. That is the challenge to educators in these transitional years before us. This book by Edmund O'Sullivan presents his response to this issue. It is the result of a lifetime dedicated to presenting a meaningful vision for education in the twenty-first century. We have taught the sciences, the humanities, the arts, religion, economics, law and politics along with the social ideals and technical aspects of contemporary life, but always there seems to be something missing.

The missing element is the relation of humans to the other-than-human components of the world that we live in. Something is not functioning properly since the multitude of living beings around us seem to be dying out. If we are educating for a world that is extinguishing so many living forms then we need to rethink the deeper forces at work in our educational programs. We cannot live simply with ourselves. Our inner world is a response to the outer world. Without the wonder and majesty and beauty of the outer world we have no developed inner world. As all those living beings around us perish, then we perish within. In a sense we lose our souls. We lose our imagination, our emotional range, we even lose our intellectual development. We cannot survive in our human order of being without the entire range of natural phenomena that surround us. One of the most foolish phrases ever invented is the phrase extolling ourselves for 'conquering' nature. One of the most perverse objectives of education has been to train students to 'conquer' the world about them.

The proposal of Dr O'Sullivan is that the primary concern of our western civilization in these times should be to move away from our ideal of 'conquest' of the earth to the ideal of 'community' with the earth. We have, in a sense, conquered the earth. Yet we find ourselves in possession of a damaged planet. We have diminished the source of our well-being. This is a critical moment not only in western civilization and in the global human community; it is a critical moment in the geo-biological story of the planet itself. In the view of competent biologists, nothing on the present scale of extinctions in the bio-systems of the planet has occurred for the past 65 million years in earth history.

In this situation we need to consider the form and purpose of education all the way from kindergarten to professional school. If, in the medieval period, theology with its heavenly concerns was the unifying concern of education; and if in the centuries since then the humanities, the sciences and economics, all with their focus on human development, have provided the education that has brought us to our present situation; then cosmology, the well-being of the earth and the well-being of the human within the earth community, must be the central concern of education for the future.

We must finally learn that it is only in the outer world of nature, with its wonder and beauty and all its numinous qualities, that the inner world of the human can be fulfilled. We came into being amidst all this splendour; only with this splendour can either our souls or our bodies be properly nourished. Education must become a way of sustaining this grandeur, not of extinguishing it.

Edmund O'Sullivan sees quite clearly that while we will need a new way of living, we need even more urgently a new way of thinking. We will need both to live with and to enjoy the energies and the beauty of the natural world. We need to know the universe story, how the universe came to be from its primordial flaring forth to the present. We need to know the story of how the earth and the continents came to be, all this along with our own human story. We need to live both with the energy and the wonder of the sun and the wind, the rivers and the waves, and with the immense number of plants that grow up from the soil; also with all those attractive and frightening animals that wander through the woodlands. We must restore the dignity and grandeur of a disintegrating natural world, Never has this been more urgent. A new century, a new millennium is opening up before ourselves and our children. It will be, we hope, a period when humans will be present to the planet in a mutually enhancing manner.

Such is the purpose of this book. It is a book concerned with the basic immensely significant vision that must guide us into the future, for when we are confronted with change at this order of magnitude, the ordinary processes of reasoning are insufficient. Although reasoning is needed, a vision is even more urgent; and vision does not come from reasoning. The shock of the situation must force us out of one context of thinking into another. This intuition, or what is referred to here as 'dream' or as 'vision', might also be thought of as coming to us from the unconscious depths of the human, from the realm that is revealed to us in our dreams. For although this context of education that is being proposed here is quite compatible with our western traditions, it forces these traditions into a new context of understanding, a primordial context that existed with indigenous peoples of the world, a context wherein they experienced themselves as members of a great family of the universe with all its components. In referring to this comprehensive context, indigenous peoples would use the intimate expression, 'All my relations'.

There is reason to believe that the world about us is ultimately a universe with feeling qualities. As Henri Frankfort, the mid-eastern archaeologist, indicated in his book, *Before Philosophy*: 'The fundamental difference between the attitudes of modern and ancient man as regards the surrounding world is this: for modern, scientific man the phenomenal world is primarily an "It"; for ancient – and also for primitive – man it is a "Thou".' This attitude has, of course, long been set aside by the modern scientific world. We are at the present time confronted anew with a consideration of what was gained and what was lost when this intimacy between the human and the surrounding world was abandoned.

When we lost our esteem for the natural world the earth became endangered in all its manifestations. The earth became a commodity, a collection of items to be bought and sold. Its nobility, its sublime, its sacred dimension was lost. The esteem of the human community disappeared. The reverence felt for the awesome qualities of nature dissolved in a world of mechanism. Only the crass measure of commercial worth determined the value of anything.

Such is the world that we have lived in. Once money values became the basic measure of worth, then the planet became subject to abuse not only in its natural phenomena, in its mountains and rivers, its coastlands and its seas, but in all its life systems; for life, even at the level of plants and the various animals, is a function of soul. Life requires something beyond mechanism, something beyond commercial worth; life requires inspiration and presence and beauty and caring and community. This should be obvious even to the most simplistic mind.

There is, we might say, a new consciousness taking shape throughout the world, the consciousness of a new age when humans would be present to the earth in a mutually enhancing manner. To share in this consciousness is, it seems, the only way to participate effectively in a future worthy of the children who come after us. If we have only a damaged planet to give them, we can at least give them a planet that is recovering its soul. We can give them a vision in which they will discover their individual selves in intimate communion with their Great Self in the beauty and wonder and numinous presence in the Universe around them. We can provide the outlines of an education programme that will guide them and their children into an age when they will renew our human celebrations with the celebrations of dawn and evening, the celebrations when the stars come out in the night sky, the seasonal celebrations when the springtime flowers bloom once again in the meadows that surround our homes.

The author here, as few people that I know, has identified the university as the place where the thinking and the vision meet, for 'without vision the people perish'. The vision in this instance must, for the first time in modern western civilization, be the vision of a universe integral with itself throughout its vast extent in space and its long sequence of transformations in time. Every being within the universe is universe-referent as regards its reality and value. The universe is the primary university. The human university is that context wherein the universe reflects on and communicates itself to the larger human community. So too the Earth, within the universe, is integral with itself and is the immediate referent as regards reality and value for every mode of being on the Earth.

Every profession and occupation of humans must establish itself within the integral functioning of the planet. The earth is the primary teacher in economics, in medicine, in law, in religion. Earth is the primary educator. Ecology is not a part of economics. Economics is an extension of ecology. Human Economy is a sub-system of the Earth Economy. So too all the other professions and occupations. Ecology is not within law. Law is an extension of ecology. So with religion. Religion is an expression of ecology. Ecology is not primarily a teaching of religion. So with medicine. Ecology is not within medicine. Medicine has its foundations in ecology. There cannot be well humans on a sick planet. Ecology is less a subject for education than the context of education. When we began to assert a human priority over the natural world we forgot where we came from; we forgot that we and all our institutions of learning are primarily in a learning position in reference to the larger world about us.

This globalization is something different from and adverse to the global-ization fostered by the industrial, commercial and financial powers of our contemporary world. Economic globalization, the culmination of these past centuries of economic development, is entering its final predatory phase. For the demands being made on the planet are far beyond what the planet can give. This globalization that manifests itself in a plundering economy is obviously a momentary achievement that can only collapse in the years ahead. Such an economy is ordered to arbitrary human demand rather than to earth possibilities. The belief has been that the knowledge and ingenuity activated in university departments and research institutes can increase the capacities of the planet without limit. Only in some vague manner is there recognition that rivers and soil and seeds, forests and seas, have limits that the most competent science cannot extend indefinitely.

What is proposed here is that there is another globalization, the globaliza-tion that recognizes the local bio-regions, and also the inherent value of each individual component of the earth community. This globalization expresses the intimate relation of the various components of the earth community with each other. The inherent value of each being and each bio-region is recognized, supported and enhanced by the other components of the community. The full wonder of the universe finds expression in the individuals and also in their mutual association. While humans have their distinctive role within this larger community, their own human well-being can be attained only within the well-being of the larger community. The human is fulfilled in the earth. The earth is expressed in the human. For humans to advance themselves at the expense of the community is to bring ruin upon both.

As soon as the university experiences itself within this context of meaning, the university will have recovered its vision of what it should be in the twenty-first century. The various schools and departments will spontaneously reshape themselves within this world of wonder and the gorgeous celebration of existence such as has not been known since the years when the universities of western civilization first came into being: celebration that finds expression in the colourful robes and the magisterial music of our annual commencement day processions.

For Eimear

and in loving memory
of my sister, Frances

. . . .

The Dream Drives the Action

We humans all over this planet, who have the privilege of witnessing a new century, are descendants of a magnificent history. For good or for ill, in our own times, we are the recipients of the legacy of 'modernity'. In our own times, the peoples of the earth are being nudged or pushed into something that is being called 'post-modernity'. There is a transformation taking place that is both exciting and fearful. But what is modernity and what is meant by a transformation into post-modernity? In his wonderfully provocative book, *A Brief History of Everything*, Ken Wilber gives us a working definition that resonates with my own understanding of modernity and post-modernity:

> The rise of modernity – and by 'modernity' I mean specifically the rational-industrial world view, and roughly the Enlightenment in general – served many useful and extraordinary purposes. We might mention: the rise of democracy; the banishing of slavery; the emergence of liberal feminism; the differentiation of art and science and morality; the widespread emergence of empirical sciences, including the systems sciences and ecological sciences, an increase in average life span of almost three decades, the introduction of relativity and perspectivism in art and morals and science; the move from ethnocentric to worldcentric; and in general the undoing of dominator social hierarchies in numerous and significant ways. (Wilber 1996: 69)

Acknowledging this side of modernity, we must also acknowledge the shadow side of its historical trajectory. One of the main theses of this book is that modernity, with all of its excellences and wonders, has reached the full fruition of its limitations. I believe we are living in the terminal stages of modern history and that we are experiencing the full force of the limitations of the rational–industrial mode which is now self-cancelling. We should not even think that it would be desirable to negate the historical forces of modernism. We are in need of an evolutionary transformation that transcends the forces of modernism and includes them at the same time. Wilber captures the sense of this transformative moment:

> But in some ways, rationality and industry, left to their own devices, have

become cancers in the body politic, runaway growths that are malignant in their effects. They overstep their limits, overrun their functions, and drift into various dominator hierarchies of one sort or another. To transcend modernity is to negate or limit these overpowering facets, while including their benign and beneficial aspects. The coming transformation will transcend and include these features of modernity, incorporating their essentials and limiting their powers (Wilber 1996: 70)

At the outset of this work, I would like to dramatize my position on the current forces of transnational economic globalization. I believe that in their present form they represent the most destructive and malignant forces of modernism. They are hydra-headed dominator hierarchies gone wild. The central overriding thesis that moves within the work you are about to read is that the fundamental educational task of our times is to make the choice for a sustainable planetary habitat of interdependent life forms over and against the dysfunctional calling of the global competitive marketplace. This work shares a point of view that is a rising tide with people and communities all over this globe (Mander and Goldsmith 1996). This emergent vision of life deeply challenges the economic globalization moving like a juggernaut in our world as we approach the new century. In Anthony Giddens' (1990) terms, the juggernaut crushes those who resist it, while frequently following a steady path, then veering away erratically in directions that cannot be foreseen. In assessing the modern world in their book *Our Ecological Footprint*, Wackernagel and Rees make the following observation about the forces of globalization:

> It seems that in today's world, urbanization, globalization and trade combine to reduce corrective feedback on local populations. With access to global resources, urban populations everywhere are seemingly immune to the consequences of locally unsustainable land and resource management practices – at least for a few decades. In effect, modernization alienates us spatially and psychologically from the land. The citizens of the industrial world suffer from a collective ecological blindness that reduces their collective sense of 'connectedness' to the ecosystems that are sustaining them. (Wackernagel and Rees 1996: 132)

This choice for what I would label an ecozoic vision can also be called a *transformative* perspective because it posits a radical restructuring of all current educational directions. To move towards a planetary education it will be necessary to have a functional cosmology that is in line with the vision of where this education will be leading us. We are at another vast turning point and we are in need of a cosmological story that can carry the weight of a planetary consciousness to where we know must move. We are living in a watershed period comparable to the major shift that took place from the medieval into the modern world. Drawing from the work of Thomas Berry

(1988), I refer to this postmodern period as the ecozoic period. The educational framework appropriate for this movement must be visionary and transformative and must clearly go beyond the conventional educational outlooks that we have cultivated for the last several centuries.

A full planetary consciousness opens us up into the awesome vision of a world that energizes our imagination well beyond a marketplace vision. Our planet is a shared dream experience. This is a final aspect of our ideas on ethical imperatives. There is much discussion of the evolutionary process and the direction of its unfolding. There is a groping aspect to this process which is neither random nor directed but creative. One of the most appropriate ways of describing this process seems to be that of dream realization. Thomas Berry (1988), reflecting on his own awe of the universe, is struck by what seems to be the fulfilment of something so highly imaginative and so overwhelming that he ventures it must have been dreamed into existence. I caution the reader at the outset not to equate my use of the word *dream* as indicative of 'the unreal', 'the symbolic' or simply a process of the 'unconscious mind'. In the many talks that we had together, Thomas Berry was trying to develop the notion that we are not motivated and energized at the level of ideas but by the deeper recesses of dream structures. He used a phrase that he attributed to Carl Jung: *the dream drives the action*. Few things are accomplished in human affairs except under the type of entrancement that can be associated with dream experience. The Christian dream created our western civilization in its medieval period. The great cultures of the world emerge not out of rational processes but out of revelatory experiences that occur in dreams or which have many of the qualities of dream experience. Only in this condition, it seems, do the more profound spontaneities of our pre-conscious genetic coding emerge in their full power and splendour.

If the dream is creative, we must also recognize that few things are as destructive as a dream or entrancement that has lost the integrity of its meaning and entered into an exaggerated and destructive manifestation. This has happened often enough with political ideologies and with religious visionaries, but there is no dream or entrancement in the history of the earth that has wrought the destruction that is taking place in the entrancement with industrial civilization. Such entrancement must be considered as a profound cultural pathology. It can be dealt with only in terms of a correspondingly deep cultural therapy.

Contemporary education lacks a comprehensive cosmology. This is one of the central ideas that I will be developing in this book. When education has drawn from the sciences, its attention has been directed to the social sciences as distinguished from the natural sciences. In most cases, educational theory and practice has borrowed from the sciences of psychology, sociology and, to a lesser extent, anthropology. What is totally lacking in modern educational theory is a comprehensive and integrated perspective that has in the past been identified as a cosmology. Thus, contemporary educational theory and practice carry with it the same blinders that have plagued modern scientific specialization coming out of the post-Newtonian period. To be sure, modern western educational thought has attempted to identify itself with humanism, but it has done so without providing a renewal of an acceptable cosmology. What I am working towards in this book is an articulation and presentation of a cosmology that can be functionally effective in providing a basis for an educational programme that would engender an ecologically sustainable vision of society in the broadest terms; what can be called a planetary vision. It is a vision that is painfully absent in our present circumstances. In his incredible work *The Spell of the Sensuous,* David Abram draws our attention to this vacuum of vision:

> Clearly, something is terribly missing, some essential ingredient has been neglected, some necessary aspect of life has been dangerously overlooked, set aside, or simply forgotten in the rush toward a common world. In order to obtain the astonishing and unifying image of the whole earth whirling in the darkness of space, humans, it would seem, have had to relinquish something just as valuable – the humility and grace that comes from being fully a part of that whirling world. We have forgotten the poise that comes from living in storied relation and reciprocity with the myriad things, the myriad *beings*, that perceptually surround us … If we do not soon remember ourselves to our sensuous surroundings, if we do not reclaim our solidarity with the other sensibilities that inhabit and constitute those surroundings, then the cost of our human commonality may be our common extinction. (Abram 1996: 270–71)

The reader should be apprised from the outset of my understanding of the notion of transformative learning which appears in the title of this work. I will start with the notion of transformation within a broad cultural context.

When any cultural manifestation is at its zenith, the educational and learning tasks are uncontested and the culture is of one mind about what is ultimately important. There is, during these periods, a kind of optimism and verve that ours is the best of all possible worlds and we should continue what we are doing. It is also usual to have a clear sense of purpose about what education and learning should be. There is also a predominant feeling that we should continue in the same direction that has taken us to this point. Here one can say that a culture is in 'full form' and the form of the culture warrants 'continuity'. We might say that a context that has this clear sense of purpose or direction is 'formatively appropriate'. A culture is 'formatively appropriate' when it attempts to replicate itself within this context and the educational and learning institutions are in synchronicity with the dominant cultural themes.

Even when a culture is 'formatively appropriate', there are times when there seems to be a loss of purpose or a loss of the qualities and features that are particular to that culture. Part of the public discourse, during times such as these, is one of 'reform criticism'. Reform criticism is a language that calls a culture to task for its loss of purpose. It is a criticism that calls itself back to its original heritage. This is a criticism that accepts the underlying heritage of the culture and seeks to put the culture, as it were, 'back on track'. When reform criticism is directed towards educational institutions we call this 'educational reform'.

There is another type of criticism that is radically different from reform criticism which calls into question the fundamental mythos of the dominant cultural form and indicates that the culture can no longer viably maintain its continuity and vision. This criticism maintains that the culture is no longer 'formatively appropriate' and in the application of this criticism there is a questioning of all of the dominant culture's educational visions of continuity. We refer to this type of criticism as 'transformative criticism'. In contrast to reformative criticism, 'transformative criticism' suggests a radical restructuring of the dominant culture and a fundamental rupture with the past.

I would suggest that transformative criticism has three simultaneous moments. The first moment I have already described as the critique of the dominant culture's 'formative appropriateness'. The second is a vision of what an alternative to the dominant form might look like. The third moment is some concrete indications of the ways a culture could abandon those aspects of its present forms that are 'functionally inappropriate' while, at the same time, pointing to some directions of how it can be part of a process of change that will create a new cultural form that is more 'functionally appropriate'.

I would say that all of the moments above, in their totality, can be called a 'transformative moment'. It is a historical moment of moving between visions. It is not the case that historical moments and their labelling go uncontested. Many would say that we are not at a transitional moment in our present historical situation as I am maintaining. Truly, we seem to be living in a time of ferment. For example, there is incredible cultural hyperactivity directing us towards the 'global competitive marketplace'. Both in Canada and the United States we have witnessed this in the decade of the 1980s. Currently, in the 1990s, the educational systems in our northern hemisphere have been the object of educational reform that is, in essence, a massively conservative endeavour. Aronowitz and Giroux (1993: 1) give us a graphic summation of this moment in their description of education in a US context: 'During these years, the meaning and purpose of schooling at all levels of education were refashioned around the principles of the marketplace and the logic of rampant individualism. Ideologically, this meant abstracting schools from the language of democracy and equity while simultaneously organizing educational reform around the discourse of choice, reprivatization, and individual competition.'

In this most recent version of 'conservative reform', there is little questioning of the 'functional appropriateness' of the dominant vision of the global marketplace in virtually any of its aspects. When there is criticism within these quarters, it is a criticism that is completely at home with the dominant cultural form that seeks a further extension of what has been in place since the beginning of the twentieth century – the dominance of the market. The educational reforms suggested in this venue continue to encourage us to tool up our educational institutions from the nation-state market to the transnational marketplace.

To embark upon a discussion of a transformative vision of education, it must be kept clearly in mind that it will involve a diversity of elements and movements in contemporary education. At this point in our treatment I will try to indicate some of the contemporary educational currents that must be part of an emergent vision of transformative-ecozoic education. To a certain extent these trends are operating somewhat separately and independent of one another. Since we are in a transitional period, in which there are many contesting viewpoints, it is important to name some of those elements that are potentially moving towards what I am calling a more integral transformative vision. I would then like to couch these elements within a broad cosmological framework which I believe will be my major contribution to the effort of offering an alternative to our present conventions in education.

My use of the term 'transformation' is both rigorous and complex. Because I am espousing an ambitious cosmological perspective, I want it understood that my use of the term transformation is not Utopian or new age from which I distance myself strenuously. All this planet seems to be yearning for is some profound and deeply needed changes that appear to be at an order of magnitude that we have not experienced heretofore. Those changes will offer many new and wonderful possibilities but we must understand that these changes will bring with them their own unique problems and, whether we like it or not, their own brutal limitations. As Ken Wilber (1996: 70) pens it: 'It will defuse some of the problems of rational-industrialization, which is wonderful, but it will create and unleash its own severe difficulties ... And so, if *this* is specifically what we mean by a coming transformation – as opposed to some wild utopian new age – then yes, I believe this transformation is definitely underway.'

We are beginning to understand that we are living in a period of the earth's history that is incredibly turbulent and in an epoch in which there are violent processes of change that challenge us at every level imaginable. The responsibility of the human today is that we are totally caught up in this incredible transformation and we have a most significant influence on the direction it will take. The terror here is that we have it within our power to make life extinct on this planet. Because of the magnitude of this responsibility for the planet, all our educational ventures must finally be judged within this order of magnitude. This is the challenge for all areas of education. For education, this realization is the bottom line. What do I mean here by bottom line? For me, the bottom line is that every educational endeavour must keep in mind the magnitude of our present moment when setting educational priorities. This demands a kind of attentiveness to our present planetary situation that does not go into slumber or denial. This poses momentous challenges to educators in areas heretofore unimagined. Education within the context of 'transformative vision' keeps concerns for the planet always at the forefront.

The wisdom of all our current educational ventures in the late twentieth century serves the needs of our present dysfunctional industrial system. Our present educational institutions which are in line with and feeding into industrialism, nationalism, competitive transnationalism, individualism and patriarchy must be fundamentally called into question. All of these elements coalesce into a world view that exacerbates the crisis we are now facing. There is no creativity here because there is no viewpoint or consciousness which sees the need for new directions. It is a very strong indictment to say that our conventional educational institutions are defunct and bereft of under-standing in responding to our present planetary crisis. In addition, a strong case can be made that our received educational wisdom suffers from what I identify as the 'loss of the cosmological sense'. Somehow this cosmological sense is lost or downgraded in our educational discourse. In truth, something was gained and we are now just coming to understand that something was lost. We are not here talking about shallow changes in fashion. We are talking about a major revolution in our view of the world that came with the paradigm of modernism.

A second consideration that I wish to bring before the reader is a certain mindfulness concerning my location as an author. By the world's standards I am located in the 'lap of privilege'. My treatment will have the necessary limitations that the present author brings to the interpretation, that is that I am white, western, male and, as of late, a downwardly mobile member of the North American middle-class. These have been my historical horizons of interpretation but my own location within them has been self-critical and self-conscious. Nevertheless, *caveat emptor*. My treatment will also interpret these structures of race, class and gender within the context of ecological concerns. A relevant quote from Susan Griffin will give the reader some anticipation of the overall sense of this location of privilege:

The awareness grows that something is terribly wrong with the practices of

European culture that have led both to human suffering and environmental disaster. Patterns of destruction which are neither random or accidental have arisen from a consciousness that fragments existence. The problem is philosophical. Not the dry, seemingly irrelevant, obscure or academic subject known by the name of philosophy. But philosophy as a structure of the mind that shapes all our days, all our perceptions. Within this particular culture to which I was born, a European culture transplanted to North America, and which has grown into an oddly ephemeral kind of giant, an electronic behemoth, busily feeding on the world, the prevailing habit of mind for over two thousand years, is to consider human existence and above all human consciousness and spirit as independent from and above nature, still dominates the public imagination, even now withering the very source of our own sustenance. And although the shape of social systems, or the shape of gender, the fear of homosexuality, the argument for abortion, or what Edward Said calls the hierarchies of race, the prevalence of violence, the idea of technological progress, the problem of failing economies have been understood separately from the ecological issues, they are all part of the same philosophical attitude which presently threatens the survival of life on earth. (S. Griffin 1995: 29)

What can the reader expect from this text? What I hope is that it will invite the reader to enter into a deep cultural and personal reflection on educational paradigms that are operating at the deeper levels of consciousness as we move into the twenty-first century. When I use the term 'paradigm' it is not to be understood as a strictly intellectual framework. In this work, paradigm brings with it the idea of 'world view' which must be understood at the intellectual, emotional, moral and spiritual levels. This work will examine the deeper recesses of consciousness that move all our current living at all levels of our social institutions and with a specific attention to the educational institutions.

The work breaks into three interrelated sections that are not to be understood in a preferred sequence even though the sections occur in a sequential order. These sections were suggested to me by the cultural historian Thomas Berry in our personal discussions together over the last seven years. In one of our conversations he said that we must educate to survive, critique and create. As we talked about these terms, I realized that they were important frames for the work that I was about to begin on a planetary educational vision. The meaning of these terms will become clear as the reader proceeds in this work.

Finally, I want the reader of this work to understand in advance what this work will not do. It will not give specific prescriptions or practices for education. Although the reader will encounter numerous examples of educational directions in every chapter of this work, they are only my own specific examples. I do not pretend, even for one moment, that I have the scope and range of all the particularities of my readers. The particular educational praxis that may be appropriate for you, dear reader, may come as a revelation to me. I feel that the specificity of contexts demands the specific creativity of the people or communities who live and work and educate in those contexts. What I hope to leave readers with is a generative vision that will challenge their own creativity in the specific educational context of their own work.

One final suggestion that the reader may find helpful. When I was writing the Epilogue, it became clear that what I was saying in it was the implicit guiding force of the whole work. It might be helpful in appreciating the guiding spirit of this book to read the Epilogue in tandem with this Prologue.

PART ONE
· · · · · · · ·
Survive

CHAPTER I

Education in a Period of Historical Decline

The basic dimensions of human prospect are survival and transformation or, to put it in conventional language, peace and development, and the two dimensions, are inextricably intertwined. The contemporary human condition is characterized by recession on both dimensions, and the vision of an integral unified human future based on bonds of solidarity and shared destiny is dimmer than ever. (Kothari 1988: 20)

As the twentieth century draws to a close, we must write an obituary for the great god Progress. We are living in the last days of the myth of unlimited growth and technoutopia, and the religion of the Mall ... Understandably, we are reluctant to give up our habit of over-consumption and our blind optimism. But the time has come for ego death and the long journey of transformation. (Keen 1994: 13–14)

Finding our place in history at the millennial turning point

We are in the terminal decade of the twentieth century and we are in anticipation of the millennial turning point which brings us into the twenty-first century. There are great expectations and equally great premonitions. Since this is a book that ultimately deals with the broad topic of education, I would say that the initial task for the contemporary educator is to 'find our place in history' before we decide what education is going to be. If there was ever a time in recent history where the understanding of historical context was necessary for doing education, our historical moment is certainly that time. All this needs explanation and elaboration, and this will be one of the initial tasks of our introductory work. The ideas on education that will be developed in this book are very much dependent on this time in which we are living. So we turn to the question, what time is it?

My first attempt at answering this question is to indicate the importance of the terminal decade of this twentieth century. We will shortly call ourselves creatures of the twenty-first century. Just by being the terminal decade of the twentieth century makes these final years important to posterity just as the terminal decade of the nineteenth century was for people entering into the twentieth century. There is a Chinese saying that is considered both a curse and a blessing: 'may you live in interesting times.' In the terminal decade of the twentieth century, we are certainly living in interesting and turbulent times. In this decade, we no longer have the luxury of the optimism of the previous decades. We are living in a period that appears to be the end of something of the order of magnitude that we do not yet fully realize.

My first way of establishing the importance of our own final decade is by going back to the final decade of the nineteenth century as a point of comparison and frame of reference. The focus will centre on life in North America and specifically on the reflections of American cultural historian Henry Adams. In the work entitled *The Education of Henry Adams* (1931 [1918]), one finds a series of reflective essays. The essay entitled 'The Dynamo and the Virgin' will occupy us here. In this essay, Adams reflects on our culture's entry into the twentieth century by making some comparisons with some of the achievements of the medieval world. He is interested in the locus of energy and dynamism which inspires a culture's creativity. Adams uses the figure of the Blessed Virgin as the focal point of the creativity of the medieval world synthesis. This energy inspired such monuments of that period as Le Mont St Michel and the cathedral of Chartres. Henry Adams, who was a nostalgic medievalist, compares these monuments to one of the symbols that would occupy the century that was coming into being – the 'Dynamo', which was being exhibited at the World's Fair at this time. The 'Dynamo' represented the perpetual motion machine; a machine that was expected to operate without entropy or shutdown. It reflected the desire to have industrial production round the clock. Adams also reflected on the cultural ethos at the beginning of the twentieth century and observed that it was extremely optimistic; one witnessed incredible faith in human powers which was absent in the medieval world synthesis. Coming into our century, there was a deep and abiding faith in the human intellect, technology and the powers of modern science. Thus, where western culture is concerned, there was an incredible belief and optimism in the forward movement of history. The idea of progress became pre-eminent and human enhancement seemed virtually assured by the powers of the intellect allied with the technology of the machine. There was a sense of great expectations.

Now let us look again at the terminal decade of the twentieth century. In contrast to the grand optimism of the terminal decade of the nineteenth century, we are living in a decade of conflicting voices and visions. There are optimists and pessimists. It is being called the age of the 'new global economic' order. These are voices of the transnational businesses (Barnet and Cavanagh 1994). From these voices we hear the necessity of competing in the marketplace of this new global world. We are encouraged to move into this world at a rapid pace and to do so competitively. There is no doubt that there is a new global economic order being created by the multinational businesses.

In contrast to this optimism, voices of stark pessimism are also being heard at this time. Robert D. Kaplan (1994), in a much discussed article in the *Atlantic Monthly*, looks at our decade and sees the 'coming of anarchy'. He uses the term anarchy in an extremely pejorative sense. He tries to demonstrate in his article how scarcity, crime, overpopulation, tribalism and disease are rapidly destroying the social fabric of the planet. A similar type of pessimism is expressed by Bill McKibben (1989) whose work is focused more on ecological disaster. The title of his book is *The End of Nature*. After reading the book you will not be surprised by its ominous title.

In looking at these conflicting scenarios Paul Kennedy, in his book *Preparing for the Twenty-First Century*, takes stock:

> Many earlier attempts to peer into the future concluded either in a tone of unrestrained optimism, or gloomy forebodings, (or in Toynbee's case) in appeals for spiritual renewal. Perhaps this work should finish on such a note. Yet the fact remains that simply because we do not know the future, it is impossible to say with certainty whether global trends will lead to terrible disasters or be diverted by astonishing advances in human adaptation. What is clear is that as the cold war fades away, we face not a 'new world order' but a troubled fractured planet whose problems deserve the serious attention of politicians and publics alike. (Kennedy 1993: 349)

Thus, a sober appraisal of our terminal decade leads to no facile conclusions for the future. The Chinese character *ji* is the symbol for both danger and opportunity. We live in a moment of challenging ambiguity.

Lester R. Brown, Director of the Worldwatch Institute in Washington, in his Foreword to the *1990 Worldwatch Institute Report* refers to the last decade of the twentieth century as the 'turnaround decade'. The turnaround refers to a radical reorientation to all aspects of our dealings with the environment that must take place in this decade if we are to avoid irreversible damage to the carrying capacities of the earth as the matrix of all plant and animal life.

As an educator, I would say that it is important to assess the accuracy and truthfulness of these conflicting voices and to find our place in history at this moment of time. Western thinking traditionally has involved the separation of natural history from human cultural history. Our major historical traditions are anthropocentric in the extreme. We have dwelt on human history outside the context of earth history. Culturally, we have a very limited cosmological sense (Berman 1981; Toulmin 1985). Even worse, when we look at our con-temporary popular culture's sense of time-span, we see a world that puts history on the junk heap in a matter of days or weeks. The world of 'planned obsolescence' makes history both meaningless and trivial. The computer on which I write this manuscript was considered obsolete within weeks of my purchasing it. This says a lot more about my culture than it says about my computer since it shows how a limited historical time-span will not serve us well in the times in which we are living.

Truly, we live in a momentous time of survival and we are in desperate need of a broad historical system of interpretation to grasp our present situation. Although we cannot predict the future, we must nevertheless make educated guesses about where our present state of affairs is leading. In this work, I will do just that. One point of reference to be considered is that of the distinguished cultural historian and ecologist Thomas Berry. In a conversation with him he spoke of our present moment in history as a 'terminal state' and also as a 'moment of grace'. In moments of grace we take danger and turn it into opportunity. In moments of grace we take decadence and turn it into creativity. Berry (1988) speaks of our present historical moment in a story context. In the present we are living between stories. He suggests that in order to survive our moment we must be prepared to take a journey into a new creative story. Berry maintains that our present cultural story, exemplified in the technical–industrial values of western eurocentric culture, is now dysfunctional in its larger social dimensions even though we continue to believe in it firmly and act according to its guidance. He insists that we are in pressing need of a radical reassessment of our present situation, especially concerning those basic values that give life some satisfactory meaning. We are in need of an integral story that will educate us, a story that will heal, guide and discipline us. The transition between stories will be referred to in the text as the movement from the 'terminal cenozoic' to the 'ecozoic'. This will be a major development of ideas in this book and it will provide the grounding for a vision of education that I will be referring to as 'transformative-ecozoic education'.

The transition between the terminal cenozoic and the emergent ecozoic periods

Webster's Dictionary gives us a sense of the ambiguity of the verb *to survive*. 'Survive' basically has a French etymology from the verb *vivre* (to live). Survive connotes a sense of how to live in a time of death, disaster or an ending of times. As we think of survival we must be acutely aware of the scope and magnitude of the context in which survival strategies are taking place. I have used the verb 'to survive' rather than the noun or adjective because my treatment will be dynamic and action-oriented even when it is being descriptive. The dynamics of survival that are developed in this chapter are formulated within the historical interpretation of the terminal cenozoic already alluded to in my introductory remarks on a terminal phase of history. The assumptions that are operating in our present historical treatment is that we are living in a profound transitional phase of history that stretches from the planetary scale to the human scale (the terminal cenozoic period). I will divide my treatment into three catagories which are interrelated even though I am treating them as separate for the moment. The three catagories of survival are planetary, community and personal.

Planetary survival In the terminal decade of the twentieth century there are numerous interpretations concerning our historical moment. Probably the most prominent and glamorized interpretation is that we are entering a global marketplace which transcends all previous power constellations; the most prominent being the nation-state. The process of globalization, which is a planetary vision based on trade and marketing, is a movement into a trans-national world view based solely on commerce. The world that is propounded under the globalization vision proceeds in a continuous manner and seems totally blind to what it appears to be doing to the infrastructures of the earth as commerce proceeds. This is a vision that will be constantly contested throughout this book. My own interpretation proceeds with the view that our present historical direction, under a vision of planetary globalization, is a morbid process that is toxic to the earth and all its inhabitants. Education that will be premised on this world view will be dysfunctional from the perspective in which this book will operate.

We are moving into a global–planetary consciousness through processes that involve terror as well as attraction (Swimme and Berry 1992). It is what Swimme and Berry call a transitional period bringing to an end a broad period of earth history that they label the 'cenozoic' and an emergence into a new period of earth history that they label the 'ecozoic'.

Signs of terror surround us today on a global scale. Global warming, ozone depletion, toxic wastes and the sundry other items of ecological morbidity prevent us from slipping back into nation-state postures that foster the movement of globalization. Our attempts at education will certainly have to be framed either to deny the terror or to deal with the incredible dangers that we are facing on this planet. In a recent publication of the Worldwatch Institute, published 1992, Sandra Postel in the introduction gives us a sense of this magnitude:

Before August 1991, few people imagined that changes so monumental could happen virtually overnight. In a remarkable series of events, the Soviet brand of communism crumbled irreparably, relegating the cold war to history. As striking and swift as these changes were, the remainder of this decade must give rise to transformations even more profound and pervasive if we are to hold on to realistic hopes for a better world. At issue is humanity's badly damaged relationship with its earthly home, and the urgency of repairing it before more lasting and tragic harm is done. (Postel 1992: 3)

For better or worse, the 1990s will be a decisive decade for the planet and its inhabitants. Faced with the magnitude of this change, we seem prone to states of denial covering the severity of the terror of our present historical moment. Terror may also generate a need to question the 'wasteworld' of a nation-state consciousness that is moving into economic globalization and its commodity-laden world order of ecological devastation. There are many tensions within the terror of our present moment. As citizens and educators alike, we live with these tensions in the backround.

In spite of the fact that there are regional differences across this planet that would indicate there are differences in responsibility for our present planetary concerns, we nevertheless know that there are vast problems facing this planet as a whole. For the past decade, Lester R. Brown (1988; 1996) and his colleagues at the Worldwatch Institute have been annually cataloguing the vital signs of our planet's health. The vital signs as catalogued in the *1988 Worldwatch Institute Report* are simultaneously revealing and ominous. If we take the indicator forest cover, we see the tropical forests are shrinking by 11 million hectares per year; 31 million hectares in industrial countries are damaged due to acid rain and air pollution. Taking the indicator topsoil on cropland there is an estimated 26 billion tons lost annually in excess of new soil formation. Using desert area as an indicator, we are coming to understand that there is an estimated 6 million hectares of new desert formed annually by land mismanagement. Our lakes tell us another story of earth desecration. Because of promiscuous industrial use, thousands of lakes in the industrial north are now biologically dead and thousands more are dying. Fresh water is another important planetary indicator of our earth's vitality. Underground water tables are falling in parts of Africa, China, India and North America as demand for water rises above amplifier recharge rates. The vital indicator of species diversity tells an astounding story. Extinction of plant and animal species together are now estimated at several thousand per year; one-fifth of all species may disappear over the next twenty years. Water quality is a major vital sign indicator over this globe affecting human populations differentially in the various regions of our earth. Today, with the exception of China, well over half of all the citizens in the majority world* do not have access to plentiful clean water supplies. The cost to human health is enormous. In one

* In this work I depart from the conventions of the first, second and third worlds by using the terms majority world and minority world. Minority world is what was formerly the first world, named so in the present context because of its much smaller numbers of peoples and population. Majority world is what was called the third world and is named so because of the larger numbers of peoples within it as well as population size.

way or another, water is implicated in multiple health problems from trachoma blindness, malaria, schistosomiais, elephantiasis, typhoid, cholera, infectious hepatitis, leprosy, yellow fever and, worst of all, diarrhoea. Dirty water is believed to be the principal transmission agent for at least 80 per cent of diseases that afflict the majority world. Even though the northern majority world has much safer water facilities, some fifty pesticides contaminate groundwater in thirty-two American cities; some 2,500 US toxic waste sites need cleaning up. Climate is also a vital sign indicator. Mean temperature is projected to rise between 1.5 and 4.5 degrees Celsius between now and 2050. Here we come up against what the experts call the greenhouse effect. Carbon dioxide is one of the most important gases in the atmosphere. When the sun's energy strikes the earth's atmosphere, much of it bounces back into space. But some is absorbed by carbon dioxide, warming the surface of our globe through what is commonly called the greenhouse effect. Carbon dioxide levels in the atmosphere have increased about 30 per cent from 1850 to 1980 and are projected to leap a further 75 per cent by 2060. All this seems to imply that these rising temperature changes will probably accompany a dramatic change in agricultural productivity for the worse, and the rise in sea levels will eventually lead to global flooding. Sea levels are projected to rise between 1.4m and 2.2m by 2100. The most recent findings as of 1995 show that global temperature has reached 15.39 degrees Celsius, breaking the previous mark of 15.38 in 1990. Finally, the upper earth atmosphere indicates numerous growing holes in the earth's ozone layer suggesting gradual global depletion could be starting and escalating risks of skin cancer on a level never before experienced (L. Brown 1988; 1996).

All of these facts and figures have been catalogued over the past decade. The educational challenge is how to bring ourselves to a sustained level of consciousness concerning these problems and to hold this consciousness at the forefront of our cultural minds. This is a difficult enterprise because we are constantly inundated with information that is not integral for a composed consciousness. We must also recognize that we have not been educated towards a planetary consciousness. Education throughout the twentieth century has been cast in a nation-state consciousness. We now see a movement beyond the nation-state, but it is not towards that of a planetary consciousness. Rather, what we have seen is a new constellation of commitments towards a transnational marketplace that goes under the rubric of globalization. This thrust towards a global consumer marketplace operates in complete denial of our planetary peril. In 1995, this global economy grew by an estimated 3.7 per cent; this is considered an impressive expansion by conventional economic standards. What is not considered in this increase of goods and services on the global scale is that it has also increased the unsustainable demands on the natural systems and resources: crop-lands, aquifers, fisheries, rangelands and forests (L. Brown, 1988; 1996). I shall be making the point in many places throughout this work that we are living in a period of contested visions. I shall also attempt to show that it is our educational task to make a conscious choice towards the vision that we will follow. The vision and dream that I will pursue are that of a transformative planetary education. We will need a much more expanded sense of literacy that can best be labelled 'earth literacy' or 'ecological literacy' (Orr 1992). This will be a major challenge for educators.

We must embed the task of earth literacy within many contexts. Even though our planet is an integral totality existing within the wonder of a larger universe, it also has the colouring of differentiated communities. One of those communities is the human community. This is the second context that we shall consider.

Human survival What happens at the planetary level of the earth community has profound implications for the human community. It is also accurate to say that what happens at the level of the human community has equally profound implications for the earth community. With all other species considered on this earth, it is essential to understand that, by far and away, the human community occupies a crucial role in both our own survival and the survival and integrity of the earth community as a totality. Brian Swimme and Thomas Berry make it very clear as to how our human presence operates on the earth at present:

> It is already clear that in the future the Earth will function differently than it has functioned in the past. In the future the entire complex of life systems of the planet will be influenced by the human in a comprehensive manner. If the emergence of the Cenozoic in all its brilliance was independent of any human influence, almost every phase of the Ecozoic will involve the human. While the human cannot make a blade of grass, there is liable not to be a blade of grass unless it is accepted, protected, and fostered by the human. (Swimme and Berry 1992)

Understanding how important the human presence is in terms of planetary survival, it is extremely important to comprehend and evaluate the differential responsibility of certain segments of the earth community in relation to our present situation. This brings us to the importance of looking at the whole issue of marginality in the context of hemispheric northern privilege. We are increasingly becoming aware of an escalating marginal underclass in the northern hemisphere. We know that homelessness is becoming epidemic in some of the large urban areas of the North. We also can conclude that marginality has class, race and gender specifications. In almost any survey of poverty and underclass in a North American context, we see that poverty and marginality predominate within lower social class designations, within groups labelled 'people of colour' and women. Thus, even within the northern hemisphere, it can be stated that there is a 'Third world in the midst of the First' (Mitter 1986). There is no doubt that the structural conditions of the emergent global economy generate marginality on a global scale. Swasti Mitter (1986) gives us a specific picture of the ironies of the global marketplace. She points out that given the rapid changes in technology and market demand in many industries, it can be easier and more cost-effective for large corporations to have facilities in areas which are not too distant from the centres of consumption and final use. This is especially so now that a sufficient reserve of cheap labour among the unemployed people of the West can assure an effective check on potential wage increases.

All of the previous considerations demand a certain nuanced understanding of how to look at the idea of hemispheric privilege. Nevertheless, we are still left with incredibly damaging statistics on the role of the North in its contribution to our global ecological crisis. Caveats taken into consideration, it is still warranted to venture a radical reassessment of the lifestyle of consumption that is prevalent in our minority world.

We must also make a differential assessment of the impact of globalization on different peoples and places. There are incredible disparities of negative impacts on the diverse peoples in our contemporary world. Serge Latouche (1993) provides us with an extensive critique on what he calls the 'grand society'. He defines the 'grand society' as the western market-oriented ideal of modernity and consumption put forward as the highest stage of human civilization. He argues that we are now experiencing, in what I am labelling the survival mode, the shipwreck of both the idea and the practices of the grand society. His position is that the shipwreck is producing ever larger and growing groups of 'castaways'. In the affluent countries in the North, not only does economic development produce ever-larger numbers of maladjusted people, but now also contributes to a rising new poor, rejects from schools, the homeless, the chronically unemployed, the de-institutionalized, and so on. There are estimates of well beyond 100 million such rich country 'castaways' (Latouche 1993).

The most devastating impacts coming from the globalization of the world economies are visited on indigenous peoples. These are diverse groups of people in all parts of our globe, numbering about 250 million at present (Burger 1990). Typically, they are descendants of the original inhabitants of an area taken over by more powerful outsiders. They are distinct from their country's dominant group in language, culture or religion. Most of them have a custodial concept of land and other resources, in part defining themselves in relation to the habitat from which they draw their livelihood. They commonly live in or maintain strong ties to a subsistence economy, and many are, or are descendants of, hunter-gatherers, fishers, nomadic or seasonal herders, shifting forest farmers, or subsistence peasant cultivators (Durning 1991; 1992). With the advancement of transnational business enterprise over the past two decades, indigenous peoples have suffered from the consequences of some of the most destructive aspects of our western ideas of development and growth. These peoples have been separated from their lands, ways of life, deprived of their means of livelihood, and forced to fit into societies that are alien to them. The story of the Americas, in relation to indigenous peoples is duplicated in almost every region of the world. Indigenous peoples are taking the lead in challenging the notion that nation-states are the foundation for either peace or environmental security. Jason Clay (1993) notes that what is at stake in our current world is not the legitimacy or survival of nations but rather the survival of peoples. Clay ventures that no single issue affects the survival of indigenous peoples as much as the state appropriation of the resources, in particular land, that indigenous peoples require if they are to survive as recognizable societies. It is the global appetite for resources that fuels the threats to indigenous peoples.

Julian Burger (1993) refers to the historical treatment of indigenous peoples as the scourge of European colonialism. We are now seeing this legacy being played out in the present. Contemporary colonialism, which proceeds in the ventures of globalization, is devastating to the everyday lives of indigenous peoples. Burger gives us a graphic picture of their state:

> In the quest for resources and land, the great wildernesses have become El Dorados and escape valves. Few of the 50 million indigenous inhabitants of the world's rain forests who depend on it for food, medicine, shelter, and income have escaped the assaults of loggers, settlers, miners, and dam-builders. In Amazonia and several Asian countries, poor farmers, squeezed off their own lands by agro-industry, have migrated in massive numbers onto indigenous peoples' territory. Today, the indigenous people of Amazonia are outnumbered 16 to 1. By early in the next century, Indonesia plans to move up to 10 million people from Java to indigenous lands on the outer islands. (Burger 1993: 4–5)

It can also be observed that a very large proportion of the major issues surrounding land use and land reform relate to the survival of indigenous peoples across the globe. Projects of the World Bank relating to hydroelectric schemes, or mining by transnationals, threaten to displace or have displaced hundreds of thousands of indigenous and tribal peoples. One example is noted by Julian Burger in State of Peoples: A Global Human Rights Report on Societies in Danger (1993). The specific project involves a series of dams being built on India's Sardar Sarovar river which has imperiled nearly 100,000 people, most being tribal peoples. The plans for these projects involve massive removal of tribal peoples from their lands without giving them land or monetary compensation. The ultimate outcome of all this movement is that these people will probably end up swelling the already vast unemployed and marginalized slum-dwelling populations in towns.

The issue here as concerns survival is at the physical, cultural and spiritual levels. This has led activists among indigenous peoples to campaign on human-rights issues at international forums. Several hundred indigenous peoples from the Americas, Asia, Africa, Europe and Oceania have been active in United Nations conferences that have considered indigenous peoples' concerns. What we are looking at here is a clash of cultures and interests that has been catalysed by the new colonialism that goes under the title globalization. At the world level, indigenous peoples have used the forum of the United Nations with mixed results and considerable suspicion. Since 1982, there has been a working group in the United Nations that deals with indigenous populations. This particular body is the only place in the UN that grants indigenous peoples an established right to speak as indigenous peoples, nations and organizations. A Draft Declaration on Human Rights and Indigenous Peoples has been produced by this body for the General Assembly. The Declaration specifically recognizes the rights of indigenous peoples against cultural genocide, defined as any form of forced assimilation or deprivation of their distinct cultural characteristics. There is also, parallel to this, a draft declaration that includes the right to protection of sacred sites, the restitution of cultural property, and the repatriation of human remains. Also incorporated are principles of greater access to and control over public services recognizing that indigenous peoples have fared far worse than any other group in the world today on almost every socioeconomic indicator (Burger 1993).

The ultimate outcome of all of the above work remains to be seen. Within the deep structure of our western colonial heritage, which is operating currently under the rubric of global economics and commerce, there must be a clear understanding that we can dismiss cultures on a global level as we march towards the global world market. One can understand why indigenous peoples may harbour suspicions of our motives. Our western colonial history warrants that suspicion and we must be aware of it.

The continent of Africa is now the recipient of the western world's fears about overpopulation and anarchy. Today, we westerners see African peoples and lands depicted in severe crisis with what Serge Latouche (1993) calls 'Afro-pessimism'. Earlier in this chapter we saw that Africans are now being looked at in Malthusian terms. For example, the American Robert Kaplan, in his article 'The Coming of Anarchy' (1994), gives us a picture of Western Africa in catastrophist terms. Kaplan discerns forces in this region which are spreading and which may well make the whole world uninhabitable. Africa is treated with an interpretation that would indicate its present plight is entirely of its own making, a result of these peoples' animism and communalism; thus the kindred blights of deforestation (linked simply to overpopulation), tuberculosis, malaria, HIV and, above all, 'teeming' black people. As Alexander Cockburn (1994: 405) points out about Kaplan's interpretation, 'where does he admit the western role in plagued economies?' Yet logging in West Africa is mostly carried forward by international companies with generous bribes to local elites, part and parcel of export-led development deemed appropriate by first world bankers.

It must be understood that Africa, and for that matter any other part of our globe today, suffers within a world economy that is predominantly run under the auspices of western hegemony. Having said that, we can now consider Africa within the context of survival. Today, Africa is being abandoned by the world that originally colonized it. The continent suffers under the weight of many scourges. Because of land use, there has been massive desertification and with desertification come the massive issues around hunger that plague this part of our globe. This continent is faced with constant misery and, as Serge Latouche (1993) says, it is the castaway of western development. Within the differentiated African communities there is an incredible variety of peoples that make for both the colour of diversity and an arena of conflict. Through its colonial legacy, Africa has been carved up into nation-states that mimic the pattern of its colonialism while covering over the vast differences of peoples. Nigeria is one case in point. It is a nation-state that harbours an incredible diversity of peoples and where conflicts among these peoples are sometimes severe. Conflicts are intensified by the sale of western arms. We also see within these conflicts the incredible hypocrisy of western nation-states. We send peacekeeping forces into these regions with one hand and arm them with the other. There is a terrible irony in the fact that UN peacekeeping forces die as the result of arms produced in the West. In African countries, as elsewhere, the spread in arms undermines democratic government, promotes human-rights violations, destroys civil society and is linked to the trade in drugs and other forms of criminality. With arms easily accessible, internal conflicts are militarized; when wars break out they are prolonged; and when wars are finally ended, peacekeeping operations are endangered and the burden of post-conflict peace-building is exaggerated by the need to try to collect millions of small arms that have been infused by western arms-dealers into the prevailing social and political disorder (Regehr 1996).

What is happening in Africa resonates in other regions of the third world. Most of the regions in the southern part of the Americas are dealing with survival issues around land reform, food, health and depletion of resources. Most of the countries in the southern tier of the Americas are ridden with debts that are impossible to repay. Debt repayment has lead to wars to secure scarcer resources and created civil war (Argentina, Uruguay, Bolivia, Peru, Guatemala, El Salvador, Mexico), and resulted in civil strife and ethnic conflicts (Peru, Ecuador) as well as the criminalization of economic activity (Colombia,

Bolivia, Peru) (Isla 1996). Ana Isla maintains that managing the debt is another way of managing the world as a market, fragmenting people's rights and using state forces as managers of crisis and polarization of conflict; thus creating conditions for massive human rights violations. The majority of these Latin American countries are obliged by the World Bank to undergo a process called 'structural adjustment' which forces them to cut back on their social welfare and educational programmes and to put the emphasis of their internal spending on export production to the first world. This process has escalated the levels of poverty in these countries and has also resulted in the depletion of natural resources. In addition to structural adjustment, a pernicious programme called 'debt swapping' or 'debt for nature' has been instituted by the creditor banks and nations. Debt for nature swaps consist of exchanging one type of debt instrument held by a creditor for certain natural resources in the debtor country. There are many consequences that relate to this activity but probably one of the most prominent is the extension of merchandization and private appropriation of natural resources previously regarded as the common heritage of the debtor country. In the final analysis, debt for nature diverts attention from the main arena of conflict, where the existing model of global wealth accumulates to the wealthy creditors, and favours extraction and transference of a significant part the debtor nation's labour, natural resources and wealth.

When we look to the minority world of the North we see a comparable redistribution of wealth going to a small group of elite people and institutions and a widening of the gap between the rich and poor. In the 1990s, we have seen a progressive development of poverty across all sectors of society with the exception of the super-rich. All of the gains that the middle-class has achieved since mid-century seem now to be eroding rapidly. We are seeing a form of structural adjustment in the North in the erosion of all major social programmes relating to health, welfare and education. We are now witnessing a degree of public homelessness and devastating poverty never before seen in almost all major cities in the North. This part of the poverty spectrum mimics the larger cities in the majority or third world. All of these indications are coupled with a breakdown in community life, forms of alienation and anomie never before encountered. Crime, drug use and other activities that threaten the community fabric are escalating on a daily basis.

In discussing issues of survival, we cannot ignore the universal plight of women and children. The issue of violence will be looked at in Chapter 5. At this point, I shall only call attention to some of the most salient findings in this area. Gender-based violence against women crosses all cultural, religious and regional boundaries. Its most pervasive form is reported to be abuse by a husband or intimate partner (*Progress of Nations* 1997). In Canada in 1987, as a specific example, 62 per cent of the women murdered were killed by an intimate male partner. Gender-specific forms of violence occur where male dominance is institutionalized in social, political and economic systems. One of the things that violently discriminates against women is the notorious practice of female genital mutilation. It is estimated that this practice is performed on 85–114 million women worldwide. The World Bank has identified violence as a major risk factor for ill-health and disease among women of reproductive age. In their overall analysis, 19 per cent of the total disease burden of women between the ages of fifteen and forty-four in advanced market economies could be linked to domestic violence and rape. Violence constitutes a comparable threat to women in the majority world but due to the relatively greater burden of disease in those regions, it represents a very low level of their total disease burden. As we shall discuss later in a more extensive treatment of societal violence, violence against children follows a similar pattern across the globe.

Personal survival Probably one of the most important factors in the breakdown of the personal world is the breakdown of the deep relational quality of not only human life but of all life forms (O'Sullivan 1990). We are now experiencing, at the end of what is being called modernity, a deep fracturing of the personal from community life at all levels of involvement. We have devised a form of economic activity, which now goes under the name of transnational capitalism, that honours no human community boundaries and is even more egregious to the boundaries of the natural world in its totality. The bottom line of all this economic activity is the creation of wealth and the making of money. In the lexicon of transnational capitalism, there seems to be no place for the creation and sustenance of community life. With the breakdown of community life, there is also a breakdown in the personal world. With the fracturing of a personal world there is also a decline in public life (O'Sullivan 1990). It is now a reality all over the globe that a significant portion of our lives is mediated by an instrument designed to advertise and sell commodities; that instrument being the mass media technology called television. With the advent of commercial television there has been a steady decline in public life. The paradox here is that the decline in public presence is synonymous with the steady advance of communications technologies. In post-Second World War history, what has increasingly occurred since 1945 is the indirect mediation of significant events through the new technologies provided in such instruments as newspapers, radio, television and, of most recent vintage, the computer, the fax machine and the Internet. It must be understood that, at the level of popular culture, the television still dominates. The dependency for connection to cultural events through television marks a ritual of privatization. The medium of television is a privatized ritual because without the encounter with real embodied events we depend on this medium as a means of relating to a wider world. It is estimated that in the typical North American family, each individual will have been spoken to by television figures more than they have been spoken to by each other (O'Sullivan 1990). It is important to note here the aims of TV productions *vis-à-vis* the viewer. The commercial interests that sponsor TV programming proceed on the assumption that there is a population of viewers who have to be formed and conformed (i.e. a passive public) to commercial and consumption values. This connection does not add up to a sense of a public life.

It must be admitted that our mass media give us a mediated access to wider world events; at the same time it can be seen that we may be left with no public access to express the significance of these events. In addition there is the phenomenon of media saturation that can invoke defences such as withdrawal and numbing. Later we will talk about the necessity for a 'civic culture' as part of a transformative vision. We will have to devise other means besides our mass media of communications to find our way back into a public life.

We seem, at the turn of the century, to be having conflicting responses to the developing world complexity. One response is to develop what Robert Jay Lifton (1993) calls the 'protean self.' This is a self that mediates with the world by recognizing its complexities and adjusting to its manifold changes. Lifton advances the idea of a 'protean self' as a response to the confusion of our times and to the widespread feeling that we are losing our psychological moorings. Rather than collapse under the threats and pulls that are part and parcel of modern life, the self can exhibit a surprising resiliency. The 'protean self' uses bits and pieces here and there and appears to be able to move with tactical flexibility, evolving a self of many possibilities and holding out a promise for the future. In such times of fragmentation and trauma as these, Lifton thinks that proteanism can awaken our species belonging; something akin to a species self. We are therefore able to assert our organic relationship to each other and to nature. That assertion, for symbolizers like ourselves, is a matter of the psyche, of the imagination. We can come to feel that we are members of a common species. We can experience, amidst our cultural diversity, that common humanity. The diversity is integral to the process.

This response to complexity and fragmentation is one of constructive resilience and adaptability. If we are cognizant of a protean response to complexity, we must also take into account that the self can also close down. Those same historical forces that evoke proteanism can also evoke more constrained and limiting visions of the self that go under the name of fundamentalism. A fundamentalist response to the complexities of our fragmented world include any movement that embraces a fierce defence of the sacred, a literal interpretation of sacred texts and a purification process of history that proceeds to name a past of perfect harmony that never was, and an equally visionary future created by a violent 'end' to impure profane history. We see the manifestations of fundamentalism today in almost all major religious practices – there is Hindu, Jewish, Islamic as well as Christian fundamentalism – and in political practices that are revolutionary or nationalistic or both, including Nazism, neo-Nazism and Communism (Lifton 1993). In our own times a fundamentalist response of the self to the fragmentation and complexity it encounters is an extreme expression of totalism and self-immersion in an all or nothing ideological system or behaviour pattern.

We know that fundamentalisn does not have staying power in human history. A country that is reared on fundamentalism usually lets go of it in the next generation. This is important for our purposes here, for we are aware that fundamentalist self-formation cannot deliver the flexibility and openness that our period of history demands. We are in need of Lifton's 'protean self', because we need a complexity, versatility and openness to the challenges that our present historical circumstance presents.

I shall conclude this section by indicating that we are going to need an educational vision that will address the conditions of all three levels that we have just discussed: the planetary, the human and the personal. We will be looking at an educational praxis that will move us past modernist conceptions of education to what I would label a 'reconstructive postmodern' vision.

Post-modern education

At this point in our discussion I feel that it is necessary to make some comparisons and contrasts between some of the recent discussions on 'postmodern education' and my discussion of the 'terminal cenozoic'. At the most generic level, the development of 'postmodern discourse' in the social sciences, education and cultural studies is indicative that there is disenchantment with the forces of modernism that is the legacy of western Enlightenment institutions and thinking. David Griffin gives us a sense of the postmodern malaise:

> The rapid spread of the term *postmodern* in recent years witnesses a growing dissatisfaction with modernity and an increasing sense that the modern age not only had a beginning but can have an end as well. Whereas the word *modern* was almost always used until quite recently as a word of praise and as a synonym for *contemporary*, a growing sense is now evidenced that we can and should leave modernity behind – in fact, that we *must* if we are to avoid destroying our selves and most of the life on our planet. (D. Griffin 1988a: ix)

When focused on educational discourse, postmodern cultural criticism has challenged a number of the central premises of modernist education. The criticism includes a suspicion of the modernist reliance on metaphysical notions of the subject, the advocacy of science, technology and rationality as the foundation for equating change with progress. Combined with the above critique is the questioning of the ethnocentric equation of judging history in terms of the triumph of western civilization; and its globalizing view that the industrialized western countries constitute a unique and superior force that can position itself to establish control and to determine hierarchies. Aronowitz and Giroux (1991) maintain that, from the postmodernist perspective, modernism's claim to authority serves to privilege western patriarchal culture on the one hand, while simultaneously repressing and marginalizing the voices of those who have been deemed subordinate or subjected to relations of repression because of their colour, class, ethnicity, race, or cultural or social capital.

The reader may ask at this point what is the relationship between the notions of 'postmodernism' and the 'terminal cenozoic'. For our purposes, it is helpful here to make David Griffin's (1988a; 1988b) distinction between 'deconstructive or eliminative' and 'reconstructive or revisionary' postmodernism. Deconstructive or eliminative postmodernism seeks to overcome the modern world view through an anti-world view; it deconstructs or eliminates the ingredients necessary for a world view. The attack on what is called the 'grand narrative' is the focal point of deconstruction. Aronowitz and Giroux (1991) give several positive features to the deconstructive turn while also pointing to some important failings. There is the potential in postmodern critique to deepen and broaden our understanding of critical pedagogy in education. The postmodern engagement with culture, difference and subjectivity provides grounds for questioning the modernist ideal of what constitutes quality of life. In declining to celebrate the master narratives of modern culture, postmodern critique raises important questions about how narratives get constructed, what they mean and how they regulate particular forms of moral and social experience. Although the present work shares some of the critical aspects of the deconstructive critique of modern world views, I am, with David Griffin (1988a), circumspect about its tendencies toward relativism and nihilism. This aspect has been subject to strong criticism and has been labelled as 'ultramodernism or mostmodernism' (D. Griffin 1988a; Spretnak 1991).

Aronowitz and Giroux (1991) point out the educational limitations of the postmodern because of its extreme suspiciousness of the modern notion of public life and of the struggle for equality and liberty which has been the foundation for liberal democratic discourse. The postmodernism of 'reconstruction' or 'revision' certainly moves beyond the Enlightenment synthesis and the breakdown of mechanistic assumptions of modernity but, in place of deconstruction as an end point, there is a reconstructive vision attempting to move beyond modern world views not by eliminating the possibility of world views *per se*, but by constructing a revision of modern premisses (D. Griffin 1988a).

I will be placing the revisioning work in this book within a cosmological orientation in which human experience and knowledge are situated in the unfolding manifestation of the universe (T. Berry 1988; Swimme and Berry 1992). I am at pains here to stress the point that this is not a new 'master narrative' so much maligned by deconstructivists. At the same time, it would be misleading to suggest that there is no narrative story in the point of view that I am venturing here. The truth of the matter is that I am, by presenting the universe story as a focal point of reference, suggesting in effect a 'grand narrative.' This is not the 'master narrative' of any one culture, but the story of the universe itself. I am attempting in this work to provide a powerful generative vision that leaves open the place for other visions and accepts as natural that diversity is a desirable value. I hope to develop, for the reader, a powerful visionary context embedding the human community within the earth community and ultimately within the universe whose very foundation goes back to the fireball. Charlene Spretnak (1991), in her attempt to create a postmodern ecological vision, notes that the elements of the universe are in our bodies; the same elements as those in trees, rocks, lions and rivers. We are aware that these myriad forms are not static, stable objects, but are an incredible number of microevents occurring within the dynamics of self-organization. Even at the atomic level, atoms exhibit articulate patterns within a vast web of relationships. Spretnak gives us a hint of where this vision is leading us and also shows how it can stand as a powerful antidote to deconstructive nihilism. Drawing heavily on Thomas Berry's ideas, she ventures that the universe in its activities produces certain manifestations among a tremendous range of possibilities and in doing so continues to create a cosmological story. Humans are not constructed world views ripe for deconstruction. We live in this universe that is dynamically acting and forge our human species identity out of 'more than five billion unique expressions of the dynamism and profound communion that fills the universe'. Spretnak (1991: 18) then ponders how this cosmological story might undergo deconstruction: 'That's merely one perspective, a deconstructive postmodernist might scoff. You could just as easily claim that we're all rigidly, unrelated, unconnected beings. One discourse is as good as the next.'

Spretnak counters this with a position that is both historical and anthropological. She observes that there is a widespread, cross-cultural occurrence of the perception of interconnectedness which makes this integral cosmological perspective more than a mere narrative of projected idealism:

It has been *experienced* by an enormous number of people in extremely varied circumstances for scores of thousands of years. The sense that the natural world is alive and that we are inherently connected with that life force is a core perception of most native people's world view, from the cultures of the Upper Palaeolithic era to those of the contemporary Fourth World. In Asia it evolved into Taoist, Buddhist, Hindu, and Confucian philosophies of organicism. That perception, that awareness of vibrant interconnectedness, lingered stubbornly despite the challenge of new ideas that spread from Europe throughout the world ...

Contemporary science itself – in the areas of biology, chemistry, physics, and chaos theory – has also concluded that subtle interconnectedness and molecular relatedness are indeed the nature of being. (Spretnak 1991: 18–19)

At this point the reader may ponder why he or she has been taken into a discussion on some of the vicissitudes of postmodern discourse. For my part, situating this work is an essential task in locating our effort in some of the more compelling alternatives to modernism. Being provided with a cosmo-logical context, the reader is alerted that this work, although postmodern in sentiment, will not be an exercise in deconstruction *per se*. This is not to say that there are no elements of deconstruction in this work. Part Two, Critique, which will shortly occupy the reader's attention, can be considered as an exercise in delimiting and deconstruction. Nevertheless, the essence of this work is not deconstruction but construction and revisioning. The ecozoic dream is an exercise in ecological reconstruction. This is the dream that drives the action of this work.

The reconstructive work that will constitute the most creative educational vision that I can mount in this work needs preparation. The new vision will develop within the womb of modernism's dying cultural dysfunctions. There must be an assessment of survival, in educational terms, that takes into account the malaise of modernity that I have presented within the planetary, human and personal levels of our current historical moment. Giving up some of the attachments to the old is as dynamic a process as that of creating something new. More often than not, detachment from the old and attachment to the new are processes that are simultaneously realized creative tensions. In the next section of this chapter, I focus on the detachment modes of survival.

The educational praxis for the survival mode

Dealing with denial, despair and loss As educators in the twentieth century, we have lived with the constant promise of a cornucopia that has been the unending optimism of our cultural dreams. Our expectations have been con-stantly stimulated while simultaneously frustrated. Going into the next century we are now facing the reality of a cornucopia that has failed in its promises of plenty. What we now face is a complete reversal and negation of our expectations. As educators, we must be cognizant of the complex psychic factors that are operating as we negotiate ourselves through this period of historical decline. The historical context is part of the dynamics of change that we are experiencing. Rajni Kothari poses a *problematique* for our current situation in world history. He identifies the *problematique* as:

Survival. Survival of the species, survival of civilization, survival of the whole
of creation. Survival of the State as an instrument of change and liberation,
identity and dignity. The *problematique* is affecting institutional structures, the
behaviour of people, their psychic responses. It is found in the currently
widespread feeling of uncertainty and insecurity at all levels, which seem to
overshadow the earlier sense of confidence and certitude – about the theory
of development, about the prospects for peace, about the continuity of human
progress, about civilization and its underlying unity. (Kothari 1988: 6–7)

To accept this *problematique*, it must be understood at the outset that formal
education in all modern societies has been in the service of the modern state,
and currently the monolithic state of transnational business. Throughout the
twentieth century, educational institutions have been embedded in nation-
state consciousness and the formal educational institutions have been aligned
to the needs and exigencies of the nation-states. Coming into the twenty-first
century there is a dramatic shift that is moving us beyond the nation-state
into a global transnational world which is part of the forward movement of
the market system of contemporary capitalism. Globalization is not of recent
origin; it is inherent in the logic of capitalism continually to expand markets.
Contemporary transnational globalization is marked by expanded markets
and communications on a global scale that was not previously imagined. The
present movement towards globalization is taking us beyond the powers of
the nation-state to a transnational market vision that increasingly challenges
the powers and sovereignty of the nation-state. What does this movement
toward transnational globalization imply for educational institutions? What
seems to be implied by the rhetoric of globalization is that education must
now act as the formative institution of transnational globalization rather than
the nation-state.

Over the last ten years we have seen a rhetoric of globalization which is
designed to create an ultimate direction for our world today. The rhetoric is
as simple as it is repetitive. All institutions and programmes must now be
designed to bring to fruition the seeming manifest destiny of the global
market. The rhetoric is couched in inevitability. The work of the educator,
within this world view, is to prepare and 'skill-train' all of us to go into and
have loyalties towards the advance of the global market. Thus, in our own
time, we are no longer hearing a rhetoric for the nation-state; our new ideal
is the transnational global market. The rhetoric for this is called globalization.

We have been saturated with a new market rhetoric that bombards us
through advertising and the mass media. We have also been saturated with
this rhetoric by our own governments who are increasingly delivering nations
over to the new global conglomerates, the free trade constellations of North
America and Europe and the Asian constellations. In Part Two of this book,
which I have labelled 'Critique', I shall deconstruct and analyse at length this

globalization process. For now, it is only necessary that the reader understand how I see its importance in the survival mode. It is my contention that the onward movement of capital-ventured globalization is deeply destructive and is the end point of a cultural synthesis that is increasingly morbid to the carrying capacities of our planet. The crucial task of the educator will be to develop an awareness that sees through the logic of destructive globalization and to combine this with critical skills to resist the rhetoric that now saturates us. Three major tasks confront the educator in the survival mode. The first is coming out of denial, the second is dealing with despair, and the third is dealing with loss and grief.

In order to deal with the educational issues of our time, we must take into consideration the location of the educator in this historical moment. The rhetoric of globalization creates a false consciousness for educators because the dream structure of the globalized mind constantly creates an optimism for the future that makes claims that all will be well if the processes of market globalization go forward. In order for this rhetoric to succeed there must be a disconnection between what the market says it is doing and what, in effect, it is really doing. There is an insistent optimism in the market vision and a rhetoric that systematically denies the disruptive effects that the trans-national market creates both locally and globally. Since the institutions of education in a society serve the conservative function of maintaining the status quo in society, it is not surprising that educational institutions are seen as allies in the current vision of the global marketplace. Today, formal educational institutions are being enlisted to prepare the next generation for the needs of the global marketplace. We are beginning to see this phenomenon across the curriculum, with the possible exception of education in the early pre-school and elementary school years. When we examine the policy goals for education in the secondary and post-secondary school system, we now see a predominance of globalization language. The deep penetration of the global market mentality is overshadowing the older language of nation-state loyalty. The bottom line now for educational endeavours is to train and prepare its clientele for the new global order. The selling language of this world view is that globalization is the key to a better future, the key to better jobs, the key to better living, and so on. While this dystopian language predominates, the reality of the situation gives us another less attractive story. The growing environmental movement has brought our attention to the complex negative impact that the unrestricted market is perpetrating on the world. Rainforest devastation, global warming, human rights violations seem to follow the market more than any of its proclaimed positive effects. In terms of wealth distribution, our world today is at its highest level of inequities. Although the global market rhetoric still boasts of a trickle-down distribution of wealth from rich to poor, the facts say otherwise. Our current form of economic development, whether it takes place within a nation or transnationally, consistently moves wealth upwards to a smaller and smaller elite group while leaving the vast majority of people both poorer and increasingly destitute (Mason 1997). It is, in practice, siphon up rather than trickle down. As regards employment in the global market, the ratio of unemployed to employed is increasing. These are just a few of the negative indicators which will be discussed in more depth in Part II. Suffice to say, for the present, there is a widening disparity between what the globalization process says it is doing and the realities of our current situation. These contradictions leave contemporary educators confused as to their loyalties and their work. This is where transformative education becomes relevant to the situation.

From a critical transformative perspective, at least four levels of consciousness must be dealt with. The first is a pre-conscious non-reflective level. The second is an emergent survival-conscious level. The third is a critical conscious level and the fourth level is a level of visionary consciousness. I shall discuss the first two levels in this chapter; the last two levels will be treated in Part Two, Critique, and Part Three, Create.

The pre-conscious non-reflective state is normative within our formal educational systems. Although educators in school systems are living with the contradictions that I have cited above, their level of awareness of the causes of these conditions is minimal. Educators, within this frame of reference, take on the project of 'skilling' students to fit into the parameters of the market. To be sure, the market is not always the paramount language in traditional schooling discourse; nevertheless, the conformity of thought that accommodates to the market is also immersed in other conformities around such areas as class, gender, race and sexual orientation. What we know in terms of educational consciousness is that, while in this state, there is no sense of the survival dimensions of our present period of history. Frequently, educators in this state of consciousness ignore or are hostile to attempts that challenge the system's present direction.

Even though the formal educational system follows the predominant received cultural norms, there are nevertheless breaks in the system that raise questions about our present directions. Emergent consciousness occurs when a person or group within our currently operating educational system questions the viability of current educational directions. This happens in a number of ways. Educators who start to take environmental issues seriously begin to challenge and prod the formal system's present silence and complicity in these areas. It can happen when issues of gender equity are challenged. It can happen when the system is challenged along issues of race. It can happen when class issues are addressed within the school system. These are just a few of the ways that an emergent consciousness can open the doors to look into the conventional slumbers of our present educational system. In the incipient stages of conscious awareness it is important to begin a deep questioning of the cornucopia of globalization. This comes when there is a connection made between the global economy's workings and the environmental and social devastation that seems to accompany its presence everywhere. This conscious-ness can be a frail reed at the beginning. It will need cultivating by education in a new social and political awareness. Since much of this new consciousness will challenge the conventional wisdom within the system, there will also be a need to prepare psychically for retaliation from members within the system who still adhere to the dominant norms. Consciousness, in the emergent survival mode, opens up at least three phenomena that must be dealt with in this mode. We are speaking of denial, despair and grief.

Coming out of denial Earlier in this chapter, we dealt briefly with the phenomenon of denial. At this point, I would like to deal with denial more specifically within the context of educational practice. In the pre-conscious state of awareness, the mechanism of denial operates in such an effective way as to insulate the conventional educator from the problematic nature of the dominant norms of our culture. When there is a break in the dominant mode of consciousness, it starts with one or more areas of awareness that bring into question the dominant norms. At a certain point, an individual educator, or group of educators, starts a process that fundamentally questions the des-tructive nature of our dominant myth structure of globalization. When this questioning process begins, we are starting down the long road of coming out of denial. At first, this process wavers back and forth. Alongside the opening up of a questioning attitude to the system, there is also a falling back into the system's myth structure. The falling back occurs when there is a loss of confidence in one's critical powers coupled with older beliefs that the system must surely be going in the right direction. After all, how can a system that comes so highly recommended be wrong? When there is an emergent ability and consciousness to question the system, the processes of denial begin to dissipate. When this process takes hold, the coming out of denial leads us into an initial state of despair.

Despair in the survival mode When educators first begin to take into account the signals of distress that are legion in our times, there is a natural sense of both deflation and despair. I spoke earlier of a failed cornucopia. Frequently, the processes of denial cover the sense of despair. According to Joanna Macy (1989; 1991), despair is a natural response to our present historical situation; it cannot and should not be banished by injections of optimism or sermons on 'positive thinking'. Our encounter with despair must be acknowledged and worked through at a deep level of the psyche. There is a difference between despair and grief that must be understood. Macy (1991) makes the comparison between the two. She maintains that despair work differs from grief work in that its aim is not the acceptance of loss; indeed, the 'loss' has not yet occurred and is hardly to be 'accepted'. But it is similar in the dynamics unleashed by a willingness to acknowledge, feel and express inner pain.

At the very onset of this process of despair work, it is necessary that we understand that our despair is not a morbid preoccupation. The natural experience of anguish and anxiety in the face of the perils of our time is a healthy reaction to the current situation. Despair is part of the process of coming out of denial. It is a dawning sense, at a level of deep awareness, that we can no longer continue in a direction that all our previous cultural learning extolled as highly beneficial and culturally meritorious.

In the context of education there must be an authentic despair that relates to the educator within the frame of reference of educational institutions. With the onset of an emergent awareness, there is an understanding that conventional educational institutions are embedded in the problematic nature of our culture's dominant values. Part of the despair work is in a deepening of acceptance that the educational institutions in which we now work are fundamentally dysfunctional within the larger arc of living values. When the logic of globalization is accepted, there is also a corresponding acceptance of the necessary nature of its negative consequences. The despair for the educator comes when there is an irrevocable realization that the system he or she is working in is not a workable or laudable one in terms of where it is going and what it is accomplishing. It is the position of this book that the present trajectory of globalization and the systems of education that seed it must be transformed and reinvented. This type of conclusion and the despair that accompanies it come from a clear assessment of what the system is truly accomplishing.

At present, we are seeing some of the rhetoric on deficit and debt penetrating into the resources of the school system in Canada. The logic of debt reduction has reached its long arm into the resources of our systems of education. Over the last five years we have seen formal school systems stripped of basic resources that allowed them to deal with issues of equity and diversity and the environment. We now have voted in conservative governments committed to globalization in programmes and policies on the one hand and the cutting to the core budgets for social and educational programmes on the other. Under a rhetoric of 'deficitism', public resources are being ravaged; our educational system is one of the many casualties. Eimear O'Neill, in addressing the Canadian context, makes some clear connections about the deficit and debt rhetoric for the Province of Ontario:

> We are told that we are cutting social programmes and restructuring government delivery of services to deal with crises around 'the deficit' and 'the debt.'

What is happening in Ontario, and across Canada, is what the World Bank terms 'structural adjustment.' This term is used more commonly in the media reports of so-called third world countries where debt to the World Bank is paid by ravaging social programmes with no expectation of maintaining human rights. In Ontario, what is being attacked is a rich network of social programmes that include livable wage support, accessible child care, quality education, programmes of violence prevention and employment equity, universal health care and shelter all of which have cushioned us from the effects of globalization felt earlier by New Zealand, Britain and the United States. (O'Neil 1998: 5–6)

Picking up on O'Neill's sense of the loss of 'quality education', a sense of specificity within these educational institutions is warranted. What is lost when the cuts are made to our current educational sectors? Almost all progressive programmes that have come into the curriculum over the last twenty years are now being compromised or savaged. These range from areas of education dealing with the environment, equity and diversity education, anti-racist education, post-colonial education, women in education. In Ontario, the funding for environmental education such as outdoor education has been severely cut or eliminated. Issues around equity, diversity and race are also being put on the back burner of current educational policy documents and discussions. All of these changes are losses to the school system and they must be addressed critically and at the same time grieved over. This brings us to the topic of loss and grief, an area that is increasingly experienced by educators within our current institutions and one that is rarely discussed.

Grief and Loss in the Survival Mode Grieving for loss is an intricate part of the life process and educational loss is a phenomenon that must be grieved for. Living in this period of terminal history, the sense of loss must be considered awesome in its scope and magnitude. I have already catalogued the sense of loss at the personal, human and planetary level. The historical position that I have developed concerning the terminal character of our history was encased in a pervasive sense of loss. This sense of living in a period of decline leaves all historical actors who become conscious of this fact in a state of loss and grieving. All of us who have been raised in the West have spent the first three-quarters of this century in a state of continuous optimism concerning the viability of our institutions. Our educational institutions were encased in the optimism that has pervaded the twentieth century. Although the globalization Utopia still moves forward on the basis of this optimism, we are now coming to see that this sense of optimism has little basis in current historical reality. All our institutions, including the educational ones, do not express an ongoing optimism. Educational institutions have been the target of massive financial cuts, leaving them depleted and demoralized. Increasingly, our public educational institutions are asked to support themselves from the

private sector. Public funds are now diverted away from educational institutions and this no longer appears as a temporary adjustment. The bottom line
for educational institutions today is that they must do more with less.

In this period of history, it is normal to have to deal with denial, grief and
loss. These are natural human responses to situations of deflation. I do not
believe that during this period of history that we need to return to a revived
optimism. Optimism is not true to our present historical circumstances. Neither
is despair. This leads me to a final reflection appropriate to the survival mode.

Tragedy is not our business

Before we move on to the critical components of this work, I would like
to make a few concluding reflections on the essence of survival. We must
firmly grasp the terminal aspects of our cultural condition and face the
momentous challenges that lie directly ahead of us. At moments like this we
become aware of some of the tragic aspects of our situation as we attempt to
accept the death of older forms. But in the end, 'tragedy is not our business'.
It will serve us well to reflect on Freeman Dyson's (1985) essay of the same
name. Dyson makes the observation that western civilization apparently has
a fascination with tragedy, and that is why spirituality in the past was a kind
of grim business, generally. We are constantly dealing with evil and good.
Dyson wrote about the sense of tragedy in terms of Robert Scott's journey
to the South Pole. Scott (1868–1912) made great preparations. In 1912 he was
already using motorized equipment. Roald Amundsen (1872–1928) was making
the journey at the same time and both explorers were in a race to see who
would get there and back first. Scott made the journey with a tremendous
amount of equipment. He went the standard way. Amundsen figured there
must be another way, and he had an instinct that Dyson identifies as 'sagacity'.
Sagacity is a bit of cunning matched with wisdom. Sagacity is really applied
wisdom. Parents have it with children. How do you deal with a child? You
need sagacity, that is, you have to be very insightful on a concrete, practical
level. At any rate, Amundsen thought about the journey and he chose an
unusual route. He also chose to go with dogs. Scott used ponies, some of the
northern breeds. Scott got to the South Pole but on his way back he got
caught in a blizzard eleven miles from the base camp. He was caught there for
five days. During that time he and his companions died. He kept a journal
which was later published. It is something to read the journal of this man
who recorded such heroism and English stick-to-itiveness, pushing forwards,
not flinching, stalwart in the face of difficulty, not giving up. This shows up in
the journal, the sense that he and his companions were committed to the
journey and it meant so much to them, to the country they represented, and
they were going to be faithful to the mission to the end.

Amundsen got there and got back, but it was Scott who became the great hero. Scott's journal, with its tragic ending, was published in 1912. During the First World War, his journal was read by English soldiers going to France for heroic combat. Scott got all the publicity. Everybody forgot Amundsen. Apsley Cherry-Garrard, a person at the base camp, went out to rescue Scott. He retrieved the journal and some other items and then covered the place with snow and ice. On his return Cherry-Garrard thought a long while before he wrote anything about it. And when he did, he reflected profoundly on this question of tragedy, and the western fascination with tragedy and with the heroic.

I repeat this story now, although it has been told so well by Freeman Dyson, because there is a feeling that we must press on with this tragic industrial world, that we are committed to it. No matter what it costs, this is the way. But Cherry-Garrard, reflecting on the Scott expedition, analysed the journey and, in a penetrating final comment, wrote this phrase: 'tragedy is not our business.' He reflected on the fascination people had with the death of Scott; he saw that Scott deserved enormous praise, but, ultimately, 'tragedy is not our business'. Scott had failed. The role of an explorer is to get there, and back, alive. It is a profound thing. Cherry-Garrard appreciated the effort put into the expedition, but ultimately it was a failure. Amundsen went, and returned, but nobody paid that much attention. As with Scott, we are caught in the tragic ending of our commercial, industrial venture. But even with death facing us with the collapse of our monumental establishment, we refuse to alter the direction we have chosen.

Like Scott and Amundsen, we too are on a journey. We are in a time of exodus. We must carry this off. We need the sagacity, as well as immense energy, to find our way into a new cultural synthesis of planetary proportions. People say we cannot do it, and the answer is that we *must* do it. There are sacrifices to be made. There is the discipline. There is the spirituality of our time that is moving us on a sacred journey. If we do not perceive the sacred nature of our journey, then we will not be able to bring about the deeper transformation needed. We need to appreciate especially the real dimensions of what it is to be a member of the sacred community in this larger sense of the term. What I am saying here poses immense challenges to every aspect of what we call contemporary education. We are challenged to a new vision that will help us through the agonies of our times. A multitude of creative processes are taking place. A healing of the earth can be observed even amid the many devastating processes that are still functioning. Much can be done. Much is being done. Even as we rewrite the story of the past and consider the realities of the present we have begun the shaping of the future.

This time it will be one of our fundamental tasks to resist the voices of the 'terminal cenozoic'. These voices have driven us out of our senses and they prevent us from looking at our situation in the critical manner warranted by our precarious situation. The voices of the terminal cenozoic turn 'waste-world' into 'wonderworld' (T. Berry 1988). In wonderworld the voices of advertising tell us that our reckless exploitation of the earth is a creative process leading to a wonderworld existence. We label this 'progress'. In order to resist the voices of the wonderworld we will have need of a restoration of a critical common sense. In the latter part of the twentieth century we have now been eclipsed by the shadow side of progress. We in the northern hemisphere have been saturated with voices that prevent us from critically reflecting on the momentous period in which we are living. It is not just the case that we have not listened to voices; it is also the case that we have been, and continue to be, saturated with the voices that propagate the values of consumption. In the context of global transformative education, we must learn to be critical of these powerful voices that direct our attention towards a consumer lifestyle that is destructive to our planet. One component of this education is the restoration of a critical commonsense. The following chapters in the section titled 'Critique' represent my attempt to develop this sense for an educational context. The following section might well be labelled *education for critical consciousness.*

PART TWO

Critique

. . . .

CHAPTER 2

Education and the Dilemmas of Modernism: Towards an Ecozoic Vision

In my introductory Prologue, I have made a preliminary assessment of the role of educational institutions in our current crisis. Let me draw the reader's attention to Thomas Berry's criteria for assessing educational institutions: 'All human institutions, programs, and activities must now be judged primarily by the extent to which they inhibit, ignore or foster a mutually enhancing human–earth relationship' (personal communication, 23 Februrary 1990).

With these criteria in mind, we can say that the modernist educational venture in all its forms, is incredibly deficient in the understanding of human–earth relationships. Since formal conventional educational institutions are tailored to the needs of the consumer industrial society, it should not be surprising that our society's present direction aligns itself with programmes and procedures that ignore and inhibit human–earth relationships. This is indeed the case and it is important that we consider the role of educational institutions in our present crisis. We must do this, for, if we neglect the historical role of educational institutions, we will be rendered blind to its impact.

Our educational institutions have been apologists for the industrial society and they are part of a broad hegemonic process for consumer dream structures. Optimism and belief in the consumer industrial society are still a part of everyday education. Here is an instance of that optimism from a 1957 Canadian textbook on the topic of the development of Canadian education: 'Disregarding world factors beyond our immediate frame of reference and control, we may look to a bright future for Canadian education. Achievements during the short period of our history have been encouraging to say the least. They should be even more impressive during the next stage of Canadian development' (Phillips 1957: 66).

Although the optimism of the late 1950s and 1960s reversed itself in the 1970s and 1980s, this turnaround had virtually nothing to do with questioning the economic industrial order and its attendant morbidity. Educational institutions were chided for their permissiveness and laxity in failing to teach the basics for a fluidly functioning industrial order. As frequently as in the past, education became the whipping boy for the changing business cycle (O'Sullivan 1980; Quarter and Matthews 1987); the scapegoat for letting down the exigencies of the plundering industrial economy. This is the gist of the recent 'back to the basics' movement (O'Sullivan 1980). The basics are the core literacy subjects of reading, writing and mathematics that are seen as prerequisites for the functioning of the industrial order.

Coming into the twenty-first century, we can see how progress through science, technology and the industrial order geared to the exploitation and consumption of the earth's resources became the major motif for the economic order of the twentieth century. Carnegie and Rockefeller had the evolutionary philosopher William Spencer lecture across the United States, making the connection between Darwin's ideas on the 'survival of the fittest' and the world of industry and business. Social Darwinism became part of the apologetic ideology for the industrial order that has led us to our present state of environmental morbidity (Hofstadter 1955). The industrialists, aided by the 'captains of consciousness' (modern advertisers), introduced this century to the marvels of endless industrial product consumption (Ewen 1976). Educational institutions have immersed themselves in the fulfilment of the needs of the industrial order. The history of American education will follow the ethos of science, technology and corporate capitalism up to the highest levels of education (Noble 1977).

One of the major apologists and proponents of this educational format was the educational historian Lawrence Cremin (1964; 1976). He observed that although there is tremendous diversity in American education, its fundamental goals are in the interest of creating equal opportunity. Equal opportunity education was defined as a fair chance for all to participate in the industrial order of democratic capitalism. Nowhere in this historical educational perspective is there a questioning of the potential down-side of the industrial order or its underlying assumptions. Even when criticism was made of the modern educational system by Marxist-oriented scholars and historians (be they from America, France, Great Britain or Australia), it was a criticism that says our present industrial order reproduces unequal opportunity and unequal access to industrial goods and services (Apple 1979; Bourdieu and Passeron 1977; Bowles and Gintis 1976; Connell et al. 1983; de Lone 1979; Katz 1968). The focus of their criticism in no way comes to terms with issues of what the industrial order is doing to the natural world on its own terms. Thus, we can readily see that all received western educational traditions, even when they differ from one another in specifics, share some common assumptions about the appropriateness of the industrial order's exploitation of the natural world for human consumption.

In the 1980s, the response to our current educational crisis was to accelerate the scenario of the new world order of globalization. In general, the answer to the problems produced by the technological industrialism of the terminal cenozoic is more industrial technique (Ellul 1964). The supposedly new panaceas are the computer and genetic engineering (Rifkin and Perlas 1983; O'Sullivan 1983; 1985). Added to the advance of computerization and genetic engineering is the larger arc of the 'global competitive marketplace'. The global marketplace is now the centrepiece of our current educational ventures and we are being asked to restructure our schools to help students to become competitive in that emergent global sphere. This is our newest version of educational reform. It has an old ring to it; the linking of schools directly to the needs of industry and business. The only difference is that, today, the yardstick is now stretched to global proportions. We have seen this business–education marriage. It has been a marriage that has contributed to the detriment of our natural world and habitat. Part of our task and challenge will be to extricate ourselves from the industrial trance state that we have been in since the beginning of the twentieth century.

The need to choose between visions

I would like to venture the thesis that the fundamental educational task of our times is to make the choice for a sustainable global planetary habitat of interdependent life forms over and against the the global competitive market-place. We are now living in a watershed period comparable to the major shift that took place from the medieval into the modern world. We are at another vast turning point and we are in need of a cosmological story that can carry the weight of planetary consciousness into where we are now moving. To move towards a global planetary education, it will be necessary to have a functional cosmology that is in line with the vision of where this education will be leading us. Drawing from the work of Thomas Berry (1988), I refer to this postmodern period as the 'ecozoic' period. This choice for an 'ecozoic vision' can also be called a 'transformative' perspective because it posits a radical restructuring of all current educational directions. The educational framework appropriate for this movement must then not only be visionary and transformative, but clearly must go beyond the conventional educational outlooks that we have cultivated for the last several centuries.

The cosmological context

Contemporary education lacks a comprehensive cosmology. This is one of the central ideas that I will be developing in this book. When education has been drawn from the sciences, its attention has been directed to the social sciences as distinguished from the natural sciences. In most cases, educational theory and practice have borrowed from the sciences of psychology, sociology and to a lesser extent anthropology. Modern educational theory lacks a comprehensive and integrated perspective that has in the past been identified as a cosmology. Thus, contemporary educational theory and practice carry with them the same blinders that have plagued modern scientific specialization coming out of the post-Newtonian period. To be sure, modern western educational thought has attempted to identify itself with humanism, but it has done so without providing a renewal of an acceptable cosmology. What I am working towards in this book is an articulation and presentation of a cosmology that can be functionally effective in providing a basis for an educational programme that would engender an ecologically sustainable vision of society in the broadest terms; what can be called a planetary vision. This new cosmology, at its mythic and visionary level, could initiate and guide the new order of earth's existence into an emerging ecozoic era. As I have already indicated, we are now at the end of the cenozoic era of the planet earth's 4.5 billion-year history. This era is rapidly ending. Not only the human aspect but, even more so, the functioning of the entire planet is being altered. All living beings are being altered in the most extensive transformation that has taken place on the planet earth in the last 65 million years. So extensive is the dissolution of the life systems of the earth during the past century, that the viability of the human being can no longer be taken for granted.

The long-term survival of our species, and of other species that share our living planet, depends on understanding the depth of what is happening to the planet at present. It is essential to admit that what is occurring is nothing less than biocide. It also depends on rekindling a relationship between the human and the natural world that is far beyond the exploitative relationships of our current industrial mode. A different kind of prosperity and progress needs to be envisioned which embraces the whole life community. All our human institutions, professions, all our programmes and activities, need to function now in this wider life community context.

It is time to evoke the emergence of a new earth period that can be identified as the ecozoic era. Even now the shift is beginning to take place in which a relationship of mutual enhancement between humans and the natural world is regarded not only as possible but essential to planetary survival. We have seen this in the various manifestations of the ecology movement and also in coexisting social justice and human rights movements. How do educators fit in with this momentous change?

Now the whole question of the educator's role in dealing with planetary crisis becomes prominent. Educators, for the most part, see themselves as practitioners who are teaching their students to function within the social order. At this historical moment, almost all educational institutions are geared towards teaching the skills necessary for dealing with the needs of the consumer–industrial phase of this terminal cenozoic period. Within this context, we can clearly say that education is part of the problem rather than part of the solution. What is needed is a radical change in perspective within educational institutions to deal with the magnitude of the problems that we are currently facing at a planetary level.

Educators have not been prepared for this momentous undertaking. They have carried out their educational tasks in the technological and industrial world that is presently our dying heritage. To cope with the magnitude of our present problems, educators must see their work within a wider historical perspective. Because educators are strongly encouraged to deal with immediate practical problems, the historical perspective that is being suggested may, at first, appear beyond their competencies. In spite of this reservation, I feel it is absolutely necessary that they ponder the broad sweep of evolutionary history that I present in my introduction. History helps us to develop perspective and, what is more, it may be an aid in changing our perspective. I have already suggested that, in biological terms, the planet earth is at the end of the cenozoic period. This period is fast coming to a close by the plundering industrial economy that humans have imposed on the planet during these past two centuries. Truly, we now have a choice either to listen to the voices of the terminal cenozoic or to follow other emergent voices that take us in the direction of transformative education.

Assessing the forces: the cenozoic–ecozoic tension

If the terminal decade of the twentieth century is a transitional moment, as I have indicated in Chapter 1, then it is very important to examine the fluctuating and conflicting forces that we are privy to in our educational venture. We know that transitional moments are fraught with ambiguities and contradictions. This is to be expected. A more pressing need is that we make a clear assessment of these forces so that we do not become simply prey to their twists and turns and that we exercise the power of choice while venturing into new and emergent directions. One of the preparations for the future is a sober assessment of the past, to see how the forces of the past are operating in the present moment. We have done some of this work in Chapter 1 but a more extended treatment is now warranted. This brings us to the present trends that have historical roots in North American education.

My concentration on the North American educational context is consistent with my framing of this work in what I have labelled 'northern privilege'. I shall examine three main currents that are operating in this cenozoic–ecozoic tension: the progressive technozoic, the conservative organic and the transformative ecozoic. It is my assessment that both the conservative organic and

Table 2.1 Educational visions

Features	Progressive technozoic	Conservative	Ecozoic transformational
Educational world view/history	Modern	Anti-modern	Postmodern
Orientation to community and natural world	Exploitive	Traditional	Reflexive/interactive
View of time	Evolutionary	Cyclical/static	Time developmental
View of space	Pluralistic	Organic essentialist	Organic/interactive
Pre-eminent metaphor	Mechanistic	Anthropological organic (human body)	Biocentric (i.e. organic web of life) 'circle of life'
View of conflict	Superficial/ameliorative	Deviant/anarchic	Creative
Contemporary educational features	Progressive	Traditional	Emergent

the progressive technozoic, for all their differences, rest solidly within the 'terminal cenozoic vision'. With that *caveat*, I hope that the reader will come away with the conclusion that my categories reveal more than they conceal; enlighten rather than obfuscate. Table 2.1 is a summary of the work of the rest of this chapter.

The progressive technozoic vision

Educational world view/history Education history in North America is strongly influenced by the political economy of the United States of America. Even when this educational thrust is in Canada, it still bears the features of American educational hegemony. There is a public commitment to the development of 'democratic citizenry'. There is also an abiding commitment to the idea of progress and its integral linkage to the technological–industrial society. This, in a nutshell, is the core of the progressive technozoic vision. It is the thesis of this book that this educational vision is now in a terminal phase and it is, thus, being called the terminal cenozoic. The vision is, therefore, a vision in decline. The major problem with this dream structure is that its contemporary proponents do not see its terminal qualities. For purposes of clarity and comparison, I shall discuss each of the prototype visions and what I judge to be some of their distinguishing features. It is important for the reader to understand that my treatment here on educational currents is schematic rather than historically accurate and exhaustive. It is my view that the educational vision of 'progressive technozoic' education is deeply embedded in the modernist dream of the 'terminal cenozoic' and must now be subject to a thorough critical re-evaluation. To do this, it is appropriate to begin with a sense of its educational history in North America.

First, the sense of the tension in the progressive technozoic stream is exemplified in the educational thinking of John Dewey and Edward Thorndike. In reading Lawrence Cremin's historical work *The Transformation of the School* (1964), one is impressed that, at the turn of this century, the educational philosopher Dewey and the educational psychologist Thorndike were two of the more salient figures in the burgeoning educational reform that was to inaugurate twentieth-century education. Both Dewey and Thorndike responded to the needs of a newly industrialized and increasingly urbanized society. Dewey's reform commentaries were ordinarily addressed to those involved in elementary education whereas Thorndike's suggestions were geared to those in the secondary level (Cremin 1964).

Dewey and Thorndike complemented one another and, combined, they provided the matrix of an educational vision that allied itself, at a fundamental level, with the march of progress that was catapulting the educational world view into the educational venture of twentieth-century capitalism. For Dewey

(1963: 216), the idea of progress was to be coupled with its twin sister 'development': 'The aim of education is growth or development, both intellectual and moral. Ethical and psychological principles can aid the school in the greatest of all constructions – the building of free and powerful character. Education is the work of supplying the conditions that will enable the psychological functions to mature in the freest and fullest manner.'

Dewey's progressive developmentalism has a contemporary ring, relating to cognitive developmental psychology as seen in the work of such theorists as Bruner, Piaget and Kohlberg (see O'Sullivan 1990). For example, Kohlberg has a deep allegiance to Dewey's ideas when applying cognitive developmental stage theory to education.

Dewey and contemporary proponents can be understood as the liberal wing of progressivism. The interest in Thorndike's (Cremin 1964) ideas take us further into a feature of education called the basics or 'back to the basics'. Unlike Dewey, Thorndike was not a philosopher and he allied all his ideas to empirical studies. He would be labelled in contemporary terms as an 'educational psychologist.' His ultimate impact on educational practice and theory was as profound and far-reaching as that of his contemporary, Dewey. Thorndike's vigorous empiricism also sparked his interest in the educational testing movement that was booming in the 1920s. Like many other psychometricians, he embarked on an elaborate programme of testing and classification of learners. It appeared that the psychological approach generated by Thorndike lent its support to many school practices in North America throughout the twentieth century. In line with 'basic education' fare, Thorndike's position was most consistent with curriculum methods that emphasized drill and repetition.

Moving from settings of learning that are based within school systems, there is also the field of adult education. Although there have been pioneers in the area of adult education who have linked their work to working-class and what is today called popular education, it must be conceded that the formal field of adult education has developed in a manner that has excluded popular movements, citizen groups, farmers and the education of labour within the terms of those movements. Some of those popular movements included the pioneer work of Moses Cody in Canada, Raymond Williams in Britain and Myles Horton at the Highlander School in the United States (Welton 1995). At the end of the war, movements such as these would not have been counted as adult education. In the post-war era, professional middle-class educators emerged who took as their task the management of the learning process in formal and professional settings. The professionalization of adult education in the post-war era until the 1980s proceeded almost entirely without a critical social perspective. Michael Collins, in commenting on conventional adult education as a field, sees it aligned with the 'cult of efficiency' (Collins 1991; 1995). In this light, the vocation of the field seemed to be preoccupied with personal and career development techniques. Much of the field falls into the category of a corporate pedagogy exemplified in such things as competency-based education and human resource development. There is an emphasis in this field on 'instrumental reason' as the prime mode of rationality.

The post-war direction of adult education relied heavily on the discipline of psychology. Following from this is its emphasis on the individual learner. Two of the major architects of this emphasis are Alan Tough and Malcolm Knowles. They developed the notion of the 'self-directed learner' with the emphasis on the individual as the unit of analysis (Knowles 1986; Tough 1981). Their work proceeded on the assumption that the individual is the primary source of his or her own learning experiences. Within this learning paradigm of the individual, they further developed the idea of 'learning contracts'. This formulation for adult learning has been immensely popular and well received within professional adult education circles. It has been implemented in many institutional settings, including hospitals, business firms, colleges, public schools and prisons. The model is, in the final analysis, trapped in its individualistic framework and thus is blind to the power dynamics of institutions. Thus this model works knowingly or unknowingly on behalf of the power of institutions.

From this capsule summary, we can draw the conclusion that throughout the history of North American education there has been an interweaving of the forces of progressivism and technology. This has been the yin and yang for 'liberal progressive reform' and 'back to the basics' reform; the upswing of the business cycle allied to the former, the downswing of the business cycle to the latter (Quarter and Matthews 1987).

The 1960s were probably the most economically expansive decade of the twentieth century. This period witnessed a renaissance in liberal-progressive thinking, while the 1990s showed a failing economy allied to 'quality education' and 'back to the basics' rhetoric. Educational criticism heard nowadays contains no fundamental questioning of the contemporary consumer–industrial order. The 'back to the basics' movement is designed to prepare students for the exigencies of the new global economic order as played out in the arena of the 'global competitive marketplace'. The bottom line is to turn out learners who can compete in this dream of the global technosphere.

Orientation to community and natural world Throughout the twentieth century, one can conclude that the progressive technozoic vision has aligned itself to the technological order of the contemporary nation-state. In its most contemporary form, we see the new global competitive marketplace of the multinational corporations. Within this venue, we see schools as the preparation ground for this new industrial economic order. Here the jargon goes something like 'the schools must prepare new learners to be competitive in the new global economic community'. There are no questions asked on the planetary sustainability of this direction. This position accepts uncritically the demands of the global market on competition and consumption. The attitude towards the natural world is fundamentally *exploitative*. It appears that our local and national community life must be geared to this global marketplace. There is no depth of reflection on how pursuit of this dream of the global marketplace may have dramatic and negative impacts on our natural habitat and biosphere. There is very little emphasis on the development of local community life and the sense that these communities also have a profound impact on the quality of our lives. Historically, this progressive technozoic model of change has been in place since the breakdown of 'traditional' societies. The idea of the market community has its origins in nineteenth-century thought. The parallels are made in the following observation of Holland and Henriot (1984: 24): 'The ideal of a well-balanced society in nineteenth and twentieth-century Europe and North America was a "market" environment in which unrelated parts interacted competitively through "free enterprise" (economics), liberal democracy (politics), and "free thought" (culture).'

Because of its enmeshment within the 'terminal cenozoic dream', the trajectory of the progressive technozoic vision, when moving towards this world marketplace, ignores the impact that this pursuit has on the environment and the exigencies of our natural habitat. In short, pursuit of the competitive marketplace must now be seen as antithetical to a viable habitat; an insult to the natural world. Local community life within this world economic community is not an end in itself but only a means to an end. That is why along with the growth of this global economic marketplace there has been corresponding destruction to community life lived at local levels (Daly and Cobb 1989). The 'wonderworld' of this competitive global community is becoming the 'wasteworld' of the local community.

View of time   There is a type of 'manifest destiny' mentality in the progressive technozoic vision. The concepts of growth, development and competition are placed in an evolutionary framework. The time-line of this vision is linear and evolutionary. There is a kind of unfolding of destiny and the best approach is to embrace the changes that destiny dictates. Change is viewed as 'progress' and proceeds along a continuum in which societies and communities are gradually moving onwards and upwards. As Ronald Reagan said long ago in his General Electric advertisements: 'progress is our most important product.' This forwards, onwards and upwards movement of history frequently makes light of the past. The past is the enemy of the future. This is the notion of progress in the idea of the 'progressive form'. Progress, in its contemporary form, is the movement into the global competitive marketplace.

View of space The dominant idea of space within this vision can be labelled 'pluralistic'. Pluralism here means that there is no idea of a collective relational whole that is seen governing each part. Thus, we see a cluster of freely operating or isolated parts. We are talking here of a 'pluriverse' rather than a universe; a 'pluriverse' whose foundation engenders the fundamental motif of 'competition':

> Functional regions are distinct and unrelated (e.g.; economics, politics, and culture). It is assumed in this model that the 'common good' is not the direct object of social concern, but results indirectly from the self-actualization of all of the parts. In economic terms, an 'invisible hand' guides competition in the 'free market' system for the benefit of all. In political terms, the parts are actuated as interest groups; in cultural terms they express themselves through 'free thought.' In this view, a healthy society is marked by individualism and innovation; it thrives in an expanding, competitive market. (Holland and Henriot 1984: 29)

In this atmosphere of pluralistic atomism, it is the role of the educational system to prepare the learner for the newly emergent market that is expanding beyond the nation-state into the sphere of the transnational corporations.

Pre-eminent metaphor Machines as an analogue for the understanding of human behaviour and institutions have been part of the fabric of scientific and social explanation in the modern world. Mechanistic explanation is based on the principles of analysis and atomism. The whole can be understood as the sum of its individual parts. You can understand the clock by taking it apart and rebuilding it from its constituent components. It is felt by some of the ecological critics that the view of the world in mechanistic terms has been one of the major factors in the deterioration of our relationship to the natural world (Berman 1981; Merchant 1980). We can also see how the metaphor of mechanism operates at the level of the organization of the schools. Much of the development of modern bureaucratic organizations has as its foundation a non-organic perspective of how parts of an organization relate to one another. There is no intrinsic relationship of parts; parts are held together by an authoritarian hierarchy and discrete horizontal status divisions.

View of conflict Although the rhetoric of competition and combat is given centre stage, we nevertheless see that when it comes to questioning the fundamental tenets of this vision there is an ameliorating emphasis on gradualism and incremental change. Therefore, any conflictual challenges to the hegemony of this system of thinking are considered to be unnecessary and therefore superficial. When ecologists make fundamental critiques of the governing global market economy as antithetical to the functioning of the biosphere, these criticisms are labelled as precipitous and an overreaction. There is a cure within this system for everything. Anything that has been done can be undone. Technology can solve the problems created by techno-logical innovation. Within the broad spectrum of this line of thinking, there is zero tolerance for conflict and critique that challenges this system's integrity. Therefore, in societies like our own, the whole area of social conflict is closely managed by politicians, business persons and ultimately, the educator who acts as the apologist of this system. Managing the challenge of social conflict and keeping it at the level of superficial change is the *sine qua non* of liberal progressive thought. Within this system, the most powerful social force is inertia. Technology and science can solve our so-called 'exaggerated environ-mental crisis'. As it is frequently put in ironic terms within this vision, 'What's the problem?'

Contemporary educational features   Because of the pluralism of this educa-tional space, educational trends are as varied as they are unrelated to one another. Their one common feature is that they all appear to accept uncritically the direction of educational change that leads us into the global competitive marketplace. The techniques are as variable as they are fragmented. For the global competitive educator, we have the global cafeteria of techniques and approaches. On the theoretical side we have the emergent area of educational theory called by its followers 'cognitive science'. Cognitive science is an amalgam of research and theory and partly an offshoot of post-Piagetian research. It is also combined with recent developments in computer simula-tion. In relation to education, it may be said that there is an assumption that the improvement of education is related to an improved and adequate science of the mind. A specific development of this type of science is the attempt to make links between the area of cognitive developmental psychology and computer systems simulation. Ulric Neisser (1967) gives an indication of the machine-metaphorical use of the computer as a guide to human under-standing: he perceives that the task of the psychologist trying to understand human cognition is analogous to that of a person trying to discover how a computer is programmed. Particularly, if the program seems to store and reuse information, the researcher would like to know by what 'routines' or 'procedures' that it is done. There have been many developments in the area of cognitive science that could be assessed over the past twenty-five years. There is also a growing scepticism about many of the attempts at simulation of the mind through machine analogues (O'Sullivan 1983). For our purposes, it is sufficient to say that this total approach proceeds with all of its variations on the assumption that the mind is independent from the natural world. It remains, therefore, locked in the Cartesian split that puts the mind over nature rather than in the natural world. There is also a penchant within this direction somehow to exceed the ordinary feats of the mind by creating organisms or machines such as robots. Here again we see a certain hubris that 'nature didn't do it right the first time'. However, some positive features are indicated in some of the directions of 'cognitive science'. For example, the cultural historian William Irwin Thompson ventures a more biocentric direction for cognitive science. In a series of edited essays entitled *Gaia: A Way of Knowing* (1987), Thompson attempts to connect the earlier work of Gregory Bateson in *Steps in an Ecology of Mind* (1972) and *Mind in Nature* (1980) to the recent work on the mind as a self-regulating autopoetic structure embedded in the natural world. This is an attempt to locate the direction of cognitive science in a 'biocentric' as opposed to a 'technocentric' path. This emergent direction is not centre stage as of yet and conventional cognitive science still reigns.

My overall assessment of cognitive science is that it continues to see the mind outside nature and possesses the hubris that it is for the 'human mind' to correct nature through the development of the technologies of the human mind. Where one of those technologies is the wedding of the mind to robotics, a note of caution is certainly warranted (Mander 1991).

Having discussed cognitive science, it is important to note that one of the more prominent directions of educational psychological theory and research extols the virtue of a view of the learner as independent of the natural world. Cognitive science is just one of the many innovations in educational research that competes for the attention of educators who desperately try to find one technical solution after another to deal with the declining effectiveness of schools in the lives of students at all levels of education. In this light, teachers are constantly hoping the next panacea will be the real thing. So we have the seeming endless parade of new techniques and workshops that extol the latest idea that promises a way out of the dilemmas of survival in the terminal cenozoic. All do their thing in the guise that whatever technique is being touted, it is scientifically based and will contribute to our uncritical forward advance through technology. This is progress and it is a progress that is extolled by the conventional advance of science and technological break-through. The question that I pose to you here is, 'What if the breakthrough is contributing to the breakdown rather than alleviating it?' C. A. Bowers makes an important critical observation about our unreflective use of science and technique in education:

> The vast number of techniques being promoted as essential to professional growth also has another effect, namely the fostering of a nihilistic attitude

where everything begins to be seen as of equal value. Without a deeper knowledge that allows issues, trends, and techniques to be put into a more reflective perspective, each technique loses its distinctness and special merit, particularly when teachers begin to realize that each year brings new dis- seminators with even more 'advanced' techniques and learning skills. What may have been found to be useful from a previous workshop, like individualized instruction or performance objectives, disappears from the list of workshop topics as new topics are added. (Bowers 1993b: 86–7)

Bowers then goes further and criticizes the progressive technocratic tradition in education for its total lack of understanding of the ecological crisis. Speak- ing again about the proliferation of techniques he stresses their tendency to foster an ecological myopia:

It also becomes part of a professional hypnosis where the events in the larger world beyond the classroom are not and cannot be fully grasped as related to what goes on in the classroom. This is particularly the case when social and environmental events cannot be related to the technique. How does the teacher connect the loss of forest cover with the classroom techniques derived from brain research, or the warming of the earth's atmosphere with 'Proactive Classroom Management?' (Bowers 1993b: 87)

As educators, we can no longer move along this path uncritically, and criticism is forthcoming from many circles. One area of criticism comes from the conservative critique of modern education. It is to this tradition or vision that we now turn.

The conservative vision

There have always been reactions to the modernist vision of evolutionary progress. Even at the onset of industrialism, with all its entrancement, there were very vocal critics of the project of modernism embedded in the techno- logical industrialism of the late cenozoic. The visionary poetry of William Blake is replete with criticism of both the Enlightenment and the fundamental tenets of the industrial revolution. There has also been a long history of 'anti- modern' reaction to the historical directions of modernism. This type of reaction has many turns and nuances, sometimes bringing together peculiar bedfellows. What is common to all the reactions, to the ideal of industrial progress, is an abhorrence of some of the negative features of the modern world as well as, frequently, nostalgia. Two of those anti-modern features coalesce in the vision of conservatism and romanticism. We will focus on the conservative dimension since it has been the most dominant form of anti- modernism in contemporary educational contexts.

From the 'conservative' side, there is an attempt to conserve the forces and institutions that were bypassed by the developments of modernism. Frequently, the conservative reaction is embedded in a position of elitism and hierarchy where there are attempts to defy some of the democratic directions of the modern world. For example, the institution of the Catholic Church was one of the main counter-positions to modernism in both the late nineteenth century and the first half of the twentieth century. There is an anti-modernest critique which labels modernism as the destroyer of traditional community values such as authority and obedience to traditional rules and customs. Thus, one aspect of the conservative critique of modernism is the perception that there is the erosion of a 'sense of community'. The other side of the reaction to modernism can be labelled the romantic revolt. The romantic revolt is highly critical of the modern dimensions of science and technology that have led to a disembodied thinking. This critique of rationalism is centred on modern thought, indicating that there is an inability to include the emotions in the development of the intellect. A further criticism is located in a sense of the loss of a body awareness and in the reification of the mind as distinct from the natural world. This results in the exclusion of vital organic processes in highly mechanistic views of the world. Thus, in both its conservative and romantic guises, a critique of modernism has always been forthcoming. Especially in its conservative aspects, the conservative–romantic vision commends the virtues of the institutions of the past. Nothing succeeds like the past.

Educational world view/history Nothing illustrates the amalgam of conservative and romantic writing on education better than the work of Henry Adams, a cultural historian, writing and reflecting on our arrival into the twentieth century. In a series of essays under the title *The Education of Henry Adams* (1931 [1918]), he reflects on the possible negative features of the dynamic industrial–technical inventiveness that he witnessed in the development of the machine technologies that were being extolled at the World's Fair of 1896. He was an historian of medieval western culture and we can see in his writing a kind of nostalgia for what was being lost in the exodus from the medieval world synthesis. We see in the core of his writings – as in those of many of the other critics of modernism – a deep suspicion towards the many directions of the modernist spirit. In our century newer forms have appeared. There has been a deep suspicion about the developments of modern technology in the work of such writers as Jaques Ellul (1964) and George Grant (1983); a wariness towards the democratization of the masses as seen in the writing of Ortega y Gasset (1957); and a protest against the general direction of education towards vocational technological ends. In the latter context, we see education critiqued because it allies itself to the forces of the modern world of industry and technology and conforms its mandate to their needs. Robert Maynard Hutchins, in defining a 'liberal education', gives us a sense of why contemporary education has become problematic.

> What is Liberal education? It is easy to say what it is not. It is not specialized education, not vocational, professional or preprofessional. Its not an education that teaches a man to do any specific thing ... I am tempted to say that it is education that no American can get in an educational institution nowadays. We are all specialists now. Even early in High School we are told that we must begin to think that we are going to earn a living, and the prerequisites that are supposed to prepare us for that activity become more and more the ingredients for our educational diet. I am afraid that we shall have to admit that the educational process in America is either a rather pleasant way of passing the time until we are ready to go to work, or a way of getting ready for some occupation, or a combination of the two. What is missing is education to be human beings, education to make the most of our human powers, education for our responsibilities as members of a democratic society, education for freedom. (Hutchins 1959: v).

And where does this conservative tradition suggest that we go to find this type of liberal education? Hutchins suggests that we find it in 'the great books of the western world'. When you look carefully at the suggested 'great' books, you realize that they are male-authored. We see here that the journey into our past is limited only to our western cultural past, a past devoid of women. That this particular approach continues to have a contemporary attraction and ring was seen in the recent interest in Alan Bloom's *The Closing of the American Mind* (1987). His book is the most recent embodiment of the 'great books tradition' of the western world. As one critic of his work puts it, 'he believes that questions about the content of education (i.e., curriculum) were settled some time ago; perhaps once and for all with Plato, but certainly not later than Nietzsche' (Orr 1992: 97). Along with his cultivation of the life of the mind through the classics of western literature, there is a scurrilous attack on American youth culture. It is, in Bloom's opinion, morally deficient and intellectually slack. These are just two negative characteristics among the numerous qualities of youth culture that he finds repugnant. In this most contemporary version of the conservation of our best male western authors, we become aware that there is nowhere in this critique of modern educational institutions a mention of issues of social justice, poverty and ecological degradation that plague the modern mind as well as the modern landscape. What is present, as with his predecessors in this tradition, is an unreflective ethnocentric eurocentrism coupled with blind gender bias. As the same critic put it:

> It is widely acknowledged that the classics of the Western tradition are deficient in certain respects. First, having been composed by white males, they exclude

the vast majority of human experience. Moreover, there are problems that this tradition has not successfully resolved, either because they are of recent origin, or because they are regarded as unimportant. In the latter category is the issue of the human role in the natural world ... Whatever timeless qualities human nature may or may not have, Western culture has not offered much enlightenment on the appropriate relationship between humanity and its habitat. (Orr 1992: 98)

This is not to say that certain aspects of a conservative perspective have no merit in addressing our present ecological crisis. For example, C. A. Bowers (1993b) identifies two lines of conservatism, an anthropocentric and an ecological strain. The tradition of Adler, Bloom and others is categorized in Bower's work as anthropocentric and he makes the same criticism of this direction that I am making here. He further identifies a tradition of conservatism that he calls 'ecological conservatism'. This is a tradition that has a deep cultural critique of our modern technological culture regarding its effects on the natural habitat. Bowers (1993b) names Edward Schumacher, Wendell Berry and Gary Snyder as exemplars of this tradition. I do not discuss this direction here, which Bowers correctly identifies as an ecologically oriented perspective, because the writers in this line of thinking have not addressed themselves to the issues of education in the formal sense. For myself, this tradition is more in line with what I will later be calling the 'ecozoic transformational'; a direction that certainly has elements of ecological conservatism within it.

Orientation to community and natural world The conservative position has an orientation towards the natural world that is simultaneously anthropocentric and traditional. It is anthropocentric in that it locates all educational objectives within the human mind. Thus, the location of educational enrichment is housed within the cultivating powers of human thought. It is the task of education to provide educational stimulus for enriching that mind. At the level of school organization (as well as the community of the school) there is the fostering of community structures that are based on tradition and hierarchy. Edward Wynne, who locates himself within the conservative tradition, suggests a list of 'traditional values' that should be incorporated into modern schooling. They are as follows:

1) The acceptance of traditional hierarchy
2) The exercise of strong adult control over children and adolescents
3) The priority given to immediate good conduct over more elaborate ratiocination
4) Great emphasis on the life of collective entities
5) Reverence for the knowledge of the past

6) The reservation of a sphere of life for sacred activities, beyond the day to day business of buying, selling, and producing
7) The equality of all community members as children of God, despite their temporal, material, and intellectual differences. (Wynne 1987: 130–2)

Although this particular catalogue of traditional conservative values might not receive universal acclaim, there are some elements of Wynne's traditionalism that apply to all. First, there is a nostalgia for a past that maintains order through hierarchy. Second, the sacred is located solely within the 'human community'. Third, there is no attention at all given to the effects that the human community is having on our natural habitat. Fourth, the human community is bound by and best regulated by traditions of the past. The way out of our present malaise is a return to the traditions of the past which, incidently, go as far back only as the Judaeo-Christian past and the advent of western culture.

View of time Time in the conservative world view is cyclical and static. There is within this perspective of time an organic biological basis for temporality that is static because of the underlying belief that nothing changes in society in any fundamental or transformative manner. The expression '*plus ça change, plus c'est la meme-chose*' is apt. Change is a cycle that repeats itself in patterns of growth–decline, birth–maturity–death, and so on. We see these change patterns in nature's rhythms, for example in the cycles of the seasons of the year. Since there is no compelling forward direction of history, as in the progressive perspective, there is no desire to bring on some glorious future. What is present is a painstaking observation of the best of antiquity. Thus, the traditional preoccupation with the past is everywhere evident.

View of space If the progressive view of space was atomistic and particularistic, the conservative position espouses a form of 'organic essentialism'. By organic, I mean here a view that society is some kind of organic unity where the whole of society is greater than the sum of its parts. By essentialist, I mean that there are some deep structural essences that are seen to be underlying all social processes. A great deal of natural law theory exemplifies the idea that there are deep structural essences that can be seen to integrate the complexities of human societies.

Pre-eminent metaphor The pre-eminent conservative metaphor is the human body as an organic totality. Using the human body as a metaphor of understanding, there is a hierarchy that is established among the parts of the body with priority given to the head. The metaphor being organic in principle, there is an understanding that the human body grows, decays and regenerates and the various parts are organically related to one another with the internal functions and external operations controlled by the head. This type of organic understanding places a strong emphasis on the hierarchical arrangements of parts and the ordering of parts based on established authoritarian structures. Hierarchy is seen as a natural underlying structure of all institutional life. Thus Edward Wynne (1987), in outlining his conservative educational viewpoint, maintains that hierarchy is a fact in all continuing organizations in our era, including schools: 'Today, there is much discussion to the effect that teachers should not properly be "authority" figures. However, parents and children alike recognize the necessary truth that teachers must play an authority role, and they are puzzled by the confusion resulting from attempts to conceal the reality of hierarchy' (Wynne 1987: 130).

What is emphasized within this view is that the ordering of the parts is based on laws activated at the top of the structure. Thus, any type of change activated from a position other than from the top of the hierarchy is seen as deviant. This is how conflict is viewed in hierarchical systems.

View of conflict In traditional systems of hierarchy, conflict is viewed within these structures as deviant and anarchic in the pejorative sense. Within hierarchical systems, there is a very marked emphasis on 'law and order'. The most appropriate response to the disorder of things is either to cushion its effects and absorb it into the present system or to reject the conflictual elements outright as in excommunication. Using the human body as metaphor, one can utilize the example of the transplant. When an organ is transplanted into the human body it is either accepted or rejected and expelled. A challenge to the body is either absorbed into the system or rejected. Thus we see, within the workings of traditional hierarchical organization, a very powerful emphasis on 'law and order', with order and harmony as the basic social virtues. Holland and Henriot give us a very clear example of the working structure using the traditional western Catholic Church:

> A landed aristocracy, hierarchically structured through nobility, high clergy, constituting a ruling elite. At best, this form of leadership served as a paternalistic guardian of the 'common good' exercising a *noblesse oblige* toward lower classes. At worst, it collapsed into despotic absolutism. In either case, its reaction to a challenge to the status quo was the same – absorption or suppression. Such rule was justified on ideological grounds by appeals to the 'divine right of kings,' demands of 'social order,' the preservation of 'tradition' and 'sound doctrine,' and the assertion that 'this is the way things have always been done.' (Holland and Henriot 1984: 34).

Contemporary educational features In the past, the preservation of the conservative traditional ethos in education was seen in the development of private elite schools. These schools housed the children of the power elite. In the traditional systems of 'elite education' there was a very strong emphasis on the value of hierarchy because it was considered the foundation for a just and ordered society. Children were inculcated into a hierarchical structure of order that they were to submit to with obedience. Furthermore, they were learning to understand that they were to be inheritors of a system where they would be the ones to give orders to others who would be their subjects. Thus, the children of the privileged acquired a sense of entitlement that they were to be the inheritors of a system of order that placed them at the top of the hierarchy. Pupils would learn the powers of governance that they would eventually apply to those who, by the very natural order of things, were below them. In contemporary education, the elite school system is only one embodiment of the traditional conservative vision. In the last ten years, there has also been a popular movement within the discourse of public education that propounds the virtues of traditionalism, conservatism and hierarchy. Edward Wynne is a vocal proponent of traditional hierarchical education within this public sphere. His description of effective schools serves as a clear example:

> Effective schools are led, we are told, by vigorous principals who clearly make known their values and policies. When necessary, these principals display determination and courage and press toward their goals in the face of resistance. Furthermore, teachers in such schools respect their principals, follow directions, and expect similar obedience from students. Such leadership does not imply poor communication or disengagement between followers and leaders. In effective schools, adults are unquestionably in control. Fair, firm, and appropriate discipline is applied. Such insistence has nothing to do with oppression. It is simply regarded as an acceptance of traditional, transitional adult responsibility and as a means of transmitting wholesome values to young persons. (Wynne 1987: 132)

Wynne's articulation of a traditional conservative vision for schooling is a contemporary reaction to the breakdown of traditional authority in the development of modernist progressive education. There is absolutely no sense that there are problems that we are facing today that are truly unique to our historical period; namely the scope and magnitude of our ecological crisis. There is no mention, whatsoever, of this incredible degradation of the natural world as a problem to be dealt with as an educational challenge. One of the more prominent problems with the conservative vision is an extreme anthropo-centrism. There is a total lack of response to the natural habitat in the discourse of modern conservative thinkers. Conservation is not the conservation of the natural habitat. Conservation within the contemporary discourse of educa-tional theory is the maintenance of the authority structures of western male white culture.

The transformative ecozoic vision

In this book, I am attempting to develop what I consider as an emergent form, a 'transformative vision'. This transformative vision contests and repudiates the viability of the global marketplace as it is currently being formulated within the transnational economic order. It is my view that this global marketplace vision cannot be a viable cultural planetary vision for the future. In essence, we are attempting to pursue a transformative ecozoic vision as an alternative to the global market vision. Here the current resurgence of the 'terminal cenozoic' is seen in the educational reform criticism of the global competitive marketeers.

The educational field of 'critical pedagogy' is one emergent educational forum that attempts to deal with the broad area of social justice issues that are embedded in inequities of power and resources along the lines of class, race and gender. In my own work, *Critical Psychology and Critical Pedagogy* (1990) and *Critical Psychology: An Interpretation of the Personal World* (1984), I attempt to show how these structures operate in educational contexts in areas such as school learning and popular movement education. The work in this area covers vital social justice concerns dealing with post-colonial and anti-racist education (Dei 1995b), class analysis and gender inequity (O'Sullivan 1990; 1984; hooks 1994; Hart 1995). There is a development of resistance education (also called counter-hegemonic education) based on the work of Antonio Gramsci (1971), Paulo Freire (1970), bell hooks (1994) and others (Aronowitz and Giroux, 1993).

There are also some similar trends in a critical standpoint that is presently being formulated in the area of adult education. A compilation of these trends in adult education can be found in Michael Welton's edited *In Defence of the Life World: Critical Perspectives on Adult Learning* (1995), and Paul Wangoola and Frank Youngman's edited *Towards a Transformative Political Economy of Adult Education* (1996). Critical adult education is a counter-movement in adult education that is presently questioning the hegemony of conventional adult education that I have discussed under progressive technocratic education. What we see in these newer critical currents is a questioning of the vision of the global marketplace, gender and class inequity, and post-colonial perspectives that question the dominance of western cultural hegemony. There is a criticism of mainstream adult education, at the level of paradigm, from the point of view of critical social theory that can be found in the works of Jack Meizerow (1995), Michael Welton (1995), Mechhthild Hart (1995) and Michael Collins (1991; 1995).

Probably one of the most prominent omissions in the critical pedagogical approach to education at this juncture of its formulations is its lack of attention to ecological issues. My major criticism is the pre-eminent emphasis on inter-human problems frequently to the detriment of the relations of humans to the wider biotic community and the natural world. The general direction of critical perspectives is towards anthropocentrism. The criticism of anthropocentrism is by no means a reason for dismissal of the vital concerns that critical perspectives pose for contemporary education. These issues must be taken forwards and fused into wider biocentric concerns. This will be a major challenge of this book in its final chapters.

Holistic education is another emergent trend in education which challenges the fragmentation of modernism that comes to us under a scientific analytical and instrumentally rational world view (J. Miller 1996). John Miller, one of the major architects of holistic education in North America, signals some of the features of holism in his introductory comments to the topic in *The Holistic Curriculum*:

> Holistic education attempts to bring education into alignment with the fundamental realities of nature. Nature at its core is interrelated and dynamic. We can see this dynamism and connectedness in the atom, organic systems, the biosphere, and the universe itself. Unfortunately, the human world since the Industrial Revolution has stressed compartmentalization and standardization. The result has been the fragmentation of life. (J. Miller 1996: 1)

Holistic educators are also very critical of the instrumental technocratic emphasis of contemporary education to the exclusion of very core aspects of life such as creativity and spirituality. Declining to identify themselves within a religious framework, there are several current treatments of education which identify spirituality as a core feature for all educational endeavours (Palmer 1993; Purpel 1989; Moffett 1994). In criticizing the shallow rationalism and value-neutral nature of modernist education, holistic educators attempt to root education in an ethical framework that goes beyond the broken surface of our lives today to a hidden wholeness. In this type of education, the intellect and spirit are integral parts of one another.

As with critical pedagogy, holistic educators are sharply critical of modernist education but for very different reasons. My conclusion is that they complement one another and should be allied. Attempting to make this alignment will be another goal of an expanded and integral 'transformative ecozoic education'.

Finally, an emergent area labelled 'global education' deserves mention. Here I am not speaking of global perspectives that prepare us for the global marketplace, but of global education perspectives that carry a planetary consciousness. The approaches to global education that I am speaking of here bear the closest resemblance to what I am calling transformative ecozoic education, in that they wed a holistic education to a planetary consciousness while maintaining a critical perspective. There are numerous instances. Budd Hall and I have done some preliminary work in the area of adult education, attempting to articulate a transformative vision in this field of adult education (Hall and O'Sullivan 1995). There is also the groundbreaking work in global education of David Selby (1995) and Graham Pike (Pike and Selby 1988) from England. The pioneering of Thomas Lyons (Lyons and O'Sullivan 1992) at the Ontario Teachers' Federation is another example. Working with teachers in the Province of Ontario, Lyons has articulated an educational vision that takes into consideration a broad cosmological perspective and combines it with an integral vision of education that includes global planetary concepts, social justice and human rights sensitivities, peace perspectives and environmental concerns.

Educational world view   At this point I would like to outline the broad features of a transformative vision that will be articulated in greater depth in the last section of this work. I have already suggested, through historical scholarship, that the loss of a cosmological sense has had profound consequences for the modern world. There is also an indication that the absence of a functional cosmology has profoundly affected the western mind-set in its treatment of the natural world. We have now reached the point where it is possible to open up a discussion on the redevelopment of enchantment or re-enchantment. There have been counter-movements to the disenchantment of the world going all the way back to Newton. Prophetic voices, from the very outset, could see the far-reaching implications of the potential down-side of the scientific world. William Blake, the mystical poet, was one of the first voices to see the underside of the Industrial Revolution. Blake was very perceptive in his poetic criticism and directed his critical gaze at Newton:

> Now I a fourfold vision see
> And a fourfold vision is given to me
> Tis fourfold in my supreme delight
> And threefold in soft Beaulah's night
> And twofold Always May God us keep
> From Single Vision & Newton's sleep!
>
> (William Blake in Schorer 1946: 5)

In the Blakean world, Newton's single vision is the principle of analysis that partitioned the natural world and left it in fragments. Sleep connoted the hypnotic character that this fragmentation would have on the perception of his contemporaries as well as on posterity. The power of this type of criticism was no contest for the powerful world view that Newton and Descartes spawned. Even into the nineteenth century, the Romantic movement would attempt to launch devastating critiques in literary circles. This in no way undercut the magnetic power of the industrial–scientific world synthesis. It is the devastating ecological crisis that has brought into question the integrity and desirability of our industrial–scientific world order. When we speak of a re-enchantment of the natural world, we are stretching ourselves to a new cosmological vision of our world. This is a world in which we can feel at home in the universe. David Griffin (1988a) gives several conditions for this cosmological reorientation: 'The formal conditions for such a postmodern cosmology, in which our understanding of humanity and nature are integrated with practice in view, include reinserting humanity and life as a whole back into nature, and regarding our fellow creatures not merely as a means but as ends in themselves' (D. Griffin 1988a: 38).

The theoretical physicist David Bohm deepens our understanding of the meaning of re-enchantment. Reflecting on the cosmological implications of the theory of relativity he conjectures:

> We speak of a whirlpool but one does not exist. In the same way we can speak of a particle, but one does not exist: particle is the name for a certain form in the field of movement. If you bring two particles together, they will gradually modify each other and eventually become one. Consequently, the approach contradicted the assumptions of separate, elementary, mechanical constituents of the universe. In doing so, it brought in a view that I call unbroken wholeness or flowing wholeness. It has always been called seamless wholeness. The universe is one seamless, unbroken whole. (Bohm 1988: 23–4)

Our modern dilemma is that we cannot re-enchant the world with a pre-modern cosmos. A pre-modern cosmology would fly in the face of the amazing advances that we have made in modern science. Morris Berman is clear that nostalgia for the past is not the solution that we should be pursuing:

> We cannot go back to alchemy or animism – at least that does not seem likely; but the alternative is the grim, scientific, totally controlled world of nuclear reactors, microprocessors, and genetic engineering – a world virtually upon us already. Some type of holistic, or participating, consciousness and a corresponding sociopolitical formation have to emerge if we are to survive as a species. (Berman 1981: 23)

This desire for a creative hiatus is seen in all areas of the physical and social sciences. David Bohm sounds a familiar call for change, remarking that our entire world order has been dissolving away for over a century. His suggestion is to forge pathways beyond the modern temper:

> I suggest that if we are to survive in a meaningful way in the face of this disintegration of the present world order, a truly creative movement to a new kind of wholeness is needed, a movement that must ultimately gives credence to a new order as was the modern to the medieval order. We cannot go back to the premodern order. A postmodern world must come into being before

the modern world destroys itself so thoroughly that little can be done for a long time to come. (Bohm 1988: 23–4)

I have been emphasizing that we are, at the present, in a transitional period in need of a functional cosmology. The difficulty is that the term 'cosmology' is so exclusively physical in its accepted meaning that it does not transparently suggest the integral reality of the universe. For the same reason, the term 'geology' does not show the integral reality of the earth but only its physical aspects. Now we do not have a terminology suited to a serious consideration of the earth. It is our task now to offer the reader a blueprint for a new cosmological sense. In suggesting an alternative, the question must be asked, 'What will be the educational features of the transformative ecozoic vision?' Here again, I will follow the conventions that I have adopted in the previous sections.

Orientation to community and natural world There is both traditional wisdom and an emergent form of knowledge that comes from the ecological sciences that suggest a radically different view of the earth community. In the past decade, there has been a resurgence of interest in the world views of Native American peoples that suggest a cosmology very different from our traditional western scientific perspective. If we take away the romanticization of native cultures (which seems also part of the current interest in indigenous ways), there is much to be learned about a proper orientation to the earth community from the traditional wisdoms of the native peoples of the Americas (Sioui 1992). I say 'wisdoms' because there is a tendency to lump native cultures into a common soup while ignoring the incredible variety and splendour of differences that we see in the multiform presence of native peoples on this continent (Burger 1990). One feature of sameness that seems to cut across these differences is that of a common understanding that the earth is not a dead resource for human consumption but a sacred community and web of life of profound intricacy. Another feature that seems to be present is a profound intimacy with the natural processes of the earth. A third feature, although not universal, is an orientation to the earth in a nurturing form where the earth is seen as Mother. Finally, there is a mystical sense of the place of the human and other living beings.

Turning from indigenous world views of traditional peoples we can also see a broadening of our sense of community as a result of the recent advances of space travel. In the Preface to the beautifully illustrated book, *The Home Planet*, the astronaut Russell Schweickart makes the following observation about the profound effect that his spaceflight had on his awareness of the planet earth:

For me, having spent ten days in weightlessness, orbiting our beautiful home planet, fascinated by the 17,000 miles of spectacle passing below each hour, the overwhelming experience was that of a new relationship. The experience was not intellectual. The knowledge I had when I returned to Earth's surface was virtually the same knowledge that I had taken with me when I went into space. Yes I conducted scientific experiments that added new knowledge to our understanding of the Earth and the near-space in which it spins. But those specific extensions of technical details I did not come to know about until the data I helped to collect was analysed and reported. What took no analysis, however, no microscopic examination, no laborious processing, was the over-whelming beauty ... the stark contrast between bright colourful home and stark black infinity ... the unavoidable and awesome personal relationship, suddenly realized, with all life on this planet ... Earth, our home. (Kelley 1988: Preface)

I beg the reader, at this point, to bear with me for a personal digression that has, I hope, didactic import. When I was a child, I had the incredible privilege of accompanying my father to Ireland, to his birthplace in County Cork, to spend three months in a farmhouse with no electricity and no plumbing. It was his house of birth and looked down on a salt-water lake with an abandoned castle on an island in the middle. The lake opened into a rapids that emptied into the Atlantic Ocean. The experience was of such significance for me that when I returned there with my wife some eighteen years later I had total recall of all the surroundings. The experience, for me, was rooted in the raw beauty of the natural world and its numinous presence. All my senses, at that time, seemed heightened. I returned many times to the memories of this period of my life as I was growing up. It was a very special place. It was, for me, an enchanted place. It was a sacred place. In mid-life I am now beginning to discover that this very earth which I call my home is a sacred place.

Indeed, the earth symbol is becoming a sacred symbol for me as for many others. Nevertheless, it is ironic that the perspective of the planet earth as our 'home planet' comes out of the military–industrial complexes of the USA and the former USSR. The perspective of the earth from outer space moved the astronauts well beyond the parochialism of their nation-state consciousness:

There is a clarity, a brilliance to space that simply doesn't exist on Earth, even on a cloudless summer's day in the Rockies, and nowhere else can you realize so fully the majesty of our Earth and be so awed at the thought that it's the only one of untold thousands of planets. (Gus Grissom, USA; cited in Kelley 1988: 18)

What struck me most was the silence. It was a great silence, unlike any I have encountered on Earth, so vast and deep that I began to hear my own body; my heart beating, my blood vessels pulsating, even the rustle of my muscles moving over each other seemed audible. There were more stars in the sky than I had expected. The sky was deep black yet at the same time bright with sunlight. The Earth was small, light blue, and so touchingly alone, our home that must be defended as a holy relic. (Aleksei Leonov, USSR; cited in Kelley 1988: 24–5)

Reflecting on the astronauts' journey into outer space, James Lovelock (1988) brought to the scientific community a new understanding of the earth with his formulation of the 'Gaia Hypothesis'. I will not go into the technical details here, but the hypothesis ventures that in its totality the earth itself is a living entity. As Lovelock points out in this hypothesis, we can now see that the air, the ocean and the soil are much more than a mere environment for life; they are a part of life itself. He believes that the air is to life as the fur is to the cat or the nest for the bird. Lovelock contends that there is nothing unusual in the idea of life on earth interacting with the air, sea and rocks. He came to his initial idea for the 'Gaia Hypothesis' when he observed an outside glimpse of the earth from outer space. Lovelock felt that this earth, in all its interactions and transformations, added up to a single giant living system with the capacity to keep itself in a state most favourable for the life upon it. It is within this wider context that we are beginning to appreciate the earth as a very special place. It is, in some very special ways, unique to our universe. The more that we explore the expanses of space, the more we are coming to recognize the incredible and exceptional beauty of our planet. There may be no other planet that has monarch butterflies, symphonic music, flowers. Our planet is inviting us to a new understanding of ourselves and our place within the earth and the larger cosmos. Louise Young, in her beautifully crafted essays on *The Blue Planet*, makes the point that we are still far from knowing the truth about our home in space but we are slowly moving towards deeper realizations:

Less than a century ago the earth was believed to be the very embodiment of stability, the unchanging background against which the drama of movement and growth and life was enacted. Men spoke confidently of the 'solid earth' and the 'everlasting hills.' Now we know that nothing is static – not the earth itself or any part of it. If we could watch a time-lapse movie of the planet's history, we would see an amazing drama of change and development: mountains being created and destroyed, sea floor ejected along the ocean ridges and consumed again at the trenches, canyons being carved by turbulent rivers, new continents split from old ones and set adrift to wander around the planet. This information has caused a revolution in our understanding of the earth and the revolution is still in progress. Those of us who know the planet that we live on must look at it anew with unjaded eyes like those of a child. (Young 1983: 5)

We are coming to understand that we are living in a period of the earth's history that is incredibly turbulent and in an epoch in which there are violent processes of change that challenge us at every level imaginable. The pathos of human life today is that humans are totally caught up in this incredible transformation and have a most significant responsibility for the direction it will take. The terror here is that we have it within our power to make life extinct on this planet. Because of the magnitude of this responsibility for the planet, all our educational ventures must finally be judged within this order of magnitude. This is the challenge for all areas of education. For education, this realization is the bottom line. What do I mean here by bottom line? For me, the bottom line is that every educational endeavour must keep in mind the magnitude of our present moment when setting educational priorities. This demands a kind of attentiveness to our present planetary situation that does not go into slumber or denial. It poses momentous challenges to educators in areas heretofore unimagined. Education within the context of 'global transformation' keeps concerns for the planet always at the forefront.

This broadening of perspective has given us a new sense of this planet in which we inhabit and one of the most profound symbols of our time is the symbol of the planet earth seen from space. Joseph Campbell suggests that this earth symbol broadens our sense of community: 'When you see the earth from the moon, you don't see any divisions there of nations or states. This might be the symbol for the new mythology to come. That is the country that we are going to be celebrating. And those of the people that we are one with.' (Campbell 1988: 32)

Finally, recent developments in the ecological sciences have also given us a broadened sense of the living earth community. Instead of thinking of the world as a set of constituent parts as in a clock, we now have an emergent sense that humans are not separated constituent parts of a dead earth. We are creatures who are embedded in the 'web of life'. This growing awareness helps us to see the human species and the human community in a larger biotic context. We are a species among other species, not a species above other species. Our western hierarchical view of the human above other species and above the natural world itself is being fundamentally challenged. Bill Devall and George Sessions (1985) see the emergence of a deep ecological perspective as a way of developing a new balance and harmony between individuals, communities and all of nature. I would say that an ecozoic vision must have as its fundamental premiss this broadened sense of community and the integral relationship that the humans have to have with it. The development of this consciousness must be one of the profound educational directions for the closing decade of the twentieth century.

View of time In my discussions of the conservative and technozoic progressive visions, I have treated time and space under separate headings. For the sake of symmetry, I will continue this distinction. Nevertheless, it must be said that with some of the current revelations of science it is more appropriate to speak in a dimension labelled space-time. Swimme and Berry clarify the idea of a 'time-developmental' context as follows:

> We have, over these past few centuries, become aware that the universe has emerged into being through an irreversible sequence of transformations that have, in the larger arc of their movement, enabled the universe to pass from a lesser to a greater complexity in its structure and functioning as well as to a greater variety and intensity in its modes of conscious expression as this can be observed on the planet Earth. This sequence of transformations we might refer to as a time-developmental process. (Swimme and Berry 1992: 223)

View of space as space-time emergence The universe is a unity that is a dynamic totality that cannot be explained by constituent parts. When I speak of unity, I mean that the way that one can understand the universe is that in all of its actions it operates as a seamless whole with a coherence that holds all things as an integral whole. This means that the various activities of the universe are interdependent and thus cannot be considered apart from one another. The universe acts in an integral manner. The systematic study of the universe as a whole demands a cosmological perspective that is interdisciplinary in nature. Our earlier treatment of modernism concluded that there is a veritable eclipse of cosmological thinking within this world view. Stephen Toulmin (1985), in his treatment of the cosmological sense, contends that the natural sciences have developed a systematic fragmentation and as a result it is no longer the professional business of any one discipline to think about 'the Whole'. It follows when discussing the universe as a totality or *whole* we are moving towards a more integral cosmological sense.

I submit to the reader that at all levels of analysis or integration of the universe, we are looking at an *interacting* and *genetically* related community of beings bonded together in an inseparable relationship in *space and time*. We are therefore talking about a universe that evolves in both space and time simultaneously. The universe, in the words of the physicist David Bohm, acts as a seamless whole. When we speak of a time-developmental universe we are attesting to the idea that the universe is an interacting and genetically related community bound together in an inseparable relationship (Bohm and Peat 1987). The universe acts in intelligible ways at all levels of interaction. When we speak of the emergence of the universe out of the primeval fireball we are not talking about some random emergence. At all levels of interactivity there seems to be a creative ordering. The universe itself is the name of that creative ordering. We can then say that the sun and the earth and the planets are bonded relationships because the universe holds them together. The same may be said of our Milky Way galaxy in relation to all of the other known galaxies. Here again we say that the universe is doing this as a fact of its primordial irreducible activity. The universe attests to the idea that everything exists and can be understood only in the context of relationships. Nothing exists in isolation (Swimme and Berry 1992).

When I say that the universe acts as a unity in space and time, I am talking about a universe that is not only present to itself simultaneously but it is also present to itself over time. We are talking about a time-developmental universe. With a time-developmental perspective we have the notion of an evolutionary emergence. Carl Sagan, in his book *Cosmos* (1980), says that humans are the product of burnt-out stars. We are the one of the many results of the evolution of the universe. Thus, the primordial energy of the fireball is the energy of all life. That same energy of the fireball is acting in the present evolution of the universe. Our universe as well as ourselves are time-developmental beings. Our present planet is the result of the evolution of the stars. We know that this process has occurred but we do not know exactly how this has come about. We can also say that the same energy that evolved in the stars has through time come to wear a human face (Swimme and Berry 1992).

What then do we mean when we say that the universe is an *interacting* and *genetically* related community of beings? When we say that the universe is an *interacting community* we are attesting to the reality that the universe is an integral reality, all the elements of which are mutually present to one another through space and time. When we say that there is a mutual presence with every other part, we are talking about a mutuality of action (interaction). This mutual presence of each element to every other element can be in the present (i.e. simultaneously or spatially) or be a mutual presence that reveals itself over time. The idea of a temporal unfolding brings into the picture a mutual presence that has an evolutionary dimension that reveals a time-irreversible genetic sequence. This genetic process is also a testimony to the integral relatedness of the universe. Swimme and Berry (1992) see the story of the universe as an integral story, not just a string of occurrences through time. They note that in the human eye we have present the elementary particles that stabilized in the fireball; we have the elemental creations of the supernova; we have the molecular architecture of the early organisms. Thus, when we open our eyes and capture light we are employing a procedure nearly identical to that invented by the plants to capture sunlight. The molecules of our eyes act similarly to the molecules of the plant leaf because our molecular structures derived from theirs. Their contention is that all past acts of intelligence are layered into present reality. In a similar vein, we may also say that the planet earth is an integral unity where each being of the planet is implicated in the existence and functioning of every other being of the planet. We now understand the planet as a self-regulating unity in which there is a 'web of life' that can only be understood as a totality. There is an incredibly intricate mystery that links everything to everything else on the planet. As humans, we are influenced by the tiniest organisms that are present on the earth from the beginnings of the planet. Simultaneously we are having a profound effect on the presence of all other beings on the earth. The intricate unity of all life processes on earth is characterized by Elisabet Sahtouris as a dance:

> The word 'evolution' when used in talking about human dancing, means the changing pattern of steps in any particular dance. A dance thus evolves when its step patterns change into new ones as the dance goes on. In exactly this sense, the evolution of Gaia's dance – Earth life – is changing patterns of steps in the interwoven self-organization of creatures and their habitats over time ... This, then is Gaia's dance – the endless improvisation and elaboration of elegantly simple steps into the awesomely beautiful and complex being of which we are the newest feature. (Sahtouris 1989: 74)

Thus, the unity of all beings on the planet exists not only in the present but also in evolutionary time. As a species on this earth we are not the dance, rather we are a part of the mysterious dance of all life.

Pre-eminent metaphor This dance brings us to a consideration of the pre-eminent metaphor for the ecozoic vision that I am about to develop. The metaphor is what is frequently referred to in ecological circles as the 'web of life' or in the native traditions as the 'circle of life'. Here, we humans are not seen as apart from the natural world as in the 'mechanistic viewpoint' (the progressive technozoic vision) or at the top of an evolutionary hierarchy as when the human body is used to signal human pre-eminence by putting the human as the head and brains of the evolutionary hierarchy (the conservative vision). The 'web of life' is an integral metaphor where life processes are seen as a seamless whole. In the web we have a deep-rooted sense of the symbiotic relationship of all living things with the human playing an integral but not pre-emptive role in evolutionary significance. Native cultures have used a term similar to the 'web': the 'circle of life'. The significance of the circle is that all beings exist within it and no one particular being has pre-eminence. Within the 'circle of life' there is a view that life must be understood in cycles. The cycles exist in sacred rather than secular time that melds the present with the past and future. For example, vision quests and dreams for native peoples reflect journeys back and forth between past and future.

View of conflict It is hard to ignore aspects of violence at all levels of the universe as we know it. The basic terms in cosmology, geology, biology, anthropology, sociology and psychology carry a heavy charge of tension and violence. Neither the universe as a whole nor any part of the universe is especially peaceful (T. Berry 1988).

Life emerges and advances by the struggle of the species for complete life expression. Humans have made their way amid the harshness of the natural world and have imposed their violence on the natural world. Among themselves, humans have experienced unending conflict. An enormous psychic effort has been required to articulate the human mode of being in its full imaginative, emotional and intellectual qualities, a psychic effort that emerges from and gives expression to that dramatic confrontation of forces that shape the universe. Thomas Berry (1988) notes that confrontation may give rise to the 'tears of things' as described by Virgil, but the creative function would be difficult to ignore.

With the advent of the human, a new violence was released on the planet (T. Berry 1988). But if in prior ages the violence of the natural world in the larger arc of its unfolding could be considered benign, the violence associated with human presence on the planet remains ambivalent in its ultimate consequences. Creativity is associated with a disequilibrium, a tension of forces whether this be in the physical biological or consciousness context. If these tensions often result in destructive moments in the planetary process, these moments have ultimately been transformed in some creative context. As human power over the total process has increased, however, and the spontaneities of nature have been suppressed or extinguished, the proper functioning of the planet has become increasingly dependent on human wisdom and human decision. The dependence began with human intrusion into the natural functioning of the land, that is, with agriculture and the control of water through irrigation. Since then a conquest mentality has been generated coextensive with the civilizational process. The conquest of the earth and its functioning was extended to the conquest of people and their lands. The sectioning of the earth and its human inhabitants is the dominant theme in the story of the planet over these many years, until now more than 160 nation-states have established their identity.

The military–industrial ventures of modern nation-states now wield a destructive power that has changed every phase of earthly existence. We have to understand that we are now facing for the first time the fact that the planet has become capable of self-destruction in many of its major life systems through human agency, or that at least it has become capable of causing a violent and irreversible alteration of its chemical and biological constitution such as has not taken place since the original shaping of the earth occurred. Thus, while we reflect on the turmoil of the universe in its emergent process, we must also understand the splendour that finds expression amid this sequence of catastrophic events, splendour that set the context for the emergent human age. This period of the human in its modern form that began perhaps 60,000 years ago, after some 2 million years of transitional human types, roughly coincides with the last glacial advance and recession. With the advent of the

human, a new violence was released on the planet. Within human consciousness, terror becomes aware of itself. Born of a conviction that the world can
be shaped in such a way that oneself or one's group can be finally protected
from violence (T. Berry 1988), humans create enormous and monstrous violence without redeeming value – violence without creativity, destruction
without integration. We are now amply aware that 'whenever creativity is
impeded, the ultimate result is not simply the absence of creativity, but an
actual positive presence of destructiveness.' (T. Berry 1988: 218). We are
contending with these forces at the present moment and we see in this creative
hiatus the ancient tension between chaos and order (Briggs and Peat 1989).
Our response must be both creative and definitive. We have not been this way
before and we will not be here at this creative moment again. This is the time-
developmental context of conflict and creativity

Contemporary educational trtends We have not been this way before and
thus it will be the objective of the rest of this book to present a positive
blueprint for an 'ecozoic education'. An ecozoic vision can nevertheless suggest
some trends in recent educational practice that will give a sense of emerging
directions. My colleagues at the Transformative Learning Centre at OISE/UT
are doing groundbreaking work to forge this vision in the area of adult
education (Clover, Follen and Hall, 1998). The educational vision that is
suggested points to a profoundly holistic and integral education that moves
beyond mechanistic atomism. A mechanistic map of the universe is no longer
helpful to our understanding of how the world works. However much we
compartmentalize for practical purposes, everything, in the final analysis, is
woven into a multi-layered, multi-dimensional web of interaction and significance (Pike and Selby 1988). At its foundation, we may speak of universe
education; an education that identifies with the emergent universe in its variety
of manifestations from the beginning until now. In this broad context our
conception of knowledge is synthetic and holistic. In contrast to the mechanistic principle of analysis that postulates the whole as the sum of its parts, a
synthetic holism suggests that the whole is a holistic educational paradigm
and holds that all things are part of an indivisible unity or whole (Miller 1996).
In addition, this holistic perspective is time-developmental in nature. We see
in holism that events are viewed dynamically and are systematically connected
in time and space. Thus a holistic paradigm is an outlook that considers that
all events can be seen from an evolutionary viewpoint. This is what we mean
when we say that we act in a time-developmental universe. It is also a perspective that does not consider that knowledge can exist apart from the physical
world. Thought is part and parcel of the natural world since human life is
embedded in nature. We would say that human thought is nature's way of
reflecting on itself. Thus holistic education within our perspective includes

within it *earth education*. By *earth education* we do not mean education about the earth, but the earth as the immediate self-educating community of those living and non-living beings that constitute the earth. With some of the above distinctions in mind we now go on to consider the sensitivities that must be developed within an integral and holistic frame of reference.

. . . .

CHAPTER 3

Modernism: the Eclipse of Cosmology and the Loss of the View of the Whole

Introduction

It is difficult for the modern western mind to fathom that, in the larger picture of the human race, it truly occupies a minority position. In his penetrating study of world religions, Huston Smith (1992) concluded that people need to believe that the truth they perceive is rooted in the unchanging depths of the universe. Yet when we look at our own cultural synthesis, we can readily see that we have lost this cosmological sense and, in Stephen Toulmin's (1985) words, 'there is a loss of the view of the whole'. With our modern outlook, with its absence of a model of the world embedded in the universe, we see the confusion of the postmodern already alluded to in Chapter 1. Even in this time of confusion there is nevertheless a need in modern science, as well as within the popular imagination, to go beyond the limitations of our modern world view. Most of us who live in the city are awestruck by the vastness of the heavens that presents itself when we have the occasion to be in the country or in a wilderness setting. Our seemingly natural awe of the cosmos is not simply blocked by external stimuli such as the background lighting of the city; we also seem to have developed internal barriers to seeing the universe as a whole. One of the objectives of this chapter is to reassess critically the forces of modernism and to show how they contribute to our present problems. This objective presupposes an interest in 'cosmological questions'. Cosmology, in its broadest sense, is a branch of philosophy which studies the origin and structure of the universe. The first objective is to show how the temper of the 'cenozoic age' has led to a veritable eclipse or covering of the world views that place cosmological questions at the centre of thinking about the universe; what the theologian Huston Smith (1992) calls the 'primordial traditions'. Our attempt here will be to show that one of the outcomes of the flowering of the 'terminal cenozoic period' was a turning away from questions that we would call cosmological. This loss of a 'cosmological sense' can be explored in several ways: first, by a discussion of the role of cosmology in pre-modern times; second, by discussing the reasons for the decline in interest in cosmological questions with the full flowering of the cenozoic period; finally, by looking at educational institutions and assessing their role in the loss of a cosmological perspective. Before doing this, let us first look at the term 'cosmological'.

The philosopher Stephen Toulmin, in *The Return to Cosmology* (1985), gives us a convenient entry point for our discussion of the term 'cosmology'. He observes that there appears to be a natural attitude taken by humans at all times and in all places when reflecting on the natural world and there appears to be a comprehensive ambition to understand and speak about the universe as a whole. Toulmin notes that, in practical terms, this desire for a view of the whole reflects a need to establish where we stand in the world into which we have been born, to grasp our place in the scheme of things, and to feel at home within it.

It is interesting when one looks at the etymology of words, how certain core concepts in this book interrelate. The etymology of the word 'ecology' refers to the study of 'home'. Thus, our attempts to situate ourselves as humans in the matrix of the earth and further in the universe is, in essence, an exercise in cosmology. This sense of wholeness is seen in the very break-down of the word universe (uni-verse) or one story. Historically, the word 'university' meant an institution where one went to experience one's place in the universe (Fox 1988). This is certainly not the university that I know. In the modern university the term cosmology appears, for the most part, to be arcane or obscure. In contemporary philosophy in the twentieth century the study of cosmology is, for all intents and purposes, absent. Nevertheless, the term has been very important in the history of philosophy in the past and will surely be so in the future because of the developments of postmodern science (Berman 1981; D. Griffin 1988a; 1988b; 1990; Huston Smith 1992; Toulmin 1985).

For our purposes, cosmology is considered to be that branch of philosophy which studies the origin and structure of the universe. Within philosophical discourse, cosmology is to be contrasted with metaphysics, the study of the most general features of reality, and the philosophy of nature which investigates the basic laws, processes and divisions of the objects of nature. To be sure, they are not mutually exclusive categories but rather different focal points. Our discussion here, however, will be more historical in nature since history provides a background context in which to deal with our present planetary problems.

Pre-modern cosmologies

The first historical indication of recorded cosmological systems is seen in the cultures of Babylonia and Egypt many centuries before the birth of Christ.

The Babylonians are, to this day, the original inventors of the calendar. The study of the sun, moon and stars was carried out for very practical purposes. The invention of the first calendar was to aid in the practice of agriculture. Astronomy, as we know it today, has its humble roots in the pursuits of hunting and agriculture. Historical scholarship on this period reveals that cosmology was an endeavour to understand the motions of heavenly bodies for purposes of survival. Cosmology in its earliest form was an effort to develop survival strategies. Thus, it was important to know what times of day that beasts of prey were available. Such an understanding could mean the difference between life and death for the hunter and the hunted. For all these reasons and more, humans were driven to note carefully the alternating cycles of day and night, thereby acquiring the first rudimentary concept of the cosmos in action (Rosen 1973).

Thus the earliest recorded interest in cosmology had several distinguishing features. The first, alluded to above, was in some of the practical pursuits of survival in pre-modern cultures. Second, there was a sense that nature was 'enchanted' and alive. This characteristic is frequently referred to as animism. In some of the pre-modern cultures the sun was considered a personified divinity. There was a substantial amount of nature worship in all pre-modern societies. Our modern interpretation is to see this as some type of primitive evolutionary form of religion.

When one assesses the later culture of ancient Greece, it is surprising to note that, for all the magnificent accomplishments of this culture, it made no significant advance over the more ancient Babylonian culture. The main contribution of Greek culture was not in the empirical realm of cosmology. Plato said in *The Republic* that one could dispense with the bodies in the heavens to obtain a real understanding of astronomy. Although Plato's influence was pernicious for an empirical basis to cosmology, he nevertheless saw cosmological considerations as fundamental to his philosophical system. What the Greek culture contributed was a philosophical emphasis on cosmological questions. More importantly, probably the greatest contribution was to establish the theses that the order we see in human behaviour stems from a foundational order in the universe. Thus, in Aristotle, the science of ethics is seen as a pursuit that is made possible because there is assumed to be an orderly universe (i.e cosmos). Aristotle's argument from design is contingent on a universe that is held by an ordered nature.

The next major juncture in pre-modern cosmologies occurs in medieval Christian times. In the medieval world we see a continuation of the enchantment of nature and of the universe. In medieval christendom we find the development of angelology. The universe is no longer divine but spiritual creatures exist in the heavens (angels) and become a part of the spheres of the heavens. Here the angelology is allied to cosmological concerns. The most significant contribution to theoretical cosmology is Ptolemy's theory of epicycles. In the Ptolemaic conception, the earth is seen as the centre of the universe. The relationship of Ptolemy's system to some of the religious currents at the time shows what a powerful influence the Church had on cosmological considerations. Angelology and cosmology were intricately intertwined in the medieval world synthesis (Rosen 1973). It was believed that all cosmic bodies were propelled on their course by an angel. In medieval times, the Christian angel replaced the pagan soul which Plato and his descendants had assigned as the driving force of cosmic bodies. By contrast, Aristotle's first mover or primary cause was incorporeal and could not itself move but operated as a catalyst that communicated motion to all cosmic bodies. Ptolemy's position was that no heavenly body received its moving power from without; they had their own vital energy within propelling them. Thus every planet was a source of its own motion, flying through space at its own pace and speed.

Our discussion of pre-modern cosmologies is in no sense historically adequate. (For a thorough exposition of pre-modern cosmologies see Rosen [1973].) I have been schematic in my treatment because it is not my purpose here to be historically exhaustive but to point out certain features of pre-modern cosmologies that have been lost with the advent of the western scientific world view. Even though pre-modern cosmologies differ widely in terms of content and form, there seem to be certain core features that separate them from the modern temper. First, they tend to be closely allied to the practical concerns of early cultures as in the case of agriculture in the Babylonian empire. Second, cosmologies in earlier times were part and parcel of the central meaning systems of those cultures. For example, the grand philosophical systems of the Greeks, as in the cases of Plato and Aristotle, centrally located cosmological concerns in the corpus of their philosophical systems. Thus, in contrast to modern philosophical systems, cosmology is a cornerstone for pre-modern philosophy from Plato to St Thomas Aquinas. Third, for good or for ill, pre-modern cosmological systems were intricately involved with the religious systems of their times. Finally, nature in pre-modern cosmologies was enchanted. For pre-modern peoples, nature and the cosmos were considered awesome and numinous. There was a simultaneous fear of and awe for the natural world which could be readily detected in their diverse cosmological systems. Along with enchantment, there is a sense of 'belonging' experienced in the natural world. Morris Berman gives an excellent sense of the meaning of enchantment in the pre-modern world:

> The view of nature which predominated in the West down to the eve of the Scientific Revolution was that of an enchanted world. Rocks, trees, rivers, and clouds were all seen as wondrous, alive, and human beings felt at home in this

environment. The cosmos, in short, was a place of *belonging*. A member of this cosmos was not an alienated observer of it but a direct participant in the drama. His personal destiny was bound up with its destiny, and this relationship gave meaning to his life. (Berman 1981: 2)

The story of the modern epic, to which we will now turn, will be a story of progressive *disenchantment* from the natural world and all that this entails.

Modern cosmological systems

Modern cosmological systems start with the post-medieval Enlightenment period taking us into the mid-twentieth century. This is the apex of what we have referred to in Chapter 1 as the final phases of the late cenozoic period. Characteristic of this period is the major cultural revisioning of thought systems that are now identified as the technical scientific–industrial world view. The movement into this post-medieval period represents a very profound change in cultural consciousness. Lewis Mumford (1961) characterizes this change from the medieval into the modern temper as one of the most far-reaching cultural changes in human history. Mumford notes that, as with other great historical junctures, the movement from the medieval world into the modern world involved a new metaphysical and ideological change en-compassing all major cultural institutions and, in essence, formed a new picture of the cosmos and the nature of the human. How did this come about and what were some of the figures and cultural forces involved?

As with all major transitional periods, certain pivotal figures become identified with the social transformation that occurred. In the case of the movement from the pre-modern to the modern world view, one of these figures was a Polish canon lawyer by the name of Copernicus. The direction of the thought of Copernicus was to undermine, in the most radical sense, the cosmological system of Ptolemy which was the foundational system of the medieval world. In essence, his cosmological system challenged Ptolemy's in which the earth was considered to be the centre of the universe. Copernicus's heliocentric position viewed the motions of the sun, moon and the planets as accounted for by the movement of the earth on its axis on a daily basis, revolving round a stationary sun once a year. The Copernican system came to full fruition with the publication of 'On the Revolution of the Celestial Spheres' in 1543. A further development of this radically different cosmological system was ventured in the work of Johann Kepler who added the notion of elliptical orbits and formulated the descriptive laws of planetary motion.

The full flowering of the Copernican system, through the later thinkers Kepler and Galileo, was to have profound implications well beyond the bounds of the science of astronomy. In today's terms we would call it a radical paradigm shift which was to be felt across all major cultural institutions. The magnitude and scope of this radical reorientation involved dethroning the earth from its place at the centre of the universe. Since the cosmology of Ptolemy was fused with the religious world view of medieval thought, religious institutions were profoundly shocked. The Copernican position meant that the earth was now only a planet among many other planets. It would no longer be in the privileged position as the site of all change and decay with a changeless universe surrounding it. In addition, there was a profound reorientation of thought in what has been called the microcosmos and macrocosmos. The close correspondence between the human (microcosmos) as a mirror of the surrounding universe (macrocosmos) was to be torn asunder in the new cosmology. As will be developed shortly, this sundering of the relationship between the microcosmos and macrocosmos became a factor in what we are calling the loss of cosmological significance. The mortal blow that the new cosmology dealt to the medieval world synthesis was that human beings no longer retained a privileged place in creation. Thus, the new cosmology was not some incremental change in ideas; it was nothing short of a revolution in thought. The ideas of Copernicus generated enormous controversy in the areas of religion, philosophy and social theory and set the tenor of the modern mind. In addition, his ideas were the catalyst for a major transition in western thought and values. In short, the Copernican revolution amounted to a major challenge to the entire system of medieval authority. In its bare essentials, the Copernican system was a total reversal of the philosophical conception of the universe that was held at that time. It was a part of an even larger transformation, involving the whole way of looking at the world; the precursor and matrix of what we have come to call the 'scientific revolution' (Harman 1988).

Willis Harman (1988) reveals the profound changes that took place in an educational comparison between the medieval world synthesis and what replaced it. He notes that in the 1600s an educated man (most educated persons were men) knew that the earth was the centre of the cosmos – the seat of change, decay and Christian redemption – while above it circled the planets and the stars, themselves pure and unchanging but moved by some sort of intelligent or divine spirits and also signalling and influencing human events by their location and aspects. A hundred years later this man's equally Christian descendant, say his great-grandson, knew (unless he lived in a Church-controlled Catholic country) that the earth was but one of many planets orbiting around one of many stars, moving through and separated by unimaginable distances – still under the overall guidance of God, but with an important difference. The outlook of the first individual was *teleological*; the universe is alive and imbued with purpose, all creatures are part of a Great Chain of Being, man exists between the angels and lower animals, and events are explained by divine purposes or by their function in a meaningful world. To his great-grandson, by contrast, it is essentially a dead universe, constructed and set in motion by the creator, with subsequent events accounted for by mechanical forces and lawful behaviours. The great-grandfather, as a reasonable man, would accept the overwhelming evidence for the working of enchantments, the occurrence of miracles, the existence of witches and other beings with supernatural powers; his descendant, with equal certainty, would dismiss all those stories as the results of delusion (Harman 1988).

Thus, the movement from pre-modern to a modern cosmology amounted to a new way of validating and seeking knowledge. The modern cosmology achieved its validation through what we would call the scientific world view. Knowledge claims about events in the world were arrived at through empirical observation and experimental testing. The final authority for all knowledge was through this experimental empiricism that has been identified with the scientific community. It is important for the reader to keep in mind the scope and magnitude of the change in world view that was ultimately to come to fruition with the ascendancy of the scientific paradigm. It took over several centuries to coalesce but, after a certain point, the chasm between the old ways of viewing the world and the new was complete.

We are now living in a transitional period as equally profound as at the time of Copernicus and we can readily conclude that a radical new cosmological vista is coming into view. It is equally as dramatic in its reorientation as was the movement from the medieval to the modern world view just described. It is difficult to depict such a momentous transition, however, when we are in the midst of it. The first task is to understand what is meant by the 'loss' of cosmology. This analysis is important because this lost sense constitutes the endpoint of the 'terminal cenozoic era'.

The loss of a cosmological sense in the late cenozoic period

> Turning and turning in the widening gyre
> The Falcon cannot hear the falconer;
> Things fall apart; the centre cannot hold;
> Mere anarchy is loosed upon the world
>
> (William Butler Yeats, 'The Second Coming')

Poets are frequently prophetic and visionary voices in our culture. William Butler Yeats, at the turn of this century, gives voice to a culture of disenchantment in his much quoted poem 'The Second Coming', with its nostalgia for wholeness. When we talk about the loss of cosmology or the loss of a sense of the cosmos we do not mean that there was a total absence of a cosmological system. The loss of a cosmological sense is for us the subjective sense that what is lacking is a perception of the wholeness and interrelatedness of things. When the poet William Blake could 'see the world in a grain of sand and eternity in an hour', he was pointing to a sense of the wholeness of things which was eroded by the development of the scientific world view. In Blake we see a poet where the relationship between the microcosmos and the macrocosmos is palpable. By the nineteenth century we see this relationship broken and fissured. Even in profoundly religious writers, such as the French writer Georges Bernanos in *The Diary of a Country Priest* (1937), we see this alienation of the individual from the natural world.

The modern world is located at a great distance from the awe and enchantment that the pre-moderns felt for the natural world, as well the enchantment of primordial peoples. We not only see disenchantment and fear in the modern mentality towards nature; also apparent is an open hostility to the natural world. Louise Young in her beautiful book entitled *The Blue Planet* (1983) indicates that there was a very strong hostility towards and repugnance for the natural world in much of nineteenth-century thinking in Europe. For instance, she reports that when Casanova travelled through the Alps he drew the blinds in his coach to spare himself the view of those vile excrescences of nature, the deformed mountains.

It is important, then, for the reader to understand how the natural world came to be regarded as such an alien and hostile place in modern thinking. A better understanding of how this attitude emerged will help us understand how we, as a culture, have assumed such a hostile view of the natural and how this is presently influencing our dealings in our planetary crisis. I shall now focus on some of the cultural factors that led us into this loss of a cosmological sense. Max Weber (1958), the great nineteenth-century sociologist, characterizes the effects of modernism as a 'disenchantment of the world' and a fragmentation of the social world due to 'bureaucratic domination'. This is for us the end point of the cenozoic period which flowered in western thought in what I shall call the 'Newtonian–Cartesian Synthesis'. We now turn our attention to this synthesis.

The Newtonian–Cartesian synthesis   For the past three centuries, the scientific world has been dominated by the Newtonian–Cartesian world view. This synthesis of thought is based on the work of the British scientist Isaac Newton and the French mathematician and philosopher René Descartes. Newton's universe was to be in the model of a machine; its core metaphor was embedded in mechanistic explanation. In his system the universe consisted of solid matter and was made up of atoms, the small indestructible particles which were said to be the building blocks of the universe. From this atomistic base, Newton developed his universal theory of gravitation. Complex questions concerning the movement of astronomical objects were resolved in questions of 'masses'. The force of gravity was that force acting between the particles. In Newton's system, gravity seems to be an intrinsic attribute of all the bodies it acts upon. The force of gravity exerts its influence instantaneously at a distance. The Newtonian synthesis combined mathematics and physics which were heretofore separate. He was a synthesizer of the work of his predecessors, particularly Kepler and Galileo. Kepler had developed laws of planetary motion in his careful study of astronomical tables. Galileo carried out his experiments to trace the laws governing fallen bodies. Newton's unique contribution was to advance the discoveries of his predecessors by combining their discoveries in the formulation of general laws of motion governing all objects in the solar system, from stones to planets. Fritjof Capra gives us a picture of this synthesis:

> According to legend, the decisive insight occurred to Newton in a sudden flash when he saw the apple fall from a tree. He realized that the apple was pulled toward the earth by the same force that pulled the planets toward the sun, and thus found the key to his grand synthesis. He then used his new mathematical methods to formulate the exact laws of motion for all bodies under the influence of the force of gravity. The significance of these laws lay in their universal application. They were found to be valid throughout the solar system ... The Newtonian universe was, indeed, one huge mechanical system, operating according to exact mathematical laws. (Capra 1983: 63)

Seeing the universe in mechanistic terms is one of Newton's legacies to the scientific world view. During the sixteenth and seventeenth centuries people were confronted with this new view of the universe which was both mechanistic and materialistic. As I have just indicated, mechanical materialism arose out of the developments achieved in the physical sciences, particularly physics. Mechanism, that is, seeing the world in terms of machine analogues, came to be seen as the most important explanatory language in the development of the physical sciences. From the point of view of mechanistic materialism, as fostered by Newton, the world consists of particles of matter in interaction. Each particle has its own existence and becomes a larger totality by addition. The totality of interactions between particles forms the totality of everything that happens in the world, and these interactions are mechanical in nature; that is to say, they consist of external influences of one particle upon another. As such, mechanistic materialism depicts the universe as nothing but a complex system of machinery; a grand machine. The mechanistic view of nature as propounded by Newton had God creating the universe and then leaving it to run like a great machine governed by immutable laws. The mechanistic view of nature was closely allied to a rigorous causal determinism. All events that occurred have a definite cause and give rise to a definite effect.

Another distinguishing feature of the scientific world view can be seen in the espousal of the principle of analysis. It is contrasted with the synthetic principle that the whole is more than the sum of its parts (a totality); a principle that we will return to later. The principle of analysis is clearly accented when the mechanical metaphor is used in inquiry. It is easy to assent to the idea that the construction of a machine is based on the sum of its parts and that the finished product can be deconstructed into its component parts (O'Sullivan 1984).

Another figure, on a par with Newton in the development of modern scientific thought, is the French philosopher and mathematician René Descartes. His philosophical system was a major response to the breakdown of philosophical discourse in the medieval synthesis accomplished by St Thomas Aquinas. Descartes' most significant contribution to modern science is seen in his extreme formulation of the absolute dualism between mind (*res cogitans*) and matter (*res extensa*). Following this formulation is the belief that the material world can be described objectively without reference to the human observer. The power of his core concepts on the formulation of modern scientific thought cannot be underestimated in both its negative and positive implications.

The cumulative impact of Newton's and Descartes' ideas had a profound impact on how we have come to view the natural world. Descartes, like Newton, viewed the material universe as dead matter and saw it operating as a machine. The implications of this world view have been astounding. Fritjof Capra gives us an idea of its scope:

> To Descartes the material universe was a machine and nothing but a machine. There was no purpose, life, or spirituality in matter. Nature worked according to mechanical laws, and everything in the mechanical world could be explained in terms of the arrangement and movements of its parts. The mechanical picture of nature became the dominant paradigm in science in the period following Déscartes ... The whole elaboration of mechanistic science in the seventeenth, eighteenth and nineteenth centuries, including Newton's grand synthesis, was but the development of the Cartesian idea. Descartes gave scientific thought its general framework – the view of nature as a perfect machine, governed by exact mathematical laws. (Capra 1983: 60)

Patriarchy and its relation to modern science It is also important to stress how the radical separation of mind and matter would affect attitudes towards all aspects of the natural world including plants and animals. The only aspect of the natural world that was considered spiritual and sacred in the Cartesian synthesis was the human mind (*res cogitans*). The human body, as with all other aspects of the material world, was considered to be nothing more than the workings of a complex machine. In this synthesis we see the radical disenchantment of the natural world in sharp contrast to the medieval world where an organic view of the cosmos was propagated in the Ptolemaic cosmology. The historian and feminist scholar Carolyn Merchant, in her book *The Death of Nature* (1980), points to the profound implications that this shift has on our understanding of contemporary ecological questions. It is her contention that the ecological model that is now developing makes possible a fresh and critical interpretation of the rise of modern science in the crucial period when our cosmos ceased to be viewed as an organism and became instead a machine. The guiding metaphor of the machine, which is at the root of our current environmental dilemma, is directly tied to the scientific and technological paradigm just identified. Merchant ventures that, in the movement into modern science, we have the reconceptualization of the universe as machine rather than as living organism which also rationalized the domination of nature as well as women. The metaphor of the earth as a nurturing mother would gradually vanish with the ascendance of the Newtonian–Cartesian world view. The machine metaphor would have a profound influence on the developing view of the natural world. As western culture became increasingly mechanized in the 1600s, the 'female earth and the virgin earth spirit' were subdued by the machine (Merchant 1995). Merchant (1980) contends that we must re-examine the formation of the world view and a science that, by reconceptualizing reality as a machine rather than a living organism, sanctioned the domination of both nature and women. We have, with the emergence of modern science, moved away from an organic understanding of nature which identified it, especially the earth, with a nurturing mother: a kindly beneficent female who brought order and plan to the universe. Alongside this conception was an opposing image of nature as a wild and uncontrollable female who rendered violence, droughts, storms and general chaos. These were conceptions that were cultivated by men, identifying chaos with the female sex and projecting human perception on to the external world. In a subsequent work entitled *Earthcare*, Merchant summarizes the transition:

> The metaphor of the earth as nurturing mother gradually vanished as a dominant image as the Scientific Revolution proceeded to mechanize and to rationalize the world view. The second image, nature as disorder, called forth an important modern idea, that of power over nature. Two new ideas, those of mechanism and of the domination and mastery of nature, became core concepts of the modern world. An organically oriented mentality in which female principles played an important role was undermined and replaced by a mechanically oriented mentality that either eliminated or used female principles in an exploitive manner. As western culture became increasingly mechanized in the 1600s, the machine subdued the female earth and the virgin earth spirit. (Merchant 1995: 77)

Thus, the first factor in the loss of a sense of a living and integrated cosmology was the development of the machine metaphor; the earth became a dead entity to be controlled and manipulated.

Another major influence on the cosmological sense was the articulation of the notion of the *individual* in the development of modern thought. With the development of the modern ideal of the *individual* we witness a breakdown in the organic totality of the person in relation to the universe. There developed in modern thought a radical break between microcosmic events and the macrocosmos. This cultural development was aligned to the atomism developed by Newton and Descartes and carried forward in the realm of social thinking by Locke and Hobbes. Where physicists reduced the properties of gases to the motion of atoms, so social theorists, as in the case of John Locke, could reduce patterns observed in society to the behaviour of individuals (Capra 1983).

Before the Enlightenment synthesis consolidated by Locke and Hobbes, we see that the notion of the individual had a radically different meaning and cultural significance. In the medieval world the notion of the 'individual' meant inseparable and indivisible. The term was used mainly in theological arguments about the Holy Trinity (Williams 1976; Storr 1988). Thus in premodern times we see the idea of the individual tied to wider cosmic ideas in theological discourse. With the development of the thought of Locke and Hobbes there is a radical break which places the microcosmic world of the individual separately from the macrocosmos. In this line of thinking the 'individual' becomes a universe unto itself and only unto itself. This crucial change enabled people to think of the individual as an absolute, cut off from the surrounding universe. Raymond Williams (1976: 135) points out: 'In England from Hobbes to the Utilitarians, a variety of systems share a common starting point of psychology, ethics and politics. It is rare, in this tradition, to start from the fact that man is born into relationships. The abstraction of the bare human being, as a separate substance, is ordinarily taken for granted.'

We have just seen how the development of the individual as an isolated cosmos with self-contained boundaries has significance for our sense of the world and how we as individuals and groups act in the world. As one can imagine, this boundary-making has a profound and lasting effect on our sense of the cosmos and also our lost sense. One other element or feature of modernism needs to be discussed before we turn to a consideration of the developments in the field of biology that were precipitated by Darwin's evolutionary theory. This feature is the effect of 'specialization' on our sense of the cosmos.

We have already seen that the pre-modern sense of the world was built on the idea of an organic unity that was replaced by a mechanistic world view (Merchant 1980). Following Aristotle, pre-modern medieval inquiry was based on an attempt to formulate general and uniform theories of change. In most instances, the medieval scholar was, for all intents and purposes, a generalist. For example, the works of Newton and Descartes were not confined to mathematics or physics. Their works had immediate implications for theology and philosophy. After the sixteenth century, however, the principle of analysis, already discussed, would be the guiding principle of inquiry. The atomistic world view which underpinned analysis allowed that all problems, of whatever nature, could be broken down into their constituent parts and studied separately and discretely. Thus, instead of trying to formulate general theories of change, inquiry became an activity of studying discrete areas and events where specific as opposed to general laws were operating. We, therefore, see the advent of specified sciences and specializations where discrete and specific laws of change could be identified. By the late sixteenth century we see specific laws of kinematics, of metallic vibration and so on emerging as separate scientific disciplines with specific rather than comprehensive theories of change. This would have a profound impact on the culture's cosmological sense.

Stephen Toulmin (1985) identifies the crucial difference between modern science and its earlier cosmological predecessors. He contends that traditional cosmology was never preoccupied with any isolated aspect of a phenomenon. In contrast, we see in the modernist world view highly specialized and distinct scientific disciplines which have continued to develop well into the twentieth century. Knowledge has become bureaucratized with very distinct and clear divisions of labour. Toulmin (1985) notes that, from the seventeenth century onwards, there would be precious few scholar-scientists who would cross the boundaries of more than one discipline. As a consequence, questions that might have been asked across a whole spectrum of disciplines have 'rarely been posed, much less answered'. Nevertheless, disciplined inquiry in modern science made impressive achievements that overshadowed the fragmentation of thought that would come in its wake. By the end of the nineteenth century, this disciplined fragmentation would cast a shadow where any attempt at a conception of the whole, as experienced in the organic world view of the pre-moderns, was abandoned. The culture's poets appear always to be the fore-runners of a cultural critique. Yeat's poem 'Second Coming' crystallizes this: 'things fall apart, the centre cannot hold'. It is a poetic indication of the loss of the cosmological sense. Toulmin gives us a sense of how this cosmology is lost in the disciplined inquiry of nineteenth-century science by personifying the banishment of the integrative cosmological task. The bureaucratized disciplinarian says to the cosmologist as natural theologian:

'You used to run a Department of Coordination and Integration, did you? Well, as you can see, we don't have any such department: all our enterprises run perfectly well without needing to be coordinated or integrated. And now, if you don't mind, would you please go away and let us get on with our work?' In short the disciplinary fragmentation of science during the nineteenth century seemingly made the integrative function of natural theology unnecessary. (Toulmin 1985: 235)

By the nineteenth century, the issue of the integration of knowledge had been sidestepped as a fundamental question. By the end of that century, the natural sciences had become fragmented into a number of largely independent disciplines, each with its separate and sometimes unique questions, preoccupations and methods of inquiry. The major outcome of this development was that the task of integration fell to no single discipline. We have neglected the interest and capacity to think about 'the whole' (Toulmin 1985). Max Weber's famous 'iron cage' quote gives us a sense of the pathos of specialization:

> No one knows who will live in this cage in the future, or whether at the end of this present development entirely new prophets will arise, or there will be a great rebirth of old ideas and ideals, or if neither, mechanized petrification embellished with a sort of self importance. For the last stage of cultural development, it might well be truly said, specialists without spirit, sensualists without heart; this nullity imagines that it has attained a level of civilization never before achieved. (Weber 1958: 182)

It must be noted that Weber wrote in the nineteenth century as an optimist.

Historical and evolutionary perspectives

Our concentration has thus far been on the epistemological systems that have made an impact on the development of modern science. One feature was the prevalence of mechanistic explanatory systems based on the principle of analysis as the fundamental mode of inquiry. To leave our survey of the loss of cosmological significance only at the level of epistemological analysis would be to ignore some of the major developments in the historical and biological sciences that were incredibly influential at the end of the nineteenth century and were to have a major paradigmatic influence on twentieth-century thought. It would be misleading to indicate that disciplinary specialization was the sole factor involved. Charles Darwin's theory of evolution would also cast a large shadow. The other major historical figure of significance for our discussion is Karl Marx.

Darwin's theory of the evolution of the species was to have a major impact on the scientific world of the twentieth century. His theory introduced a time consciousness in the evolution of all life forms and placed the genesis of species within the natural world. His system of thought was to challenge the major tenets of the Judaeo-Christian formulation of the origin of the human in relation to divine creation. To talk about humans as emerging natural forms without having recourse to the intervention of a divine creator was anathema to the religious mentality of the nineteenth century. For Darwin, humans evolved from lower species and as an evolving form had better survival capabilities than their ancestors. Species survived because they were better fit to survive (natural selection). When Darwin originally formulated his theory of the evolution of life forms, he was seen to be making descriptive statements rather than interpretive ones. It is only relatively recently that we are able to show how all observations are 'socially constructed' and are, therefore, systems of interpretation (Hofstadter 1955; Rifkin and Perlas 1983; Worster 1977). One of Marx's major contributions to western thinking was to show how systems of thought (interpretation) were related to the economic systems of the societies in which they were embedded. Following from this link between interpretive system and the economic base, we can interpret Darwin's evolutionary theory within that light. In a contemporary analysis of Darwin's theory of evolution, Jeremy Rifkin and Nicanor Perlas note that there was a remarkable resemblance between Darwin's description of evolution and of workings of the industrial production process where machines were assembled from their individual parts:

> While it would be grossly unfair to suggest that Darwin knowingly borrowed concepts of industrial assembly, his theory of biological evolution did indeed reflect a similar method of production in nature. Each new species was seen as an assemblage of individual parts organized into new combinations and arrangements and with additional improvements designed to increase both their complexity and their efficiency. (Rifkin and Perlas 1983: 98)

As Rifkin and Perlas point out, it is difficult to fault Darwin for his reliance on machine imagery. There was an overwhelming presence of the machine in nineteenth-century English life. In addition, I have already indicated that the machine was also the central metaphor in the modern scientific world view of both his contemporaries and his immediate predecessors. Darwin likened himself to the Newton of biology, in that he successfully transformed the idea of a mechanical universe into a mechanical theory of the origin and development of the species. Again the comparison between the pre-modern and modern cosmologies in this context is striking. Before the age of the machine, living creatures were viewed as 'wholes'. This traditional view of nature was overthrown and replaced with a radically new conception, compatible with the new form of industrial production. Darwin came to view living things as the sum total of lifeless, inanimate parts 'assembled' together in various functional combinations. Darwin admitted that it was no longer possible for him even to imagine that living creatures were created whole and in their entirety (Rifkin and Perlas 1983: 100–1).

Darwin was to consolidate mechanism into his evolutionary perspective, thereby turning living organisms into machine-like objects. This was, in effect, the ultimate in the desacralization of nature which severed the slim strands of animism that still remained in people's cosmological world visions (Rifkin and Perlas 1983).

If Darwin was influenced by the social forces of production of his time, he was also, at the same time, an important influence on the legitimation of the industrial social order in which he lived. His theory of evolution, with its emphasis on natural selection and survival of the fittest, would resonate with the social order of industrial capitalism. Richard Hofstadter (1955) gives us an excellent account of how Darwinism became 'Social Darwinism'. The 'captains of industry', the likes of Carnegie and Rockefeller, would have the Darwinian philosopher Spencer (Darwin's nephew) lecture on how the Darwinian notion of 'survival of the fittest' fitted in with the ethos of cut-throat competition that prevailed in the productive order of industrial capitalism. In this view the human and natural world are in habitual conflict. But it was not only capitalists who took up Darwin's theory of evolution. Marx and Engels were also to use Darwin's theory for their own ideological purposes. Marx felt that Darwin's theory served as a basis in the natural sciences for the class struggle in history. Thus Darwin's theory of evolution has the underlying motif of conflict and competition: 'Darwin's cosmology sanctioned an entire age of history. Convinced that their own behaviour was in consort with the workings of nature, industrial man and woman were armed with the ultimate justification they needed to continue their relentless exploitation of the environment and their fellow human beings without ever having to reflect on the consequences of their actions' (Rifkin and Perlas 1983: 103).

We must be aware here that our educational institutions are based on some of the powerful presuppositions that we have just outlined. From them it can now be concluded that our present educational synthesis is based on the received wisdom, or lack thereof, of a trajectory of modernism. Later I shall indicate how our present educational establishment serves the need of an industrial world view now becoming defunct. The wisdom of all our current educational ventures in the twentieth century serves the needs of our present dysfunctional industrial system. Our present educational institutions, which are in line with and feeding into industrialism, nationalism, competitive individualism and patriarchy, must be fundamentally put into question. All of these elements coalesce into a world view that exacerbates the crisis that we are now facing. There is no creativity here because there is no viewpoint or consciousness which sees the need for new directions. It is a very strong indictment to say that our conventional educational institutions are defunct and bereft of understanding in responding to our present planetary crisis. In addition, a strong case can be made that our received educational wisdom suffers from what we have been calling the 'loss of the cosmological sense'. Somehow this cosmological sense is lost or downgraded in our educational discourse. In truth, something was gained and we are now just coming to understand that something was lost.

I am not talking about shallow changes in fashion; I am talking about a major revolution in the view of the world that came with the paradigm of modernism. These major dimensional changes profoundly altered the way we moderns view the world and thus changed how we have come to educate our progeny. Well into the last part of the twentieth century one could still find optimism about the progressive nature of the industrial and scientific revolution. However, the world that had stabilized itself with the hubris of modernism cloaked in science, capitalism, industrialism and technology has now become problematic. Morris Berman (1981), an astute observer of modernism's decline, points out that the problem is that a whole constellation of factors – technological manipulation of the environment, capital accumulation based on it, notions of secular salvation that fuelled it and were fuelled by it – has apparently run its course. In particular, the modern scientific paradigm has become as difficult to maintain in the late twentieth century as was the religious paradigm in the seventeenth. The collapse of capitalism, the general dysfunction of institutions, the revulsion against ecological spoilation, the increasing inability of the scientific world view to explain the things that really matter, the loss of interest in work, and the statistical rise in depression, anxiety and outright psychosis are, in Morris Berman's terms, 'all of a piece'.

What has been propounded in this chapter is the idea that a major shift took place between the 'pre-modern' and 'modern world' cosmologies that has had profound consequences for our thinking and actions regarding the natural world. I have indicated that the modern scientific tradition depicted nature as a non-living entity to be manipulated, controlled and exploited. We could also come to understand that with the idea of 'the loss of cosmological significance' we have a corresponding 'disenchantment' with the natural world and our relations to it. The disenchantment with nature, at a most fundamental level, means denying that nature has any aspects of subjectivity, feeling and experience. Nature is fundamentally an 'object' and not 'subject'. Thus nature when addressed by the human is referred to as an 'it' rather than a 'thou'. The awe and reverence towards nature, so prevalent in pre-modern world views, is totally absent in the modern world. With nature as object rather than participating subject, we have a sense of alienation that was not seen in pre-modern cultures.

Disenchantment also means that nature has no inherent intention or purpose intrinsic to itself; intention and purpose exist only in the intentions directed towards nature by humans. Thus the natural world is seen to have no purpose or direction outside the human designs that are made on it. This, then, makes nature a means to human ends rather than an end unto itself. The modern scientific perspective that has come down to us via Newton and Descartes has left no role in the universe for purposes, values, ideals, possibilities and qualities, and there is no freedom, creativity, temporality or divinity. This has led to an unprecedented movement towards nihilism and despair. In a sense, the ethos of modern science has led to ironic outcomes regarding the integrity of human thought. Mechanistic science, in the process of disenchanting the natural world, has also disenchanted itself. The scepticism of modern science has opened the door to despair and cynicism that have turned on the very processes of science itself. This is seen in some of the extreme trends in deconstructive postmodern criticisms. The implication is that if all human life is ultimately lacking in meaning and purpose, then science, as one of its activities, must share in this lack of ultimate meaning. In the nascent stages of the modern scientific world view, scientific findings were held to be true under limited circumstances. Today, however, some of the post-modern criticisms of science have led to a more complete scepticism (D. Griffin 1988a).

Disenchantment presents even deeper problems than epistemological ones. At the level of cultural practices we have seen that humans, in assuming a detached, amoral stance towards the natural world, were led to a reckless exploitation of nature; the consequences of which are now being experienced as an ecological crisis. It is fundamentally important not to externalize our present crisis. It is the world view of western thinking that is fundamentally at issue and is the root cause of the environmental crisis. We are at its very centre. The environmental crisis is part and parcel in everything we believe in and act upon. It is, as it were, in the very fabric of our lives (Evernden, 1983). It is imperative for us to understand that the environmental crisis is not extrinsic and outside us as if it were an external phenomenon; in its present form and magnitude it radically and fundamentally calls into question our cultural world view based on technological innovation for the purposes of competitive marketing for consumer consumption. The decadence of our industrial–technical–consumer world is fundamentally seen in the shadow that it casts; the shadow of planetary destruction. Seeing and believing in the world from a disenchanted perspective opens up a dead world of matter to be exploited and manipulated. The sense of awe and reverence appears to be lost in our present attitudes towards the natural world.

In addition, we must assess, at the personal level, the profound effect that the value of *individualism* has had within the context of disenchantment. The modern definition of the individual as an autonomous social unit is a product of the consensus achieved by liberal social theory. In liberal social theory, individuals are seen as separate autonomous monads that are unique unto themselves. The primary position of the 'state of nature' is characterized by Hobbes as solitary, whereas the individual contracts socially out of fear of survival. The creation of society is based on a contractual arrangement of separate individual entities who, in Hobbes' words, are social atoms. This atomization which is so characteristic of the liberal idea of individualism would have profound implications for modern thought.

When Locke applied his theory of human nature to social phenomena, he was guided by the belief that there were laws of nature governing human society similar to those governing the physical universe. As the atoms in the gas would establish a balanced state, so human individuals would settle down in a society in a 'state of nature.' Thus the function of government was not to impose laws on people, but rather to discover and enforce the natural laws that existed before any state was formed. According to Locke, these natural laws included the freedom and equality of all individuals as well as the right to property, which represented the fruits of one's labour. (Capra 1983: 69)

The down-side of individualism is now being felt at all levels of cultural life.* The self-encapsulated individual that we have just described has profound implications for the loss of the cosmological sense that links individuals to the wider community and subsequently to the universe itself.

Educational vision: the re-enchantment of the natural world

For well over three centuries we have been, as humans, attempting to separate ourselves from the organic processes of the natural world. With the Cartesian turn the mind was elevated over nature and it was the work of the mind to wrest secrets and powers from the natural world. By separating the human self from a larger inclusion in nature and the universe we have proceeded to deepen the chasm of alienation of the human from the natural world. Our conception of historical time has become truncated and our sense of interest in the larger evolutionary processes of the universe and the earth has been muted. As Thomas Berry (1988) says, we have become autistic to the voices of the natural world. The sense of the organicity of the natural world must be revived. There must be a shift in the emphasis of sciences away from the dichotomies of the modern Cartesian system to a postmodern science that is based on a dynamic open system framework that is both organic and holistic. In opposition to a framework that separates values and facts, a more holistic interpretation brings facts and values together in dynamic inter-action. The natural world must be known and revealed in our relations with it, in the sense that we are participant–observers rather than detached viewers. The tacit unconscious dimensions of the mind must be valued, and descriptions of the world must be a mixture of the abstract and concrete, with qualitative description taking precedence over quantitative description. The mind must be considered to be part of the natural world and the mind\body, subject\object relationships must be aspects of the same process. Finally, logic must be both\and rather than either\or. Organicity must be reintroduced

---

* My treatment of 'individualism' ignores its many positive features. See Taylor (1991).

within a postmodern system where living systems are not reducible to components and where nature is considered to be alive.

The location of the human world as a participant world in the deep creative unfolding processes of the universe opens our horizons to the revelatory mysteries of nature. In moving into the deep participatory processes of the universe, we experience a greater appreciation of all aspects of reality. As humans, we will be able to experience our place in nature as part of a complex 'web of life'. The dynamic processes experienced in the 'web of life' open our human vision to the wonderful interplay of all natural phenomena and their interrelatedness. In later chapters, I suggest an overarching vision that embeds the ongoing living processes of the earth in an emergent expanding universe. By opening up our human lives to the grand story of the universe, we offer an integral story of how human history embeds itself in the creative emergence of the universe. We are made of star stuff. The largest vision of an expanding evolutionary universe locates our human history in the wider context of the history of the earth. We are not only star-lings, we are also earthlings:

> In the photographs of the earth from space the planet looks like a little thing that I might hold in the hollow of my hand. I can imagine it would feel warm to the touch, vibrant and sensitive. Born of stardust, this handful of matter has evolved throughout the eons of geologic time. Like a butterfly taking shape within its chrysalis, the parts have rearranged themselves, taking on new forms. Diversity has increased, and simplicity has given way to elaborately integrated complexity. Beneath the mobile membrane of cloud and air are a storehouse of splendors and and a wealth of delicate detail. There are rainbows caught in waterfalls, and frost flowers etched on windowpanes, and drops of dew scattered like jewels on meadow grass, and honeycreepers singing in the jacandra tree ... Time flows on ... the planet continues to spin on its path through the unknown reaches of space. We cannot guess its destination or its destiny. This beautiful blue bubble of matter holds many wonders still unrealized and a mysterious future waiting to unfold. (Young 1983: 266)

At this point in time, the educational venture needs to experience *human* activities as a continuation of the creativity that brought about the emergent galactic systems and shaped the elements; that brought the planet earth into existence within the solar system; that brought forth life in the fantastic variety of its manifestations; that awakened consciousness in the human order, that enabled the great cultural sequence to take place. There is an unbroken continuity in the creative process throughout this total expanse of universe development. In our very physical and psychic constitution we are totally involved in that single, vast, creative process that reaches across all the distances of space and from the beginning of time to the present. Human involvement in this vast creative process finds expression in poets and musicians, in religious personalities, and in our continuing effort to constitute a human mode of social and individual being. It is this understanding of the universe that enabled this vast human effort to take place and it is this understanding that constitutes also our basic resource for structuring a new planetary order that we are calling the ecozoic age. As mentioned previously, the new origin story, the supreme achievement of the scientific effort of these centuries, must be completed by a sense of the psychic as well as the physical dimensions of the evolutionary process. But, once this is done, a vision strong enough, vital enough and sufficiently inspiring to support the effort is required. This integral creation story is completed by an awareness of its numinous and psychic aspects from the beginning. Our task is to understand this process in some depth in the educational venture into the ecozoic age.

The great advantage of the current universe story is its universal availability. While it emerged originally out of a western cultural context, it is not intrinsically related to any traditional culture. It is sustained on its own evidence. Already this story is the functional basis of education on a universal scale even though the story is generally understood simply in its account of the emergent physical universe. Along with improvements it often brings in the form of medicine and health care, nutrition, improvements in agriculture, a stronger sense of social justice, better means of transportation and communication, it must be said that this story of the universe is also frustrating to traditional societies everywhere. It is a contamination to religion, a cause of moral breakdown, a disruption of social order, a source of psychological confusion and emotional upset. Along with western technologies it leads to commercial exploitation of the people and to devastation of the natural environment.

The total impact is multivalent and filled with contradictory effects. Yet there is no likely way into the future that does not take as its basis the more integral form of this new vision of the universe. The burden of western civilization is to integrate this story in its creative aspects and to develop it into a more central creative instrument for the future course of the human venture.

From the point of view of an educational venture, one notes historically that the creative genius of the earlier processes of the earth, as well as its principal instrument of education, is through genetic coding. This coding guides the unfolding of the life process in the individual and the species. The ultimate creative genius of the earth at this level is the master plan of the total biospheric interaction of genetic codings and the mutation process whereby new codes are developed within the interplay of the various living and non-living energy systems. Creativity at this level, as well as freedom at this level, is wonderfully instructive for understanding freedom and creativity in the later human phase of their development.

As with the universe, the full expression of the human takes place through a sequence of major or macrophase developments, in addition to the variety within any single level of its development. Certain moments of creativity correspond with the mutation processes at the pre-human level. So we have in our time the cultural macrophase development from the cenozoic to the ecozoic age. As all creativity involves being seized by an archetypal reality in the unconscious depths of the universe, so now we are being seized by a new revelatory experience that is coming to us in the new origin story and its fulfilment in this latest communion phase of the universe. Any retreat to monoculture is a failure in evolutionary nerve. We certainly do not need the 'new world order' of the United States as presented by President George Bush at the end of the Gulf War. If anything, it will be our educational task, to cultivate resistance to a truncated American vision of world culture: 'To speak of a global cultural force does not mean the loss of cultural diversity: a global ecological ethos and ethic can be developed within the context of a diversity of living cultures and traditions' (Mische 1989: 15).

We are indeed free in the manner of this achievement, but we are mandated by the larger coding of life and of consciousness towards certain unique achievements that are possible in our times. Just as the shaping of the planet earth is a one-time affair that can never be repeated; as the emergence of life took place in conditions that were themselves consumed by the earliest living beings and can never again occur in the natural world; as consciousness emerged at a certain moment and the transition from pre-human consciousness to the human mode of consciousness can never again be expected; so with the creative cultural moments that we have indicated, these are absolute achievements, unique and unrepeatable. This can be seen in the creation of the great classical religious cultures. The moment can never be repeated.

So, too, with the scientific–technological period a transition has been made. The planet itself has been changed, all living forms are affected, the deepest realms of human consciousness are permanently altered. We can carry forward the scientific observation and experimental process but the transition from the classical to the scientific age will never again take place.

The movement into the ecozoic age will, of its very nature, be creative in its direction. While we have been speaking about an all-encompassing vision, we must constantly be aware that the emergent evolutionary story is at every level a story of differentiation, subjectivity and communion. The re-enchantment of the natural world will not be accomplished by a return to older ways of thinking and acting. We will not be able to romanticize or imitate indigenous peoples' participatory mystique with the world. We cannot copy world view systems that we do not occupy or live in. We nevertheless must appropriate certain aspects of wisdoms from the past. We must have a sober accounting of the wisdom and sagacity of cultures that have preceded us.

Although magic, religion and mystical traditions were prey to errors and follies of the spirit, they nevertheless carried within them a wisdom of the awareness of humanity's organic embeddedness in a complex and natural system. This type of appreciation does not abolish modernity, but it may help us transcend it. The major problem is for us to discover how to recapture older wisdoms in a mature form (Berman 1981; 1989).

Modern scientists are beginning to understand that traditional indigenous wisdom is often extremely sophisticated and of considerable practical value. Native science preceding our own western systems has developed systems for identifying, naming and classifying soils, plants, insects and other elements of local environments and deriving medical and economic benefit from them. These systems are powerful illustrations of the benefits of their acute observations. Knudtson and Suzuki (1992), in distilling the differences between native and scientific knowledge, give us the sense of the quality of enchantment embedded in native knowledge. They list the following qualities as a basis of comparison:

1. Traditional native knowledge views the natural world as holy rather than profane, savage, wild, wasteland or property.
2. Native wisdom is imbued with a deep sense of reverence for the natural world with an absence of the desire to exercise human domination over it.
3. Native wisdom sees spirit as dispersed throughout the cosmos and not embodied in a single monotheistic supreme being.
4. The native mind tends to view the universe as the dynamic interplay of elusive and ever-changing natural forces, not as a vast array of physical objects.
5. The entire natural world is seen as somewhat alive and animated by a single life force.
6. From the native perspective, there is a profound sense of empathy and kinship with other forms of life, rather than a sense of separateness from them and superiority over them. Each species is seen as richly endowed with its own singular array of gifts and powers, rather than as pathetically limited compared to human beings.
7. Finally, there is a tendency to view the proper human relationship with nature as a continuous dialogue of horizontal communication between humans and other elements of the cosmos rather than as a monologue one-way vertical imperative.

Our cultural history with the indigenous first peoples of the Americas has been marked by arrogance and disrespect for a world view that for the most part we neither understood or appreciated. We are now coming to see, with the help of postmodern deconstruction, that we have ignored world views that were rich in cosmological significance. The above summary of the world views of indigenous peoples can give us a new appreciation of the historical and contemporary significance of native cosmologies. A postmodern education, embedded in an ecozoic horizon, would engage and tap into the profound significance of indigenous knowledge. It should be of real educational interest to enter into dialogue with world perspectives that have rich cosmologies. The outcome of these dialogues would, no doubt, be open-ended. This type of education would not be a romanticizing of native ways. Rather, it is expected that new and more enriched perspectives would be generated. For our own specific educational world view, it would be an opening and appreciation of world views and peoples other than our own. It would be an exercise in cultural humility that has been too long in coming.

An important dimension of a transformative educational vision is based on the assumption that the primary educator is the whole earth community. Currently, our concern for the natural world is based on its utility and we are lacking a sense that the natural world in which we are embedded is much more than a utilitarian margin. The disenchantment with nature has left us with a view of that world based primarily in terms of its physical dimensions. There is a sense of urgency for a wider perspective than the physical because our predominant scientific perspectives have developed an enormous volume of information about the natural world in its physical aspects and our corresponding powers to control it. This is a very one-sided perspective and it affects our educational programmes at their deepest levels. What is currently being suggested in educational circles is either traditional or reform principles. As we noted in Chapter 2, there are suggestions that we go back to the examples of traditional civilizations and we are invited to rediscover our educational principles in the humanities. We see this in *The Closing of the American Mind* (Bloom 1987) which I have already critiqued. There are also suggestions that we turn back to the spiritual and moral traditions of the past. This corner is occupied by the religious new right. There is also the wonder world that is projected by science and technology. Hope is given here as the pragmatic adaptation to the world through acceptance of its imperatives as known through the physical sciences, politics, economics or sociology. Finally, education has relied heavily on the guidance of the psychologies of one persuasion or another.

The vision of education that is being developed in this book moves into a perspective that I call 'transformative ecozoic' and one of its foundational characteristics is a functional cosmology. Thomas Berry (1988) notes that there are difficulties here for the educator on first blush. He notes that presently the term 'cosmology' is exclusively physical in its accepted meaning and therefore does not indicate the integral reality of the universe. He further notes that the term 'geology' falls short because it does not indicate the integral reality of the earth, but only its physical aspects. What Berry points to is the need for a functional cosmology that indicates the integral reality of the universe. This brings us to our second elaboration of a transformative ecozoic vision. I paraphrase Thomas Berry's work at some length because he crystallizes, for educators, what will be elaborated upon in later chapters of this book. In his initial ideas for a functional cosmology he suggests a fourfold evolutionary process. First of all, there is the evolution of the galaxies and the elements. Second, the evolution of the solar system and the earth with its molecular and geological formations. Third, there is the evolution of life in all its variety. Finally, the evolution of consciousness and the cultural developments of the human order. The whole process represents a unity:

> from the first imaginable moment of cosmic emergence through all its subsequent forms of expression until the present. The unbreakable bond of relatedness that makes of the whole a universe becomes increasingly apparent to scientific observation, although this bond subsequently escapes scientific formulation or understanding. In virtue of this relatedness, everything is intimately present to everything else in the universe. Nothing is completely itself without everything else. This relationship is both spatial and temporal. However distant in space and time, the bond of unity is functionally there. The universe is a communion and a community. We ourselves are that communion becoming conscious of itself. (T. Berry 1988: 91)

An adequate description of the earth must also include each and every aspect. The simpler elements are not known in their fulness until their integration into more comprehensive modes of being is recognized.

When we speak of education within this larger universe context, it must be seen as a pervasive life experience. Formal education programmes cannot fulfil all of these requirements. At the same time, formal education must be transformed so that it can provide an integrating context for total life functioning. At the higher levels of formal education, what is needed are processes of reflection on meaning and values, carried out in a critical context. At the present moment it is clear that the university expresses a universe context. Accuracy would demand that we call our institutions of formal education 'multiversities' rather than universities. Our universities today flounder for want of a larger and more comprehensive context. Having no adequate larger context in which to function, our higher educational institutions operate within a splintered and fractionated world view. One of the most common solutions to this vacuum is in the reinstatement of past forms of humanistic studies in a core curriculum, a curriculum which includes philosophy, ethics, history, literature, religious studies and some general science. At this point in our own cultural history, these attempts at an integral education do not appear to evoke a sense of committed identification and no unifying paradigm appears on the horizon. As a result, effective education does not take place.

In closely examining this moment of crisis, Thomas Berry (1988) suggests that we need to return to the story of the universe. He maintains that for the first time the peoples of the entire world, insofar as they are educated in a modern context, are being educated within this origin story. The universe story provides the setting in which children everywhere – whether in Africa or China, in Russia or South America, in North America, Europe or India – are given their world and their personal identity in time and space. While the traditional origin and journey stories are also needed in the educational process, none of them can provide the encompassing for education such as is available in this new story, which is the mythic aspect of our modern account of the world. The story tells us how the universe has emerged into being and of the transformation through which it has passed, especially on the planet earth, until the present phase of development was realized in contemporary human intelligence.

The plenitude of this universe story is the basis for all educational endeavours and is the proper context for the entire educational process. At the same time, the story must also be understood within the limits of personal and social development. Thus, it can be appreciated within a human developmental context. How the elementary, secondary and higher education student will appreciate it will depend upon the developmental stage of each person. We should not be surprised that the elementary and secondary student will not appreciate the story in a fully reasoned and reflexive manner; at the university, the processes of human maturity allow for its penetration at a more profound level. It is important to note at this point that our deepest educational endeavours and commitments would be grounded in a story that has a cultural, historical and cosmological context of meaning that can be accepted on a broad scale by persons of different ethnic and cultural backgrounds. The universe story is a 'grand story' but not a 'master narrative'.

. . . .

CHAPTER 4

Ringing in Our Ears and Invading Our Souls: Reflection on the Dream Structure of Our Western Cultural Mantras

As we move forwards, I shall attempt to make connections with cosmology, economics and the development of modern educational thought. For now, I would ask my readers to prepare themselves for a shift in what I would consider a careful study of some of the sacred symbols of modern western societies. I return to my use of the label 'terminal cenozoic'. I use this term to indicate that what we are dealing with in our time is more than the appellation postmodern or post-industrial. What is now being terminated is an incredible period of earth history and not simply a phase of human history. Even though it is becoming apparent that there is a radical turning point which involves a termination in the historical earth process, we nevertheless find a rhetoric of denial in the language of the global marketplace.

In this chapter we take a critical look at some key words that are part of the everyday lexicon of the 'new economic order'. These sounds ring in our ears. We hear the words so repeatedly that I liken them to a series of mantras. In many of the major spiritual traditions throughout the world, there is the employment of a repetitive sound in order to help foster a certain elevation of spiritual consciousness. In the Hindu tradition we frequently hear of the sound 'Om'. In the Buddhist tradition there is a repetition of the sounds of the zen koan. Frequently the zen koan is presented as an incomprehensible riddle to be repeated, such as: What is the sound of one hand clapping? In the Christian tradition there is the Lord's Prayer as well as the intonations of the Gregorian chants. The role of sound in the development of consciousness can either elevate one's spiritual condition or lower one's spiritual awareness. This chapter will examine a number of sounds that are repeated in contemporary culture through the mass media which, in my opinion, evoke a state of consciousness that propagates the 'consumer–industrial society'.

I have made the connection between the consumer–industrial society and its larger arc as the terminal cenozoic. When I speak here of the terminal cenozoic, I am referring to its latest embodiment which now reaches beyond the nation-state. This is the modern development of transnational corporate businesses that fly under the flags of the 'new world order' or the 'global competitive marketplace'. This historical phase has some pre-eminent symbols that evoke the latest version of our consumer–industrial consciousness. The repetition of these symbols as sounds are the work of the gurus of the terminal cenozoic. I am speaking here of the creative branch of consumer–industrial capitalism: the advertisers. The cultural historian Stuart Ewen (1976) calls the people who occupy the advertising branches of capitalism the 'captains of consciousness'. They do not sell products. Their job is to elicit a state of consciousness that encourages positive attitudes towards industrialization and a corresponding desire to consume the products of industry. In contemporary world culture, as advertised by the proponents of the 'new global marketplace', there is a constellation of symbols and sounds akin to mantras that attempt to create an entrancement with a consumer consciousness. At the level of the global economy, it involves a supreme dedication to the movement of the greatest amount of natural resources, with the greatest possible efficiency, to the consumer economy and to the 'waste heap'. The latter is not a source of new life by way of fertilizing fields and farms but, as the historian Thomas Berry (1988) points out, at best, a dead end and, often, a toxic source of further death.

The increase in the speed and volume of this activity is the basic norm of what we now refer to as 'modern progress'. The progress symbol comes to us within a constellation of mutually supportive symbols. The supporting symbols of the progress myth, as I see them, are growth, development, globalization, competition and consumption. These symbols and sounds serve as the mantras of the terminal cenozoic, disguising the terminal nature of our current cultural synthesis in that they extol and propagate the consumer–industrial order. It will be my task here to take these symbols out of their honorific context and submit them to critical scrutiny. I will do this in sequence, starting with the notion of progress.

Progress

Although the idea of progress can be traced backed to classical antiquity in western thought, it nevertheless has had a very powerful role to play in modern western thought since the Enlightenment (Ginsberg 1973). At its deepest level of meaning, it signifies belief in a linear unfolding of perfection. This unfolding moves forwards historically and takes on the notion of stages of progress. Each subsequent stage of history (here we are talking about western history) is a further unfolding and an increment of the stage that preceded it. The idea of progress especially took hold in the seventeenth century and almost all major political, social and scientific theories developed in western culture have incorporated the notion of 'progress' in their lexicon (Wiener 1973). It should be pointed out that Marxism and capitalism share this symbol in their own particular interpretations of history. The theologian Mircea Eliade (1959) traces the germ of linear development to our Judaeo-Christian heritage. This core religious conception is seen in the emphasis on the linearity of history that was further developed in western culture during the Enlightenment, which extolled its own period of history by the use of the term 'progress'.

In the nineteenth century, the progress idea was further developed by Darwin's theory of evolution and Marx's conception of history. From the moral sciences, it was developed by the French thinker Auguste Comte. The popular reading of Darwin's theory of evolution was made by his nephew Herbert Spencer who extolled evolutionary progress by blessing cut-throat business competition as a way to advance the winners of history. The best survive and these are the ones that have competed the best. He gave lectures on this theme in the United States at the invitation of Andrew Carnegie (Hofstadter 1955). Marx also used evolutionary ideas in the development of his conception of history. For him, history proceeded in progressive stages and each stage of history is an advance over the previous phase. Although Marx was profoundly critical of capitalism, he nevertheless saw it as an advance over all previous types of historical economies. What binds Marx and Darwin together is the sense that western culture is the most advanced economic evolutionary form. Thus, western cultural institutions are the high point of history's progressive development as seen by all modern western systems, even when they are at odds with one another as in the case of Marxism and capitalism (Said 1993).

The temperament of the nineteenth century can be seen as waxing lyrical about the notion of progress. Nevertheless, it will be the last century to embrace the idea of progress unequivocally. Two world wars and the Holocaust, plus the agonies of our own times, have seriously undermined any facile use of this idea. Nevertheless, in the 1980s we saw how the free market liberalism of the governments of Ronald Reagan in the USA, Margaret Thatcher in Great Britain and Brian Mulroney in Canada propagated the highly questionable ideas of progress through economic growth.

The Reagan years in the United States were a replay of Ronald Reagan's years as the voice-over for the General Electric advertisements that I saw in the early days of television. The slogan for General Electric was 'progress is our most important product'. This could well be said about some of the rhetoric of the Reagan White House. He had changed little from his acting days, but his rhetoric took on a much more ominous significance. It is ironic that by the end of his term in office he could no longer speak of the USSR as the 'evil empire'. It seemed to dismantle itself of its own accord before our very eyes. Its undoing may well be the undoing of advanced capitalism that seems to be guiding the world into the twenty-first century.

From the perspective that I have been developing, it can be argued that capitalism and Marxism share a common heritage, rooted in the inner recesses of the Enlightenment, that ultimately compromises the natural world. If we look at state socialism's treatment of the natural world, then we can see how both systems are detrimental to the natural world. The cultural historian Christopher Lasch (1989) is deeply critical of both capitalism and Marxism. Lasch's perspective is in accordance with the perspective that I am developing; namely, that neither Marxism nor capitalism holds much hope for the mounting problems that threaten to overwhelm us. He ventures a judgement as to what may be the fundamental problem. It is the contention of Lasch that both systems have erred in their common commitment to the idea of progress. It is easy to see why capitalism's common heritage with socialism has fundamental flaws so as to leave both traditions on the waste heap of planetary history. It is at the level of the planet that one can see that both world views have ultimately wreaked havoc on the natural world. With this consideration in mind, it is ludicrous to listen to the prophets of the new world order of transnational capitalism.

Since the cold war ended, we have been hearing that capitalism is victorious and now should have free rein to fulfil its historical mission. And what is that mission? As it turns out, capitalism and its attendant companion liberalism have placed only a minor emphasis on democratic participation. As Lasch notes, the major goal of liberalism is not democratic participation; rather, it accents the right to enjoy the good things of life. The modern state seems to place the right to goods over the right to participate in civic life (Lasch 1989: 28). Thus the modern state, backed up by the modern school, is in the business of developing consumers of goods rather than active participatory citizens. Lasch shares my pessimism about the global marketplace:

> Liberalism ultimately presupposes the creation of a global market that embraces populations formerly excluded from any reasonable expectation of affluence. But the prediction that 'sooner or later we all will be affluent', uttered so confidently a few years ago no longer carries much conviction. The global circulation of commodities, information and populations, far from making everyone affluent, has widened the gap between rich and poor nations and has generated a massive migration to the West, where the newcomers swell the vast army of the homeless, unemployed, illiterate, drug ridden, derelict and effectively disenfranchised. (Lasch 1989: 29)

If this is the case, it is astounding how well the consumer culture is still marketing itself on a global scale. We see this idea embedded in two other related concepts of the progress myth: growth and development. If progress is the direction of historical movements, the ideas of growth and development are the dynamics which move cultures to higher stages of progress. We shall now examine the ideas of growth and development simultaneously in their most recent forms.

Growth and development

The concepts of growth and development are complementary and mutually supportive at a practical level, which is why I have treated them simultaneously in this chapter. The concepts of growth and development are intertwined and frequently defined as one by the other in a circular process. The idea of 'development' generally designates the economic process associated with modern industrialization. According to their degree of economic activity, we distinguish the more developed and the less developed nations of the world. The present world economic situation has witnessed a certain imperative that the less developed nations share more extensively in the economic development that has taken place in the more advanced nations. Development itself is considered not only desirable but also a necessary process for attaining a truly human quality of life. The roots of both growth and development go back to the nineteenth century. Edward Said (1993), in his masterful treatment of culture and imperialism, makes a close connection between growth and development and imperialism. In the twentieth century, 'growth' and 'development' have become acceptable code-names for imperialism. At its core level, imperialism is a process whereby one or more nations take on the task of developing another nation or nations. As regards this process, it will be our task to examine critically this lofty objective because it will tell us something about how power works at a global level. In this century, especially since the end of the Second World War, growth and development have become honorific ideas. Lester Milbrath (1989) has an excellent treatment of these concepts and it is his contention that these are some of the most powerful geopolitical symbols of our time. As ideological symbols, we can see how powerfully they operated in popular discourse. Milbrath invites us to see how the process goes unquestioned in the popular imagination. He notes that there is a constant injunction to continue growing in economic output, in population, in prestige, in strength, in stature, in complexity. Growth is associated with development, health and progress. Progress defined as growth is believed to be inevitable and good. Some people even believe that if we do not grow then we will die.

As you can see, these symbols support one another and move together as constellations. Thus, you rarely see one on its own. Almost always, these symbols are projected as very positive and inviting. Therefore, it is initially difficult to look at them in a critical manner. Nevertheless, it will be my task to move the reader in critical directions.

Rowledge and Keeth (1991), following an analysis by Schaef (1987), develop the thesis that these constellations of symbols follow an addiction model. The addiction model indicates that we must have such things as growth and development. Addiction involves necessity and so there is a compulsion to grow and develop. Like a drink that the alcoholic thinks he *must* have, growth and development are seen as something that we *must* have. As regards economic growth, both individuals and societies seem to follow this addiction model. As with all major addictions, there are active perpetrators and co-dependents. The perpetrators are in the 'producer' role and the co-dependent takes the role of the 'consumer'. Of course, these roles can change in different contexts.

There is one major index of our addiction and it is seen in our use of the growth index GNP (gross national product). We are constantly hearing the term as an index of economic health. If the GNP rises or grows then we are led to believe that economic development has taken place. There are so many problems and absurdities attending the use of GNP that it is surprising that it still remains a hallowed term in conventional economic circles. (For excellent critical treatments on the GNP, see Daly and Cobb [1989]; Ekins [1992]; Henderson [1992]; T. Berry [1988]; Waring [1988].)

For my purposes here, it is necessary to appreciate the historical trajectory of growth and development in their most recent post-war manifestations if we are going to understand the dynamics of these notions. Wolfgang Sachs (1992) has given us the most thorough archaeology of the notion of development and from this we can see the powerful cultural and economic forces in which it is embedded. Sachs takes us to the White House during the post-war administration of Harry Truman for the origin of the modern meaning of development. He gives us the most recent vintage of this concept by looking at the inauguration speech of President Truman in which he defined the largest part of the world as 'undeveloped' areas. Sachs points out that, in that moment, Truman established a pivotal concept which crammed the immeasurable diversity of the South into a single category: underdeveloped. For the first time, the new world view was thus announced: all the peoples of the earth were to move along the same track and aspire to only one goal – development.

Truman's vision of post-war development was that greater production was the key to greater prosperity and peace. It was also the beginning of the United States becoming first among the imperial nations (Barnet and Cavanagh 1994; Said 1993). Sachs (1992) points out that it was within the corridors of the State Department during the post-war period that 'cultural progress' was absorbed by 'economic mobilization' and 'development', and the result was enthroned as the crowning concept. Modern civilized nations could be measured by their level of production. There was also a belief that development need not be linked to the presence of natural resources. In fact, a society could be considered 'underdeveloped' when it failed to develop or extract its natural resources. In Truman's view, people as well as whole societies could be considered objects of development. This was, in essence, how the American model of society was to be projected onto the rest of the world. In this very context, the definition of 'poverty' began to define whole peoples. Poverty, defined from the point of view of the industrialized nations of the world, came to be understood as a lack of spending power that could be elevated by 'economic growth'. Under this definition of poverty, whole societies have been pressured and forced to reorganize themselves into modern money economies supposedly competing on the world market. Development politicians of the industrialized world viewed 'poverty' as the problem and 'growth' as the solution. This definition of 'poverty' was fundamentally flawed when it failed to distinguish between frugality, destitution and scarcity. Wolfgang Sachs gives us a lucid description and clarification of this distinction. For Sachs, *frugality* is the mark of cultures free of the frenzy of accumulation. Everyday necessities are gained from subsistence production with only a small part being purchased on the market. He offers us the following picture:

> To our eyes people have rather meager possessions, maybe the hut and some pots and Sunday costume, with money only playing a marginal role. Instead, everyone has access to fields, rivers and woods, while kinship and community duties guarantee services which elsewhere must be paid for in hard cash. Despite being in the 'low income bracket' nobody goes hungry. What is more, large surpluses are often spent on jewellery, celebrations or grandiose buildings. In a traditional Mexican village, for example, the private accumulation of wealth results in social ostracism – prestige is gained precisely by spending even small profits on good deeds for the community. Here is a way of life maintained by a culture which recognizes the state of sufficiency; it only turns into demeaning 'poverty' when pressurized by an accumulating society. (Sachs 1992: 11)

Sachs maintains that *destitution* is a state that is precipitated by frugality when it is deprived of its foundations. This includes the infrastructures of life such as community ties, land, forest and water. These are important pre-requisites for subsistence without money. When these essentials are removed, destitution ensues. *Scarcity* is a phenomenon that has arrived in modern times. Scarcity effects only urban groups caught up in the money economy as workers and consumers and whose spending power has fallen below a certain poverty line. Urban populations living in scarcity have a precarious situation that seems to spiral only downwards. Societies of scarcity are in a predicament that makes them vulnerable to the whims of the market. Simultaneously, a scarcity society is forced to live in a situation where money assumes ever-increasing importance. It is a downward spiral when the capacity to achieve through one's own efforts gradually fades, while at the same time desires, fuelled by glimpses of high society, spiral towards infinity; this scissor-like effect of want is what characterizes modern poverty.

Instead of continuing to preach the gospel of modern economic growth and development, it is Sachs' contention that we should concentrate on more frugality and lessen the shackles of destitution produced by modern 'development'. Currently, politicians have seen 'poverty' as the problem and 'growth' as the solution. They have not acknowledged, up to this point, that they have largely been working with a concept of poverty fashioned by the experience of commodity-based need in the northern hemisphere. With the less well-off *homo oeconomicus* in mind, they have preached growth and often produced destitution by bringing numerous cultures of frugality to ruin. For the culture of growth can be erected only on the ruins of frugality, and so destitution and dependence on commodities are its price (Sachs 1992).

While all this is true, we still are lacking both the understanding and the discipline required to establish an integral development process. A process of this kind would enrich human life in some integral manner while avoiding the disintegrating effects of development on the human community as well as on the planet itself. Laments in more developed societies over the disruption consequent upon the new industrial processes are balanced by the urgency in the less developed societies for relief from their more immediate afflictions. Relief seems to be promised in and through the development that could be made available to them through the more developed societies. These so-called advanced societies have, all too frequently, depressed the other societies by exploitation of their resources as well as their personal abilities and energies. This exploitation, in its most recent vintage, has gone under the name of the 'structural adjustment policy' of the World Bank and the International Monetary Fund (IMF).

Development, in this context, rides on the backs of three powerful assumptions. The first is that western science is the only way of understanding the world. This, in effect, dismisses the wisdom of most of humankind. The second is that progress and development, using this scientific world view, are essentially embodied in the increasing output of market commodities. The third is the relatively recent invention of the 'nation-state' which is sovereign within its artificial borders and which allows 'development' to be imposed on its subject populations (Ekins 1992). Development is therefore an alliance between governments and other powerful interests in the North and governing elites of the South, many of whom were converted to the northern view of development during the colonial period and whose image is in the likeness of the most 'developed' country, the United States. Paul Ekins (1992) outlines the mechanisms that were set up between the North and the South to achieve this end; debt, trade and aid. From the point of view of the North, this triad has been enormously successful. In reference to third world debt, northern interests have been finding unlimited resources that can be extracted from the South, when certain conditions prevail. One such condition is the foreign loan which enables southern elites to finance a variety of self-aggrandizing projects. Contrary to banking practices and natural justice, repayments are extracted by IMF-imposed 'structural adjustment' programmes from labourers and the resources of the poorest people; those who have no share in the loans themselves. It must be noted that 'aid and trade' has very similar effects; aid being promoted through bilateral GATT arrangements, and structural adjustment through the IMF. If development is defined as a means of further enriching already existing government programmes and multilateral institutions, such as the World Bank, and trade is being imposed by the ideology of free trade through institutions controlled by the relatively rich irrespective of the effect on the poor, then aid, trade and debt have proved to be powerful development tools (Ekins 1992). But it is not the development that is valorized by the northern partners in the exchange. Because of its negative effects, Vandana Shiva (1989) has labelled this so-called development process as 'mal-development'.

Before ending this critical treatment of growth and development, it seems important to consider two other connections. First, I am referring to the effects of the development of militarism and its influence on modern development ideas. Second, we must also make some preliminary judgements on the new field of genetic engineering. As regards militarism, it must be acknowledged that no modern discussion of issues around 'development' is complete without mentioning the corrosive effects of modern militarization. Current military spending in the world stands at about US$1,000 billion per annum or $1.9 million per minute (Epp-Tiessen 1990). Making the link between militarization and underdevelopment, Ester Epp-Tiessen (1990) gives the following statistics on world military spending. The global military establishment accounts for 5.6 per cent of the world's gross national product, and employs approximately 25.7 million people in the armed forces alone. An estimated 57,000 nuclear weapons stockpiled worldwide contain 1,000 times the explosive power used in all wars since the introduction of gunpowder. Epp-Tiessen (1990) makes special note of the pace of militarization in the third world. As an example, in the 1960s, 22 of the 78 independent developing countries were ruled by military governments; by 1988 the number had risen to 64 out of 113 or 57 per cent. Taking the 1960s as a reference point, military spending by third world countries increased fivefold in constant prices. As a result, developing countries now absorb 82 per cent of the world's arms transfers. The connection of militarization to underdevelopment or mal-development is no less striking: Epp-Tiessen (1990) believes that militarism contributes to underdevelopment in many ways. Even more significant than the individual consequences is the manner in which militarization strengthens the various mechanisms whereby the industrialized nations of the North engage in the exploitation of the South. It is important to see that compounding the foreign debt of developing economies by gearing production towards exports and away from urgent local needs, by contributing to dependence on the IMF, and by fostering authoritarianism and repression, serve to reinforce the structure and dynamic of a world hierarchy of power supported by the militarization of the third world. Epp-Tiessen (1990) concludes that, at a very basic level, militarization makes for underdevelopment by integrating the developing countries into a global economic order in which they are destined to be losers. Within this perspective it is not difficult to see that the trajectory of modern development in the eurocentric–western mould is, to say the least, problematic. George Dei (1995b), for example, gives us an African critique of western development strategies pointing out that this development for Africans has led to strengthened unequal dependency relations between African societies and the West. It has also reinforced and maximized the system of control, exploitation and inequality within African societies.

Dei (1995b) and Shiva (1989, 1995) both suggest an alternative to a euro-centric view that is reminiscent of a different paradigm of development suggested in 1975 by the Dag Hammarskjold Foundation of Sweden (Ekins 1992). Called 'Another Development', the Foundation outlines five key features of the alternative. First, this alternative development is oriented towards satisfying people's fundamental human needs (Henderson 1992; Ekins 1992; Daly 1973; Daly and Cobb 1989; Roberts 1993; Georgescu-Roegen 1971). Second, it is a development enacted by the people concerned, based on their knowledge, experience and culture, rather than development imposed by outside influences. David Korten (1991) has labelled this 'people-centred development'. Third, development, in the alternative paradigm, based on self-reliance, is achieved largely through the mobilization of local resources to meet perceived local needs. Fourth, it is ecologically sound (Roberts 1993; Quarter 1992). Finally, fifth, development strategies must be achieved only where fundamental reforms are made both in domestic power relations and in international development institutions such as the World Bank and the IMF. This development fundamentally challenges the hegemony created by the current programmes of aid, trade and debt that are presently devised by the international competitive economic order.

It is to be noted that the most recent pronouncements of the Brundtland Commission, summarized in *Our Common Future: The World Commission on*

Environment and Development, there is clearly a sensitivity to the above tenets of the alternative paradigm in what this Commission labels as *sustainable development*. Although the concept of sustainable development put forth by the Commission is particularly sensitive to the dimensions of development affecting the planet's ecological balance, it nevertheless does not extricate itself in any fundamental way from the economistic paradigms of development, maintaining that sustainable development can move ahead, to a 'new era of economic growth' (Brundtland 1987). Alas, the Commission allows us to have our cake and eat it too.

Even while efforts are being made to advance the quality of life, we need to reflect more profoundly on the entire process of development. The human community must accept the discipline that is needed to avoid the greater and more absolute disasters that threaten us if development is not dealt with properly.

I have indicated, in passing, the role that science and technology have in modern development. Before finishing this critical analysis of western ideas on development, it is important to deal with the latest dimension of development: the world of biotechnology and genetic engineering. In this context of the present dysfunctional development of western science and technology, we must proceed with extreme caution. This area of endeavour is not just a new trend but, rather, we are experiencing genetic engineering as an area of great cultural and planetary consequence. In their critical appraisal of these new developments, Jeremy Rifkin and Nicanor Perlas (1983) observe that civilization is experiencing the historic first moments of the next age of history. The media are already treating us to glimpses of a future where the engineering of life by design will be the standard operating procedure. Even as the corporate laboratories begin to dribble out the first products of bio-engineering, a subtle shift in the ethical impulse of society is becoming perceptible. As we begin to reprogramme life, our moral code is being similarly reprogrammed to reflect this profound change in humanity's organization of the world.

Biotechnology is often dated from the first cloning of a gene in 1973 and its expression within a foreign organism a year later. In the 1980s the first human-made life form, and the accompanying life processes, were successfully patented, solidifying the base for what has turned out to be the business of biotechnology (Menzies 1989). While biotechnology has made impressive advances in the past several years, it must be acknowledged that nature at the microscopic level is still an unchartered frontier. In the context in which we speak, there are several reasons for grave concern about the present developments in biotechnology. One is that biotechnology is being developed almost exclusively within the military–industrial complexes around the globe and it is also almost solely restricted to private industrial investment and development.

The number of unclassified US Department of Defense projects using genetic engineering technology and monoclonal antibodies has risen from zero in 1980 to over one hundred in 1984; spending on the US programme increased by over 900 per cent between 1979 and 1986. Over one hundred corporate laboratories plus eighteen US government laboratories are now involved in this work. There is virtually a total absence of public discourse on ethical issues as a result of biotechnological development being confined to these two sectors. It is reasonable to conjecture that destructive power and profit are the main engines driving the exploitation of this new area of knowledge development. Although a science in its nascent stages, biotechnology is growing rapidly and is virtually publicly unmonitored. Heather Menzies (1989) makes the following observation about the rapid developments in this area. She maintains that, in its social construction, biotechnology is unique. From one perspective, it is still at a very early stage (by analogy where manufacturing was over a century ago). But already its development is being telescoped. Instead of growing slowly, allowing at least some hindsight and sober second thought along the way, it is being force-fed into an advanced stage of industrial development.

The shorter view of these accelerated developments, more often than not, short-circuits considerations of their long-term environmental and social consequences (Suzuki and Knudston 1988). Combined with the short-sightedness of the industrial profit motive there is also the presence of monopoly control over the research and development by biotechnology multinationals. These private companies are involved in medical diagnosis, agriculture, chemicals and fermentation. Projecting to the year 2000 in the area of seed marketing, there will probably be monopoly control by twelve seed and chemical multinational giants. At a time when there was a call for biodiversity at the Earth Summit in Brazil in 1992, these same multinationals were creating monopoly control over world seed production and creating a seed monoculture by reducing diversity. For example, as a result of monopoly control over seed production in the last twenty-five years, seventy-five types of vegetables available during the early twentieth century, approximately 97 per cent of the varieties of each type, are now extinct. The precious few that are left are under patent protection by a small number of multinationals (*New Internationalist* 1991; 1997).

The second reason for concern is that biotechnology is being carried out within the cosmology of what we have called the terminal cenozoic. We are still caught up in the paradigm of mechanism. Jeremy Rifkin and Nicanor Perlas (1983) make some of the parallels in the area of human genetic engineering and raise some fundamental questions of concern. They point out that the idea of engineering the human species is very similar to the idea of engineering a piece of machinery. An engineer is constantly in search of new ways to improve the performance of a machine. The fundamental task is to eliminate all imperfections. The whole idea of setting limits to perfectibility is alien to this enterprise. Rifkin and Perlas go on to point out that with human genetic engineering we get something and we give up something. In return for securing our physical well-being, we must also accept the idea of reducing the human species to a technologically designed product. Finally, there are profound reservations about the cosmological perspective in which genetic engineering is being carried forward. The development of biology from the nineteenth century was the most recent recurrence of a cosmological stance that has for centuries attempted to put humans above and beyond the intricate web of life. It may be that, instead of moving ahead into the alteration of our genetic coding, we should pause to consider the guidance that we can get from it. Thomas Berry (1988) points out that we seldom consider going to our genetic coding for guidance because we are too busy trying to alter and manipulate our genetic designs. Our culture makes us generally unaware that genetic coding provides the basic psychic and physical structure of our being. Our genetic coding determines not only our identity at birth; its guidance continues also in every cell of our bodies throughout the entire course of our existence, guidance manifested through the spontaneities within us. Berry concludes that the functions of science and technology, at the human level, must be subordinated to the larger scientific and technological processes developed by the earth during the past billions of years. These larger scientific and technological processes of the earth are already threatening a massive retaliation for the abusive interference recently brought about by the human phase of scientific and technological processes. The present toxic elements saturating the planet constitute the method by which the earth is disciplining, educating and warning the human community to observe more carefully the basic rules of 'development', whether this be in the eastern or western, the northern or the southern regions of the globe. At this same time, the earth is inviting human participation in the next phase of the continuing cultivation of those immense forces that have given the earth its past splendour and which are capable of new forms of magnificence if only humans will listen to the earth's directives from deep within their own being (T. Berry 1988). With these final caveats we go on to the mantra of globalization.

Globalization

'The human world appears to be going global and we must keep up with this new direction. We need to be primed for competition in the new global marketplace.' You can read or hear statements like this almost daily in one or the other of our communication media. It is now the new religion for trans-national business and, as we shall see, it is a recapitulation of the Social

Darwinism of the last century with the same undemocratic standards and values (Hurtig 1991). There is rhetoric about a 'level playing field' which has the ring of justice to it. Here international trade is likened to a sports playing field where if the slope goes one way it gives advantage to one of the contestants, if it goes the other way the advantage is to the opposite team. In the transnational business context, for example, the field is thought to advantage one state when there are subsidies given to an industry, allowing it to reduce the price of exports. In this context the so-called justice of the level playing field demands that the subsidy be withdrawn (J. Smith 1993). In practice, however, justice is caricatured. As Barnet and Cavanagh (1994) point out, the subsidies are very broadly defined to include things such as regional development programmes, generous unemployment insurance benefits, and even publicly funded health care. Trading partners can argue that because these benefits are provided by the state, employers receive a hidden subsidy. To level the field these programmes must be bulldozed (J. Smith 1993).

Our politicians also speak of the 'new global order' in many of their rhetorical flourishes. Globalization is now being inserted into public discourse. The public discourse on competitive globalization is fuelled by our communications mass media. The western press is called the 'free press' and it has the pretensions of democratization. Noam Chomsky and his co-author Edward Herman (1988) have challenged this assumption in a powerful critique of western mass media and their pretentions to being democratic and free. Herman and Chomsky fundamentally refute the postulate that the media are democratic; they build their own thesis that the western press and the so-called American free press are in the business of manufacturing consent for the modern imperial mission of transnational business. Therefore, they dispute the American mass media's boasts that they are independent and committed to discovering the truth. They develop a case that mass media are not in the business of truth at all, rather they merely reflect powerful groups as they propagate their corporate agenda all over the world. The frequent boast of the so-called democratic press that it is based on unbiased professional and objective criteria, does not hold up under careful scrutiny. They go on to demonstrate that the powerful corporate interests in the world fix, for the general populace, the premisses of discourse, deciding what the general populace is allowed to see, hear and think about. Corporate interests also 'manage' public opinion by regular propaganda campaigns that are played out in advertising, programming and news reporting (Chomsky 1989a; 1997; Herman and Chomsky 1988). These media are in no way democratic in terms of access and it can be safely concluded that they follow the trajectory of transnational corporate agendas (Chomsky 1997; Schiller 1983). This has been called electronic colonialism (Chomsky 1997; Schiller 1983).

In the global context, the new world order is complemented by the new information order. When carefully studied and analysed, this new information order has been characterized as a monoply of the western industrialized nations (Chomsky 1997; Schiller 1983). When western hegemony of the new information order is questioned and criticized, there is an incredible backlash from the western governments, business and press (Chomsky 1997; Schiller 1983; McPhail 1981). There is a claim that these hegemonically controlled structures which buttress the corporate agendas of the West are the only real free media. Taking commercial television, as a particular instance, we see that it sells its audiences to goods producers with carefully determined ratios of so many thousands of viewers per advertising dollar. Advertisers refer to the programmes as the 'free lunch' which entices the consumers to come out and see the commercials. Any threat or criticism to this process is seen as a tampering with 'free television' (Chomsky 1997; Schiller 1983).

Throughout this century, mass media public relations professionals have been busily developing and refining techniques to unfold the desired agenda for their corporate and government clients; creating positive images and repressing the darker and seamier side of their activities (Nelson 1989). In the latter part of the twentieth century, we see the incredible ascendance of the United States of America. The USA is now the single most imperial power in the world. Herbert Schiller (1983) notes that what lends sophistication to the US imperial power today is its dependence on a marriage of economics and electronics, which substitutes in part for the earlier 'blood and iron' foundations of the more primitive conquerors. It is no exaggeration to say today that the conditions under which information is purveyed in the United States are controlled by concentrated private economic power (Schiller 1983). Broadcasting is therefore our century's way of getting out the apologia for corporate dreams. This dream structure has been solidified by the incredible advancement of information technologies, especially television. From a global perspective, the most marketable cultural commodity is the American way of life (Barnet and Cavanagh 1994). Western transnational advertising is a multi-billion dollar industry, and it offers what may be the only product that we currently cannot avoid. The dream structures of its messages seep into our subconscious and permeate all levels of societies throughout the modern world. The popular culture of the USA has a monopoly in the global communications market. With its sheer weight of numbers and the enormous concentration of its programmes, the USA literally dominates the world. In the countries of the South, we see a stranglehold of American images because American reruns can be marketed and sold at much cheaper prices than indigenous programmes (*Distress Signals* 1986; Barnet and Cavanagh 1994). All things considered, it is not unrealistic to say that the United States of America represents the first imperial power to operate at a planetary level.

All that being said, we must still closely examine the meaning of this use of the term 'globalization'. We have to look at this term critically and see where the global ideas are leading to. There is a certain glibness that accompanies this term and it is worth our while to be on the lookout for 'globaloney' (a term attributed to Clare Booth Luce).

This has been called the age of globalization (Barnet and Cavanagh 1994). There is a plethora of social forces that are converging on one another to make the world a lot smaller. The sense of the global has come to us from two separate vantage points. The first point of reference took place over twenty-five years ago when we saw the pictures of earth from outer space. These photographs gave us the sense of the earth as a total entity and offered a unifying metaphor that awakened a planetary consciousness for many. There was the sense that all members of this lovely blue planet were interrelated and in an intricate web of life that probably existed nowhere else in the universe. I would like to make a distinction here by looking at the term globalization in two contexts: 'new economic order' and as 'planetary organicity'. The second usage or vantage point is the new global economy of transnational business which is also referred to as the new economic order. I label this as one of the essential mantras of the terminal cenozoic period. Transnational corporate rhetoric, which comes from the myriad advertising agencies and is seen day after day and night after night on our mass media, is a language that hides the entropy in which it is implicated (Nelson 1989). In reflecting on global corporate activity, when we get past the rhetoric and look deeper into these activities, we see a path of destruction. Marcia Nozick (1992) does not wax lyrically on these matters. As regards the trends in global economic development, we see very disturbing scenarios. One outcome of transnational globalization is that it creates the opposite of the wealth that it claims to be bringing to the world. We can see that the present developments in global economic restructuring are creating a growing, permanent underclass of disenfranchised, dispossessed people (Nozick 1992). This frame of reference has brought the earth together as a global marketplace. This is the world of transnational business. Its preoccupation is with trade, commerce and the competitive edge in every type of merchandise that the human mind can conceive of and fabricate. Jeremy Rifkin (1991) gives his assessment of the overriding negative consequences of the transnational business. He maintains that the chief impediment to a new biospheric temporal and spatial orientation is the multinational corporation. The giant global companies represent the final institutional stage of mechanistic consciousness and geospheric thinking. In both their operating procedures and objectives, the multinationals epitomize the values and assumptions upon which the modern world view is based. Their role in the world and their impact upon the world need to be understood, critiqued and ultimately contested if society is to have any hope of entertaining a new biospheric consciousness.

Using the earth planet symbol, the new transnational market ventures now fly under this symbol as if it were its flag. But behind this symbol is not the organic totality that we read about as the earth as Gaia; a more sinister process hides behind the camouflage and confuses the average citizen. As Barnet and Cavanagh depict it:

> We are all participants in one way or another in an unprecedented political and economic happening, but we cannot make sense of it. We know that we are supposed to think globally, but it is hard to wrap the mind even around a city block, much less a planet. No wonder we are at the mercy of buzzwords and sound bites. 'Globalization' is the most fashionable word of the 1990s, so portentous and wonderfully patient as to puzzle Alice in Wonderland and thrill the Red Queen because it means precisely whatever the user says it means. (Barnett and Cavanagh 1994: 13–14)

If 'nationalism' was the overarching ideal at the turn of the nineteenth century, it is 'globalization' that is taking us into the twenty-first century. It will be our educational task to get a handle on it because it now serves to mystify rather than inform. Somewhere out there is a global marketplace that we all are to be competing in and God help those who are unable to maintain their competitive edge. The nation-state at the turn of this century is no longer a sovereign entity. Transnational businesses can work around nation-states and it is usually nation-state leaders that make the transnationals' work much easier by entering into trade blocs. Thus we have the European Economic Community (EC) in Western Europe and what appears to be a North American trade bloc with the acronym NAFTA (North American Free Trade Agreement). Even when we look at the positive features of this new world order we see that it is a system that works for a small minority of people. Certainly, global integration is a mixed blessing even when we put a benign face on it. Barnet and Cavanagh in their excellent treatment of globalization note that integration of national economies bring very mixed blessings. They summarize it this way:

> in the late twentieth century there is strong evidence that, as national economies become increasingly intertwined, nations are breaking up in many different ways, and no alternative community is yet on the horizon. For some regions and city blocks all around the world, globalization brings unparalled prosperity. For others on another continent or just across town the consequences are crushing poverty ... As traditional communities disappear and ancient cultures are overwhelmed, billions of human beings are losing the sense of place and sense of self that gives life meaning. The fundamental political conflict in the opening decades of the new century, we believe, will not be between nations or even trading blocs but between the forces of globalization and the territorially based forces of local survival seeking to preserve and to redefine community (Barnet and Cavanagh 1994: 22).

What Barnet and Cavanagh are saying here is very important. They are clear as to where the forces of transnational globalization are taking us. Ultimately, we are taken back to where we started and that is the locale where we build our community life. We can now build our local community within a consciousness of a planetary community that sees all of us living in one world. This idea, of course, needs developing and it will constitute the work of the latter part of this book. In the meantime, we will all have to keep our sniffers out for the 'globalony' that will be dished out in large portions by the global giants who will inundate us with propaganda about the beauties of their global marketplace.

Competition

Webster's Dictionary defines the word 'compete' as seeking or striving for something (as a position, possession or a reward) for which others are contending. This is one of the most powerful words utilized by capitalism in all its transformations going back to the mid-nineteenth century and up to the present. Adam Smith saw in competition the invisible hand that regulated all trade and commercial transactions. Competition was to take place in the marketplace unencumbered by other institutions such as the state. It is at this point that Adam Smith and Karl Marx diverged; Marx seeing the need for competition to be controlled by the state. For capitalism, competition is one of the main driving forces of the market. We hear our politicians and business gurus telling us constantly that we must maintain our 'competitive edge' or we will fall behind and drop out of the race. To make the competition fair the playing field must be levelled as already indicated.

It is necessary to examine this term in its political and historical context. We have to go back to the nineteenth century where the term was organically linked to capitalism. Darwin's theory of evolution had an element to it whereby a species' longevity was the result of a mechanism called 'survival of the fittest'. I have already indicated that this mechanism became the rationale for Social Darwinism (Hofstadter 1955). In the social context it is considered part of the nature of things that the fittest should survive and prosper. This gave tremendous legitimacy to the cut-throat competition of the business world. There were very strong reactions to Social Darwinist formulations of competition in the beginning of the twentieth century and there are ample critiques of it in contemporary historical and scientific thought (Rifkin and Perlas 1983; Hofstadter 1955; Kropotkin,1895). The truth of the matter is that Darwin did not espouse the 'Social Darwinism' of his day. For Darwin, the struggle for survival brings out cooperative instincts. This notion of co-operation was developed by the Russian Prince Kropotkin (1895) in his classic *Mutual Aid*. Arguing on both historical and scientific grounds, he arrives at a place very different from competition in the development of species. He argues persuasively that love, sympathy, sacrifice and cooperation play an immense part in the progressive development of moral feelings. Now even contemporary thinking in biology, anthropology and palaeontology follow Kropotkin rather then Herbert Spencer and T. H. Huxley in arguing for the pre-eminence of cooperation over competitiveness in the evolutionary development of life forms (Margulis 1987; Margulis and Schwartz 1982; Sahtouris 1989).

These developments have had very little impact on the rhetoric of transnational business. The global competitive marketplace is resilient because it is valorized by big business through the mass media and it is done relentlessly day and night.

Consumerism

The culture of consumption and unchallenged and unbridled capitalism that has overtaken the world at the end of the twentieth century is profoundly destructive within its own frame of reference. Without a new vision, we will continually see the breakdown of living structures and the termination of many life forms and eventually our own. I have called this stage of history the terminal cenozoic. It is also a culture that does not satisfy many of our fundamental human needs.

The complexity and apparent diversity of our own culture makes one cautious about venturing a definition of a culture as a simple *commodity culture*. It is true that in all cultures and at all times human groups have demonstrated an interest if not in commodies *per se*, then in decor. Usually an interest in commodities was restricted to the clan, tribe or class that could afford the luxury of that interest. It is only within the last half of this century that an interest in commodities has crossed over into all classes as well as underclasses. When I say that interest is pervasive, it does not mean that people have large varieties of goods and services; it is just that most people want and desire commodities even though they cannot have them. The global marketplace capitalism is characterized by its obsession with the commodity form.

The psychologist Phillip Cushman (1990) maintains that our post-Second World War period shifted away from a Victorian, sexually restrictive self to what he refers to as an 'empty self'. He believes that the post-war era in North America has experienced a significant absence of community and a tradition of shared meaning. The result is a lack of personal conviction and worth, and these absences are embodied as a constant, undifferentiated, emotional hunger. Cushman maintains that the economy and the power structure thus impact on the personality. In the post-war period, we see the emergence of an 'empty self' that seeks the experience of being 'filled up' by consuming goods, calories, experiences, politicians, romantic partners and empathetic therapists in an attempt to counter the growing alienation and fragmentation of our era. This outcome is prescribed by the exigencies of the post-war economy which is premissed on the continual consumption of non-essential and quickly obsolete items and experiences. This type of economy thrives on having people experience a strong need for consumer products. In addition, it is premissed on disposable income where an uninterrupted flow of money is buttressed by a continual motivation to spend it (Cushman 1990). One of the institutions that addresses the modern contemporary self is that of advertising.

Advertising is the systematic cultivation of certain needs and wants that help sell commodities, whether they be goods or services. We are now moving into a global culture which moves itself forward by incessantly creating commodity needs in every nook and cranny of this earth. Global culture can also go under the name of mass culture because the cultivation of the need for commodities is directed towards every part of the globe in one form or other.

In order to produce the enormous quantities of goods and services we have to create a population of people vulnerable to need-messages, called consumers. Consumption becomes the predominant motif of that culture's concerns. The market mechanism of mass production creates incredible social injustices. In earlier chapters, I have documented the inequities that it has created between the rich minority and the rest of the majority world. It is creating degradation and destitution for peoples all over this planet. They are driven off lands, their lands are depleted, and their labour is exploited Even in affluent countries, we are losing, in an escalating manner, our basic infra-structures of housing, health and social welfare. Governments no longer take care of the commonweal but are accommodated to the needs of transnational businesses which have no loyalty or interest in local communities. Certainly within our western world, we have a breakdown in a sense of community life that leaves us open and vulnerable to the mediated culture of television. Michael Lerner (1996) gives us a memorable picture of our community in his discription of a typical middle-class family in the United States. He maintains that, for many, after the workday, there is a pained absence of shared spiritual and ethical vision and of deep mutual recognition. Many people thus seek solace in the malls or in television. They imagine that their freedom now consists in not having next-door neighbours tell them how to dress or live; meanwhile they have their wants shaped by a constant flow of media images as they soak in a steady diet of indoctrination from their television. With a sense of irony, Lerner sees these newly 'freed' human beings increasingly finding their sense of freedom from the consumer choices that they are encouraged to make in the market. Corporate interests, recognizing this growing estrangement, sell products by offering the image of connection with others through the purchase of various commodities and lifestyles. Thus, the freedom obtained through this process increasingly feels empty, and people are, in fact, trapped and dominated by a subtler but equally coercive power, now operating by shaping their consent rather than by opposing it.

For a number of centuries, western culture has taken itself to be the highest point in human cultural evolution. The British, when colonizing Asia and Africa, saw their activities as 'the white man's burden'. In our century, western culture created the notion of developed and underdeveloped to put itself at the top of a scale of evaluation. Western culture has judged the world beyond it on the basis of productive capacity to extract natural resources and to create commodities for a being that we refer to as a consumer. A culture was considered backwards if it were not industrialized, modernized and attuned to the use of western technology and scientific expertise.

In some quarters, we are now coming to see the limitations of the western world in so far as it fulfils some of our fundamental human needs. In our recent past we could say that our culture was a very good provider at the subsistence level. In this last decade of the twentieth century we are clearly seeing a breakdown at the level of subsistence in relation to the existential needs of being and having. For example, food banks and shelters for the homeless are increasing at a rapid pace as we listen to the hype of globalization. When we look at the need for protection, we can say that western societies have dealt adequately with the needs for being, having, doing and interacting in the post-war period. At the present moment, there is clearly a deeply felt erosion of some of our assumed social care systems. Our health benefits are being depleted, social protection programmes savaged, and there is an attack on the pensions system which increasingly leaves a population of elders vulnerable. We also see a diminishing public space for interacting and this has led to a falling off of a public life.

The need for affection has become very problematic in our society. There is a diminishing sphere of affection ties. More and more, the intimate family has become almost the sole place for intimacy and affection. When we consider the need for understanding we can say the existential needs of being, doing or having are met depending on one's social class, race or gender and their interaction. It is important to note that our society operates on a hierarchical level. We see the development of an underclass escalating in the midst of what we have called affluence. Increasingly, education becomes more elite. Participation is very low in our consumer society in all four existential categories of being, having, doing and interacting. We are experiencing an incredible decline in public community life. The culture of television is becoming the predominant mode of interacting. There is a decline in political participation at all levels of government and in many of our western nation-states there is a declining participation in voting. To be sure, there are differences as regards different areas. For example, rural settings normally have a sense of community solidarity that we do not often find in cities. Idleness (my choice would be leisure) at all levels of existential needs is absent in our modern society. The pace of life and the compulsion towards speed and movement have made our society a high stress battleground for competing demands on our time. The need of creation is met in our society but at the level of interaction we seem to have less and less space for expression and temporal freedom. Probably one of the most serious deficits in our society today is its inability to meet the fundamental need for identity. The sense of belonging in modern societies is very low. Fragmentation and isolation make it difficult for persons to have a sense of belonging and continuity. Finally, the need for freedom seems to be met, in the so-called free societies, on very superficial levels. The most serious area is in the category of having where the notion of equal rights is central. Through our economic march towards globalization, we are creating an ever-increasing underclass where there is chronic unemployment and marginal labour at best. For blacks, indigenous peoples and women there is a continued lack of equal access that seems to continue despite movements for equal rights.

In summary, it is important to get a sense of how our society meets fundamental human needs. We are the subject of propaganda when we swallow the belief that our society is the highpoint of a cultural evolutionary process. When we seriously consider our needs and how they are met, contemporary society is lacking in some of the important essentials.

'Shop 'til you drop.' This is the task of the new global consumer. We are already seeing this in the new churches of globalization: the new global shopping centres that are appearing around the world (Barnet and Cavanagh 1994; Mander 1991). These centres are looking for consumers not citizens; a subject that we shall return to. It does not matter if people have no means because they have seen 'the good life' on television and this 'good life' adds up to North American culture. *Dallas* and *The Cosby Show* appear on television screens everywhere. The 'American dream' is exported all over the world (Barnet and Cavanagh 1994; Mander 1991). It is ironic that, at the present time, most of the major American broadcasting systems are predominantly owned by the Germans and the Japanese. As businesspersons they are not overcome by national pride. They market the television of the American way of life because it is the land of the consumer's dream. Even though American television is really no indication of what the everyday life of an American happens to be, there is a dream structure built into programming that has an appeal in all the cultures of the world. It is a dream that is limited, to say the least, bordering on a monoculture. It is therefore accurate to say that the vision of America as a free nation of consumers of the products of the good life is a cultural ideal that has now reached global dimensions. Several years ago, an Israeli professor audited one of my summer classes. In dealing with the topic of media influence she noted that on her kibbutz the communal meetings had to be changed from Friday to Saturday because their meetings were being held at the same time as *Dallas* was showing.

Television is by no means the sole mediator of popular culture but, in the latter part of the twentieth century, it is, without doubt, the most powerful mediator of cultural values that shapes what we call our commonsense view of reality. In television as a cultural mediator, we can see our culture's dominant story and vision rehearsed (i.e. ideological and Utopian symbols).

Let us first note that the communicator on the television addresses us as individuals rather than groups. We are individuals who have a right to own, a duty to consume, and the cultural task of believing that this is the best of all possible worlds. It is the cultural story of 'consumer capitalism' and the main cultural memory is that we have consumed yesterday and therefore have a right, indeed an obligation, to consume today.* We also come to learn that there are those who know more and those who know less; as a viewer, we happen to be the one who knows less. We are never asked to use our judgement. We are to rely on the judgement of 'experts'. At the level of viewing we come to realize that although all people are equal, some nevertheless are better than others. Thus merit becomes an essential caveat to our notion of equality. Therefore, at the level of media images, men are said to be equal to women. At the same time, the portrayal of men's roles in contrast to women's roles shows the male species to be more important and significant. The same applies when capital and labour, whites and blacks, first and third worlds are considered.

Further, one of the dominant actors within our culture is not a person, but technology. Although it is not a person, it is personified and we come to believe that technology accomplishes cultural tasks. For example, a multinational such as 'United Technologies' presents advertisements depicting 'technology' as a cultural actor and transformer of our world. Here we come to believe that 'technology' creates culture rather than being the byproduct of a cultural consensus. What is absent from all of these commercials is the 'human agency' and judgement which decides how our technological inventions come to

---

* In North America and especially the United States, the celebration of the victory of capitalism over socialism masks the major chronic problems that exist as a result of unbridled industrialism. The victory of the free market should give no solace to peoples in the western democracies. Wild capitalism will breed a competitive jungle with the uncompensated inequalities and exploitation that we see in the western hemisphere. The demise of socialism illustrates only that modern societies cannot be run on a single principle, whether that of planning under the general will or that of free market allocations. Our mass media communications are now involved in a non-reflective advocacy of the free market mechanism. It is presented as the commonsense view of the future directions of economies all over this globe. For a more thorough discussion of this topic, see Taylor (1991).

fruition. For example, nuclear reactors do not just happen; rather, they are the outcome of human decisions which are not shown in these commercials.

As we have already indicated, the progress vision gives us the sense that we go forwards gradually but inevitably. We can move forwards best by not questioning the integrity of the dominant cultural story. Thus the agents of Utopian change remain the same as the agents of the cultural story. They are capitalist white men from the first world. Progress achieves equality by melding all within the confines of the dominant myth. This is done by exploiting nature or manipulation. This is the cultural myth of mastery over stewardship. In addition, the Utopian symbol of progress constantly erodes the cultural story by tying it to the 'myth of consumption'. The products or the effects that we have acquired from products are constantly eroded by new products for consumption. Thus, the car, toothpaste or stereo that we bought yesterday are no longer adequate given the new line of commodities. The only stability in the story is the process of consumption itself. Although it is never the centre stage of TV programming, it is intimated that lethal armaments, although undesirable, are inevitable necessities for the maintenance of progress. I might add that cultural myth-making can be done in the privacy of your own living room where the communication is private and unquestioned. Thus, a public political life in which we make judgements is not encouraged. The TV frequently eclipses the need for public rituals that go beyond addressing the individual by providing quasi-public events such as the Super Bowl in the USA. It is interesting that a sports event of this kind could assume such prominence. However, upon closer scrutiny, it becomes clear why this is so. The event extols the nation with a flag ceremony, male dominance, technology, competition and merit rewarded in the game's star system. There is even a moment of 'ideological silence' before the playing of the national anthem.

Commercial television, then, if looked at carefully, allows one to codify the dominant cultural story and vision. This is the dominant story and vision because commercial television is the forum for the most powerful commercial interests in our society. Companies sponsor the programmes. They pay to communicate to the viewer the mythic structure of capitalism, the foundational myth of our consumer–industrial, commodity-driven culture. For those who would challenge this dominant cultural story and vision, there are important and crucial pedagogical tasks to be accomplished in order to deal effectively with the wonderworld of consumer capitalism presented on the mass media. A critical pedagogy that seeks to challenge this powerful dominant myth cannot ignore its elements of attraction. The attraction is that it presents *wasteworld* as *wonderworld* (T. Berry 1988). We learn from the *Prison Notebooks* of Antonio Gramsci (1971) that the dominant cultural myth of consumer capitalism is held together by consent from within the populace. This is clearly the case within liberal democracies where a docile consent mitigates the need for harsh coercion. The main organs of this consensus in our contemporary period are the mass media communications systems. Schooling also plays a significant role but it takes a back seat in the age of the 'tube'. Thus, a critical pedagogy that would challenge these powerful voices of the dominant myth of our capital consumer–industrial order would ignore these media's influence at its peril.

But the dominant cultural story and vision do not exhaust the stories and visions within a complex culture such as our own. Within any culture, oppositional stories and visions always exist. This is the role of critical pedagogy as it is designed to be, an education that cultivates critical commonsense.

If the main motive of advertising is to create consumers, the encouragement of creative critical human action will also be an agenda to be shortcircuited.

> The power to dominate a culture's symbol producing apparatus is the power to create the ambience that forms consciousness itself. It is a power we see exercised daily by the television business as it penetrates virtually every home with the most massive continuing spectacle human history has ever known. Wittingly and unwittingly, this business and its client industries set the stage for a never ending performance stripping away emotional associations that centuries of cultural experience have linked to patterns of behaviour, institutional forms, attitudes, and values that many cultures and subcultures revere and need to keep vigorous if they are to survive. (Goldson 1977: 14–15)

What we need today is a new understanding of what it is to be a citizen. Citizens are active agents and not passive consumers. The fundamental task of commercial radio or television is not to cultivate our human powers of understanding through human action but to channel our desire for purposes of the consumption of capital products. Thus, the direction of modern advertising is to eclipse the 'human act' by shortcircuiting consciousness, human intentionality and creative human intentions which may not be consumer-oriented.

The mantras of globalization that we have just discussed at some length are reflective of the deep cultural and economic forces that proceed under the aegis of globalization and are moving through the world like a tornado. It is a deep destruction which must be resisted critically while attempting to bring into existence more life-affirming and life-making forces. One of the components of a new vision is a resistance to a destructive older vision. Having assessed the powerful forces of globalization, we are abundantly aware that there must be deep criticism and resistance to these destructive forces that are overrunning the world at present. What follows are several dimensions of critical resistance education.

Critical resistance education within the contexts of privilege and marginality: the majority–minority world context

The development of the idea of 'global privilege' entails a certain containment in definition at the outset. Global privilege demands a structural understanding of the so-called free market economy that stretches its tentacles over every inch of this planet. We are talking here of patterns of exploitation and consumption in the global marketplace. The discussion of global privilege in a hemispheric context entails certain limitations and caveats. At the outset the idea of 'privilege' will be assessed within the geopolitics and economics of the world economy. Therefore the initial development of the idea of hemispheric global privilege initially proceeds in the absence of a detailed analysis of gender and race privilege as well as class privilege. It must be acknowledged that in the northern hemisphere there are large sectors of the population who are seriously disenfranchised. When we talk about the South, traditionally called the third world or the underdeveloped world, it is recognized that there are elites who live in the same conditions of privilege as their northern confrères. The appropriate expression here is 'that there is a third world in the first world and a first world in the third world'. There is also a well-developed feminist analysis that locates the global economic system in a system of 'patriarchal privilege' (Mies 1986). All of these caveats must be kept in mind as we develop the idea of 'hemispheric privilege'; yet in a world economic context we can justifiably venture an argument for northern privilege that is helpful to the present context because it locates our educational challenges in a global–planetary context while giving specific local geographic parameters. After this is done, we will consider how marginality and underclass fit into this overall analysis.

Here are some figures for the reader to ponder. The northern hemisphere consumes about 80 per cent of the world's global resources, while three-quarters of the world's population who live in the southern hemisphere share what is left. In one year, the average person in the West is likely to: (i) consume more than 264lb of paper, compared to an average consumption of just 17.6lb per person in the third world; (ii) consume over 990lb of steel compared with 94.6lb in the third world; (iii) purchase energy equivalent to almost 6 tons of coal compared with 0.5 tons in the third world (*New Internationalist* 1990).

In the context of dumping poisons, western industry produces vast amounts of toxic wastes, much of which is dumped in the third world. For example, since 1986 over 3 million tons of toxic waste have been shipped from western Europe and North America to other countries outside those hemispheres (*New Internationalist* 1990).

As regards water usage and wastage, westerners waste between 30 and 100 gallons of water daily. The average North American flushes away more water every day than a Madagascan uses in three months. The United States and Canada are the two most rapacious countries in the world in terms of water consumption and waste. The next in line for this wastage is western Europe (*New Internationalist* 1990).

In terms of energy consumption, the USA has just 6 per cent of the world's population but consumes 30 per cent of the world's energy, compared with India where 20 per cent of the global population use only 2 per cent of the world's energy. (*New Internationalist* 1990).

All of the facts and figures above give us a portrait of what I am calling northern hemispheric privilege. More specifically, hemispheric privilege may be more accurately called the structural global economic privilege of the northern hemisphere. We have for the last thirty years been saturated with the twin concepts of development and underdevelopment. In location, the northern hemisphere is considered the developed world and the southern hemisphere or third world is the underdeveloped world. Most of the theories about development and underdevelopment rest on the assumption that the northern developed nations are in some ways advanced and the southern hemispheric third world is underdeveloped and lacking. It is now becoming clear that what we call development in the northern hemisphere is the major source of underdevelopment in the southern hemisphere. It has been labelled maldevelopment and overdevelopment by critics (Shiva 1989; Max-Neef and Hopenhayn 1989). It is also the major factor in the desolation of the earth. I think it is essential that we abandon the concepts of development and under-development and focus on privilege in the northern hemisphere and its effects not only on the southern hemisphere but on the planet as a whole. In my opinion it will be necessary to see that northern hemispheric privilege is the single most important threat to planetary survival. One of the most important forms of learning for peoples in the northern hemisphere involves emancipating and decoupling themselves from this privilege. This decoupling from northern hemispheric privilege includes all of the North, both rich and poor, men and women, whites and people of colour. We are not talking about giving up Mercedes Benzs and mink coats. In terms of the world's economic system, almost everyone in the North is rich. In comparative terms even our destitute are well off.

Critical resistance education for survival and emancipation from privilege

What is our order of magnitude today when we speak in terms of survival? In our present moment, we are talking about the survival of the life systems of the planet within which our own survival as a species is secured. We are living in a period where the terror of loss is striking. If we do not survive we

will take countless other species with us. This is the most fundamental aspect
and the foundational cornerstone of the order of magnitude of survival at the
present moment. Added to this order of magnitude is the fact that we are
living in a momentous transition in human history. Coming to the end of the
terminal cenozoic, we are living in its decadent phase. It has not been before,
nor is it the case now, an easy task to live in major historical transitional
periods characterized by decay and downturn. Nevertheless this is our legacy
and we must make appropriate responses to the radical upheaval that characterizes our unique situation. As painful as this may sound, survival must be
carried out within the devastation of the ruined infrastructures of the consumer industrial order. Our responses will vary depending on our location in
the present world order. Up until now, it should be noted that when we speak
about survival we almost always are talking about freedom from want and
freedom from oppression. Indeed, these types of freedoms are the work of
over two-thirds of the peoples of the planet living in the third world and an
increasing number of peoples in the first world. What I would like to consider
here is freedom or emancipation for people of privilege in the northern
hemisphere. Also freedom from the planetary sweep of the consumer ethic of
the North that is projected across the planet, from the poorest *favelas* of Recife
in Brazil all the way to the slums of Calcutta. We are now aware that the
consumer lifestyle is emulated all over this planet. Robin Leech's programme
the *Lifestyles of the Rich and Famous* is extremely popular in all areas of the
world. Conspicuous consumption in this programme is put up as the ideal for
all humans even when this lifestyle is impossible to achieve for over 95 per cent
of the world's population. As Alan Durning (1992) so aptly suggests, the
planet would be laid to waste long before the world could achieve the American
Dream. We have an educational task to see through and beyond the destructive
visions and values of 'consumerism' and I call this task the *emancipation from
privilege*. I would contend that it is one of the major educational tasks for
peoples living in the so-called developed world. Indeed, we can say, from the
previous statistics quoted, that the lifestyle of privilege is the cancer of the
planet. In the *1992 Worldwatch Institute Report* the following observation is
made about the countries of privilege:

> Thus far, global environmental politics has been characterized more by foot
> dragging and denial of problems than by cooperation. Few rich countries have
> acknowledged that they have caused the preponderance of environmental
> damage, and therefore have the responsibility to underwrite most of the trans-
> ition to global sustainability. The United States has stonewalled even modest
> efforts, such as setting targets to reduce carbon emissions as part of ongoing
> negotiations to protect global climate. (Postel 1992: 5)

What privilege gives is a seeming immunity to certain events. The privileged are also steeped in what psychologists have labelled 'denial'. From the point of view of learning and reassessment, 'denial' presents us with a grave cognitive deficit. It is the position of not only not knowing but also not knowing that one does not know. The denial within the context of global privilege has had a devastating planetary impact. In the northern hemisphere we do not see ourselves as dangerous and we constantly indulge ourselves with the luxurious and at the same time dangerous idea that we are 'more developed' than the rest of the world. Through the mass media we attempt to export our lifestyle all over the planet. We elect politicians to tell us that everything is basically in order. We tune out any communication that challenges our affluent lifestyle. Therefore we need to be emancipated from the denial of our position of privilege. In her article in the *1992 Worldwatch Institute Report* entitled 'Denial in a Decisive Decade', Sandra Postel makes the following observation about denial:

> Psychology as much as science will thus determine the planet's fate, because action depends on overcoming denial, among the most paralysing of human responses. While it effects most of us in varying degrees, denial runs particularly deep among those with heavy stakes in the status quo, including the political and business leaders with power to shape the global agenda. This kind of denial can be as dangerous to society and the natural environment as an alcoholic's denial is to his or her own family. Because they fail to see the addiction as the principal threat to their well-being, alcoholics often end up by destroying their lives. Rather than facing the truth, denial's victims choose slow suicide. In a similar way, by pursuing lifestyles and economic goals that ravage the environment, we sacrifice long-term health and well-being for immediate gratification – a trade-off that cannot yield a happy ending. (Postel 1992: 4)

Centrality and marginality in the context of privilege: critical resistance education as border pedagogy

Centrality is the power location of the position of privilege. Power and knowledge are understood to emanate from the centre towards the margin. The position of centrality is occupied today by western culture (the developed minority world), white, heterosexual men. The marginal position is occupied by non-western culture (the underdeveloped majority world), people of colour, women, children and persons of gay and lesbian sexual orientation. Within the context of centrality and marginality, people in the privileged position have the power to name the world. In other words, the centrality of the position of privilege defines the normative structure on not only the centre but also the margins. From the point of view of power equity, centrality is in a dominance position in relation to the margins. From an epistemological perspective, the centrality of the position of privilege allows for the pre-emptive importance of the privileged position in the definition of the total problem. Thus for peoples and groups that occupy the central position of privilege, there is a sense that their positions are more important and epistemologically superior within a world of discourse and power. Here we find the pre-emptive importance of the centre in the definition of the world. Thus, the first world or the developed world has the solution to problems of the third world or underdeveloped world. Also we see this in the prioritization of western, white, male culture over non-western, non-white cultures, and women. The major vulnerability of these positions of centrality and pre-emptiveness is that they are the foundation for ethnocentrism, racism and sexism in our world today. A critical look at centrality and marginality issues moves us into a position to challenge all positions of centrality and privilege.

Aronowitz and Giroux (1991), in their work *Postmodern Education*, offer a pedagogy that suggests a way of transforming the pre-emptiveness of privileged position. They call this form of education 'border pedagogy'. Border pedagogy is a subset of critical pedagogy that offers educators the opportunity to engage the multiple perspectives that exist within the totality of privilege and marginality. In order to dislodge the pre-emptiveness of privilege, 'border pedagogy' suggests that the learning situation engage multiple references that constitute different cultural codes, experiences and language. Border pedagogy attempts to educate students in the reading of these different codes.

In suggesting the processes of border pedagogy, Aronowitz and Giroux indicate that this pedagogy does more than simply provide a forum for students to explore the intricacies of power implicit in all locations of power. Border pedagogy, in addition, provides opportunities for teachers to deepen their own understanding of the discourses of various positions in both the centre and the margins in order to effect a more dialectical understanding of politics, values and pedagogy across a complex 'difference terrain'. The long-term proposition of this type of critical pedagogy will involve the educator in an in-depth examination of positions of power and how they affect the educational process. It is to this type of reflection on power that we now turn.

CHAPTER 5

Dimensions of Power: Education for Peace, Social Justice and Diversity

In this chapter I intend to introduce the notion of dominator cultures and discuss some of the structures that maintain them. My treatment will attempt to elucidate the ecological implications of four of the main dominator structures in our own times. They are the structures of patriarchy which lead to sexism, the structures of racial superiority which lead to racism, the structures of class which lead to class exploitation, and the structures of anthropocentrism which lead to habitat and species loss. These structures of domination are not to be considered in any way exhaustive.

Location of privilege

Before embarking upon a discussion of the structures of patriarchy, race and class, it is necessary to locate my own placement within these structures of power and domination. I am a white, heterosexual male of European descent and am part of the middle-class. In areas of both discourse and public practice, I occupy a position of privilege. Being white, I am not subject to the racism that people of colour experience on a daily basis and this applies no matter what position they occupy in the structures of gender and class. Being male, I am not subject to the negative effects of the structures of patriarchy which make power and male privilege a given. Being heterosexual, I am not subject to the paranoia directed towards men with homosexual preferences and therefore not a direct victim of homophobia. Being a member of the middle-class, I am not subject to the effects of class structures that people of more marginal economic means encounter. In my position of privilege, I am spared, for the most part, from being a victim. Because of my position, I am frequently a victimizer without being conscious of the effects of my position of privilege. Marilyn Frye (1983) names this position of privilege the 'arrogant eye'. With this occlusion of perception, one can organize everything seen into one's own frame of reference to the exclusion of any other. The position of arrogance allows for ignorance of the other because this ignorance has no consequences for the arrogant perceiver. Conversely, those who occupy a position without privilege must have a very intricate knowledge of those in positions of privilege in order to survive. It is therefore understood that it takes a great deal of cognitive, emotional and spiritual work for the one occupying the position of privilege to break free of it in order to embark upon more inclusive perceptions of the other.

The baggage of privilege that I bring with me does not disqualify me from addressing the topic of oppression in my treatment of education and ecology. Sexism and racism are ecologies of violence and domination. Any treatment of education today that ignores or sidesteps the topic of racism will, of necessity, be incomplete. To tackle the topic of ecology without due consideration of racism would be a source of studied ignorance that would indicate a perspective based on the presence of a position of privilege. Marilyn Frye would call this kind of ignorance 'studied ignorance' because it is an ignorance that is both dynamic and active. She illustrates this in her discussion of racism in white America:

> Ignorance is not something simple: it is not a simple lack, absence or emptiness, and it is not a passive state. Ignorance of this sort – the determined ignorance white Americans have of American Indian tribes and clans, ostrich-like ignorance most white Americans have of the histories of Asian peoples in this country, the impoverishing ignorance most white Americans have of Black language – ignorance of these sorts is a complex result of many acts and many negligences. (Frye 1983: 118–19)

With that understanding in mind, it is hoped that my attempts here to discuss the structures of patriarchy, race and class will meet with a modicum of success.

Ecology, war, patriarchy and the institutionalization of violence

Riane Eisler, in the preface to her book *The Chalice and the Blade* (1988: xiii), puts the following questions to herself and to her readers: 'Why do we hurt and persecute each other? Why is our world so full of man's infamous inhumanity to man and to woman? How can human beings be so brutal to their kind? What is it that so chronically tilts us toward cruelty rather than kindness, toward war rather than peace, toward destruction rather than actualization.'

One of the more facile responses to these questions is that violence and cruelty are a part of the makeup of the human. We will not pursue that line of thinking here; nevertheless, it is necessary to pay close attention to the issue of violence if we are going to pursue the questions we will be addressing in this chapter with any degree of depth. At the other extreme to 'essential' violence is the view of human nature as 'infinitely perfectible' and in the process of evolutionary change. This is also a facile view of human nature and the incredible violence of the twentieth century seems to contradict or, at least, question our ideas about human progress and perfectibility.

My treatment of violence and destruction will follow a different path as I develop and weave together different facets. Violence will take on different shades and hues as we consider the subtleties of the issues and problems in which it is embedded.

Violence within the cultural context of the human

Having recognized the cosmological context of violence and creativity, we are, nevertheless, left with the complexity of the pervasive presence of violence of humans towards one another. Because of the incredible saturation of violence and hatred within our own period, it is frequently assumed that violence and force dominate the human endeavour. The violence of humans towards one another, both personally and culturally, belies any facile belief that the human race is any better off in this century than in its predecessors. The incredible use of arms and weapons, the holocaust of Jews in Germany, the killing fields of Cambodia, the atrocities of Bosnia, the proliferation of massive amounts of nuclear weapons along with conventional weapons, to name just a minuscule set of examples, can lead one to the conclusion that the human race trades in violence. Certainly, the track record of the twentieth century indicates that there is very little evidence that humans are a peaceful species; peace and non-violence being rare exceptions. At this level of analysis, we are left with very depressing conclusions about the long-term possibilities of the human. Military establishments all over the planet have justified their existence by saying that war and violence are endemic to the human project. Within this view of the world, the question to ask about war and violence is not whether they will occur but, rather, who will survive. From the military point of view, at the very best, it is said that the presence of war machines may act as a deterrent. The catchphrase here is 'the best defence is the presence of a good offence'.

Within the more recent developments of historical scholarship, this morbid interpretation of human history is being called into question (Eisler 1988; Gimbutas 1974; Stone 1976). This scholarship is bringing about a new interpretation of western history which broadens our understanding of human experience and especially our understanding of some of the factors that attract or deter cultural violence. The most recent scholarship in the historical understanding of cultures is seen in the development of interpretations of patriarchy (T. Berry 1988; Eisler 1988; Gimbutas 1974; Stone 1976). In an historical time dimension, pre-patriarchy refers to the matricentric period of Old Europe that apparently flourished around 6500 BC and extended up to the Aryan invasions around 3500 BC. Patriarchy is coterminous with the advent and extension of western civilization and its time location is the last 5,000 years. Post-patriarchy is considered an emergent form of history taking place in the present and moving into a future that is said to be beyond patriarchal structures of extreme hierarchy and identified with total participatory govern-ance and emergent form of global participatory culture. The reader must be cautioned that the stuff of human history does not in reality divide into such neatly arranged sequences. Nevertheless, the pattern just suggested gives a provisional intelligibility which will allow us to understand further our topic at hand.

Dominator cultures The construct of 'dominator culture' has recently been introduced in the writings of Riane Eisler whose work involves an historical interpretation of cultural violence (Eisler 1988; Eisler and Loye 1990; Noble 1992). Eisler draws on recent developments in historical scholarship, especially from the work of Marija Gimbutas (1974) in her historical treatment of goddess cultures. What comes out of her historical work is a very different under-standing of the presence of human violence in the longer trajectory of human history. In drawing on the work of Gimbutas, Eisler ventures that when you look at early Palaeolithic and Neolithic societies where there seems to be a predominance of goddess worship, there appear to be no signs of sexual inequality or dominance. This finding stands in marked contrast to modern historical cultures coming to us in the Judaeo-Christian synthesis. Our own historical prehistory appears to stem from worship of a father god. The Judaeo-Christian heritage, with its emphasis on a father god worship, also carries with it a gender dominance of male privilege. This hierarchy of male dominance is accompanied by the presence of violent social structures. Eisler maintains that where one finds male dominance, there is also the presence of the institutions of private property, slavery and agrarian agriculture. By contrast, there are archaeological data that seem to support extremely egalitarian societies in the cultures that have antedated our own (i.e. the Palaeolithic and Neolithic). These cultures also appear to have an absence of violence (Eisler 1988; Eisler and Loye 1990). One can draw from this work a more hopeful view of history where it is reasonable to venture the interpretation that war and violence are not inevitable to our human story. With this hopeful interpretation in mind, we are nevertheless led to a very critical perspective on our own historical legacy which appears to be deeply embedded in a hierarchical conception of power that comes specifically from the structures of patriarchy. In its simplest interpretation, patriarchy is a system of power in which men dominate. Eisler names our own patriarchal structures of power a 'dominator model'. A dominator model expresses a hierarchy of power based on the threat or the use of force. She makes an important distinction between a dominator hierarchy and other hierarchies seen in nature that she calls 'actualization hierarchies':

> The term *domination hierarchies* describes systems based on force or the express or implied threat of force, which are characteristic of the human rank orderings in male-dominant societies. Such hierarchies are very different from the type of hierarchies found in progressions from lower to higher orderings of functioning, such as the progression from cells to organs in living organisms, for example. These types of hierarchies may be characterized by the term *actualization hierarchies* because their function is to maximize the organism's potentials. By contrast, as evidenced by both sociological and psychological studies, human hierarchies based on force or the threat of force not only inhibit personal creativity but also result in social systems in which the lowest (basest) human qualities are reinforced and humanity's higher aspirations (traits such as compassion and empathy as well as striving for truth and justice) are systematically suppressed. (Eisler 1988: 204)

The dominator society is laced through all our social, cultural and economic institutions. In looking at the western historical heritage we can see the dominator form in the four patriarchal establishments that have been in control of western history over the centuries. The four establishments are the classical empires, the ecclesiastical establishment, the nation-state, and the modern corporation (T. Berry 1988). All of these institutions have been, in their historical makeup, exclusively male-dominated and created primarily for the fulfilment of the human as envisaged by men. Historically, women had a minimal, if any, role in the direction of these establishments (T. Berry 1988). Currently, there is a rising awareness of our predicament and of patriarchy's role in creating this predicament. Concurrent with this rising awareness are attempts to dismantle or avert the dominator structures. It is to be noted that the strong feminist movement of the last two decades has accomplished a great deal in raising our culture's awareness of the destructive effects of patriarchy throughout contemporary society (Milbrath 1989).

Modern science and the dominator system The development of modern science is accompanied by the mentality and mind-set of the dominator system as seen in the major establishments of western culture. In theory, scientific endeavours have the pretence of freedom from values but this is not borne out in everyday practice. In all modern nation-states, we see the wedding of the scientific enterprise with the military establishments. Science, as an institution, is supported by military objectives and receives support from the military. Lester Milbrath (1989) maintains that almost all organized scientific efforts have a dominator motive: control of nature, military power, economic growth, economic power, beating the competition, maximizing prestige and honour, and making money. Science would do well to think much more seriously about values.

One area that merits investigation and reflection is the way science reorders human experience around the dimensions of order and power. Carolyn Merchant (1980) ventures the interpretation that the mechanistic world view in modern science has had a profound influence on how we view order and power. She maintains that order was attained through an emphasis on the motion of indivisible parts subject to mathematical laws and the rejection of unpredictable animistic forces of change. Power was achieved through immediate active intervention in a secularized world.

This notion of power saw its achievement in human artifice where the human gained control over the natural world. In achieving this control we can see the human project of modern science as domination over the natural world. Merchant (1980) moves further into a discussion of gender and domination. She notes that when nature is treated as the feminine, any attempts at controlling the natural world are advanced with a project of subjugating women as part of the natural world. Violence and force are integral to this project (Merchant 1980). A similar interpretation of the modern western scientific project is made in the work of Vandana Shiva (1989). It is her contention that modern science is a consciously gendered activity. For Vandana Shiva, science and masculinity are associated with the domination of nature. Maria Mies and Vandana Shiva (1993) see the extension of science today in the work of gene and reproductive technologies. They maintain that the spirit of inquiry within these disciplines breaks down the last boundary that has heretofore protected the human person from the violent invasions of analysis and also from becoming a mere object of research. Mies and Shiva (1993: 52) go on to offer a new orientation for science that leads in a very different direction. If the old science was one of limitless inquiry, the new science is one that recognizes limits: 'In a limited universe, therefore, there can be no infinite progress, no infinite search for truth, no infinite growth unless others are exploited.'

This is not the direction of conventional modern science. We will move on to examine the destructive violence that follows in its wake when it is joined to the military project.

Modern warfare, environmental devastation and patriarchy Military establishments are paradigm cases of dominator cultures. Based on force and violence, they are also the home of gendered patriarchy. Military cultures are deeply enmeshed in the cult of masculinity. Conventional military doctrine follows the structures of the dominator model. There is an assumption that only a (strong) military system can effectively deter force and the threats of force

(Galtung 1982). Almost all the personnel of military establishments within and between nation-states who define 'national security' are men (Seager 1993). From a feminist analysis, part of the male agenda in defining 'national security' is to protect the hegemony of male privilege in the institutions of war (Seager 1993). Increasingly, since the middle part of the twentieth century, war has taken a deliberately sinister environmental turn. In modern warfare, it can be said without exaggeration, wreaking environmental destruction has become an intricate part of its planned strategy. It is estimated that the world's armed forces are quite likely the single largest polluter of the earth (Renner 1991). Instances of this type of devastation are now legion and environmental destruction has become part of planned military strategy.

As early as the 1950s we see the British army using chemical herbicides and defoliants for military purposes in its anti-insurgency campaigns in Malaysia. In Vietnam, the American military dumped approximately 25 million gallons of defoliants and environmental toxins over the course of the war. The most recent war in the Persian Gulf pitted the US-led multinational coalition of armed forces against the army of Iraq. The war had a very short duration but the effects on the whole area were nothing short of devastating. The war left large parts of Iraq, Kuwait and Saudi Arabia in almost total devastation. Within a period of a week, Iraq's urban infrastructure was reduced to a rubble by the most intensive air bombardment in the history of modern warfare. In every major settlement in the country, coalition bombing destroyed water supply systems, electrical systems, fuel supplies, food stocks, sewerage systems, transportation systems, and public health delivery systems (Seager 1993). The whole Gulf area suffered extreme environmental damage due to numerous oil spills. Oil fires in Kuwait carried massive pollution in the area at a scale never previously seen. Total impact and damage to this area, as a result of this military encounter, will not be fully calculated because its continuing impact will never see the light of day. Dead men as well as dead environments do not tell stories.

When we take a look at our own continent for signs of militarism and environmental devastation, we can see a picture no less frightening than in the Gulf region. Central America is a case in point. The environmental problems that have emerged from this small region are deeply rooted in a long history of natural resource plundering by foreign corporations operating in consort with local elites. There is also a simultaneous presence of military force used to sustain and protect the activities of local elites and at the same time protect foreign economic interests and investments. The collusion of these forces and their effect on the life of this region have been nothing short of catastrophic; ecological collapse is a consequence of the fact it is one of the most heavily militarized regions in the world (Seager 1993). Most of the armed conflicts are focused on land use and land reform. Each day human rights violations, increase, relating to the estrangement of peoples from their land. In Central America today, a small coterie of land owners control the land use of most of these small countries. People are virtually driven off their land for the production of cash crop agriculture to suit the over-indulged food needs of the US population to the north. The exploitation of land and the deforestation goes on at such a furious pace in this region that it is projected that by the year 2025 there will be no tropical rainforests anywhere in Central America (Seager 1993). The global significance of the Central American environmental tragedy is not just local to the region. The rainforests in this area have a planetary significance characterized by the World Health Organization as 'the lungs of the planet'. Destruction of the rainforests, loss of wildlife, and environmental degradation threaten global health at the same time as they create widening zones of unsustainability, deepening poverty and social inequities in a region plagued by a history of resource-based social injustice (Seager 1993).

Nuclear wasteland   When we catalogue all of the different ways in which military operations have had an impact on the environment and human health, nuclear weapons production and testing is the most severe and enduring. Michael Renner (1991: 145) makes the following contrast: 'While the effect of toxic waste is relatively localized, the spread of nuclear debris is global, and while hazardous substances will be with us for generations, plutonium has a half life of 24,000 years. Even if nuclear arsenals were abolished tomorrow, their waste products cannot be.'

The beginning of the nuclear age of the military started with the Manhattan Project which resulted in the bombing of Hiroshima and Nagasaki. These bombings ended the Second World War and also represented the beginning of the nuclear age. Although there have been peaceful projects in the use of nuclear energy, the vast majority of research and development has been in the development and testing of all manner of nuclear weapons throughout the cold war period from 1945 until well into the 1980s. From the very beginning, the US government's nuclear projects were cloaked in secrecy and tenacious resolve. Witness the words of Thomas Murray, a member of the Atomic Energy Commission in 1955: 'We must not let anyone interfere with this series of [nuclear] tests – nothing' (Renner 1991: 145).

This statement was made in closed session and it is emblematic of the priorities of both the East and West in the early days of the cold war. Since nuclear projects were under the shirt-tails of the 'national security' doctrines of both superpowers, the door was open to a huge build-up of nuclear arsenals, uranium mining, warhead design, testing and deployment. In addition, the architects of the nuclear industrial complex knowingly compromised the health and safety of workers in the industry, as well as that of soldiers and residents near nuclear sites. The devastating impact on the environment, peoples and the natural world is only now being closely appraised and catalogued. The painstaking work of Rosalie Bertell, which is carefully documented in her book *No Immediate Danger* (1985), catalogues the full impact of low-level radiation all over the world that has been parented by the nuclear industries of the cold war. She introduces the idea of 'omnicide' since her findings concerning the long-term effects of nuclear radiation lead her to the stark conclusion that we are headed for species annihilation. This would be a relatively swift (on the scale of civilization), deliberatively induced end to history, culture, science, biological reproduction and memory. With a pathos characteristic of the whole book Bertell (1985: 2) makes the following judgement: 'It is the ultimate human rejection of human life, an act which requires a new word to describe it, namely omnicide. It is more akin to suicide or murder than to a natural death process.'

It is not my task here to give an exhaustive survey of the military's war on the natural world. That task has been done elsewhere and well (Bertell 1985; Milbrath 1989; Renner 1991; Seager 1993). Rather, what I would like to do in concluding this section is to consider again the role of patriarchy and its specific cultural context. Although the presence of patriarchal structures depicted in dominator cultures all around the globe have wreaked havoc and violence in an unprecedented manner in our century, it must be pointed out that the violence of nuclear armaments, be it through testing and use, stockpiling or disposal, is the work of men in the western cultural tradition. Other cultures have participated in the arms race but their leadership is under the hegemony of the western superpowers. This leadership has been white and male. The original Manhattan Project had an illustrious cast of some of the finest scientists of the western world. These men, mostly from the natural sciences and particularly physics, were intellectually sophisticated and urbane. They were the best and the brightest. They and many of the scientists that would work in military laboratories all over the western and eastern bloc throughout the cold war would share many things in common and one of these common characteristics was the fact that they were virtually all male. The language of the arms race, as we shall see, took on the characteristics of the male culture that was pervasive in these research laboratories. Carol Cohn (1987) spent a summer with male experts who were involved in the development of nuclear strategies. She noted that their language, at first, was impenetrable, filled as it was with particular words and acronyms. For example, the inventors of the first atomic bomb called their first test the 'Trinity', after the patriarchal Christian imagery of the Godhead. The Holy Trinity signifies God the Father, Son and Holy Ghost, the male forces in creation. This quasi-divine language gave the personnel involved a sense of being in a special priesthood; so much so that in the later development of cold war nuclear programmes reference was made to the 'nuclear priesthood' (Cohn 1987).

Primal images of birth were used in many of the projects. More often than not these followed the lines of a male initiation rite. The personnel and scientists at Los Alamos referred to the atom bomb as 'Oppenheimer's Baby', and the hydrogen bomb at Livermore was referred to as 'Teller's Baby' after the Hungarian Third Reich expatriate scientist Edward Teller. This language was pervasive and part of the everyday working patois of the labs. For example, a briefing officer in relating his enthusiasm for a satellite project commented: 'We'll do the motherhood role – telemetry, tracking and control – the maintenance.' The birthing lineage in the nuclear weapons industry was totally male-dominated. Disparagement of women was also seen in some adverse remarks made against Teller by his detractors. Those wanting to downplay Teller's role referred to him as the bomb's 'mother' and awarded Stanley Ulam the title of 'father', Ulam being the scientist who 'had the important idea and inseminated Teller with it'. Teller only 'carried it after that'. In a distorted sort of way, patriarchal thinking was such that these men felt that the bombs that wreaked such incredible horror on Hiroshima and Nagasaki were their babies, 'Little Boy' and 'Fat Man'. In the early phases of nuclear testing, Cohn (1987) indicates that the bombs were not only the progeny of the attending scientists, but emphatically male progeny. Before knowing that the bomb would work, their anxiety over its success was illustrated: 'They hoped that the bomb was a boy not a girl – that is, not a dud.' Following the success of one of the first test runs, General Groves wired Secretary of War Henry Stimson: 'Doctor has returned most enthusiastic and confident that the little boy is as husky as his big brother.' Stimson then wrote to Winston Churchill saying, 'Babies satisfactorily born.' In 1952, after the successful test of a hydrogen bomb named 'Mike' in the Marshall Islands, Edward Teller enthusiastically wired Los Alamos saying, 'It's a boy.' Cohn (1987) reflects on the overall history of these early bomb projects and notes that it is permeated with imagery that confounds man's overwhelming technological power to destroy nature with the power to create. What an incredible piece of irony!

Such institutions maintain a deeply adversarial view of life permeated with struggles for power and the absence of any overall significance. Only power matters. When referring to the adversary, death becomes 'collateral damage'. Language inversion is pervasive. There are 'surgically clean strikes'. President Ronald Reagan referred to one nuclear ballistic missile as 'the peacemaker'. That remark was in reference to the MX missile that carried ten warheads, each with an explosive power about 250 to 400 times that of the bomb that levelled Hiroshima (Cohn 1987).

Sexual language and imagery are also part of the working language. Ads in airforce magazines catalogue common male anxieties. There were ads that promoted weapons as 'big sticks', or 'penetrators'. From the Pentagon a target analyst explains that plans for limited nuclear warfare were doomed because 'it's a pissing contest – you gotta expect them to use everything they got'. After India entered the nuclear world it was remarked that 'she had lost her virginity' (Cohn 1987).

What is finally most appalling is the profound truth that these conventionally educated, intelligent men were not even concerned with their own survival. Power was the single most salient dimension that pervaded their lives and seemed to govern their perverse visions. Cohn (1987) points out that when a group of men create a discourse that excludes human life in its calculations, it is virtually impossible to expect that discourse to reflect human concerns. Cohn finishes her article with some important conclusions concerning the transformation of male discourse if we are to have a less violent world. She believes that those who seek a more just and peaceful world have a dual task before them. First there is deconstruction which requires close attention to, and the dismantling of, technostrategic discourse. The dominant voice of militarized masculinity and decontextualized rationality speaks so loudly in our culture that it will remain difficult for other voices to be heard until that voice loses some of its power. Second, the reconstructive task is to create compelling alternative voices – diverse voices whose conversations with each other will invent those futures.

Violent discourse reflects the presence of a culture of violence and is present in both capitalist and socialist social orders. When comparing the capitalist social orders of the West with the eastern bloc socialist orders, one is struck by the incredible similarity that they demonstrate on the dimensions of power, violence and patriarchy. The cold war, on both sides, was an exercise in patriarchal dominator power. Although capitalist and socialist systems are dissimilar in many aspects, they converge on the use of power and violence in the resolution of social conflict. Because both share a common linkage, their attitudes towards resource extraction in relation to the natural world are very similar indeed. At the level of the nation-state and alliances of the nation-state, these social orders have wreaked ecological devastation on the natural world (Handa 1982). Violence, power, and domination have been the pervasive outcomes of the cold war and, with the fall of the eastern bloc Socialist states, there has been no reprieve from violence as capitalism marches forwards into the twentieth-first century. The triumph of capitalism in no way heralds the abatement of violence and patriarchal domination. Although we have a somewhat altered venue of violence with the curtailment of the cold war, state warfare, ethnic violence within states, arms production and the distribution of arms for 'hot' wars, and the violence of the trajectory of the new global economic order, leave us in our present violence-enmeshed state.

It is safe to say that we are going into the twenty-first century locked in an embrace with violence. The projections that were made for the twentieth century stated that it would see a triumph for human progress and the rationality of the human. We do not bring a legacy of progress and rationality as we enter the next millennium. The new global market of transnational capitalism which is now covering the globe boasts of many things; however, it does not boast of peaceful social structures. Violence is accepted as part of the fabric of the global competitive marketplace where there must be winners and losers at all times. Violence and domination, it now appears, come with the territory of modern life and institutions. Violence devastates us at the global level but also reaches into the very fabric of our personal lives. It is to the prospect of personal violence that we will now turn.

Patriarchy and the ecology of men's violence

The etymology of the word ecology is 'eco' meaning home and 'logos' the study of home. We live our lives in nested hierarchies of community. The earth is our home, our community is our home, and the intimacy of our family is also our home. When we think of home, the idea of safe boundaries comes to mind. Ideally, our home is a place where nurture, succour and affirmation are experienced. It is not a spatial location but rather a region of nearness with boundaries that give us security and trust. We can say, then, that our house is our home. We can also say that our 'body' is our home. Violence is, within this context, a process that violates those boundaries of trust and security. Rape is violent not only because it is a physical violation but, more so, because it is a violation of those boundaries of self that give us trust and security in life. It is a deep invasion of the spirit and we are well aware that violations of the spirit do great damage.

There is an ecology of violence. This is an inversion of our natural affinity for conditions which enable us to trust in the basic goodness of life. Patriarchy is a system of domination not only because it is an institution of power. Domination is also characterized by violation of boundaries. When this occurs one can say that we are living in an institution or institutions of violence where males are the prominent boundary breakers. Therefore male violence under conditions of patriarchy is an ecology of violence. An ecology of violence is a home in violation.

We have just studied the ecology of violence under patriarchy that has created systematic violation of the natural world at the planetary level. Let us now turn to the microcosm.

Intimate violence Data in the United States compiled by the Department of Justice in 1991 indicate that while women are less likely to be victims of violent crime than men, they are six times more likely to be harmed by an intimate (French 1992). In Canada, the vast majority of family violence is perpetrated by men on women and children in the household (Lynn and O'Neill 1995). When violence takes the form of sexual abuse it is found, in Canada, that 98.8 per cent of the perpetrators are male and 1.2 per cent are female. Incest is a form of violence that is only just becoming recognized in terms of its scope and magnitude. It is now becoming clear that it is wide-spread and not class-linked (French 1992). Men of every class and educational level rape little boys and girls; girls being the primary target. The over-whelming majority of serial murderers are men and most mass murders are committed by men, frequently focused on women (Mies and Shiva 1993).

Lynn and O'Neill (1995) who minutely catalogue the Canadian data on intimacy and violence, feel that male violence cannot be understood unless you place family relations within a particular economic and political system. They venture the idea that with the development of industrial capitalist states came the separation of community life into the public world of work, law and politics and the private world of family and intimate relationships. Follow-ing from this public and private fissure, there was a concomitant separation of men and women from each other in terms of their work, their relative access to the public world, and their involvement in the ongoing vicissitudes of family life. Lynn and O'Neill (1995) advance the notion that in an advanced capitalist country, such as Canada, men have lost the power over their own work. In the conditions of work under capitalism, men appear to have been conditioned not to rebel against oppressive, exploitive work situations and feel safer to express their anger in the home. The use of violence in the home appears to maintain the previously unquestioned sex-role hierarchy and is condoned therein.

The above findings apply not only to North America; the problem of men's violence is global in proportions. Angela Miles (1996: 117) reflects on the global context: 'All over the world women are beaten, raped, burned, sexually abused and harassed, mutilated, confined, forced into marriage and into preg-nancy, sold into prostitution and pornography, aborted after aminocenteses, killed as infants and as adults, denied food and medical treatment and education, and forced to work without pay *because they are women*.' She notes that from the point of view of a global context, the forms of this abuse vary across cultures, classes and nations, but violence *per se* is universal.

Patriarchy and the exclusion of women and the environment from the UN System of Accounts (UNSNA) In *If Women Counted: A New Feminist Economics* (1988), a groundbreaking work by Marilyn Waring, economics and accounting are systematically submitted to a feminist critique. This critique of the United Nations System of Accounts (UNSNA) does more than point out the exclusion of women's unpaid work and the intrinsic value of the earth from national accounting: 'The United Nations System of National Accounts (UNSNA) and its rules and regulations govern the measurement of national incomes in all countries. It is my confirmed belief that this system acts to sustain, in the ideology of patriarchy, the universal enslavement of women and Mother Earth in their productive and reproductive activities' (Waring 1988: 14).

In focusing her attention on some of the absurdities in the way in which economists measure growth, Waring points out how military expenditure, and especially wars, count as growth despite the loss of human life. Environmental disasters, such as the Exxon Valdez oil spill, increase growth while the preservation of the earth and its resources are given no value in the market. Thus, the cost of cleaning up the mess increases the gross national product while no value is given to the land that is devastated or the species that are lost through the spillage. This summarizes direct violence. We turn now to the more pervasive form of culturally mediated violence.

Mediated violence: the mass media There is a culture of violence that is mediated through mass media. These media include newspapers, tabloids, television drama and sports, movies and video productions. The incidence of violence in the mass media is more than one finds in real life. For example, newspapers can create a sense of a crime epidemic that promotes a menacing portrait of the world (Gerbner 1970). By far and away, men and boys are the most prevalent perpetrators of violence in the mass media (Fiske 1978). If one considers television alone, there is a hierarchy of violent depictions. One of the most common forms of television violence is that of battery. This is closely followed by homicide, pointing a deadly weapon, aggravated assault and fraud (Fiske 1978).

In the most recent research on US television programming, conducted at four universities, the conclusion reached was that 'psychologically harmful' violence is pervasive on broadcast and cable TV programmes. This study was funded by the cable industry itself and was based on a scientifically selected sample of about 2,500 hours of programming. It found not only that the majority of programmes contained some violence, but that the context in which violence occurs can have harmful effects. The study demonstrates that the risks of viewing the most common depictions of televised violence include learning to behave violently, becoming more desensitized to the harmful consequences of violence, and becoming more fearful of being attacked. Perpetrators of violent acts on TV go unpunished 73 per cent of the time. When violence is presented without punishment, viewers are more likely to learn the lesson that violence is successful. Most violent portrayals fail to show the consequences of a violent act. The findings show that 47 per cent of all violent interactions show no harm to victims, and 58 per cent depict no pain. Longer-term consequences such as financial or emotional harm were shown only 16 per cent of the time. Some 25 per cent of violent incidents on TV involve the use of hand guns, which the study concludes can trigger aggressive thoughts and behaviours. Finally, few programmes containing violence emphasize non-violent alternatives to solving problems.

The work of Gerbner (1970) in the USA in the area of television violence is concerned with the mass-produced messages of television as an active part of our cultural and social environment. Gerbner's findings are quite startling. His studies report that 80 per cent of all television drama contains violence, that 50 per cent of the leading characters committed violence, and 60 per cent were victims of it. Older people were more likely to be victims of younger perpetrators. There are also class, gender and race indicators. Middle-class white groups were least likely to commit or suffer violence. In terms of race, the findings show that 50 per cent of white Americans committed violence, compared to 60 per cent of white foreigners, and 67 per cent of non-whites. Victims of violence followed the same order as perpetration above. Gerbner (1970) also noted that 'cool efficiency' and, to a lesser extent, manliness and youth appear to be the chief correlates of success and virtue in an impersonal, self-seeking and specialized structure of violent action. The cultural signifiers directed towards young men show how the development of images of manliness is gained through actions of violence. In the area of film entertainment, films depicting violence are the popular choice of male teenagers. One of the rites of passages for male teenagers is to be able to remain cool as they watch extreme violence.

It should be noted here as we conclude this section on patriarchal structures how deeply violence is textured within them. There is an ecology of violence that weaves its way through male cultures on a global scale. It is present in all of the structures that glorify the male gender. It is present in academic institutions and in prisons. Although it takes on many different manifestations because of varied contexts, the common denominator is domination of women, children and the earth itself. The same dominance that goes into the violence of nations is present in the violation of bodies. It is nested in all of our institutions of power from the government to the boardroom to the military–industrial complex to the school room.

Racism

Diversity, difference and peoples   We think of the modern world as being divided into nation-states and that differences between peoples are seen in the differences between nations. Nation-states, however, are poor indicators of the diversity of peoples on this earth. Here we can honour an important distinction between 'nations' and 'states' made by Bernard Nietscmann in the

Cultural Survival Quarterly (cited in Mander 1991). He catalogues that, at present, there are 3,000 native nations contained within the borders of 200 states which assert control over those peoples. Under international law, a nation comprises peoples of common heritage, language, geography, culture, political system and desire for common association. With this distinction in mind, one can delineate two very different geopolitical mappings of peoples and countries of the world. The first is the commonly understood one of large recognized states and their attendant peoples, often described in terms of 'three worlds'; the second is a quite different one of more than 3,000 enduring peoples and nations who exist beneath the imposed states (Mander 1991). It should be noted that the world's more than 3,000 distinct peoples are nowhere registered or recognized internationally. Their existence, territories and defensive struggles are largely invisible. What is visible is the *multinational stated populations* that have become internationally recognized as 'peoples' and 'nations', even though they have none of the characteristics of either.

It is important to acknowledge the diversity of peoples who inhabit the globe because there are known forces of convergence that are threatening this diversity, creating a kind of world 'monoculture'. The powerful cultural dictates of this world economy are making the survival of peoples a precarious venture to say the very least (Lorde 1990). In our own times it is important to understand how difference can be utilized perniciously. The pervasive existence of a 'global profit economy' has no small part to play. Audre Lorde captures the sense of how this global profit economy is working in our contemporary era:

> Institutionalized rejection of difference is an absolute necessity in a profit economy which needs outsiders as surplus people. As a member of such an economy, we have *all* been programmed to respond to human differences between us with fear and loathing and to handle that difference in one of three ways: ignore it, and if that is not possible, copy it if we think it is dominant, or destroy it if we think it is subordinate. But we have no patterns for relating across our human differences as equals. As a result, those differences have been misnamed and misused in the service of separation and confusion. (Lorde 1990: 281–2)

This type of unequal dominance constitutes the very structure of racism; the subject to which we will now turn.

Systemic racism The greater part of western European history conditions us to see human differences in simplistic opposition to each other: dominant/ subordinate, good/bad, up/down, superior/inferior (Lorde 1990). In a society where good is determined by profit margin rather than human need, there must always be some group of people who, through systematized oppression, can be made to feel surplus, to occupy the space of the dehumanized inferior.

Racism is the belief in the inherent superiority of one race over all others and thereby the right to dominance (Lorde 1990). Vulnerability to this belief system appears to have been a fundamental problem for human beings throughout human history. This belief system leads to dominance, subjugation, slavery and all manner of human violence. Racism, more often than not, is based on skin colour but this is not the whole story. Even within colour boundaries that are the same, different groups have set up racial dominance on grounds other than colour. The historical presence of anti-Semitism against Jewish people is ample evidence that racism can be exercised based on characteristics other than colour. The inter-ethnic conflicts in Northern Ireland, Iran, Iraq, Rwanda and Yugoslavia, to name just a few, connect racism to tribal, religious and economic conflict. All of the latter are laced with the historical spectre of colonial legacies. Our treatment here must honour the nuances of these different conflictual fields.

A prominent part of my treatment of racism here will be across boundaries of colour. It is therefore necessary to mark some of the more perplexing aspects of racism that operate within colour boundaries. In order to deal with the perplexities of the definition of racism, Carole Ann Reed (1994), distinguishes between narrow-focused racist analysis (i.e. narrow-focused anti-racism) and broad-based racist analysis (i.e. broad-based anti-racism). Narrow-focused analysis usually takes as its reference point certain key moments in history which appear to be traceably causal. In the case of the racism against indigeneous peoples, Columbus' discovery of America is a moment in the continent's history where the birth of the racism against indigenous peoples was initiated. Here racism was used for the purposes of monetary exploitation of the newly discovered lands and peoples (Reed 1994). Colour was the most easily recognizable distinction between the 'new' and 'old' world people and it is ventured that this characteristic was given a hierarchical social signification. Thus, those with lighter skin colour from the old 'civilized' European world were said to be inherently superior to the darker-skinned inhabitants of the new world (Reed 1994). In this historical moment, racism was tied to the colour of skin between two different peoples. The 'broad-based' interpretation links racism to other social justice agendas that are not traced to historical moments that have ended in racism but instead are linked to other physical, cultural and religious dimensions. Reed (1994) articulates differences by noting that skin colour is one signification that has been used among others: for example, the eye shape of the Japanese and Chinese people, and the supposedly distinctive noses of the Jewish people.

Two examples of broad-based racism will be given here: Rwanda and conflict in Northern Ireland. In the spring and summer of 1995 a programme of massacres took place in the African country of Rwanda. The massacres took place with lightning speed, mostly using machetes. It is estimated that from the original population of 7,700,000, at least 800,000 were killed in just a hundred days. (Phillip Gourevitch describes the massacres:

> By comparison, Pol Pot's slaughter of a million of Cambodians in four years looks amateurish, and the bloodletting in the former Yugoslavia measures up to no more than a neighbourhood riot. The dead of Rwanda accumulated at nearly three times the rate of Jewish dead during the Holocaust. Members of the Hutu majority group began massacring the Tutsi minority in early April, and at the end of the month dead Tutsis were easier to find in Rwanda than live Tutsis. The hunt continued until mid-July, when a rebel army conquered Rwanda and brought the massacres to a halt. That October, a United Nations Commission of Experts found that the 'concerted, planned, systematic and methodical' acts of 'mass extermination perpetuated by Hutu elements against the Tutsi group' in Rwanda 'constitute genocide'. (Gourevitch 1995: 78)

The background and complexity of this tragedy cannot be explored here, but several things should be noted in passing. First, the massacre was preceded by a history of inter-group conflict since the waning of colonial rule during the late 1950s. Although there were no clear colour differences between groups there were certain identifiable differences in physical characteristics; the Tutsis are taller and more angular and the Hutus smaller in stature with larger body mass. I am by no means attempting to say that physical differences constitute an identifiable cause for the problems. There was also a colonial heritage that encouraged inter-group conflict. At this point, I wish to stress that racial conflict can be generated by complex factors when colour is not the abiding feature of difference.

Northern Ireland is a second example of racism that does not follow colour boundaries. It has been one of the examples of chronic conflict in modern western European history, and it continues to rage. It is presented as a religious conflict but this appears to be a surface pretext. Both the Catholic and Protestant factions claim that the differences are not only religious they also are differences in peoples. There may be some pretext for these differences; for example, the Ulster Protestants are transplants from Scotland and French Huguenot stock. All that being said, social class differences play a significant role; the Protestants having always been favoured by English colonial rule and having better jobs and housing. The effects of the colonial heritage of British rule can by no means be discounted and deserve significant historical consideration. Ireland was the first colony of the British Empire. It might well be said that the British prastised their brutal colonial treatment on the Irish before they took their show on the road to India and Africa. Wherever the British went, their colonial legacy was laced with racism towards whichever subject people they were imperializing. A typical sense of the racism of the English toward the Irish is seen in a statement that was made by Queen

Elizabeth I's Crown historian concerning the defeat of the Spanish Armada. In commenting on the Spanish retreat, he noted that some of the Spanish fleet washed up on the shores of Ireland, where they were 'eaten by the savages' (Dawson 1956).

Colonialism, imperialism and the deep structures of global racist domination
Racism like sexism is an essential ingredient in cultures of domination. With racism we always find the presence of hierarchial systems of power when the dominant group subjugates the non-dominant group along lines of some perception of racial difference. Difference within the context of racial stereo-typing occurs when a dominant group marks out another group for some form of subjugation. This subjugation occurs along cultural, political, educational and economic lines. What we see in the context of racist dominator structures is a violence visited on the dominated culture that is destructive to body, mind and spirit. Difference is in no way celebrated for its positive aspects of diversity, but, rather, differences are grounds for negative attribution and discrimination (Dei 1994; 1995a). How this is done is something to behold in itself. The idea of race and particularly the dominator concepts embedded in racist ideological structures have complex historical roots. In the case of occidental racism, it is accompanied by a background history of western colonialism and imperial reign. Edward Said (1993), in examining the colonial and imperial structures of the Orient and Africa, notes that the whole system is premissed upon the subordination and victimization of the native. First, there is a self-forgetting joy in the use of power to observe, rule, hold and profit from distant territories and people. Second, there is the ideological rationale for reducing then recon-stituting the native as someone to be ruled and managed. Third, there is the presence of the idea of western salvation and redemption through the West's 'civilizing mission'. This aspect was supported by 'idea experts'. Here we find the missionary, the teacher, advisers and scholars. Fourth, there is the security of a situation that permits the conquerers to avoid looking at the violence that they perpretuate. Finally, there is a process which takes place after the native inhabitants have been displaced from their historical location on their land and their history is rewritten as a function of the imperial culture.

Edward Said (1993: 132) concludes that all of the above, taken together, create an amalgam of the arts of narrative and observation about the accumu-lated, dominated and ruled territories whose inhabitants seemed destined never to escape, to remain creatures of European will. Developing further the groundbreaking ideas of Said, Homi Bhabha (1990) makes some important connections between racism and cultural discourse. He contends that, in its colonial moment, racist stereotypical discourse provides structures of govern-ance that split knowledge and the exercise of power. Some of these discursive practices recognize the differences of race, culture and history as elaborated by stereotypical knowledges and racial theories, or administrative colonial experience. With the preceding in mind, there is an institutionalization of the ideologies of race stereotypes regarding the colonized people. The overall impact of the complex practices of colonialism renders the colonized population both the cause and the effect of a closed system of interpretation that justifies the rule of the colonizer in quasi-moralistic terms. The colonizer sees himself, in relation to the colonized, as on a 'civilizing mission' or enduring 'the white man's burden' (Bhabha 1990). There is a world view embedded in this process and it is to this that we will now turn.

Racism and the world view of western culture Audre Lorde (1990) stresses that the vast legacy of western European history has conditioned us to see human differences in simplistic opposition to each other. We are therefore left with a set of oppositions: dominance/subordinate, good/bad, up/down, superior/inferior. These oppositions are embedded within our cultural ultimacies. As Lorde points out, society premisses good in terms of profit rather than in terms of human need. There must, of necessity, be a group or groups that can be made to feel as though they are surplus by systematized oppression and who are made to occupy the space of the dehumanized inferior. 'Within this society, that group is made up of Black and Third World people, working class people, older people, and women' (Lorde 1990: 281). To Lordes' list I would single out and add aboriginal peoples. It is from the aboriginal peoples that the 'New World' countries have appropriated territories and their highly distinctive cultures, resulting in pervasive stereotypical images of these peoples and an idealization of the colonizers (eurocentrism). This experience of eurocentrism and the misuse of power at the heart of racism includes justifying stolen land, a model of planned inequality, and a rationalization for continuing to disenfranchise minority groups (Zarate 1994).

It must be noted that western culture is not the only culture with these types of oppositions. Nevertheless, the western cultural world view brings to the conditions of racism its own peculiar makeup. For over 500 years, western cultural ideology has been operating on the assumption that it has a civilizing mission for the world. There is an assumption within this mission that occidental culture is the 'centre' and all other cultures are the 'margins'. A further assumption is that the 'margins' must be assimilated to the 'centre' and this has become the operating assumption of western culture *vis-à-vis* the rest of the world. Within this frame of reference, cultural differences do not exist to be celebrated and nurtured. Difference is not the opening to exploration and knowledge of the other on its own terms. Rather, from the position of the centre, difference is something to be assimilated or suppressed. Assimilation of the margins to the centre does not take place under conditions of reciprocity or cooperation. In terms of Lorde's oppositions, the centre assumes the position of dominance and the margins are relegated to subordinate status. With the good/bad opposition there is again a dichotomization. The cultural ideology of the West takes for itself the high road of 'goodness' and relegates all outside people to the margins labelled as dark, ignorant and bad. With the oppositions of up/down and superior/inferior, we see the conceits of the West as more 'evolved' and 'superior' when compared to the cultures of the margins. All this amounts to a process of domination that locates all positive characteristics within occidental culture.

Environmental racism Environmental racism refers to the systematic degradation of land or peoples which follows from the processes of systematic racism. Systematic racism in environmental terms means that specific lands and peoples within lands are the recipients of some form of environmental degradation that can be attributed to the fact that the peoples and their lands are the subjects of historical racism. Environmental racism is carried out at both a global and a local level.

At the global level, the West's treatment of Africa is an example of historical and contemporary environmental racism. The whole history of racism that is presently visited on people of colour goes back to the ignominious history of the slave trade. The colonialization of Africa by western nations is a process of exploitation that we are only beginning to recognize as we start to see the collapse of the western myth of superiority in relation to other continents. Europeans began their explorations of Africa after 1795. Invasions then followed between the years 1880 and 1900. The conquering European powers divided up the the African continent, imposing boundaries which split some ethnic groups and locked others together. Local systems of government were disrupted by the imposition of taxes and by appointing subjected chiefs to administrate them. Western colonial nations flooded Africa with cheap industrial goods such as cotton, metal wares and firearms, thereby inhibiting local production. They traded liqueur which brought alcoholism and discouraged local food production by promoting cash crops like peanuts, cocoa and bananas. At the same time, they cultivated markets for imported foods such as sugar. This web of ensnarement is the legacy of the West to Africa which continues up to the present. The British considered its colonialism as 'the white man's burden'. They couched their colonial dealings in a rhetoric that portrayed them as being on a civilizing mission for the black man. Somehow, Africa was to be improved by its exposure to the civilizing influence of the West. The facts point to a different conclusion. Today, for example, Africa is poorer than it was thirty years ago and getting poorer still. Famines, droughts and wars are commonplace. No longer a site of importation, global bankers seem to be writing off Africa in the global economic market (*New Internationalist* 1990). In place of imports, many African nations are now becoming the dumping ground for the toxic waste of the West. African countries, strapped by economic burdens and poverty, allow toxic dumping for cash. Toxic dumping is also done without permission and often undercover. Ships from western countries, loaded with toxic waste, frequently have to negotiate themselves into African ports, being *persona non grata* anywhere else in the world.

The case of indigenous peoples presents the single most disadvantaged and discriminated-against group in every society. In both rich and poor societies, they have suffered the most severe marginalization both in historical and contemporary times (Burger 1993). The effects of the colonialization of European peoples on the indigenous peoples of the Americas is now seen historically as a disaster. This colonial legacy is repeated wherever European colonialism has visited: Australia, New Zealand, the Pacific, Africa and Asia, including the vast area in the east and north of the former Soviet Union. Julian Burger (1993) reflects on the pervasiveness of this legacy using government statistics from across the world today:

> In New Zealand, indigenous peoples are seven times more likely to be unemployed than the average person; 50 per cent of prisoners are Maori although Maori make up only 9 per cent of the population. In Australia, Aboriginal people have a life expectancy of 20 years less than the average and are 14 times more likely to go to prison. Indigenous people make up 60 per cent of Guatemala's population but only 150 out of the 25,000 students who are in higher education. In Canada, infant mortality among indigenous people is over twice the national average. (Burger 1993: 4)

Indigenous peoples are also bearing the brunt of the effects of environmental degradation as a result of plundering industrialism. Forest loss, mining, dams and military activity are just a few of these activities. Indigenous peoples live in these fragile environments and are the first to suffer the effects of this war on the ecosystem (Burger 1990). Their intimate relationship with the natural world leaves them particularly vulnerable. Burger catalogues the areas of ecological vulnerability:

> Large-scale logging leaves them no forest and thin soils which are soon leached by tropical rains. Mercury used by gold prospectors in Amazonia has poisoned as much as 1500 km (930 miles) of their river system, killing fish and causing illness among thousands of Indians. About 5 million tons of toxic waste, including fluoride emissions from aluminium smelting are dumped daily into the St. Lawrence river, Canada, causing miscarriages, birth defects, and cancer among Mohawk Indians. Indigenous people of the Pacific (and Arctic) have borne the brunt of the dumping of radioactive waste (as well as nuclear testing). Johnson Island, home to 90,000 Pacific islanders, is the site of a U.S. toxic waste incinerator. Toxic emissions leak into the sea, polluting the entire food chain. (Burger 1990: 120–1)

Environmental racism, with regards to indigeneous peoples, is a global phenomenon. We can see from the catalogue above the systemic nature of environmental racism that depends on the land and cultures as the global economy is being pursued. Its contemporary manifestations reach deep into the historical fabric of western societies, leaving indigenous peoples the victims of western cultural values and practices.

Finally, one can also encounter 'environmental racism' in the midst of urban settings. C. A. Bowers (1993a) argues that ecological devastation, within urban settings, has its deepest impacts on the minority populations who live where environmental abuses have been tolerated for decades. He notes how, in urban settings within the United States, these differential impacts move along racial lines. Thus, 60 per cent of African American and Hispanic youth in the United States live near hazardous waste sites; and in urban areas they are twice as likely to be exposed to dangerous levels of lead poisoning than are white youth.

Class

Although the notion of class has multiple origins, its salience in modern times comes from Marxist social and economic theory. Within the context of Marxist theory, class signifies a group of persons having, in respect to the means of production, a common economic relationship that brings them into conflict with other groups having a different economic relationship to these means (Bottomore 1983). Thus we have slaves and masters, serfs and lords, proletariat and capitalists that are understood to be classes that cross the span of ancient, medieval and modern times. Class structures have subordinate classes or sub-classes distinguished besides and within the primary ones. Marx applied the term class to the following groups: feudal nobility, wealthy bourgeoisie, petty bourgeoisie, small farmers, proletariat, agricultural labourers. For Marx, the notion of class was a uniquely prominent feature of capitalist societies (Bottomore 1983). Marx's theory of class conflict was historically specific and contextual. On his evolutionary scale, capitalism was an advanced state of economic development. Thus the class conflict that he postulated between the proletariat and the capitalist class in western culture was the most advanced state of evolutionary development. In his piece called 'The Asian Mode of Production', Marx contended that non-western societies would have to advance to capitalist modes of production before they could move on to socialism (Handa 1982). The powerful critique that Marx made of capitalism's exploitation of the proletariat was felt over the globe. When Marx was writing at the turn of the century, industrial capitalism was in its most exploitative mode. It was the age of *laissez-faire* capitalism where exploitation of workers was transparent and rapacious. With the advent of socialist revolutions in both Russia and China, governments of capitalist countries started to regulate capitalist appropriation of citizenry. The greedy underbelly of raw market force capitalism was curtailed by government regulations. In North America, unions enabled workers to bargain collectively and organize for worker benefits from the capitalist class of owners. In western democracies, governments developed social benefits in health and other social areas to cushion against the effects of unchecked market capitalism. Thus western democracies, in response to socialist revolutions, put a human face on capitalism. The face was labelled 'neo-capitalism'; a response to the *laissez-faire* capitalism that preceded it.

The post-war period provided the testing ground of the conflicting ideologies of western capitalism and eastern bloc socialism. The contending powers behind the competing ideologies held one thing in common. Both socialism and capitalism embraced the hegemony of the western industrial mode of production. They were also on a common path as regards the exploitation of the earth's natural resources and share equally in the post-war desecration of the natural world. The arms race and the consumer race have exacted a toll on this earth which brings into question the post-war optimism of western capitalism and eastern socialism. Now, in the latter part of the twentieth century, we have seen the demise of state socialism. Capitalism claims itself to be the 'winner' of the cold war. With this new opening to unbridled and unchallenged capitalism, we have witnessed a return to earlier forms of captitalist appropriation. The reappearance of a *laissez-faire* liberalism brings with it a deep suspicion of the neo-liberal turn. The neo-liberal turn was the enclave of government-imposed regulations to protect the public with respect to industrial activities (anti-pollution, safety, health controls, and so on) (Cox 1991). All of these controls now appear to be on the road to being weakened and dismantled. Under the mantle of neo-liberalism, state sector employees made great gains in collective bargaining and wages and they are now becoming front-line targets for budgetary restraint. People on welfare and non-union workers are being hit by reduced state expenditure and by unemployment. The farm and small business sectors are in conflict with banks and with government as affordable finance becomes increasingly unavailable to them. The safety nets in these sectors appear to be disappearing (Cox 1991). We are progressively witnessing these dramatic sectorial changes within the heart of capitalism. Today, in the affluent North, we see high levels of unemployment, corporate downsizing, falling real wages, greater dependence on part-time and temporary jobs without benefits, and the weakening of unions, creating a growing sense of insecurity in the middle-class (Korten 1995). There is a growing despair among the young, especially from minority races, of finding even minimally adequate jobs. Youths who have advanced degrees and technical skills have seen their jobs evaporate in downsizing and no longer believe that education and job training lead to steady jobs. Northern economies are now being squeezed by the mechanisms of the global competitive marketplace. This malaise is happening at the centre.

What is happening outside the centre, in the periphery? The periphery in the recent past was called the 'third world', or the 'underdeveloped world'. These are the names given it by the powers of the centre. In the context of the idea of 'global privilege' that we have developed thus far, I would also use the expression of the world living under the privileged and silenced by the privileged. From the critical perspective adopted in this book, the periphery is best called the world of the 'overexploited' or the 'overdeveloped' world (Sachs 1992). It is sometimes named the South, meaning not only a geographical location but also a whole constellation of peoples living throughout the world in marginal economic conditions. Although the terms 'first world' and 'second world' are out of fashion today, it is still possible to speak of the 'third world' as the world that is on the periphery of the international economic community. It is those groups of nations which, during the process of establishing the present world order, did not become rich and industrialized. In the context of the North's rhetoric of privilege, we have called this world 'underdeveloped' because it did not enter into the abundance of the developed world. Always within the frame of reference of the developed and underdeveloped world is the idea that somehow the underdeveloped world of the South lacked the essential motivation and know-how to become developed and privileged. Always absent in this discourse is the idea that the development of the North is tied to the systematic underdevelopment of the South. The major source of economic activities between the North and South at present is that the North systematically demands the extraction of vital resources from the South to the North and returns to the South consumer goods and environmental waste and pollutants from the North. David Ransom in a recent issue of the *New Internationalist* (1992) gives a very good picture of how this works:

> To the free-market economists of the North it all makes perfect sense. Goods come and go as they please, and disposing of Northern toxic waste in the South is cheaper and easier than it is in the environmentally-conscious North. This is the way the North–South trade usually works – and has worked for the past decade. During this time heavily indebted Southern countries have been required by the World Bank to follow what are called 'structural adjustment' policies. These policies demand exports of any kind in exchange for credit. If you have natural resources like copper or wood, then you must produce more of them and cheaper. Because everyone else is required to do the same thing there is a glut on the world market, your exports get cheaper and cheaper and so you must export more and more. The net result is that the North gets plentiful raw materials – cheaply – and therefore doesn't have to worry about conservation – while the South is left with torn up forests, polluted rivers,

gigantic holes in the ground and an impoverished people living in an almighty mess. All that's new is that the South now has the option of importing toxic wastes as well as exporting raw materials. (Ransom 1992: 6)

It is within this context that critical voices from the South are justifiably suspicious of the use of the term 'global'. Vandana Shiva, speaking of issues related to the 1992 Earth Summit, makes the following caveat:

The Motto for the North at the UN Earth Summit and other global negotiations seems to be: 'What is yours is mine; what is mine is mine.' This lopsided view of a common future is made easier by the idea of the 'global.' Through its global reach the North exists in the South. The South, however, exists only within itself. The South can only exist locally, while only the North exists globally. (Shiva 1992: 26)

Because of the limitations of public communications media in the North, we are not aware of critical voices from the South. The 'global mass media' are really the monopolized hegemony of northern communications conglomerates that speak of the South within the limitations of the northern hemispheric world view of world capitalism. As readers and viewers of world news in the northern hemisphere, we are given world views within the limited confines of the northern hemispheric press communications which are controlled by vested interests of monopoly capitalism. We do not hear voices other than our own, in the wider world–cultural sense. Our press voices are northern and euro-centric and therefore ethnocentric.

Critical voices from the South would interfere with dominant northern hemispheric corporate industrial interests. Some of the major human rights atrocities committed throughout the third world are against dissenting journalism. Critical journalism in the South is a life-threatening activity of such vast proportions as to be one of the highest categories in the work of Amnesty International (Chomsky 1989b).

It is necessary to remind ourselves constantly that the voices of industrial plundering that are at the apex of the northern economies are not *our* voices and they do not speak for the vital interests of humanity. We must therefore emancipate ourselves from the privileged media of the North which bring us our day-to-day wonderworld of consumerism. One way to do this is to attempt to hear the voices of the South, of the underprivileged. Although this is difficult, it is not impossible if we exert ourselves. These are healing voices because without social and economic justice there will be no sustainable development that includes prospects for long-term planetary survival.

Serge Latouche, (the French economist and social theorist, maintains that there is no longer a 'third world'. He says that in the modern economy of the global marketplace, the idea of a developing third world is defunct. Latouche (1993) contends that in place of a third world, there are now three 'fourth worlds'. The first world that Latouche enunciates is a world that exists inside the womb of the affluent nations. It is a world of suffering and stress created within the daily life of the affluent societies; a world where there is ever greater and greater material suffering; a world where the poor and the destitute exist within the world of affluence. New technologies have created unemployed workers with no rights. We are witnessing an unprecedented development of 'modernized poverty' that has, in turn, stimulated the rise of drugs, crime and insecurity. The exact figures are not known but it is estimated that the poor are counted at 40 million in Europe. By adding the 20 or 30 million North Americans who live below the poverty line, and the poor in eastern Europe, we go well beyond 100 million. The second group of 'fourth world' outcasts identified by Latouche are the native minorities throughout the developed world. Here we have such peoples as the Lapps or Sami of the Great European North, the Eskimos or Inuit of Canada, Greenland and Alaska, the Aborigines of Australia, Melanesian natives, and the Tsiganes (gypsies) spread all over the continent of Europe. These peoples constitute a collection of cultures who are very much minorities, scattered across several nations and resistant to modernization. These peoples have their land appropriated for multinational projects or used as the sites of toxic dumping. The third group of peoples belong to those societies that are called 'least advanced' or 'least developed'. By far and away the most numerous, their rejection is not confined merely to isolated individuals or ethnic groups, but extends to whole nation-states and their populations. These are the countries of the South that are crushed by debt burdens. Today no one seriously thinks that these debtor nations can still join the international leap-frog competition and catch up with the others. In the context of trade, the whole continent of Africa is now being written off as a trading player in the world market, we only hear of Africa when there is a coup d'état or a famine. Latouche crystallizes the commonality of these three worlds:

> In spite of the gulf that separates them, the three 'Fourth Worlds' exhibit a certain number of common traits. They are all victims of progress, all in a situation of internal exile under the sway of planetary modernity. The sub-proletariat of the West, aborigines on reserves, or uprooted people in the LDC's, are all different examples of objectively identifiable outcasts from the great banquet of over-consumption who live out their sentence in their im-provised cultures of poverty ... They can no longer be considered merely as small isolated groups in the midst of a rich society; they constitute an *other* society. (Latouche 1993: 42)

We have now reached an impasse in the world economy. The era of colonizing open frontiers is in its final stage. There is nowhere else to go on this planet. Colonization of lands is no longer a physical possibility. All we have left in this new information age is the colonization of the mind. In the wake of the affluent society, we have the wreckage of the terminal cenozoic.

The integral webbing of gender, race and class

Up to this point, we have considered gender, race and class as separate sites of domination and power. In reality these social forces are, more often than not, systematically related to one another. Taken singly or combined, they are integral parts of the dominator structures. Consider Marilyn Frye's description of a birdcage:

> If you look very closely at just one wire in the cage, you cannot see the other wires. If your conception of what is before you is determined by this myopic focus, you could look at that one wire, up and down the length of it, and be unable to see why a bird would not just fly around the wire any time it wanted to go somewhere. Furthermore, even if, one day at a time, you myopically inspected each wire, you still could not see why a bird would have trouble going past the wires to get anywhere. There is no physical property of any one wire, *nothing* that the closest scrutiny could discover, that would reveal how a bird could be inhibited or harmed by it except in the most accidental way. It is only when you step back, stop looking at the wires one by one, microscopically, and take a macroscopic view of the whole cage, that you can see why the birds do not go anywhere, and then you will see it in a moment. It will require no great subtlety of mental powers. It is perfectly *obvious* that the bird is surrounded by a network of systematically related barriers, no one of which would be the least hindrance to its flight, but which, by their relations to each other, are as confining as the solid walls of a dungeon. (Frye 1983: 4–5)

The birdcage provides us with an image of how gender, race and class interact; in the social reality of oppression and domination, these dimensions are woven together in an intricate pattern. Thus, the dominator pattern of patriarchy does not exist separately from the race and class domination. At the level of social and political reality, these patterns of domination are integral to one another and work together in intricate patterns of oppression.

Our description of the three levels of the 'fourth world' reveals the ongoing devastation that the global economic system has been visiting on certain segments of the human species. We must now face up to a more inclusive devastation that is part and parcel of our economic trajectory. The natural world and the other species of our planet have also been the recipients of the rapacious pillage of the global marketplace.

Education, equity and difference

The presence of difference and diversity within the earth community and the human community is a matter of fact. It becomes a problematic issue for educators when issues of social power are recognized and addressed along lines of difference. In a closely argued piece which connects cultural diversity and the ecological crisis, C. A. Bowers (1993a) maintains that the two major changes that will dominate the educational/political scene over the decades ahead are the growing awareness of and pride in distinct cultural identities, and the ecological crisis. Addressing the field of teacher education, he stresses the point that these two dimensions are not to be seen as pulling in separate directions:

> While on one level the two phenomena appear to be separate and distinct, and thus requiring different responses, they are, in fact, related. Both, for quite different reasons, signal that the assumptions underlying modern culture are no longer sustainable. The viability of the earth's ecosystems is being seriously threatened by the technological practices and ever expanding demands on nonrenewable 'resources' deemed necessary by the modern individual. And the myth of personal success that prompted generations of people to turn their backs on the web of relationships and patterns that constituted their ethnic heritage by entering the competitive and highly individualistic mainstream culture is now becoming increasingly illusory. Unemployment, drug use, alienation, structural poverty, stress, and toxin-induced illnesses represent the reality that now overshadows this myth. The flaws in this modern form of consciousness are now being challenged by both environmentalists and groups attempting to recover their ethnic identities – African Americans, Hispanics, and Native Americans (Sioux, Nez, Perce, Cheyenne, etc.). To put it another way, the ecological crisis and the emergence of ethnic consciousness have their roots in the same dominant cultural values and practices that are now seen as increasingly problematic. (Bowers 1993a: 163)

In the final part of this chapter, I shall consider four areas of difference that must be addressed in any critical transformative education for our time. Difference will be examined here within the context of four concerns for an education that is non-sexist, peaceful and non-violent, anti-racist and class conscious. Although other areas of difference are of equal importance, for example, education around sexual orientation, ability, and so on, our present treatment will focus on the four concerns mentioned above.

Anti-racist education Although the notion of clear racial difference lacks any strong scientific evidence, we must nevertheless acknowledge that, at the level of everyday life, the social effects of operating out of a 'race' position are incontestible. There are powerful social meanings to race which are anchored particularly in the lived experiences of minority groups in white-dominated societies (Dei 1996). When the issue of race is raised within the context of its consequences and social effects, it is sometimes contested on the grounds that you cannot have racism if you do not have races. This is not the experience of many groups who have lived with the reality of racism as it exists in the world today. Educators must not overlook the painful aspects of living on the receiving end of structures that mark people on the basis of their perceived race. Racism as a social process of exclusion and discrimination can operate with vitality in the absence of clear lines of demarcation between racial groups.

Racism is a system of privilege existing between human groups which allows one group to have pre-emptive power and placement over another. To discuss the phenomenon of racism in our own society, we must open up for discussion the whole system of 'white-privilege'. In western societies, whiteness and the privilege of white skin is taken for granted (Dei 1996). White privilege brings with it enormous social, political and economic benefits due to the dominance position of being white. Today, anti-racist education calls into question white privilege and the ideology that supports it. This questioning can be an entry point for white people to join the debate around issues raised by anti-racist education. White educators who embark on anti-racist education can bring forward the questions: 'How is whiteness delineated and read in the schools and in the wider society?' and 'Why is white culture so dominant that some students are led to think they are in the majority in the world?' (Dei 1996). Anti-racist education attempts to do more than merely question the systemic basis of white privilege; there is a pro-active movement to educational endeavour that seeks to open a forum or space. As the anti-racist educator George Dei (1996: 28) puts it: 'anti-racism calls for creating spaces for everyone, but particularly for marginal voices to be heard. It calls for dominant groups in society to listen to the voices of subordinated groups.' Thus, anti-racist education must define, conceptualize and perceive 'difference' from the standpoint of those who occupy the margins of society and continually have to resist their marginality through collective action. This involves the educator in the question of just how to teach difference in an educational context. George Dei ventures the following scenario in the teaching of difference:

> Difference must be taught in a way that allows people to acquire the strength to work collectively for transformative change. Difference should be taught in a manner that recognizes our individual and collective strengths. Difference should not be taught in a manner that renders exotic and romanticizes the 'other.' We recognize our difference in order to learn from each other … A related question concerns the extent to which an emphasis on differences can aid or impede a politics of social transformation. There is little doubt that a politics of similarities can mask forms of social injustice. In an ideal world we could not deny the importance of connecting on the basis of our commonalities. After all, we should be able to 'visualize a community' in the midst of difference and diversity. It is important *not to confuse diversity with divisiveness*. However, highlighting or privileging difference, in a manner that engenders divisiveness, is not a virtue of diversity. (Dei 1996: 37)

Anti-racist education recognizes the diversities and complexities of racism in the world today. This allows us to understand Edward Said when he remarks that no one today is purely one thing (cited in Dei 1996). Within this complex situation we must deal in multiple strategies. There will also have to be specific choices implemented in a given situation as to how the struggle against social oppression will materialize. George Dei (1996), in addressing this complexity, gives the following example. He points out that by choosing to focus on anti-black racism we are not to negate the struggle against anti-Semitism. As he points out, they are both forms of racism that an anti-racist struggle has to confront. Our task is to be able to connect these struggles and also to relate anti-racism with other forms of social oppression and the broader political economic questions. With that in mind, one must be aware of the powerful social effects the globalized economy has on community life.

In the Canadian context, current national and global restructuring has profound implications for schooling and this is most clearly seen in relation to racial minorities, women and economically disadvantaged youth. This situation sets one minority group against another and here difference is the matrix for racism among minority groups (Roman and Eyre 1997).

At another order of magnitude is the complex interweaving of other dimensions of difference. This order of complexity demands that when we consider racism, it must be within a more integrated understanding of oppressions and how they are interlocked. George Dei calls this type of anti-racist analysis 'integrative anti-racism'. He states:

> An integrative anti-racism approach is based on the principle that myriad forms of oppressions are interlocked and that a study of one such system, racism, necessarily entails a study of class, gender, sexual inequalities, homophobia and ableism ... The complex nature of oppressions, and the interchangeability of the roles of 'oppressor' and 'oppressed' in different situations, necessitate the use of an integrative anti-racism approach to understanding social oppression. This approach is informed by the knowledge that individual subjectivities are constituted differently by the relation of race, class, gender, age, disability, sexuality, nationality, religion, language and culture. (Dei 1996: 56–7)

Studying racism in an integrative manner raises some important questions about social inequality and prevents any attempt at a facile understanding of these complexly interwoven phenomena. In a world that is increasingly becoming integrated in communities of peoples where 'difference' is the norm, education around issues of anti-racism will gain increasing importance.

Non-sexist education As with the discussion of anti-racist education, the topic of gender relations within an educational context must be seen in an integral context. At the level of everyday life, gender relations are experienced by particular individuals within contexts of race, ethno-cultural background, class, age, ability and sexual orientation. This makes it imperative, at the outset, to go beyond simple generalizations about men and women and to consider the specific context within which their life experiences are embedded. Sexism is the institutionalization of privilege along gender lines. In the context of contemporary education, we may speak without equivocation about 'male privilege'. The prioritization of male privilege exists within the institutions of patriarchy that we have already looked at in this chapter. Patriarchy is seen as the institutionalization of male dominance in vertical structures of hierarchy. Within educational institutions, privilege is given to teaching and learning styles more closely associated with white, male, middle-class experience. This privileging often ignores the strengths of girls and women in the curriculum. In addition, women's skills are not recognized and rewarded, neither in education nor in the wider social context. Male privilege operates within educational institutions when, with the same education and skills as a man, a women gets paid less and has less power and responsibility. We also see, in relation to women, that occupations that employ a large number of women pay less for the same skills than occupations which employ a large number of men. Sexism is one of the major barriers to achievement. Because of persistent perceptions that academic achievement is not feminine, many young girls and women frequently do not perform to their full potential. We also continue to see substantial differences in enrolment and participation rates for some fields of study; most notably, engineering, the applied sciences, technologies and trades are areas that are almost completely dominated by men (S. Wolf 1994). A critical transformative educational process must address and surmount the problems of inequality that are sanctioned in conventional educational institutions. This is one dimension of an education that is non-sexist in orientation.

A second major area that a critical transformative non-sexist education must address is the pervasive violence that exists in institutions that socialize students in a male culture. Women and children, as we have already discussed, are the recipients of this violence on a horrendous scale. One of the more serious forms of violence within the modern school system is sexual harassment. Frequently this type of male violence is treated within the school as harmless. 'Boys will be boys' is a phrase often heard and used as an excuse for sexual harassment (S. Wolf 1994).

When patriarchy is the norm, then the top of the hierarchy is a white, male heterosexual. All sorts of violence and selection are carried out within the normative structures of patriarchy. Within the norms of patriarchy, there are high correlations between position and gender and this positioning or favouring of males is legitimized by the culture through its political, economic, religious and educational institutions. The institutions of patriarchy, like any other deeply violent social formations, combine direct, structural and cultural violence in a vicious triangle. Patriarchy is not only an institutional structure that protects male privilege, it also serves as a legitimizing institution for the perpetration of male violence. In order to address the pervasiveness of patriarchal violence there must be a deep and profound exploration of how dominance and subordinance operate along gender lines. There must be a deep questioning and study of the background cultural factors that end up in male violence and in their domination of women. The institutions of patriarchy have been challenged by the women's movement and that is an opening towards change that is necessary and, at the same time, long in coming. But change in this area, if it is to be effective, must be initiated by men in our culture who have come to see how male misogyny and privilege work against both men and women. What we need is an education that will challenge male privilege but also give us a vision of a partnership between the sexes that has power equity as its basis. The recent work of Riane Eisler and David Loye in *The Partnership Way* (1990) and the 'New Dynamics' workshops inspired by the work of Carole Pierce and Associates are suggestive approaches that move on a path to power equity between the genders (Pierce 1994). In the final analysis, non-sexist education must examine gender inequity at all levels of the social life in which it is embedded. A break in the hegemony of patriarchal power will help us forge a vision of education where equity is the norm rather than the objective.

Education and class in the context of globalization

We have already made some preliminary remarks about class and have considered it as an integral dimension of difference along with race and gender. Now I would like to consider some educational issues that relate to class in a critical transformative framework. From experience we know how difficult it is to address class issues in educational contexts. bell hooks (1994) maintains that nowhere is there a more intense silence about realities relating to class differences than in educational settings. We see very clearly in western democratic societies a silence and resistance in addressing class issues (Aronowitz and Giroux 1993; Bourdieu and Passeron 1977; Bowles and Gintis 1976; Dale and Esland 1976). Within the North American context we see a mythological sense that school is for everyone equally. We know, at the level of legitimation and everyday practice, that educational systems socially sort along lines of gender, race and class. Western liberal ideology masks the oppressive nature of our educational institutions. In the last twenty years there has been a development in education that codes the intricate systems of oppression. Initially inspired by the work of Paulo Freire (1970), groundbreaking work on pedagogy and oppression, there has been further development of a critical perspective that systematically raises issues of domination, such as the class issue in educational contexts (Collins 1995; Livingstone 1987). I have indicated earlier that the class issue has taken on new meaning in the context of the globalized economy. Education in our present situation of globalization has come full circle back to the task of training the future workforce. After years of neglect, business and governments have discovered training. Educational institutions are being pummelled by business and government for a poor track record as trainers of students for the global job market. Jim Turk (1992), Director of Education at Ontario Federation of Labour, notes that education and training are less a cause than an effect of economic decisions. He maintains that emphasis on education and training is more likely to flow from a vibrant and fully industrialized economy than be a factor to bring it about.

It is important to locate class within a critical perspective that looks at the restructuring of unbridled capitalism in a global economic framework. The Australian educator Griff Foley (1993) fosters the critical framework that I am proposing at both 'macro' and 'micro' levels. At the 'macro' level he proposes that we examine educational policy that is being driven by the globalization process. He contends that the globalization of production has transformed the welfare state into a competitive state. What Foley sees happening in the movement towards a competitive state is a transformation of education from a citizen's right into an instrument of economic policy. At the 'micro' level, people are seen as instruments of production whose value comes from their training for the needs of the marketplace. Foley sees a need for a radical educational approach that will help people turn away from the dominant 'technicist' formulation of 'restructuring' and pay attention to what workers and the unemployed are actually experiencing and learning in the process of capitalist reorganization. A critical education that is formulated within a class perspective must move in the direction that shows clearly what economic restructuring is doing. It must be developed within local and national contexts that develop effective counter-strategies which show how globalization and 'restructuring' are clearly an impediment to a just society. Foley reminds us that capitalism, built as it is on the exploitation of the many by the few, is opposed to the general interest. We must also understand that there will be no secure and long-term reformation of capitalism in the interests of the many. We are reminded by Foley to reflect on our experience of the 1980s. Then capitalism was inherently unstable and destructive. It recovers from its periodic crises by intensifying the exploitation of labour. Foley raises again, in our own times, the question 'Whose side are you on?' He challenges adult educators:

> Do we adult educators choose to work with and for, capital, by accommodating ourselves to, with whatever qualifications and continued rhetorical resistance, the language and techniques of a workplace restructuring which is so clearly driven by the interests of capital? Or do we take the far more difficult task of

striving to develop forms of education which really do serve the interests of working people? (Foley 1993: 4)

In the era of globalization with its rhetorical flourishes and mantras, we risk being seen as naive by developing a position counter to the hegemonic voice of capitalist restructuring. We must make it clear that what we are about, as critical educators, is anything but naive. A critical education that is class conscious must examine closely how the world economy of transnational business is the basic cause of the steady decline in viable work all over the world. Jeremy Rifkin, in his book *The End of Work* (1995), addresses the worldwide increase in unemployment which is now at its highest level since the great depression of the 1930s. Rifkin points out that the number of people who are underemployed or without work is rising sharply as millions of new entrants into the workforce find themselves victims of an extraordinary high-technology revolution. He notes that sophisticated computers, robotics, telecommunications and other so-called cutting-edge technologies are fast replacing human beings in virtually every sector and industry, from manu-facturing, retail and financial services, to transportation, agriculture and govern-ment. Rifkin also notes that many jobs that are displaced in the workforce are never coming back. Blue-collar workers, secretaries, receptionists, clerical workers, sales clerks, bank tellers, telephone operators, librarians, wholesalers and middle managers are part of an older economic workforce that are now destined for extinction. Although some new jobs are being created, Rifkin points out that they are, for the most part, low-paying and generally temporary employment. In the contemporary global labour force, there is a polarization into two potentially irreconcilable forces: one being an information elite that controls and manages the high-tech global economy, and the other, the growing numbers of permanently displaced workers who have very little hope or prospects for meaningful employment in an increasingly automated world.

Richard Barnet (1993) points to this job crisis as an arena where some of the most fundamental questions of human existence are being raised. He antici-pates that there is an enormous amount of work waiting to be done by human beings: building decent places to live, exploring the universe, making cities less dangerous, teaching one another, raising our children, visiting, comforting, healing, feeding one another, dancing, making music, telling stories, inventing things and governing ourselves. But much of the essential activity people have always undertaken – to raise and educate their families, to enjoy themselves, to give pleasure to others, and to advance the general welfare – is not packaged as jobs. Until we rethink work and decide what human beings are meant to do in the age of robots and what basic claims on society human beings have by virtue of being here, there will never be enough jobs.

Both Barnet (1993) and Rifkin (1995) point out that some elements of a global strategy for reorganizing work are beginning to take shape. Rifkin suggests that we move beyond the delusion of retraining for non-existent jobs. He urges that we begin to ponder what, up to this point, was unthinkable – to prepare ourselves and our institutions for a world that is phasing out mass employment in the production and marketing of goods and services. He puts forth an idea that we must begin seriously to redefine the role of the individual in a near workerless world.

Educators in formal areas of schooling, adult educators in universities and non-formal settings, educators in unions and those who are advocates for the homeless and unemployed, face daunting issues confronting the relentless and destructive fallout of global restructuring. Educators who have grasped the critical task of being at the edge of new global strategies for reorganizing work outside the destructive restructuring of economic globalization must summon the courage and the imagination to face the human assault on human beings. We will consider these issues in more depth in a later chapter which considers issues related to 'quality of life education'.

Peace education: dealing with conflict and violence

Peace and conflict are words that cannot be looked at without a context. Correspondingly, the idea of a transformative peace education also carries with it a complexity and intricacy which demand careful thought and consideration. The earlier parts of this chapter have given the reader a sense of the scope and magnitude of the violence that is manifest in all aspects of the contemporary world. Although the complexities of a peace perspective is a world unto itself, my specific view of a transformative peace education is that it is an education that deals creatively with the complexities of conflict and violence. Here again, we will see that peace education is not a separate direction from the other concerns that we have looked at, such as racism or sexism. Peace education, when it is identified as such, is an integral education that will address the multitudinous areas of modern life where conflict and violence meet (Bickmore 1997). It is not my purpose here to enter into an exhaustive discussion of the complex dimensions of peace education. My task here is to connect peace education issues to the wider context of transformative education that I am setting out in this book. Three sites or contexts of peace and conflict will be considered. The contexts are the global/planetary, the regional/local and the personal.

At the planetary level, we see conflict and violence that are pervasive (their complexity has already been elaborated in Chapter 1 and throughout this chapter). What must be grasped from an educational peace perspective is the deep underlying conditions that generate violence at the planetary level. One major factor that serves as a deep underlying causal condition is anthropocentrism. Anthropocentrism or 'homocentrism' is an exaggerated sense of the pre-emptive importance of the human in relation to all other species. As an orientation to the world it is another illustration of the existence of a dominator culture. There is a deep desire at the very core of western scientific culture to dominate and control all natural processes. It should be recognized, in our present discussion, that not all human cultures can be characterized as anthropocentric. Almost all traditional or tribal cultures appear to carry on a very intimate relationship with the natural world and the other species within the natural world. These cultures are also characterized by their intimate relationship with the universe at large.

Western culture appears to be very different from traditional cultures in relation to the sense of intimacy with the natural world and the universe. The natural world, within western cultural myths, became a sphere that had to be tamed. This taming was built on an adversarial relationship to the natural world. Frederick Turner (1980) characterized this as 'the western spirit against the wilderness'. Brian Swimme and Thomas Berry (1992) maintain that the educational survival needs of our present time involve a journey into intimacy with the universe. Western educational tradition has accomplished the polar opposite of intimacy. In truth, our educational journey is a pilgrimage into estrangement. We have been taught to see ourselves as separate and detached from the natural world. When we talk of our existence we speak of it as standing out from and separated from the universe and the natural world. This is the disenchantment that we have spoken about above. Looked at from this perspective, human consciousness is conscious in so far as it is seen as separated from the universe and the natural world. When one considers the world view of western thinking, we see the world outside our consciousness as silent and inert; dead matter to be manipulated and controlled at our fancy. The world outside human consciousness is an object to be used at our species' discretion and within the terms of our own needs and preferences. The only intimacy within this world view is human intimacy. Here we are locked into anthropocentrism. The only other voice besides our own is the human; all other aspects of the natural world outside the human are silent and speechless. Because we see the universe outside the human as having no voice, it follows that we have no capacity for intimacy with the natural world. We are not aware that we are living on the surface of things. This is part of the arrogance of western education. We look at cultures that profess an intimacy with the world outside human consciousness as primitive and underdeveloped. We see this clearly in the case of indigenous peoples. Their intimacy with the natural world, their closeness and reverence for the animal and plant world, are seen as retrograde within the modern temper. What we in the modern western scientific tradition have failed to see is our very limited capacity for communion with the world outside the human. The western educational tradition has trained us to see only the human world as subjects. But what if the universe is a communion of subjects and not a collection of objects (Swimme and Berry 1992)?

Habitat and diversity What are the consequences of this orientation to the natural world? First, consider the implications of habitat destruction. So far as is known, we are the only green planet in the universe. Since our appearance on the earth, we, as a species, are implicated in the destruction of a rich heritage of land base that will grossly impoverish the earth's green cover in a twinkling of geological time (Myers 1984). By the end of the twentieth century, deserts are likely to have expanded by a full two-thirds and we will have eliminated at least one-third of our tropical forests. We appear on the brink of destroying our inheritance of coral reefs, mangroves, estuaries and wetlands. In the name of human welfare, we will tear up, chop down, drain, poison or develop other precious lands. The events above are not 'acts of God' but the result of human artifice. Various pressures within the human community bring this about. Poverty in one part of the world is matched by consumer greed elsewhere. To meet the complexity of human needs in our present society we have ventured on to a highway of overexploitation of our natural habitat. The findings now indicate that when some tropical forests are removed they do not readily re-establish. With soil cover disappearance and the loss of critical stock nutrients, a forest cannot regenerate. Desertification is irreversible or it comes at a massive cost. Far more is at risk than we might think possible. For example, when certain sectors of the biosphere, notably tropical forests, coral reefs and wetland ecosystems serve, by virtue of their biotic richness and their ecological complexity, as 'powerhouses' of evolution, we are impoverishing the future course of evolution (Myers 1984). Specifically in the case of tropical forests, which harbour a disproportionate share of the earth's biological diversity, there is the dramatic focus of concern about mass extinction. The outright clearing of tropical forests by settlers in search of land for cultivation and by commercial logging operations producing timber for trade and domestic needs may directly cause the extinction of one-fifth of all plant and animal species by destroying their habitat (Wolf 1988). The deep pathos concerning the importance of biological diversity is articulated by John Ryan in a piece on biological diversity in the *1992 Worldwatch Institute Report*:

> Complex beyond all understanding and valuable beyond measure, biological diversity is the total variety of life on Earth. No one knows, even to the nearest order of magnitude, how many life forms humanity shares the planet with: roughly 1.4 million species have been identified, but scientists now believe the total number is between 10 million and 80 million. Most of these are small animals, such as insects and mollusks, in little explored environments such as

the tropical forest canopy or the ocean floor. But nature retains its mystery in familiar places as well. Even a handful of soil from the eastern United States is likely to contain many species unknown to science. (Ryan 1992: 9)

We are in the process of destroying species without ever understanding their vital importance. There are estimates that by the year of 2050 half of all species today could be extinct (Seager 1995). Other species are living components of vital ecological systems (ecosystems) which provide humanity with indispensable free services and whose disruption could lead to the collapse of human civilization (Ehrlich and Ehrlich 1981). At present, well over 90 per cent of all species that have ever lived have disappeared. They have become extinct by natural processes. When humans began hunting animals for food, commerce and sport, extinction ensued because of the disruption of the natural environment. In the process, the extinction rate soared to about one species per year in the twentieth century (Myers 1984).

In our own time, when natural environments are being destroyed and degraded on every side, the extinction rate is rising to about one species per day or even higher. It is estimated that by the end of this century, we could lose a million species. It also appears to be a real possibility, that by the middle of the next century perhaps a quarter of all species may be lost. What is the scope and magnitude of this loss? Norman Myers (1984: 154) attempts to give us a sense of scale: 'In its scale and compressed time span, this process of extinction will represent a greater biological debacle than anything experienced since time began. It will massively exceed the "great dying" of the dinosaurs and their kin, together with associated organisms, 65 million years ago, when a sizable share of the Earth's species disappeared.' We are in a headlong trajectory of species loss that will ultimately halt the course of evolution itself. It is cryptically put by two scientists who catalogue this loss, observing that 'dying is one thing, an end to birth is something else' (Myers 1984).

As the project of economic globalization goes forward, we can see that insensitivity to the destruction of the natural world is callous. Almost all major nation-states are in complicity with this destructive process. On the global level, consciousness of the destruction of the natural world and resistance to it come from women's groups. Women appear to be our critical consciousness educators in the areas of environmental devastation. Joni Seager (1993) observes that women are the backbone of virtually every environmental movement group around the world. With few exceptions, women constitute approximately 60 to 80 per cent of the membership of most environmental organizations. We know this also to be the case in virtually all aspects of peacekeeping in our contemporary world (Seager 1995). Specific examples are noteworthy, as illustrated in Joni Seager's (1993) compendium of examples of women from all over the world:

The prominence of women as catalysts and leaders of the grassroots environmental movement is a global phenomenon: in India and Kenya, it is the
women-led movements that are fighting to save forests. It was an ad-hoc group
called Mothers of the Aral Sea that helped to bring international attention to
the catastrophe of the disappearing Aral in the former USSR. Women in the
Ukraine and across Europe took the lead in forcing their governments to
acknowledge the seriousness of the Chernobyl nuclear accident and its fallout.
Women are in the forefront in virtually every community group in the U.S.
and Canada organizing around toxic wastes. (Seager 1995: 264)

Based on the examples that I have given, we can expect that women
involved in planetary peace issues will be exemplars of peace education efforts.
They will form a new type of leadership not encased within the violent
structures of patriarchy.

Turning concerns for peace education to the regional/local level opens up
a world of conflict and violence that stretches from one end of this earth to
the other. We have elaborated on the violence that is being visited on indigenous peoples. There are complex conflicts between peoples within and across
nation-states. There are violent conflicts that affect particular hemispheres.
We see these zones of conflict in all areas. Examples pervade. Northern
Ireland, Bosnia, Rwanda, and the region of Central America, Algeria, Nigeria
are just a few. The arms industry supplies the weapons to fuel local and
regional conflicts. For example, between 1965 and the mid-1980s, third world
military expenditure increased faster than in western countries and accounted
for a greater proportion of the gross domestic product, an average of over 4
per cent (*World Guide 1997/1998* [1997]). The human cost of all these conflicts
is astounding. One of the outcomes of regional conflicts is the development
of a distinct global population of peoples who are labelled refugees. The term
refugees has a specific definition in international law: 'A person unable or
unwilling to return to his/her homeland based on reasons of race, religion,
ethnicity, membership of a particular social group, or political opinions.' Their
numbers have risen from 17 million in 1991 to more than 27 million at the
beginning of 1995 (*World Guide 1997/1998* [1997]).

There are no pat prescriptions for peace education given the complexity of
local and regional situations. Peace education and conflict resolution must be
tailored to the contours of the region or locale where it is initiated. I would
like to give examples of peace education efforts, one from Central America
and one from Northern Ireland. The peace education programme in Central
America comes out of the work of Abelardo Brenes-Castro (1988; 1996) and
colleagues and goes under the name of 'The Culture of Peace and Democracy
in Central America'. In response to the initiatives of peaceful resolutions of
conflict in Central America, the University of Peace in Costa Rica has encouraged a programme of peace education dealing with the specificity of the

region of Central America. Since 1988, this programme has been involved in a lengthy education initiative that deals with issues of peace and sustainabilty as worked through the region of Central America combining efforts in Costa Rica, Guatemala, Honduras, El Salvador, Nicaragua, Panama, Honduras and Belize. The 'Culture of Peace' programme has produced an integral model for peace, democracy and sustainable development that is being launched in the region in formal and informal education settings. This programme has produced more than thirty texts and numerous pedagogic guides. These guides are being used in workshops throughout the region, particularly by community leaders and people involved in the media. The programme has also commenced to address educators in the formal school system in several of the countries in the region. All participants in the training process deal with issues such as basic human needs, rights and obligations, personal development, and policies of life and communal spirit. There are workshops dealing with issues around peaceful resolution of conflicts, Gandhian non-violence techniques and the development of more harmonious relations between men and women. This educational peace project attempts to support marginal communities in the use of non-violent methodologies to solve their regional economic, political, social and personal problems. One of the workshops is called 'For a Journalism of Gender', and deals with women and media. This particular workshop takes into account that the conventional media's interpretation of reality is frequently based on partriarchal codes (*Dialogue* [1996]). The 'Culture of Peace' programme deals with peace education issues in a comprehensive and integral manner.

I will now cite an example of peace education in Northern Ireland that deals with regional conflict of a more focused and specific nature. The peace programme initiative exists in County Antrim in Northern Ireland in an institution called Correymeela.

The initiating vision for Correymeela started with a Protestant minister, Ray Davey, from the town of Lisborne, Northern Ireland. His initial pastorate was as a chaplain at Belfast University in the mid-1960s. He was resident in Belfast in 1968 when the conflicts erupted between Protestants and Catholics in Northern Ireland. Very sensitized to the violence that surrounded him in the North during this time, he purchased a property in the mountains of northern Antrim which now goes under the name of Correymeela. Correymeela has been, for the last thirty years, an institution of peace and non-violence dedicated to a Christian ecumenical aproach to peaceful resolutions and understanding between Catholics and Protestants in the North. This particular institution accepts as a basic premiss that there is a spiritual dimension to peaceful and non-violent resolutions to conflicts. Its present director is Colin Craig who related to me the details of Correymeela's history and its work.

Over these past thirty years, Correymeela has been an inspiration to young people in the North of Ireland that opens an area of new vision and hope in future Protestent and Catholic relations. From the point of view of Correymeela, there are three basic elements for peace: peacekeeping, peacemaking and peace-building. Peacekeeping is a prerequisite to communal peace. You need a base from which to operate. It is taking the immediate violence out of the situation so that other factors can operate and come forth. Peacemaking is fundamentally a political task. It is about equity, diversity, equality and justice. Lastly, there is peace-building which is the relational reality. If peace could be paraphrased it would be as people affirming and experiencing connectedness empathetically. It has to be based on the everyday lived experience of people. It has to be done out of encountering each other's stories. In Colin Craig's present observations, he maintains that there has been a steady erosion of community participation and involvement of the young. There seems to be the loss of a deep sense of place and connectedness which helps young people to commit themselves to the community life of their locale. There also appears to be a loss of a sense of the fact that young people can make a difference to the ongoing life of their communities. This is the reality of 'alienation' and the loss of relatedness.

In thinking about this contemporary reality of youth and commitment, the Correymeela staff has devised a new programme labelled 'The Odyssey'. It is about a journey and it has been designed knowing that people long for a greater reality than the local community, the Northern Irish Community, the European Community. There is the sense that there is a wider cosmological community that Craig identifies with Thomas Berry's *Universe Story* (1988). Operating from the basic foundation that the 'universe story' is the story from which all other cultural stories come, 'The Odyssey' is an attempt to imagine and create a four-part programme. Groups which participate in this four-week programme comprise diverse people from all walks of life in Northern Ireland, except, possibly, parents with young children. There is also a balance of Catholic and Protestant, nationalist and unionist. The first part of the programme is 'Building the Story'. This part initiates 'The Odyssey' wherein people tell their own stories, the stories of their locale, the stories of their uniqueness. The story starts to build when people attempt to weave their stories together. Through the discussions they attempt to build a collective communal story based on the individual stories of the participants. At the end of that week, all the participants will be asked to pack some simple clothing and prepare themselves for a week-long journey in an ancient Irish skin boat called a *curragh*. They are asked to participate in a journey along the northern coast of Ireland from Lough Swullagh all the way back to the shores of Ballycastle where Correymeela is located. This journey is designed to be a stripped-down learning process very close to the group's sense of survival. It is designed to give people a sense of strenuous work within the context of an arduous journey. While on this journey, it is noted that the participants cross the border of the North and South of Ireland which goes unnoticed in the turbulent waters that do not speak of boundaries. People learn on this journey to work together at a very raw level of survival awareness. People have to depend on each other on this journey if they are to complete it safely. Many of the cultural and religious differences that exist within a group of participants are subsumed in the tasks of the ongoing journey. A Catholic and a Protestant must synchronize their efforts at the oars if their movement forward is to be accomplished. What all the participants perceive on this journey is the rhythm of the earth, the rhythm of the sea, the rhythm of the coast.

When the journey is completed, the third part introduces the idea of service. This gets us back to the idea that there is service and commitment owed to the communities of the participants. In the third week there is a sustained work commitment that runs all day. Service is offered at shelters, daycare centres and homes for the aged. There is tutoring offered. This segment is for the re-engagement of community commitment.

Finally, in the last week, there is the round-up and integration called 'The Giving of the Keys'. Keys stand for knowledge, experience, yourself and sharing. All the participants do the integrative work that attempts to bring together the total experience of the last several weeks. The key represents for each of the participants the opening of a door into a new vision. The emphasis on vision at this point is practical. The integration work involves post-programme work suggested by 'The Odyssey' experience just completed. The emphasis is on a vision that walks and has feet.

When we move to the level of the personal in considering peace education we are talking about the structures of intimacy as well as one's relationship with oneself. The most prominent area where some form of peace education is warranted is the area of intimacy between men and women and the intimacy structure of the family. This chapter has outlined in detail the deep and pervasive violence that develops from the structures of patriarchal dominance. When this structure of domination operates at the level of intimacy, we witness a pervasive violence that victimizes women and children everywhere. Peace education at the level of intimacy must address male violence. What is personal and intimate is not private. All of us face, at a public level, the effects of violence of men against women and children. Given the public outcome of this violence, it is appropriate to address it at the level of public schooling. Given the nature of violence that I have alluded to, we see a need to address these issues both within and outside school contexts.

We are now beginning to see schools address the problem of sexual harassment. Programmes that address harassment in the schools have developed the viewpoint that the issue of sexual harassment can never be separated from the larger issue of gender equity in education (Larkin 1997). Sexual harassment is a reflection of the devaluing of girls that occurs both within and beyond the educational setting. We are also beginning to see a variety of sexual harassment resource materials for educators. Here in Canada there are materials available at both the elementary and high school levels.

Gender equity and issues of harassment must be addressed in peace education (Larkin 1997). There is also a great deal of work to be done in the area of male violence outside school structures. Prisons, social service agencies and psychotherapeutic settings must also be prepared to deal with the pervasiveness of the problems that this type of violence produces.

In addition to dealing with men's violence towards women and children, we must also confront the enormous violence that men perpetrate on one another. There must be educational spaces both inside schools and out that confront the destructive misogyny of male role socialization in our society. For most men, particularly when young, there is a running dialogue of doubt about masculinity (Kaufman 1997). Michael Kaufman accents the state of terror that forms part of the regime of male socialization. He states:

> There is enormous terror that other boys will discover one's own fears. There is also the enormous fear of ridicule and violence at the hands of other boys. There is enormous fear of other males ... We have a word for this fear of other males, and that is homophobia. Of course, the term 'homophobia' is more commonly used to refer to a fear, or hatred, of gays, lesbians, and bisexuals. I don't want us to lose sight of this specific and important meaning. But I do feel that this specific form of men's homophobia is a product of the broader fear of other men and the fear of not being 'manly enough.' In a culture that defines manhood as an ability to dominate women, dominate other men, control one's own unruly emotions, and display the heterosexuality that is compulsory in our society, it is no surprise that for many men, particularly when they are young, there is an active hatred of homosexuality. (Kaufman 1997: 17)

It is not my task here to go into the depth and intricacies of a programme dealing with the violence of men. What is important at this point is for the reader to recognize that any detailed programme dealing with the violence that we encounter in our society will, of necessity, address the violent socialization of men.

PART THREE

Create

The Planetary Context of Creativity: Educational Vision in a Cosmological Context*

Unless we live our lives with at least some cosmological awareness, we risk collapsing into tiny worlds. For we can be fooled into thinking that our lives are passed in political entities, such as the state or a nation; or that the bottom-line concerns in life have to do with economic realities of consumer life-styles. In truth we live in the midst of immensities, and we are intrically woven into a great cosmic drama. (Swimme 1996: 60)

Introduction

We have just completed a radical and fundamental critique of conventional education in the latter decades of the twentieth century. I brought to your attention the grave dangers of pursuing educational ventures that are simply fostering the activities of the new global economic marketplace. All too often, a picture of the planet taken from outer space is used as a logo for transnational economic activity. The planet is talked about as a globe but this is insufficient in its dimensions. The globe as presented by the entrepreneur gives one the sense of something that is being connected either through human enterprise or human communications. Companies like IBM and American Telephone and Telegraph make advertising claims about bringing the globe together as a result of their corporate ventures and communication systems. Setting aside the idea of the globe as simply the terrain of economic enterprise, it becomes possible to see our planet earth as a single multiform unity, as it was before humans ever inhabited it. We are planetary creatures rather than global

---

* The 'cosmological context' introduced in this chapter is drawn heavily from the work of Thomas Berry. For several years Thomas Berry and I met and discussed, at length, his cosmological vision which culminated in *The Universe Story* jointly published with Brian Swimme. In the last section of this book, I weave his ideas on cosmology to address an educational context. I do this by elaborating and interpreting his 'Twelve Principles' which in their nascent form preceded *The Universe Story*.

creatures. Our planet earth occupies a place in the universe. We are desperately in need of a planetary consciousness which will locate us within the creative processes of the unfolding universe story. We are not in need of globalization consciousness. This statement will need elaboration and justification.

We need a unique kind of creativity for our educational ventures today. Conventional education during this century has not prepared us for this moment with all of its dangers and promises. The human venture has always been a turbulent process, but this seems especially true in our own time. It is possible to observe that our destructive violence, as well as vast creative forces, pervade all human affairs and all earthly forms of existence. We live in a world of forces that are very difficult to comprehend. Within this swirl of forces, out of which both the earth structure and human history are made, it is important that there should never be an absolute conquest of any one of these opposed forces by any other. The difficulty in recent centuries is that, through science and technology, we have obtained extraordinary control over the other forces, especially over the forces of the natural world. The result has been a dangerous and precarious dominion over the earth that, for a while, has had both positive and negative consequences. A momentous phase of human history has taken place. Courage, inventiveness and power have been shown to achieve what could hardly have been dreamed of in former centuries. We command nuclear energy. We travel into space. We know the genetic coding process. We are also in the process of destroying the carrying capacity of the earth for our species as well as the larger biotic world.

It is unfortunately not clear whether, at this moment, we are awakening to the fact of our own vulnerability and to the consequences of our own activities. If this were to start happening we would begin to produce a type of reflection that western humanity has not known for centuries. Perhaps it is even a kind of reflection we have never known before. In the wisdom born of this reflection lie the future hopes of both the human community and of the earth process.

Since the main area of disturbance is the biosphere of the earth, it is in the realm of biology that much of the most significant reflection is taking place. Out of this reflection has come the perception that the entire earth can best be understood as a single organic reality. The components of the earth are inter-dependent and delicately attuned to each other in their vital functioning. This constitutes an amazing echo across the centuries, not only of Plato's experience of the universe as a single vital organism; it is also an echo or a reawakening of the primordial experience of humans when consciousness first awakened within them. By entering into the metaphase of the biological sciences we gain entry into a new age of the earth, a new period of human history, a new creative interplay of the contending forces about us (Swimme 1984).

This is our historical moment, a precious moment, this moment when the ancient communion of the human with the natural world finds new expression. Thomas Berry (1993) calls the terminal decade of the twentieth century a 'moment of grace'. He is basically saying that moments of great danger can also be considered moments of creative opportunity. We can no longer speak of the end of history, write Ilya Prigogine and Isabelle Stengers (1984), 'only the end of stories'. In our present situation one could say that we are living in between stories, the modern story and an emergent story that we do not fully comprehend but must nevertheless envision. This is the 'creative' part in our idea of education that challenges us, at this moment, to survive, critique our current dysfunctional state, and create and envision vibrant structures to address our vital needs.

Planetary consciousness: the necessity of a cosmological context

Modern western culture is probably the first culture to attempt to function without an overriding view of the cosmos. In fact, as we have seen in Chapter 3, there has been disenchantment with the cosmological context that has developed in modern western thinking. Frequently, from our western point of view, we have labelled cultures as retrograde for having a larger cosmology embedded in mythic structures. Most of the social sciences at the end of the last century labelled peoples with mythic interpretations of the universe as primitive. This served more than one purpose. From a scientific point of view, it established western scientific thinking as superior to the thinking of other existing cultures. The label of primitive also gave European cultures an excuse and apology for their imperialism and colonialism (Said 1993).

We are now living in a watershed period comparable to, if not even more dramatic than, the major shift that took place from the medieval into the modern world. We are in a transition from the modernism that I have described in Chapter 3 to a postmodern world view whose characteristics we only vaguely see at this point. I call the movement into this postmodern perspective the ecozoic period. The educational framework appropriate for movement into this period must be visionary and transformative and clearly must go beyond the conventional educational outlooks that we have cultivated for several centuries. It is understood that anything approaching a 'grand narrative' will be viewed with more than a modicum of suspicion. The postmodern critique of 'grand narratives' appears to be not only suspicious of past narratives but is also, in its deconstructive moment, suspicious of suggested 'grand narratives' for the future. Donna Haraway (1991) suggests that all grand narratives that present themselves as true stories are potentially sources of violence and oppression. Her contention is that difference rather than commonality of a universal is the operant critical analytic lens for viewing society. This type of critique exposes us to the inherent ethical dangers that are potential in any new large vision, including the one that I will be venturing in this chapter. I differ from Haraway in my present attempts to offer a larger cosmology because I feel that difference must ultimately be understood in an integral manner. I therefore believe that there are compelling reasons to attempt what David Griffin (1988b) calls a reconstructive postmodern vision. It must be done with humility and openness. In the light of the destructive consequences of the grand narrative of the global marketplace, it is necessary to proceed, with all due caution, with a vision that is comprehensive in scope and magnitude, to counter the destructive totalizing monological system of the market vision. But that is not the whole story for venturing a new vision. As the philosopher Arran Gare articulates:

> it is not enough to defend a new cosmology in opposition to the cosmology that has underpinned modernity. It is necessary to articulate this in such a way that it can effectively challenge the hegemonic culture, so that it can orient people in practice, in their daily lives, to create an environmentally sustainable civilization. To do this it will be necessary for a new grand narrative, a grand narrative formulated in terms of the cosmology based on a philosophy of process. (Gare 1995: 139)

When Gare uses the word 'process', I equate it with my meaning of transformative vision. Gare further points out the paradox that has resulted from our loss of faith in grand narratives, and all narratives to some extent. What has been revealed in this loss of faith is the importance of narratives for the constitution of subjects, social organizations and societies. These narratives, even in their demise, show how we only know what to do when we know what story or stories we find ourselves a part of. Following from this underpinning, to know what to do about the environmental crisis requires the creation of stories which individuals can not only take up and participate in but which will also reveal to them why there are the problems at this moment, how they arose, how they can be resolved, and what role individuals can play in resolving them (Gare 1995). Personal and bioregional stories will be necessary but not sufficient. Given the present momentum of the global transnational competitive vision, more will be required. We need stories of sufficient power and complexity to orient people for effective action to overcome environmental problems, to address the multiple problems presented by environmental destruction, to reveal what the possibilities are for transforming these and to reveal to people the role that they can play in this project. The scope and magnitude for such a project cannot be underestimated as Arran Gare makes clear:

> In order for such stories to 'work,' to inspire people to take them seriously, to define their lives in terms of them, and to live accordingly, such stories must be able to confront and interpret the stories by which people are at present

defining themselves and choosing how to live in an environmentally destructive way. It is also important to reveal how power operates, and show why those individuals who are concerned about the global environmental crisis are unable effectively to relate their own lives to such problems. The new grand narrative must enable people to understand the relationship between the stories to which they define themselves as individuals and the stories by which groups constitute themselves and define their goals, ranging from families, local communities, organizations and discursive formations, to nations, international organizations and humanity as a whole. (Gare 1995: 140)

What follows is the grand narrative as articulated in several publications by Thomas Berry (1988) and Brian Swimme (1984; 1996). It must clearly be understood that the authors do not see their telling of the story of the universe as the definitive narrative. In discussions with Thomas Berry, he makes it clear that the story of the universe can never be told in a single once-and-for-all way. The universe is a text without a context. So, the diversity of storytelling of origins and the universe are stories within The Story. The Story, in capitals, is the ground for all of the stories that have been told over the ages. In each age, the universe impinges on the consciousness of peoples in unique ways. The scientific story of the universe that we are articulating in our times is a unique rendering that could happen only in our time. The empirical basis of the story makes it very compelling for the consciousness of the modern world view. The story that I will now describe is the cosmological context that I feel should accompany an educational vision that has a larger vision for a planetary context.*

The universe story

When I suggest the work of Brian Swimme and Thomas Berry's (1992) rendering of *The Universe Story*, I do so provisionally and with humility. It has a grandeur for me in its scope and magnitude, but it is not a 'grand narrative' to replace other stories of origins. This is readily acknowledged by Swimme (1996: x) when linking his work with the older wisdom traditions: 'It may be too much to hope that science itself will become a wisdom tradition, but perhaps we are already witnessing the creation of a comprehensive cosmology, one grounded in our contemporary understanding of the universe, and yet subtle enough to interact harmoniously with the more ancient cultural traditions.'

---

* As this work goes to press, I have come across the work of Donald W. Oliver and Kathleen Waldron Gershman (1989) which offers a very interesting cosmological perspective inspired by the process philosophy of Alfred North Whitehead. Although my entry point is different from theirs, they are nevertheless moving in the same direction that I am suggesting here. Let a thousand cosmological flowers grow.

I do not know the fullness and complexity of all origin stories in existence. They are the products of a myriad of peoples on the planet. My choice of a specific origin story for elaboration must be understood in the light of my location. My scholarship is steeped in the traditions of the West. I do not want to be dismissed because of my location. It is for the reader ultimately to assess whether I occupy my location in a critical and reflective manner. Having said that, I build upon the work Swimme and Berry's (1992) 'universe story' as my entry point into a broader cosmological context. I have found that this point of entry has opened up a system of larger meaning that I hope will create an organic planetary context for educational endeavours and that transcends the myopic vision of the global marketplace. The story form that will be rendered shortly comes from some of the recent work in astronomy and physics and cultural history. In that regard, it is located within a western scientific per-spective. To be sure, it is only one way to tell the universe story. My choice of this cosmological orientation does not exclude other versions of the universe story. A sense of plurality and diversity should be accented when we are involved in comprehensive storytelling. Just a few examples are suggested.

The reader may find it of interest to read Elisabet Sahtouris's *Gaia: The Human Journey from Chaos to Cosmos* (1989) or the Native Canadian historian Georges Sioui in his *Amerindian Autohistory* (1992). The reader may also want to engage the very vibrant dialogues that are now taking place between Native American elders and modern physicists. For example, one contemporary physicist who worked with Albert Einstein has noted that many North American aboriginal languages contain, in their structures as well as in their expressive capabilities, a sophisticated post-Einsteinian understanding of the universe that English is often unable to capture (Ross 1996).

Keeping the above understanding in mind, this chapter proceeds to describe and summarize some of the features as presented by Berry (1988; 1989) in several independent works, in addition to Swimme and Berry's (1992) col-laborative effort. My take-off point is to elaborate on a cosmological view through an interpretation and elaboration of Berry's (1989) 'Twelve Principles for the Understanding of the Universe'. These principles are indicative of dynamic evolutionary developments in the life of the universe, the planet earth, and the intra- and inter-species development of the human within evolutionary processes. The twelve principles are as follows.

Principles

1. The universe, in its full extension in space and its sequence of trans-formations in time, is best understood as 'story'. For the first time we have a story in the twentieth century with scientific precision through empirical observation. The difficulty is that scientists have until recently given us the

story only in its physical aspects not in the full depth of its reality or in the full richness of its meaning. The greatest single need for the survival of the earth or of the human community is for an integral telling of the Great Story of the Universe. This story must provide in our times what the great mythic stories of earlier times provided as the guiding and energizing sources of the human venture.

2. The universe is a unity, an interacting and genetically related community of beings bound together in an inseparable relationship in space and time.

3. The voices. The universe as a whole and in its various modes of expression speaks to us of itself and of the deep mysteries of existence. Everything radiates a manifestation both of itself and of the numinous mystery that all things bear within them. This capacity for ordered self-development, for self-expression, and for intimate presence to other modes of being must be considered as a pervasive psychic dimension of the universe from the beginning.

4. The three basic tendencies of the universe at all levels of reality are differentiation, subjectivity and communion. These tendencies identify the reality, the values and the directions in which the universe is proceeding.

5. The universe has a violent as well as a harmonious aspect; but it is consistently creative in the larger arc of its development.

6. The earth, within the solar system, is a self-emergent, self-propagating, self-nourishing, self-educating, self-governing, self-healing, self-fulfilling community. All particular life systems must integrate their functioning within this larger complex of mutually dependent earth systems.

7. The human emerges within the life systems of the earth as that being in whom the universe reflects on and celebrates itself in a special mode of conscious self-awareness. The human is genetically coded towards a further transgenetic cultural coding invented by the human community in a remarkable diversity in the various regions of the earth. This diversity of cultural elaboration in the various peoples of the earth is communicated to succeeding generations by both formal and informal educational processes.

8. Domestication. Transition from an integral presence in the natural world to the beginnings of permanent villages and control over the forces of the earth through agriculture and domestication of animals took place some 12,000 years ago. This period, generally known as the Neolithic period, was also the beginning of pottery, weaving and new ways of fashioning stone implements. The major shaping forces of human societies were manifest at this time in the intellectual, imaginative and emotional developments that ever since have characterized the various human societies.

9. The classical civilization. This is the period of progressive alienation of the human from the natural world, although from the beginning the basic forms of human development were in intimate association with the rhythms

of the universe. The rise of cities with extensive populations, more elaborate religious expression in ritual and architecture, the extension of intellectual, religious and moral reflection, the development of specialized social functioning, the increase in centralized government, the invention of writing, and greater technological expertise; these achievements were centred in the eastern Mediterranean, the Indus valley and later the Ganges valley, and the Yellow river in North China. Later in the western Mediterranean and European areas. Also in Central and South America.

10. The scientific–technological–industrial phase of human development had its beginnings in Europe and in North America. In this period the violent plundering of the earth took place. The functioning of the earth has been profoundly and permanently altered by human agency in its chemical balance, in its geological structure, in its biological systems. The atmosphere and the water are extensively polluted. The soils of the earth are wasted through erosion, road building, industrial establishments, shopping malls and waste disposal practices. The earlier mystique of the earth vanishes from consciousness.

11. The ecozoic age. In the period that we are now entering a new intimacy is sought for the integral functioning of the natural world. The dominant anthropocentricism of the scientific–technological phase is, by necessity, being replaced with an eco-centrism. We are, at the moment, in the inaugural phase of this period and we are witnessing new programmes instituted for integrating human technologies with the technologies of the natural world. A sense of the larger inter-species social order is starting to develop.

12. The great liturgy. The newly developing ecological community needs a mystique that will provide the high exaltation appropriate to the existence of such a stupendous universe and such a glorious planet as that on which we live. This can be found in the renewal of human association with the great cosmic liturgy in the diurnal sequence of dawn and sunset as well as the great seasonal sequence, and the great hydrological cycles. This recalls to mind the earlier ritual celebrations of the classical period, although now these celebrations will take place within a new story of the universe and its emergence through evolutionary processes.

The above principles are indicative of dynamic evolutionary developments in the life of the universe, the planet earth, and the intra- and inter-species development of the human within evolutionary processes.

The twelve principles are elaborated and deepened in Swimme and Berry's subsequent work, *The Universe Story* (1992). The elaboration of the first four principles is the work of this chapter.

Principle 1 locates the story in the depth of origin. The 'universe story' starts with the Big Bang. Here we see the telling of the story of the universe

15 billion years ago when a great flash filled the vast sea of infinite space. In each developing phase of existence a primordial energy blazed that would never again come forth with such intensity. With this incredible happening, the universe billowed in every direction, and as the energized hadrons and leptons entered a stable form of existence, they quickly participated in giving birth to the first atomic beings, hydrogen and helium. After the stars took shape as oceans of fire in the heavens, they went through a sequence of transformations. Some eventually exploded into stardust out of which the solar system and the earth took shape. Earth gives a unique expression of itself in its rock and crystalline structures and in the variety and splendour of living forms until humans appear. This is the moment in which the unfolding universe becomes conscious of itself. We bear the universe in our being as the universe bears us in its being. The two have a total presence to each other and to that deeper mystery out of which both the universe and ourselves have emerged (Swimme and Berry 1992).

In contrast to alienation and isolation, the universe story brings with it a profound sense of the relational quality of the unfolding process of evolution. This is the highlighting feature of Principle 2, integralism.

To speak of the universe as a unity means that it is a dynamic totality that cannot be explained by its constituent parts. It further means that the universe is coherent in terms of all its actions. It follows from this that the various activities of the universe are interdependent and thus cannot be considered apart from one another. The universe acts in an integral manner. The systematic study of the universe as a whole demands a cosmological perspective that is interdisciplinary in nature. Our earlier treatment of modernism concluded that there is a veritable eclipse of cosmological thinking within our western world view and heritage. Stephen Toulmin (1985), in his treatment of the loss of the cosmological sense, contends that the natural sciences have developed a systematic fragmentation and as a result it was no longer the professional business of any one discipline to think about 'the Whole'. It follows that if we are discussing the universe as a totality or *whole*, we are attempting to revision an integral cosmological sense. At all levels of analysis or integration of the universe, one is looking at an interacting and genetically related community of beings bonded together in an inseparable relationship in space and time. We are, therefore, talking about a universe that evolves in both space and time simultaneously. The universe, in the words of the physicist David Bohm (1988), acts as a seamless whole. When we speak of a time-developmental universe we are attesting to the idea that the *universe* is an interacting and genetically related community bound together in an inseparable time and space relationship. The universe acts in intelligible ways at all levels of inter-action. When we speak of the emergence of the universe out of the primeval fireball, we are not talking about some random emergence. At all levels of interactivity there seems to be a creative ordering. The universe itself is the name of that creative ordering. We can then say that the sun and the earth and the planets are bonded relationships because the universe holds them together. The same may be said of our Milky Way galaxy in relation to all of the other known galaxies. Here again we say that the universe is doing this as a fact of its primordial irreducible activity. The universe attests to the idea that everything exists and can be understood only in the context of relationships. Nothing exists in isolation.

When it is said that the universe acts as a unity in space and time, Swimme and Berry (1992) are talking about a universe that is not only present to itself simultaneously but is also present to itself over time. This is what is meant by a time-developmental universe. With a time-developmental perspective there follows the notion of an evolutionary emergence. Carl Sagan, in his book *Cosmos* (1980), can say that humans are the product of burnt-out stars. We are one of the many results of the evolution of the universe. Thus, the primordial energy of the fireball is the energy of all life. That same energy of the fireball is acting in the present evolution of the universe. Our universe, like ourselves, is a time-developmental being. Our present planet is the result of the evolution of the stars. We know that this process has occurred but we do not know exactly how it has come about. We can also say that that same energy that evolved in the stars has through time come to wear a human face (Swimme and Berry 1992).

What, then, do we mean when we say that the universe is an *interacting* and *genetically* related community of beings? The universe as an interacting community attests to the reality that the universe is an integral reality, all the elements of which are mutually present to one another through space and time. Thus, there is a mutual presence with every other part; a mutuality of action (interaction). This mutual presence of each element to every other element can be in the present (i.e. simultaneously or spatially) or be a mutual presence that reveals itself over time. The idea of a temporal unfolding brings into the picture a mutual presence with an evolutionary dimension that reveals a time-irreversible genetic sequence. Again, going back to the fireball or the Big Bang, we can see the universe beginning from a numinous speck, billowing in a fireball, constellating into the galaxies, then, in second generation planetary systems, erupting into life, and sparkling with a conscious self-awareness. This genetic process is also a testimony to the integral relatedness of the universe. Swimme and Berry maintain that the story of the universe is an integral story, not just a string of occurrences through time. They give the example of the human eye. Here we have present the elementary particles that stabilized in the fireball, we have the elemental creations of the supernova; we have the molecular architecture of the early organisms. When we open our eyes and capture light we are employing a procedure nearly identical to that invented by plants to capture sunlight. The molecules of our eyes act similarly to the molecules of the plant leaf because our molecular structures derived from theirs. All the past acts of intelligence are layered into present reality. When Swimme and Berry say that the 'universe acts', they mean the whole living universe, the present as well as the past.

From this we may conclude that our planet earth is an integral unity where each being of the planet is implicated in the existence and functioning of every other being of the planet. We now understand the planet as a self-regulating unity in which there is a 'web of life' that can only be understood as a totality. There is an incredible intricate mystery that links everything to everything else on the planet. As humans, we are influenced by the tiniest organisms that are present on the earth from the planet's beginnings. In Principle 3 we call this Voice.

Thus we observe that the history of humans on the earth is recent and the psychic dimension that is revealed is one that allows the psychic to be conscious of itself. Carl Sagan attributes a responsibility to the human species for their peculiar psychic ability:

> For we are the local embodiment of the Cosmos grown to self awareness. We have begun to contemplate our origins: starstuff pondering the stars; organized assemblages of ten billion billion billion atoms considering the evolution of atoms, tracing the long journey, by which, here at least, consciousness arose. Our loyalties are to the species and the planet. We speak for the Earth. Our obligation to survive is owed not just to ourselves but also to that Cosmos, ancient and vast, from which we spring. (Sagan 1980: 345)

Recently we have come to know the earth within the context of a more comprehensive knowledge of the universe itself. Berry (1988) offers us the idea that through our observational sciences we have commenced to understand just how the earth was born out of the larger processes of the universe, how life appeared, and finally how we ourselves emerge into being. But if we have such scientific knowledge we are often lacking in any deep feeling for the mystique of the earth or any depth of understanding. Berry attempts to capture this understanding when he directs our attention to the stars in the sky, the birds in their playful flight through the air, the fish in their serene drifting through the sea, the flowers blossoming in the fields. He suggests that as we experience the fragrance of the honeysuckle in the evening, listen to the rising and fading resonance of the cicadas while we watch the fireflies signalling to each other, our most immediate feeling is of the awesome mystery of things.

In spite of these possibilities for depth and understanding, we nevertheless have difficulty with this sense of mystery. Berry (1988) feels we no longer understand the voices speaking to us from the surrounding world. Our intense scientific preoccupations along with our relentless commercial exploitation of the planet have left us insensitive to the natural world in the deeper emotional, aesthetic, mythic and mystical communication it is making to us. Berry labels humans as autistic persons who are enclosed in themselves so tightly that they cannot get out of themselves and nothing else can get in. Presently, we are so enclosed in our human world that, as a society, we have almost completely lost our intimacy with the natural world. As children we become literate in reading human language while remaining illiterate in the language of the world about us. Also we become socialized in the human community while we remain alienated from the larger society of living beings.

Principle 4 provides the location of where value lies. Swimme and Berry (1992) maintain that values are determined by the human sensitivity in responding to the creative urgencies of a developing universe. At a most fundamental level, the universe produces variety in all its creations. Developmental differences can be seen not only in individuals but also in social structures and in historical periods of our development. Humans are presented with a problem in this creative context because there is no absolute model for individual development. Personal realization involves a unique creative effort in response to all those interior and exterior forces that enter the individual's life. Also, in relation to each historical age and each cultural form, there is a need to create a reality for which there is no pre-formed model; there are no finished answers but only striving forward at each moment and simply opening to a larger life.

The universe is considered to be coherent and intelligible throughout the total extent of space and the entire sequence of its time-development. What first impinges on human consciousness is a web of relationships which is the matrix for the emergence of life. There is a new understanding of values that return us to consider the significance of the more traditional context of story as a source of understanding and value. It is of the utmost importance that the next generations become aware of this larger story and the sacred values that have been present in an expanding sequence over this entire time-scale of the world's existence. Within this context, all our human affairs, all professions, occupations and activities have their meaning precisely in so far as they enhance this emerging world of subjective intercommunion within the total range of reality. Within this story, a structure of knowledge can be established with its human significance from the physics of the universe and its chemistry through geology and biology to economics and commerce and so on, to all those studies whereby we fulfil our role in the earth process. In this larger process, Swimme and Berry (1992) consider that there is no other way of guiding the course of human affairs except through our discovering the human role in this grand evolutionary process.

Principle 4 expresses that there are three interrelated basic tendencies of the universe at all levels of reality. They are the interrelated tendencies of differentiation, subjectivity and communion. These tendencies identify the reality, the values and the directions in which the universe is proceeding (T. Berry 1989). Establishing this comprehensive context is important in any consideration of human affairs, for only in this way can we establish any satisfying referent in our quest for a viable presence of the human within the larger dynamics of the universe. There is the supposition that the universe itself is the enduring reality and the enduring value even while it finds expression in a continuing sequence of transformations. In the context of transformation, Swimme and Berry (1992) indicate that a deep cultural pathology has developed in western society that has now spread throughout the planet. A savage plundering of the entire earth is taking place by industrial exploitation. Thousands of poisons unknown in former times are saturating the air, the water and the soil. The habitat of a vast number of living species now finds that the harm done to the natural world is returning to threaten the human species itself, and this is on a comprehensive scale (Brown 1988).

Our earlier discussions of the current planetary crisis indicated that *we* are the planetary crisis. At this time in the evolution of the planet we boldly say that the planetary crisis is a consequence of our limited awareness. We seem to be caught up in limited awareness of our actions in relation to the planet and the universe. The identification of the person with the planet comes from an understanding that one's personal identity is intertwined with an awareness of our relationship to the planet and to the universe as a totality. The foundational experiences of all of the major religions point to an intimate relationship between the person and the cosmos. The intimacy of this relationship allows us to say that 'the needs of the planet are the needs of the person'. We may extend this relationship by saying that 'the rights of the person are the rights of the planet' (Roszak 1978). If this relationship holds true, then we are able to say that personal development is integrally related to planetary development.

Differentiation can be seen from the articulated energy constellations we call the elementary particles and atomic beings, to the radiant structures of the animate world, to the complexities within planetary systems. We find a universe of unending variety. So various is the universe that the history of humanity can be understood as an ever-increasing differentiation of consciousness. Thus, the human species is seen as arising from the earth as matrix; the presence of the humans is just one unique articulation of an infinitude of differentiations in the universe. Further, within the human species we see an endless variety of peoples who have their own unique articulation within cultural and biological contexts. We refer to this type of articulation as gender, race or ethnicity. Further still, each person is part of an endless differentiation within the human species. Thus, it can be said at the personal level that each person is a unique expression of the universe unfolding.

Subjectivity means that the universe consists of subjects; centres of sentience and spontaneity. Teilhard de Chardin (1959) referred to subjectivity as the 'within of things'. The poet Gerard Manley Hopkins (1959) called this dimension of subjectivity the 'inscape'. The notion of a *subject* is a source of autonomous activity in the universe. The idea of soul seems also appropriate here. One can therefore say that humans share subjectivity with plants, animals and the elements (Swimme and Berry 1992). Spontaneity refers to the self-organizing capabilities of a living universe at all levels. The subjectivity of the human is seen in our conception of the 'human self' as a centre of self-organizing and self-regulating activities that are seen in the organizing of biological and cultural activities of the human species.

It is important to consider 'sentience' along with spontaneity for the full understanding of our use of the term subjectivity. The thorny question to discuss is the dividing line between sentient and non-sentient beings. Descartes, as we have seen, drew the line at the level of the human. Contemporary science is more inclusive, including mammals such as whales and dolphins. Swimme and Berry (1992) assume that all visible matter has the capacity for sentience, at least epigenetically. The notion of epigenesis means that we can say that intelligence and sentience were in latent form from the very beginning of our universe. The interpretation of epigenesis (that qualities arise from latent capabilities of forms) also speaks of the direct relationship between the powers of the early earth and the potential sentience entirely absent from those powers. Thus our presupposition that the rocks, air and water, just by being what they are, flower into sentient beings. At the very least, we can say that future experience in a latent form belonged to the activity of a rock. By attributing sentience and spontaneity to all matter we are left with a sense that there is a dimension of subjectivity that is present in matter itself at all levels. From this point of view, one may consider all aspects of the natural world in intimacy. This allows us to consider that all aspects of the natural world may be addressed as 'thou'. The notion of the Gaia hypothesis (Lovelock 1988) gives us reason to assume that the very earth itself is a living, spontaneous and sentient entity that can be addressed in intimate terms. If this is the case, then the personal world extends beyond the human community. We will have more to say about this later.

Communion signifies the deep relational quality of all reality. To be, is to be in relation. Much of our existence finds ultimate fulfilment in relatedness. The intricacy of our personal world is embedded in community. Much of our existence finds ultimate fulfilment in relatedness. We can see this in the intricate mating rituals the natural world has invented. So much of the plumage, coloration, dance and song of the world come from our relationships of true intimacy. The energy that we and other animals bestow on this work of relatedness of being, the attention that we give to our physical appearance alone, reveals the ultimate meaning of the communion experience (Swimme and Berry 1992).

The loss of relationship and the consequent alienation is a kind of supreme evil in the universe. Swimme and Berry (1992) indicate that to be locked up in a private world, to be cut off from intimacy with other beings, to be incapable of entering the joy of mutual presence was, in previous times, the very essence of damnation. Today we refer to this damnation as alienation. This alienation is cultivated when there is an extreme emphasis on individuation in the differentiation process or when the basis of our subjectivity is undermined (O'Sullivan 1984; 1990). The former is characterized as egocentrism while the latter is characterized as autism. What we see today in contemporary western values is the embodiment of alienation. Thus in a world of vast diversity, with its promise of an equally vast diverse relatedness, modern humans find themselves shut up in a world of egocentrism and autism, incapable of any deep or sustained contact with the world outside the self. Even when there is a sense of community, the community is limited to the human; the world outside the human is excluded. This truncated sense of community is labelled anthropocentrism. Its subjective correlate is individualism; the alienated exaggeration of the differentiation process when considered independently from *communion*. In my work in the area of critical education, I considered it very important to address the historical development of the idea of individualism because of its central value in modern consciousness. In addition, we must assess, at the personal level, the profound effect that the value of *individualism* has within the context of disenchantment. The modern definition of the individual as an autonomous social unit is a product of the consensus achieved by liberal social theory. In liberal social theory, individuals are seen as separate autonomous monads that are unique unto themselves. The primary position of the 'state of nature' is characterized by Hobbes as solitary, where the individual contracts socially out of fear of survival. The creation of society is based on a contractual arrangement of separate individual entities who, in Hobbes' words, were social atoms. This atomization which is so characteristic of the liberal idea of individualism would have profound implications for modern thought (O'Sullivan 1990).

> When Locke applied his theory of human nature to social phenomena, he was guided by the belief that there were laws of nature governing human society similar to those governing the physical universe. As the atoms in the gas would establish a balanced state, so human individuals would settle down in a society in a 'state of nature.' Thus the function of government was not to impose laws on people, but rather to discover and enforce the natural laws that existed before any state was formed. According to Locke, these natural laws included the freedom and equality of all individuals as well as the right to property, which represented the fruits of one's labor. (Capra 1983: 79)

The down-side of individualism is now being felt at all levels of cultural life. The self-encapsulated individual that we have just described has profound implications for the loss of a cosmological sense that links individuals to the wider community and subsequently to the universe itself.

Educational vision in a planetary context

The astronaut Gus Grissom made the following observation looking back on the earth from outer space: 'There is a clarity, a brilliance to space that simply doesn't exist on Earth, even on a cloudless summer's day in the Rockies, and nowhere else can you realize so fully the majesty of our Earth and be so awed at the thought that it is only one of untold thousands of planets' (cited in Kelley 1988: 18).

Grissom here is speaking out of a planetary understanding. I believe that educational vision in the twenty-first century must be accomplished within a planetary context. We live on a planet and not on a globe. When we look at the universe story that we have just depicted, we encounter an organic totality and not a cartological map. We are one species living on a planet called 'Earth', and all living and vital energies come out of this organic cosmological context. The globe is a construct of human artifice. Before 1492, cartographical procedures for mapping commerce routes were flat. For Europeans, Colombus moved the mapping systems for commerce from a flat surface to a globe. The globe is a mapping device made for commerce today. The language of globalization is first and foremost for commercial purposes. For all of the major issues that we have discussed in the chapters under Part II: Critique, the language of globalization was the background context. The major fundamental shift in our time is that power structures on the globe have moved from national state business (including military business) to transnational business. All over the world, at this moment, nation-state governments are delivering their governments to transnational business (Barnet and Cavanagh 1994; Clarke 1997; Clarke and Barlow 1997). We cannot therefore dispense with global language and it is absolutely necessary that it be the subject of deep order cultural criticism at a world level. At the same time we cannot be confined to globalization visions even as a sole corrective. At the planetary level, we move beyond geosphere to biosphere. Jeremy Rifkin refers to this as 'biospheric politics':

> The transition from a mechanistic to an organismic image of the earth and the accompanying shift in attention from the geosphere to the biosphere fundamentally alter the human perception of time upon which all definitions of human security are based ... The linear time frame of geospheric politics will have to be bent into the cyclical loop of the biospheric processes. The notion of an ever-accelerating rate of production and consumption rushing into an

open-ended cornucopic future has led us to the present environmental and economic crisis. In the name of progress, we have mortgaged our planet's future and made our children's world far less secure. Reorienting the time frame of human culture to make it compatible with the circadian, lunar, and circannual cycles of the biosphere will mean rethinking the most essential features of our temporal values. (Rifkin 1991: 264–5)

How can the universe story that we have just encountered give us a sense of temporal direction that Rifkin suggests is necessary? I would suggest that the universe story can help to guide and direct our educational vision. It provides the basis of a functional cosmology for a planetary vision. The story evokes creative energy. In this context learners need, above all, an attraction that entrances and moves them. The basic purpose of the story is to enable us to interact more creatively with the emergent processes of the universe as experienced today (T. Berry 1988). This story potentially provides not only the understanding and the sense of direction that we need, it also evokes an energy needed to create this new situation. It must be repeated constantly that we are not now dealing with another historical change or cultural modification such as those we have experienced in the past. The changes we are dealing with are changes on a geological and biological order of magnitude. The educational vision must be at this order of magnitude.

This emergent time-developmental perspective that the universe story provides has profound implications for an educational vision. Education can no longer be considered a closed process of knowledge accumulation. There is no set curriculum that withstands the test of time. New educational challenges present themselves with the ongoing evolution of life. When and if we are able to look back on the present moment, we will see that we had our own creative response to the ongoing evolution of all life. A time-developmental perspective does not allow us to say that 'there is nothing new under the sun'. What we are now coming to realize is that we pass this way once and education in the late twentieth century has its one-time only challenges. Thus, when the educator insists that we begin our educational vision in a time-developmental context we develop a tradition that seeks educational insights framed within our very best knowledge of the universe.

Further elaboration on Principle 3 can bring us to a realization that education must now involve a journey into intimacy with the universe. The planetary context for education involves that kind of journey. The western educational tradition has accomplished the polar opposite of intimacy. In truth, our educational journey has been a pilgrimage into estrangement. We have been taught to see ourselves as separate and detached from the natural world. When we talk of our existence, we speak of it as standing out from and separated from the universe and the natural world. Deep ecological perspectives are allied to each other by what they accept and what they reject:

In contrast to reform environmentalism which attempts only to treat some of the symptoms of the environmental crisis, deep ecology questions the fundamental premises and values of contemporary civilization. Our technological culture has co-opted and absorbed all other criticism, so that parts may be questioned but not the whole, while deep ecology as a fountain of revolutionary thought subjects the core of our social existence and our thinking to piercing scrutiny. Deep ecology recognizes that nothing short of a total revolution in consciousness will be of lasting use in preserving the life-support systems of our planet. (Seed and Macy 1988: 38).

In their study of the many facets of deep ecological perspectives, Devall and Sessions (1985) discuss the poet Robinson Jeffers. Noting that Jeffer's poetry was deeply influenced by his place of dwelling on the Californian coastline of the Big Sur, they point out that his poetry gave *voice* to the rivers, mountains and hawks of that coastline. Devall and Sessions quote Jeffers on his view of the world:

I believe that the universe is one being, all its parts are different expressions of the same energy, and they are all in communication with each other, therefore part of one organic whole. (This is physics, I believe, as well religion.) The parts change or pass, or die, people and races and rocks or stars; none of them seems to me important in itself, but only the whole. The whole is in all its parts so beautiful, and is felt by me to be so intensely in earnest, that I am compelled to love it, and to think of it as divine. It seems to me that this whole alone is worthy of the deeper sort of love; and there is peace, freedom, I might say a kind of salvation, in turning one's affections outward toward this one God, rather than inwards on one's self, or on humanity, or on human imaginations and abstractions – the world of spirits. (Devall and Sessions 1985: 101–2)

Jeffers represents a form of pantheism that may be problematic for some readers. This is not the place for discussion of his world view. Nevertheless, we see in his thinking a sense of what I am calling a cosmological horizon.

The movement into the ecozoic age will, of its very nature, be creative in its direction. While we have been speaking about an all-encompassing vision, we must constantly be aware that the emergent evolutionary story is at every level a story of differentiation, subjectivity and communion. The re-enchantment of the natural world will not be accomplished by a return to older ways of thinking and acting in the world. We will not be able to romanticize or imitate indigenous peoples' participatory mystique with the world. We cannot copy world view systems that we do not occupy or live in. We nevertheless must appropriate certain aspects of wisdoms from the past. We must have a sober accounting of the wisdom and sagacity of cultures that have preceded us. Although magic, religion and mystical traditions were prey to errors and follies of the spirit, they nevertheless carried within them a wisdom of the awareness of humanity's organic embeddedness in a complex and natural system. This type of appreciation does not abolish modernity, but it may help us transcend it. The major problem is for us to discover how to recapture older wisdoms in a mature form (Berman 1981; 1989). We are beginning to see such attempts in the re-engagement of aboriginal wisdom seeking to decolonize from the Eurocentric mind-set of western culture (Graveline 1998). Further, modern scientists are beginning to understand that traditional indigenous wisdom is often extremely sophisticated and of considerable practical value. Native science preceding our western systems has developed systems for identifying naming and classifying soils, plants, insects and other elements of local environments, and for deriving medical and economic benefit from them (Knudtson and Suzuki 1992).

Because of the deep understanding of earth processes and a frame of reference which is planetary in vision, it will be both prudent and wise for educators to pay careful attention to indigenous wisdom because of its rich and varied planetary emphasis. At this moment, our cultural history with the indigenous first peoples of the Americas has been marked by arrogance and disrespect for a world view that for the most part we neither understood or appreciated. We are now coming to realize, with the help of postmodern deconstruction, that we have ignored world views that were rich in cosmological significance. The summary above of the world view of indigenous peoples can give us a new appreciation of the historical and contemporary significance of native cosmologies. A postmodern education, embedded in an ecozoic horizon, will engage and tap into the profound significance of indigenous knowledge. It should be of real educational interest to enter into dialogue with world perspectives that have rich cosmologies. The outcome of these dialogues would, no doubt, be open-ended. This type of education would not be a romanticizing of native ways. Rather, it is expected that new and more enriched perspectives will be generated. For our specific educational world view, it will be an opening and appreciation to other world views and other peoples. It will be an exercise in cultural humility that has been too long in coming.

A further dimension of educational vision stems from an assumption that the primary educator is the whole earth community. Our concern for the natural world is based on its utility and we are lacking in a sense that this world of nature in which we are embedded is much more than a utilitarian margin. Disenchantment with the natural world has left us with a view of that world primarily in terms of its physical dimensions. There is a sense of urgency for a wider perspective than the physical because our predominant scientific perspectives have developed an enormous volume of information about the natural world in its physical aspects and our corresponding powers to control it. This is a very one-sided perspective and vision that affects our educational programmes at their deepest levels. What is currently being suggested in educational circles is either traditional or reform principles. As we have already indicated, this deep cosmological awareness is seen most vividly in primal peoples' oral tradition where there is a celebration of the wonders of the natural world. There are also the more celebrated naturalist writers of the North American continent of the nineteenth century and the early part of the twentieth century. These include such men as Thoreau, Whitman, Muir as well as the more recent writings of Edward Abbey (1982) and Aldo Leopold (1949). In this venue we can also include such writers as Barry Lopez (1986), Loren Eiseley (1960; 1972; 1978) and Lewis Thomas (1975; 1980; 1984).

The eco-feminist tradition also appears to carry with it a deep sensitivity for communicating and giving voice to the natural world. One can see this in such diverse writers as the scientist Rachel Carson (1962), the naturalist Annie Dillard (1974; 1983) or the eco-feminist and naturalist Deloris La Chapelle (1988). The latter has developed rituals for bonding with the earth to restore this lost identification with the natural world. When you look at the naturalists who have had notoriety, we see only the presence of men. With the advent of an eco-feminist movement, we are now coming to understand that the voices of women have not been heard. Women poets sensitive to the voices of the natural world seem to abound when one looks carefully. There is now a very powerful woman's voice speaking for the natural world (S. Griffin 1978; 1995). The most recent work of Susan Griffin, *The Eros of Everyday Life* (1995), carries with it a sense of and the necessity for the connecting again to the natural world that I am fostering here. What is important about Griffin's work is how she clearly connects to the natural world and to human social movements. She points out to us a nascent consciousness that is developing between a sense of care for the natural world and a caring for human society:

> If human consciousness can be rejoined not only to the human body but with the body of the earth, what seems incipient in the reunion is recovery of meaning within existence that will infuse every kind of meeting between the self and the universe, even the most daily acts, with an eros, a palpable love, that is sacred. (S. Griffin 1995: 9)

We are now beginning to see that there is a weave of thinking coming from diverse voices that gives a sense of a wider and deeper connection to the earth and its place in the wider story of the universe. Attention to these voices is of the utmost importance for those who pursue alternative visions to the global marketplace. The former view the earth as a sacred presence in the universe; the latter simply treat the earth as dead matter for human exploitation.

What does this suggest to the educational needs of the present moment?

What is needed for a planetary perspective on education, at all levels, is a profound reorientation of our thinking that is symptomatic of a 'paradigm shift'. Robert Ornstein and Paul Ehrlich (1989) suggest that we need a radical shift in our normal way of perceiving ourselves and our environment. They suggest that we have to look at ourselves in the long view and understand an evolutionary history of millions of years, rather than the fleeting history that is taught. Thomas Berry (1988), when addressing education at a post-secondary level, suggests that something akin to the story of the universe would be the proper context of the entire educational process. He suggests a sequence of courses. The first course would present the sequence of evolutionary process phases that the universe story encompasses. Thus, we would see in its expanse, the formation of the galactic systems, the formation of the earth within the solar system, the emergence of life in all its variety upon the earth, and the rise of consciousness and human cultural development.

The second course would address human cultural developments and introduce the learner to envisage a comprehensive human development in its historical stages as well as its cultural differentiation. The learner would be encouraged to see the continuity of his or her own personal development in the prior development of the universe, of the earth, and of all human history. As relates to a planetary consciousness, Berry (1988) maintains that this process of learning encourages the connection of personal identity in historical time and cultural space.

A third course might deal with the differentiated historical aspects of the great classical cultures that have dominated human development over the past several thousand years. Although these cultures have been widely differentiated in the cultural patterns that cover the planet, they have accomplished throughout the Euroasian, American and African worlds certain definitive achievements. In the different parts of the world, a special emphasis could be given to knowledge of the spiritual traditions to which they are heirs.

A fourth course suggested by Berry is the study of the scientific–technological phase of development. What is specifically under observation during this recent phase of history is the dominance of the human over the natural world. This has culminated in a decline in the sense of the numinous aspects of the natural world in favour of a dominant preoccupation with human reason, human power and the mechanistic view of the universe. Correspondingly, it is a period of study which witnesses a profound social consciousness where our globe is affected by political, social, economic and religious adjustments that have shaken the planet with unique severity.

Berry also proposes that the curriculum look closely at what he labels the emerging ecozoic period. Here Berry is asking us to return, in a new way, to a planetary consciousness that challenges the globalization vision that we have been critiquing throughout this work. Berry ventures that study should be directed towards re-establishing the human within its natural context. Within this curriculum there must be an abiding concern for the integral functioning of the biosphere, the healing of the damage already done to the dynamics of the earth, and the fostering of a renewable economic order by integration of the human within the ever-renewing cycles of the natural world, as they are sustained by solar energy.

Finally, a sixth course would address the origin and identification of values. This course would seek to discover within our experience of the universe just what can be the foundation for values. Such a foundation for values would supply a human and planetary context for the creative venture that we are facing. Berry feels that the educational process itself would have, through this overall programme, a cultural, historical and cosmological context of meaning that can be accepted on a broad scale by persons of different ethnic backgrounds.

If we look at the broad thrust of secondary education in western societies, we see how the powerful impact of globalization has penetrated into the dream structure of contemporary education. Public schooling dedicated itself to the needs of nation-states in the past. With the advent of globalization, public schooling has now become a new terrain for the affairs of corporate profit. The recent ascendance of neo-liberal governments, as in the USA, Canada, New Zealand, Mexico and Chile, to name just a few, has seen the advent of the privatization of public schooling. These types of governments have set national agendas which move towards the labour market demands of transnational corporations while, at the same time, relinquishing their commitments to fund public education. This has been leading all sectors of public education towards privatization and slowly but surely bringing education under the hegemony of the corporate agenda. What must be pointed out most forcefully here is the blatant fact that corporate visions are devoid of any semblance of the planetary consciousness that we have been examining in this chapter. It would be fair to say that there is an all convergent literacy encouraged by the global corporate agenda. It is a literacy of profit and the bottom line. Governments that espouse a neo-liberal agenda, like the present Progressive-Conservative government in Ontario, Canada, are attacking traditional education and suggesting that the curriculum be shifted drastically towards corporate needs. An Ontario arts education writer captures the mood:

Welcome to the new educational dogma. Things may be bad in schools, and getting worse, but the sure way to fix them up quick is to get computers ... Business types, futurists and fellow travelers of the $1.4 trillion information technology industry constantly remind us that unless our schools get wired, and fast, our kids will all end up working with squeegees and sleeping under bridges.

If funds were no problem, computers in schools would be an interesting experiment, just as TV and film strips were in the sixties. But in most public schools, buying new expensive technology usually means sitting on something else. (Evereet-Green 1997)

The compromise is frequently done at the expense of arts education, music, outdoor education and environmental education, to name just a few of the casualties.

To foster a transformative education that is embedded in an agenda of 'planetary consciousness', it will of necessity have to be a vision that resists the corporate visions of an infinitely exploitable planet. Much of this resistance education has been suggested in previous chapters. At the same time, a more positive programme for public education must be offered which fosters a sustainable education within a planetary vision.

As with the programmes suggested in higher education, a similar set of concerns is appropriate for secondary level education. This chapter has suggested that all education be couched in a cosmological context. This broadened context immediately frees us from the contemporary stranglehold of the global market. The story of the universe is not a story of markets. It is a dynamic story of origins and creativity. The creativity involved in the telling of the universe story is that we are opened to an educational vision that expands our cultural awareness and gives us a certain freedom of distance from the imperial demands of our present globalization mania. If the universe is taken as the ultimate context of all education, then a course that deals with the unfolding processes of the universe is essential. Related and complementary courses that connect with the universe must also be made available. Astronomy, earth science, evolutionary sciences of life both in chemistry and biology move to a more central stage in a secondary school curriculum context. Historical studies of the earth's history that focus on what native peoples call the circle of life open up a history of diversity that honcurs and identifies the incredible variety of plants and species that inhabit this planet. All courses that address, in some way, a planetary context will also need to accent the interdependence of all life. Time spent in visionary expansion is valuable in its own right. It also serves to counteract the single vision of our current fractured cosmology of mechanism, dominance and exploitation. A planetary consciousness may be built upon by developing courses that examine the planetary consciousness that pervades the mythic structures of American First Nations peoples. A coupling of indigenous science with contemporary earth science is currently a new area of exploration and its outcome should be the subject of courses that deal with planetary concerns.

The area of literacy must also be re-examined in the revisioning of education in our time. The earlier forms of literacy of print and numeracy are still important for education and they are the literacies that are most valued within conventional education. In Chapter 4, we developed the sense of a resistance education under the title of 'media literacy'. In the present context, we are in need of a new literacy focus that relates to planetary concerns. David Orr (1992) uses the term 'ecological literacy' in this regard. Let me say in regard to a literacy of the planet, the last part of this work will be, in part, an exercise in ecological earth literacy.

One very important way to develop an embodied planetary consciousness is to develop a sensitivity to and knowledge of the bio-region in which one is living. I would suggest we put our curriculum education in the context of the bio-region. The emphasis on knowledge of the bio-region is a counterforce to the movement towards globalization because knowledge of local place and context is at the core of a bio-regional emphasis (Sale 1980; 1985; Plant 1989). The context for a bio-regional literacy education is envisioned by the very splendour of earth. In introducing the idea of the bio-region, Thomas Berry (1988) maintains that the earth context not only activates our interior faculties, it also provides our physical nourishment. The air and water and soil and seeds that provide our basic sustenance, the sunshine that pours its energies over the landscape, these are integral with the functioning of the fruitful earth. Physically and spiritually we are woven into this living process. As long as the integrity of the process is preserved, we have air to breathe and water to drink and nourishing food to eat.

The difficulty has come from our subversion of this integral life community, supposedly for our own advantage. In this process we have torn apart the life system itself. Our technologies do not function in harmony with earth technologies. We force the soil with chemicals to produce beyond its natural rhythms. Having lost our ability to invoke natural forces we seek by violence to impose mechanistic patterns on life processes. In consequence of such actions, we now live in a world of declining fertility, a wasted world, a world whose purity and life-giving qualities have been dissipated.

Berry (1988) proposes that we foster an interaction with the earth community as participating members and that we foster the progress and prosperity of the bio-regional communities to which we belong. Here we note that a bio-region is an identifiable geographical area of interacting life systems that is relatively self-sustaining in the ever-renewing processes of nature. The full diversity of life functions is carried out, not as individuals or as species, or even as organic beings, but as a community that includes the physical as well as the organic components of the region. Thomas Berry (1988) identifies the bio-region as self-propagating, self-nourishing, self-educating, self-governing, self-healing and self-fulfilling. He maintains that each of the component life systems must integrate its own functioning within this community to survive in any effective manner.

The first function, self-propagation, requires that we recognize the rights of each species to its habitat, to its migratory routes, to its place in the community. The bio-region is the domestic setting of the community just as the home is the domestic setting of the family. The community continues itself through successive generations precisely as a community. Both in terms of species and in terms of numbers, a certain balance must be maintained. For humans to assume rights to occupy land by excluding other life forms from their needed habitat is to offend the community in its deepest structure. Even further, it is to declare a state of warfare which humans cannot win since they themselves are ultimately dependent on those very life forms that they are destroying.

The second bio-regional function, self-nourishing, requires that the members of the community sustain each other in the established patterns of the natural world for the well-being of the entire community, and each of its members. Within this pattern the expansion of each species is limited by opposing life forms or conditions so that no one life form or group of life forms should overwhelm the others. In this functioning of the community we include, for humans, the entire world of food gathering, of agriculture, of commerce and of economics. The various bio-regional communities of the natural world can be considered as commercial ventures as well as biological processes. Even in the natural world there is a constant interchange of values, the laying up of capital, the quest for more economical ways of doing things. The earth is our best model for any commercial venture. It carries out its operations with an economy and a productivity far beyond that of human institutions. It also runs its system with a minimum of entropy. There is in nature none of that sterile or toxic waste or non-decomposing litter such as is made by humans.

The third function of a bio-region is its self-education through physical, chemical, biological and cultural patterning. Each of these requires the others for its existence and fulfilment. The entire evolutionary process can be considered as a most remarkable feat of self-education on the part of planet earth and of its distinctive bio-regional units. An important aspect of this self-educational process is the experiential mode of its procedures. The earth and each of its bio-regions has performed unnumbered billions of experiments in designing the existing life system. Thus the self-educational processes observed in the natural world form a model for the human. There is presently no other way for humans to educate themselves for either survival or fulfilment than through the instruction available through the natural world.

The fourth function of a bio-region is self-governance. An integral functional order exists within every regional life community. This order is not an extrinsic imposition but an interior bonding of the community that enables each of its members to participate in the governance and to achieve that fullness of life expression that is proper to each. This governance is presided over in much of the world by the seasonal sequence of life expression. It provides the order in which the blossoming and exuberant renewal of life takes place. Humans have traditionally inserted themselves into this community process through their ritual celebrations. These are not simply human activities but expressions of the entire participating community. In human deliberations each of the various members of the community should be represented (T. Berry 1988).

The fifth function of the bio-regional community is self-healing. The community carries within itself not only the nourishing energies that are needed by each member of the community; it also contains within itself the special powers of regeneration. This takes place when forests are damaged by the great storms or when periods of drought wither the fields or when locusts swarm over a region and leave it desolate. In all these instances the life community adjusts itself, reaches deeper into its recuperative powers and brings about a healing. This is done whether the damage is to a single individual or to an entire area of the community. Humans, too, find that their healing takes place through submission to the discipline of the community and partaking of its nourishing and healing powers.

The sixth function of this life community is found in its self-fulfilling activities. The community is fulfilled in each of its components, in the flowering fields, in the great oak trees, in the flight of the sparrow, in the surfacing whale, or in any of the other expressions of the natural world. Then there are the seasonal modes of community fulfilment, the mysterious spring-time renewal. In conscious celebration of the numinous mystery of the universe expressed in the unique qualities of each regional community, the human fulfils its own special role. This is expressed in religious liturgies, in market festivals, in the solemnities of political assembly, in all manner of play, in music and dance, in all the visual and performing arts. Out of all this comes the cultural identity of the bio-region.

A world that will resist and transcend the forces of globalization lies in acceptance and fulfilment of the educational role in all six of these community functions. The change indicated is the change from an exploitative anthropocentrism to a participative biocentrism.

Finally, we turn to elementary education and the world of childhood. We frequently encounter a sense of the world of the child as limited and parochial. Within this conception of the child's horizon we would be led to believe that the child's powers are not developed to encounter the universe. This appears not to be the case. One of our great western childhood educators, Maria Montessori (1973), believed that the child must encounter the universe at the deepest level of its being for deep educational grounding. On first appearances the telling of the 'Great Story of the Universe' may strike some readers as far-fetched as a fundamental objective for the education of young children. However, Maria Montessori encourages a cosmological context as a fundamental theme for the education of children between the ages of six and twelve years. She encourages us to give children a vision of the whole universe. This vision of the whole, demonstrating how all things are part of the universe and connected with each other to form one whole unity was felt by Montessori to be an aid in helping the child's mind to become focused. It also stops children from wandering in an aimless quest for knowledge. What Montessori points out is that without this anchoring there is a loss of a view of the whole that leads to a fragmentation of the child's mind. Children are satisfied when they find that they are centred in a universe and not in their own egocentricity. This centring in the universe story has profound educational consequences:

> If the idea of the universe is presented to the child in the right way, it will do more for him than just to arouse his interest, it will create in him admiration and wonder, a feeling loftier than any interest and more satisfying. The knowledge he then acquires is organized and systematic, his intelligence becomes whole and complete because of the vision of the whole that has been presented to him, and his interests spread to all, for all are linked and have their place in the universe on which his mind is centered. (Montessori 1973: 10)

For Montessori, education that is based within a cosmic story is not something wholly novel to our time. Rather, wherever there has been education in the real sense of the word there is a vital connection to stories that tell of the creation of the world and the place of the human within it. These creation myths can now be developed on a scientific plane that deepens and extends all of their earlier pre-scientific endeavours. Most important, from our sense, is that 'the dream drives the action'. Montessori places a fundamental emphasis on the cultivation of the imagination and particularly on the role of the telling of the universe story. The imaginative vision is quite different from mere object perception, for there are no limits placed on the imagination. It also links the cultivation of the imagination with the intelligence of the learner.

One can also see in the pioneering work of Edith Cobb, in her *The Ecology of Imagination in Childhood* (1977), the importance of the child's sense of the natural world in the development of creative and inspired thinking in adulthood. Through the investigation of memories, Cobb believes that the child appears to have experienced a momentary sense of discontinuity, a revelatory sense of continuity, and an immersion of her whole organism in the outer world of forms and colours and motions in a time dimension that is nonparticularized. Cobb sees this as a natural phenomenon and part of the growing powers of the central nervous system. It is her contention that the child's experience of the sense that time and space have been momentarily suspended appears universally and should not be dismissed as a charming recollection. Although standing alone, this type of study is not definitive, you get the sense when you read the *Oxford Book of Mystical Poetry* that mystical poets such as Blake, Wordsworth, Manley Hopkins and others had similar experiences. Wordsworth's Ode, 'Intimations of Immortality from Recollections of Early Childhood', demonstrates the deeper sense of the cosmic connection of childhood:

> Our birth is but a sleep and a forgetting:
> The Soul that rises from us, our life's Star,
>   Hath had elsewhere its setting,
>   And cometh from afar:
>   Not in entire forgetfulness,
>   And not in utter nakedness,
> But trailing clouds of glory do we come
>   From God, who is our home:
> Heaven lies about us in our infancy!
> Shades of the prison-house begin to close
>   Upon the growing Boy,
> But he beholds the light, and whence it flows,
>   He sees it in his joy;
> The Youth, who daily farther from the East
>   Must travel, still is Nature's Priest,
>   And by the vision splendid
>   Is on his way attended;
> At length the Man perceives it die away,
> And fade into the light of common day.

We can see from this ode the child's expanded horizon. Knowing that this horizon exists, we must be prepared educationally to move within a new vision of earth community. This poses an interesting challenge for educators as to the scope of our sense of community. Charlene Spretnak poses this question to the educator and proceeds to elaborate on her own version of an answer:

What if we were educated to nurture awareness of our inseparable relatedness? In effect, young children would be allowed to continue their natural perception of the world as a realm of inherent relatedness instead of suffering through the educational process of displacing holism with the notion that mind is totally discrete in each of us rather than being immanent in the larger biological network. Young children feel a magical connection with other people, animals, trees, and flowers that could, through the progression of years in a cosmologically grounded educational system, be gradually enlarged to include knowledge of the ways relatedness is explored by mathematics, science, literature, the social sciences, music, fine arts and so forth. (Spretnak 1991: 188–9)

It is not within my expertise to write on how an expanded vision of primary education would be situated within a planetary context. I nevertheless suggest to those interested in this pursuit, that a reading of James Moffett's *The Universal Schoolhouse* (1994) and the groundbreaking work of David Hutchinson (1998) are very helpful in this regard.

Summary

In this chapter I have attempted to offer the reader a context for an educational vision embedded in a functional cosmology that is designed to initiate a deep planetary consciousness. This planetary consciousness attempts to embrace a very different view of the earth than the current view of the planet as a global marketplace. I have emphasized throughout this work the necessity of going beyond educational visions that are embedded in market economy globalization. This is vital because of our cultural addiction in the present moment to a truncated view of our place in the wider universe and to our limited appreciation, as a species, of our place on this earth. It was not my purpose here to offer a facile formula for a new vision of education with planetary sensitivities. At the same time, it is only fair to the reader, after hearing all my criticisms of conventional education, that I offer a provisional story of the universe that offers a vision susceptible to correction and expansion. Because I do my work from a position of privilege, I have been at pains to offer a sense of diversity when venturing an expansive story such as the one I have just suggested. It is important to understand that the location of the story and the telling of it must be kept in mind. I leave open to the reader a point of entry into the story on their own terms. Majority world, minority world, the gendered world, the world as located within class, race and peoples must be taken into account. I have alluded to some of these different locations in this chapter when discussing the world views of indigenous peoples, deep ecologists and eco-feminists.

My next task is to show how the larger arc of the story of the earth is integrally related to the universe story; how both these stories are integral to the development of the human story and our personal stories.

. . . .
Education for Integral Development

This chapter contains a comprehensive discussion of the notion of 'integral development'. The words integral and development have been carefully chosen. In spite of the very critical analysis of the concept of development in Chapter 2, there is still a core need to retain a conception of development in our treatment of a vision of transformative ecozoic education. It is one thing severely to criticize western conceptions of development, it is another to try to conceive of education in the absence of an overarching conception of development. Therefore, if my treatment of education is to include a conception of development, it will be necessary to articulate it in a way that transcends the limitations of western ideas. What I intend to do in this chapter, then, is to present 'integral development' and link it to the creative evolutionary processes of the universe, the planet, the earth community, the human community and the personal world. Integral development must be understood as a dynamic wholeness where wholeness encompasses the entire universe and vital consciousness resides both within us and, at the same time, all around us in the world. Development therefore involves our entry into this larger soul of the world or the *anima mundi* (Sardello 1994).

The fundamental idea of development presumes that all living processes are always in dynamic states of growth, decay and transformation. The ideas of evolution and development are different sides of an underlying dynamic. Evolution basically means that all living forms evolve and exceed themselves. Development connotes the dynamic energy that drives the movement of evolving forms. The word growth is used in tandem with development when evolving forms move to higher levels of complexity and integration and can be seen as such. I use the term integral development rather than holistic or integrated development because of the creative dynamic and evolving nature of the processes. The term holistic places an undue emphasis on harmony and integration. My sense of the term integral is that it connotes a dynamic evolving tension of elements held together in a dialectical movement of both

harmony and disharmony. An integral model of development will be generative and open-ended, offering an understanding of evolutionary processes
that includes a critical role for stress in the transformation of evolving systems.
Here, I am drawing on the theory of 'dissipative structures' presented by Illya
Prigogine and Isabelle Stengers (1984) in initiating a new science of wholeness
based on chaos.

To understand the fundamental nature of Prigogine and Stenger's theory
of dissipative structures, we must proceed with the assumption that all evolving
forms are open systems whose forms or structures are maintained by a
continuous dissipation (consumption) of energy. Dissipative structures are
based on what Prigogine and Stengers call the principle of order through
fluctuation. From an evolutionary point of view, these fluctuations explain
irreversible processes in nature and movement through ever higher orders of
life. All systems, including human beings, contain sub-systems that are continually fluctuating. All dissipative structures can well be described as an
integral system of *flowing wholeness*. Integral development refers to a pattern
of linking processes involved in the organization of a system or structure. We
can observe that any living system is connected at various points; the more
complex the living dissipative structure, the more energy is required to
maintain its connections. Any system at any given moment can operate in a
state of equilibrium or dis-equilibrium. The continuous flow of energy through
a system creates fluctuations within it, many of which are absorbed or adjusted
to without altering the system's structural integrity. But, if the fluctuations in
the system reach a critical level, the system becomes sufficiently turbulent so
that the old connecting points no longer work; the system transforms itself
into a higher order, one with new and different connecting points. The
dissipation of energy creates the potential for a sudden reordering of the
system. The parts reorder into a new whole and the system escapes into a
higher order. Each new level is more integrated and connected than the
preceding one and requires a larger flow of energy to maintain it. Every time
there is a transformation, the system becomes still less stable and therefore
more susceptible to further change (Prigogine and Stengers 1984). One can
say here that development promotes further development.

Following from these current ideas on evolutionary processes we can now
appreciate the need to keep some conception of development in mind even
though, in some ways, our western use of the idea has brought it into
disrepute.

Integral development and creativity

Thomas Berry's (1989) fifth principle deals with development and creativity.
The universe has a violent as well as a harmonious aspect; but it is consistently

creative in the larger arc of its development. Evolution does not carry its venture, so to speak, in a placid unfolding of structures. It appears that the processes of evolution are carried out as a dynamic emergence that entails both stability and disequilibrium. From our previous discussion of dissipative systems theory, we understand that when a system reaches beyond its present structure towards new orders of self-organization, it becomes creative in its self-organizing. This creative process of self-organization is called autopoiesis. Autopoiesis refers to the characteristic of living systems to renew themselves continuously and to regulate this process in such a way that the integrity of the structure is maintained (Jantsch 1984). It is helpful, at this point, to link the wider connection of our meaning of integral development with the expansive processes of creativity embedded in the unfolding of the universe story.

The entire creative sequence of evolutionary development, from the beginning, is revealed in the three basic principles as set out by Thomas Berry (1989). To reiterate, the three basic principles are differentiation, subjectivity and communion. These three principles exist as dynamic emergent evolutionary processes and, at a most fundamental level, define the very essence of creativity itself. When we are talking about contemporary creativity we note that it consists of activating, expressing and fulfilling the universe process, the earth process, the life process and the human process within the possibilities of the historical moment. Our own historical moment demands that we come to grips with the self-regulating autopoietic processes of our planetary system. As humans, we are now in need of a consciousness that allows us to see our self-regulation within the larger autopoietic processes of the earth which is our matrix or, if you will, our mother. Our treatment of the idea of integral development is to see it initially within the light of principles of differentiation, subjectivity and communion.

The universe did not become a homogeneous smudge, but a world of identifiable and structured beings radiant with inner intelligibility and individual identity. What is essentially implied by this principle, the principle of differentiation, is sensitivity to variety in all levels of the evolutionary process. The principle of subjectivity points to the interiority of differentiated processes. While differentiation distinguishes from others, subjectivity gives the interior identity and formation, the inner spontaneity, the in-dwelling self of every being, its immediacy with ultimate mystery. Subjectivity expresses the autopoietic nature of living things. Out of this inner world of self-regulation comes the freedom which is so minimal in its earlier physical expression that it seems non-existent although its presence is revealed as the ascending sequence, as developments take place leading to the variety of living forms and eventually to the human where inner freedom of a high order is attained.

It is within the context of the human that the principle of subjectivity takes on a psychological context. Certainly the domain of phenomenological psychology is most closely connected with aspects of subjectivity and consciousness (O'Sullivan 1990). Nevertheless, it is appropriate to include the area of cognitive developmental psychology within our framework of subjectivity. Here we are talking about the seminal work of Chomsky in language, Piaget in cognitive development and Kohlberg in the area of moral development (see O'Sullivan 1990). The problem that we find with all of the above is that there is not a deeply relational quality to their theories and they collapse the element of community which is our third fundamental principle. Thus, psychology as it is developed currently absolutizes subjectivity to the detriment of differentiation and community.

Finally, the principle of communion is pervasive in the emergent evolution of the universe. Already there is by force of gravity, and of other energy bonds, a communion of articulated realities of the universe. The atomic structure within itself is a communion of particles. So with the stars in their galaxies, so with the components of the planet earth, so with the variety of living forms which are interwoven in an enduring web of life. So, too, with the human. As with differentiation and subjectivity, so with communion. This attains its highest expression in human consciousness, in the centre of emotional attraction, and in human aesthetic feeling. We cannot underestimate how important our sense of communion is for the deeper needs of our very existence. It is fundamentally important to understand what the loss of communion means for us in our daily living. The intricacy of our personal world is embedded in community. Much of our existence finds ultimate fulfilment in relatedness. We can see this in the intricate mating rituals the natural world has invented. So much of the plumage, coloration and dance and song of the world comes from our relationships of true intimacy. The energy that we and other animals bestow on this work of relatedness of being, the attention that we give to our physical appearance alone, reveals the ultimate meaning of the communion experience.

Integral development and the self-regulating dynamics of the earth system

In our modern western scientific heritage, we have looked upon the earth as a dead entity that was totally susceptible to human control and artifice. We are just beginning to become conscious of the fact that the earth has a deeper evolutionary trajectory that goes well beyond any human designs that we have had on it. Our most recent scientific knowledge has brought us to an understanding about our planet that reveals a much more subtle capacity for autopoiesis and self-regulation. The Gaia hypothesis serves as an example to illustrate this point. Formulated by the British biochemist James Lovelock

(1979; 1988), it states that the planet earth is a living entity with its own unique self-organizing and self-regulating powers. The self-regulating powers of the earth are seen through the regulation of its vital signs; specifically, through the regularity of the earth's surface temperature. It appears that the average temperature of the earth varies between 60 and 100 degrees Fahrenheit. Despite drastic changes in the atmosphere, the average temperature has remained within the above range for hundreds of millions of years. If at any time in the earth's history the temperature went beyond these limits the earth would have extinguished.

The stabilization of oxygen concentration within the earth's atmosphere is about at the level of 21 per cent. It seems that this optimal balance is necessary for the maintenance of life. If the atmospheric content of oxygen was below the 21 per cent level, the larger animals and insects would not have had the energy for survival. If the oxygen content of the atmosphere rose above the 21 per cent level damp vegetation would burn.

It also appears that there is regulation of the amount of salt in the oceans. Currently the oceans contain about 3.4 per cent salt. This particular figure has remained constant even though salt is constantly being washed away by rivers. If the figure had gone above or below the limit of 3.4 per cent, life on earth would be radically different and most likely would have been extinguished.

The presence of a small quantity of ammonia in the atmosphere is needed to neutralize the strong sulphuric and nitric acids. The result of this neutralization is that rain and soil remain at optimal levels of acidity for the preservation of life.

Finally, the existence of the ozone layer in the earth's upper atmosphere shields life on the surface of the earth from the damaging effects of ultraviolet radiation which damages the molecules essential for life.

Lovelock's (1979; 1988) postulation of the Gaia hypothesis is just one example of how the earth operates in a self-regulating capacity. Some would argue that the maintenance of life on our planet has been the result of coincidence rather than the homeostatic self-regulating processes of the earth. If we liken the earth's homeostatic systems to our own bodily functions, then coincidence seems to be stretching the point. Our own bodies behave in a well-ordered manner and, it would appear, with purpose. Sweating, eating, shivering and breathing appear to be coordinated integral processes that preserve our homeostasis and help us to survive and grow. Since these autopoietic processes work at the level of body functioning, it certainly does not seem far-fetched for Lovelock to suggest that similar processes are self-regulating at the level of the planet. The Gaia hypothesis advanced by Lovelock assumes that the earth is a self-regulating, self-sustaining system, continually adjusting its chemical, physical and biological processes in order to support life and its continuing evolution.

At this point I would like to consider the activities of the human species within the self-regulating dynamics of our planet. If we consider our current human presence on this earth, then the reader can entertain our interacting activities with the earth from the point of view of dissipative systems dynamics discussed previously. Peter Russell, in *The Global Brain*, makes the following observation:

> Looking at humanity from the perspective of dissipative systems, we can see that the two principal characteristics of a major fluctuation seem to be present: increasing through flow of energy and matter, combined with high entropy. We are now consuming energy and matter like never before, with all the ensuing problems of resource scarcity and depletion. At the same time, the entropy produced by humanity has shot up, resulting in increasing disorder both within society and the environment. (Russell 1983: 65–6)

Russell believes that the human presence on this earth appears to be rapidly approaching the breaking point moving towards two possible outcomes: breakdown or breakthrough. It has been one of the assumptions of this book that we are in a period of high dissipation that I have labelled the terminal cenozoic. We must understand both the promise and the precariousness of our situation. If we have a breakthrough we will embark on a new system of integral development that I have indicated to be an ecozoic period. If we are going to move in this direction, we will have to cast off the old systems of development that have treated our earthly matrix in a manner which now jeopardizes our continuing presence on this planet. Our human intentions for an integral development that will allow us to bring forth our species project in a mutually enhancing human–earth relationship demands that we become acutely aware of the powerful self-regulating activities that are inherent in the evolutionary processes of earth activities. Thomas Berry's sixth principle (1989) addresses the nature of the earth's autopoiesis. He suggests that the earth, within the solar system, is a self-emergent, self-propagating, self-nourishing, self-educating, self-governing, self-healing, self-fulfilling community. Furthermore, all particular life systems must integrate their functioning within this larger complex of mutually dependent earth systems. The earth is thus a dynamic and organized entity in the universe with its own centre of organization and development.

The earth as *self-nourishing* is based on our understanding that the universe is energy in action. In defining the earth within the solar system we need to think in terms of what the earth does. Most fundamentally, the earth within the solar system nourishes itself. All nourishment is the earth/sun system consuming itself. The sunlight born of the stellar nuclear fusion becomes the green leaf, the root and flowering fruits, that become the flesh and blood of animals, that become the constelled genetic strands of the prokaryotes, that become the elements of the air, that turn into the leaf lit by the sun. Oak tree and whales and penguins and the grasses sprout into existence through participation in these cycles of self-nourishment that form the earth/sun system, where what is waste for one species becomes nourishment for another, so that the circle of life endlessly repeats in an unbroken sequence of transformation.

The earth as *self-educating* assumes that learning via evolutionary processes is a self-educating process. It is precisely the educational dimension of earth that provides it with such radiance and splendour when compared to any other planet. This genetic probing and sensitivity and capacity for remembering can be considered our supreme power; and, as humans with our prolonged period of learning, we need especially to reflect on the nature of education which takes place as part of the community process.

The earth as *self-governing* indicates that the earth community must integrate the human species with the enveloping earth community; the integration beginning with a comprehensive respect for each species within the life world. The natural world before emergence of the human was a totally participatory community of qualitatively different species. Each species governs the whole and is governed by the whole.

Finally, the earth as *self-healing* signifies that the earth community carries within itself unique powers of regeneration. The healing of the earth community has two basic dimensions that are intertwined: there is a need for the healing of the earth as a whole, and there is the need for the healing of the human considered as a particular species. In both of these related endeavours, the context for healing is the universe as a whole. The powers of healing, the powers of regeneration and the powers of renewal are rooted in the primordial realities of the universe, the earth and the human species.

Human emergence and integral development

We must understand our human presence on this earth as an integral part of the evolutionary processes of the universe and the evolution of planet earth. In Thomas Berry's (1989) seventh principle of the universe, there is an articulation of human emergence. According to Berry, the human emerges within the life systems of the earth as that being in whom the universe reflects on and celebrates itself in a special mode of conscious self-awareness. The human is genetically coded towards a further transgenetic cultural coding invented by the human community in a remarkable diversity in the various regions of the earth. This diversity of cultural elaboration in the various peoples of the earth is communicated to succeeding generations by both formal and informal educational processes.

Humans emerge in the processes of evolution as a species unique to planet earth. In broad evolutionary terms, humans are a one-time, one-place species.

In saying this we acknowledge that the human being emerges at a specific time in the development of the universe and also is restricted to a particular place. When we say place we acknowledge that humans are uniquely creatures of the planet earth. This means that in the unfolding of the universe humans emerge at a specific time and place. We, as a species, are peculiar creatures of planet earth. We are the creation, in time, of the earth's unique unfolding. While we say that the earth is a one-time, one-place event in the evolution of the universe, we can also say that the human species is unique in its time and place in the cosmic unfolding. Not until the earth is saturated with life in such a dazzling complexity of form could something like the human arise. The human being is not only an earthling through and through in the sense that every molecule and every organ and every physiological action pattern has been woven out of the living strands of our planet; it is also true to say that the human being is a time-specific expression of the earth in its luscious existence 4 million years ago, when the continents had reached an eco-systemic complexity never before attained and, for all we know, never again to be experienced. Out of a paradise of beauty and elegance, the earth seemed to have surpassed itself again in an ecstatic self-display that we call the human.

The earth is the central locus of the evolutionary process within our planetary system. It appears that the possibility for the earth was contained in the evolution of the galaxies and the elements; second, we see its actual birth in the evolution of the solar system; third, it is the container for life in all its variety; and fourth, it generates the evolution of consciousness and the cultural developments of the human order.

It is especially important in this discussion to recognize the unity of this total process from that first unimaginable moment of cosmic creation until the present. This unbreakable bond of relatedness is increasingly apparent to scientists, although it ultimately escapes scientific formulation or understanding. By virtue of this relatedness, everything is intimately present to everything else in the universe. Nothing is completely itself without everything else. This unity prevails over the boundaries of space and time. The universe is both communion and community. We ourselves are that communion in a special mode of reflective awareness.

The invention of human community Instinctively, humans perceived themselves as a mode of being of the universe as well as distinctive beings in the universe. This is what we mean when we say existence. The emergence of the human was a transformative moment for the earth as well as for the human. As with every species, there was a need to establish its niche, a sustainable position in the larger community of life, the need for food and shelter and for clothing. There was need for security, the need for family and community context. This need for community was quite special in the case of humans since humans articulate a unique mode of being, a capacity for thought and speech, aesthetic appreciation, emotional sensitivities and moral judgement. These combine in a cultural shaping which establishes the human in its specific identifying qualities.

Whatever the cultural elaboration of the human, its basic physical as well as psychic nourishment and support came from the surrounding natural environment. Human society in its beginnings was integral with the larger life society and the larger earth community composed of all the geological, biological and human elements. Just how long this primordial harmony of the very early period endured we do not know beyond the last 100,000 years of the Palaeolithic period. Some 10,000 years ago, the Neolithic and then the classical civilizations came into being. It must suffice here to indicate that with the classical and generally literate civilizations of the past 5,000 years, the great cultural worlds of the human developed, along with vast and powerful social establishments whereby humans became oppressive and even destructive of other life forms.

We must be very aware, at this time of our earth history, that the human presence on this earth has taken on a variety and diversity of forms through its brief evolutionary history. We seem to be an open-ended species that has the capacity for the invention of ourselves along a number of different paths. The reason that I am stressing the inventiveness of human–earth relationships is to have the reader sensitized to the fact that we have invented and reinvented ourselves many times during the course of our brief history on this earth. Today we need to be able to project a new vision of ourselves in relation to our presence on this earth. In our modern era, we have invented tools and devices that are bringing us to a disastrous scenario within the earth context. Our hope, in this moment, is that we will be able call upon our capacities of invention and creativity in order to forge a presence that is mutually enhancing in terms of an integral human–earth relationship.

That the human emerges out of the planetary process and is dependent on the planetary process in its basic laws of development is quite evident, especially during the earlier phases of the human enterprise. More so than other life forms, the human had to discover its proper identity and its role within the earth process and within the life community, both by instinct and by thought processes. Humans needed to frame for themselves some sense of the natural world, how it came into being, how it functioned, and what the proper role of the human might be. These perceptions were presented in stories that narrated the creation of the universe and the events leading up to the present. Within this context the human could proceed with its self-identification, and establish patterns of action coordinated with the surrounding universe.

The difference in these stories resulted from and further enhanced the distinctive life styles whereby various peoples related to each other, to the natural world about them, and to the numinous powers that provided their ultimate explanation for the emergence of the universe and for its patterns of activity. Through their various myths and through their rituals, based largely on the seasonal transformations of the natural world, the various societies established their functional presence within the surrounding universe. The differences in these myths and rituals reflect the diversity of life experience of the various peoples and the special features of the geographical region they inhabited.

Neolithic invention In Principle 8, domestication represents a transition from an integral presence in the natural world to the beginnings of permanent villages and control over the forces of the earth through agriculture and domestication of animals (T. Berry 1989). The advent of the invention of domestication appears to be about 12,000 years ago.

With the emergence of language, the history of the human community has been a search for an appropriate cultural niche in the earth's life. This search for an ecological niche raises some fundamental issues as to where human beings are in the natural order. With domestication we see a process of development in humans attempting to forge a place within the natural world (Swimme and Berry 1992). We must attend to some historical aspects of domestication in order to underline its importance. We are able to estimate that the first humans on earth were hunters and gatherers who travelled in groups of between twenty and forty members. The time frame for humans in this phase takes us back 20,000 years. At this point we see a dramatic change taking place that affected the presence of the human for ever as regards their relationship to the natural world. A new power was exercised by the human; one with profound consequences that altered the history of the earth. We are referring here to the human's power to domesticate the world in specific ways. Domestication, in simple terms, involves the altering of the genetic structure of plants and animals. At the outset, this altering of the genetic structure was carried out without conscious awareness or forethought. But if one looks at the history of domestication into the present, what is involved is a dramatic reversal in forethought so that we now have an incredibly well-developed science of 'genetic engineering'. At the beginning, we could call the origins of domestication humble. The first animal domestication took place probably 20,000 years ago. With the knowledge that the modern-type human goes back 50,000 years and the understanding that little or no cultivation occurred in the first 30,000 years, one can begin to appreciate the advance in human understanding required for domestication to take place.

In its embryonic stages, domestication was nothing more than a hunter's preference for a particular animal or species of animal. Domestication further developed when humans began to breed the animals *per se*.

In a similar manner, the early humans' gathering of plants and seeds proceeded to the point where the connection was made between plants' small fluffs and the next season's plants. What began as a most natural event – a shadowing of a herd, casting seeds – ended in the complete transformation of the planet. The human species is the only species on the planet earth that has developed domestication into a systematically controlled science. Genetic engineering is nothing more than a more completely controlled example of domestication. What nature did spontaneously, humans now must do with complete deliberation and the expenditure of physical and psychic energy, leading to those social stresses we find at the present time. Here is the place where the human species has found difficulty in establishing a proper niche for itself in the natural world. Because of the difficulty in finding a niche in the natural world, humans are sometimes referred to as *natural aliens* (Evernden 1983). Domestication, in its totality, has become a two-edged sword. As humans provided themselves with foods and other materials for the enhancement of their lives, they simultaneously stripped the earth of its wild vitality. For example, compare here the characteristics of wild versus tamed (domesticated) species of animals. Through the process of domestication, we have conscious, self-reflexive awareness that can be considered creative in so far as a wide variety of species of plants and animals were created. Alternatively, the wilderness of 4 billion years was replaced by a bovine plasticity of domesticated species (Swimme and Berry 1992). With the transformation of the genetic structures of plants and animals, we can see that the human species also alters its nature in some fundamental sense. We see with domestication a transformation, the magnitude of which alters the very nature of the human community. It is precisely because domestication led to different species, to different relationships between the human and the non-human, to different relationships between humans *per se*, to different destinies for animal species, to different destinies for the plant world, and to different destinies for the human worlds, that one can regard the dynamic of domestication as one of macro-transitions of the universe. Indeed, with the scientific development of genetic engineering we have a further intrusion of the human into natural processes. It is a profound responsibility to have developed the capability to alter radically life's processes.

The classical civilizations The domestication process continued into what has come to be known as 'civilization'. The ninth principle opens up a discussion of the classical civilizations (T. Berry 1989). The most distinctive developments that took place in this transitional period occurred in the region known as Old Europe, an oval-shaped region with its axis from the mid-Italian peninsula across to the Dneiper river, an area identified in some detail in the studies of Maria Gimbutas (1974) and the commentaries of Riane

Eisler (1988). Here, for several thousand years from around 6500 BC to 3500 BC a civilization evolved that was apparently lacking in the aggressive warring qualities and the social oppression we see in later civilizations that began further to the East. The weapons and walls of these civilizations to the East seem to have been missing in the early period before the advent of what is labelled western European civilization. The social structure and functioning of these goddess-oriented civilizations seem to have been more integral in terms of their masculine–feminine relationships. These were also more participatory societies when compared with societies embedded in hierarchical structures.

Besides its social achievements, this period was distinguished by its high intellectual and cultural attainments as well by its artistic accomplishments and its highly developed mythic and ritual self-expression. This early civilization reached its height in Crete in the fourth century BC. Its historical significance is such that a reappraisal of the cultural possibilities of the human in terms of its capacity for peaceful self-expression needs to be undertaken. The civilization of this period provides a standard against which later civilizations need to be judged. In its fullest expression, the Cretan civilization may have reached a height of humanity that has never been surpassed in the western world in its aesthetic qualities, the well-being of the people, its social harmony, and the sublimity of its mythic and ritual self-expression. That this was a goddess-oriented civilization is especially significant (Eisler 1988). The civilizations that follow move in a very different path. It is not our purpose to articulate a historical treatment of the many early civilizations. These civilizations take us back to Sumer and through early European and native civilizations in various parts of the world. It takes us through all of the modern religions. What is important here is that the entire sequence of changes be understood as the interval between the beginnings of domestication until the rise of the sciences. It is the rise of the world view that would henceforth begin the final subjection of the land sphere, the water sphere, the atmosphere and the life sphere by the mind-space.

Apart from the earlier developments of Old Europe, especially the brilliant developments in Crete, the period of the classical civilizations extended from 3500 BC until AD 1600. This civilizational period of the past 5,000 years can now be seen in its comprehensive dimensions as an identifiable part of the human process which exists within the parameters of the late Neolithic period dated some 5,000 years ago, and the scientific–industrial age that begins some 300 years ago.

This period should be considered as a biological phase in earth history, since the civilizational process is a transformation not only of the human but also of the ecosystems of the planet. The classical period constitutes a 5,000-year phase of earth history, a period when the life of the continents as well as the structures and functioning of these life systems were severely influenced by human presence. The civilizational process introduces a new phase in the history of the earth. All these various developments need to be kept in mind since the planet earth, as an integral mode of being, is affected in its entirety by the transformations that take place in any of its parts.

The modern world The tenth principle opens the discussion of the modern western world (T. Berry 1989). In the movement into the modern world starting in the sixteenth and seventeenth centuries, the western world entered upon an investigation of the earth and universe that would come to surpass in significance all other such investigations carried out in earlier times. However irreplaceable the insights and perspectives of the classical civilizations, here was a new form of knowledge, one that went beyond the horizons of traditional thought. We have extensively discussed this particular horizon as modernist thought in Chapter 3. We have already indicated that the modernist world view has had a profound effect on our orientation towards the natural world. Modernist thought has been especially effective in penetrating into the physical dynamics of the universe. We can now conclude the modern scientific enterprise brought human understanding to a point where humans now had to confront the possibility of finally and fully understanding the actual dynamics of the universe, not by means of pure fancy, or idle speculation, or mythic invention, or abstract philosophy, but by means of a rational quantitative theory tied to and refined by the actual empirical data.

Modernism began with this storm of confidence issuing forth when Europeans found the way in to a new understanding of the universe. We have already seen that the change in consciousness resulting from the modernist outlook demanded that traditional knowledge as well as traditional ways of obtaining knowledge were either thrown into question or fully rejected. Scientific knowledge led to a frustration of pre-modern societies everywhere. Science came to be an adversary to religion, a cause of moral breakdown, a disruption of ancient social orders, as well as a source of psychological confusion and emotional upset. Modernism, coming through the scientific enterprise, destroyed or skewed pre-modern economics, law and politics.

The full significance of the scientific venture is multivalent and full of contradictions and paradox. The scientific approach to knowledge had an aggressive dimension from the very beginning. The mechanistic orientation of much of modern science swept the world clear of all soul and thus eliminated for centuries the emotionally rich communion experience pre-modern peoples enjoyed in the natural world. And by conceiving the world as a machine, humans shaped by modern science were free to manipulate nature in any way they wished without regard for the non-human world. With the culmination of modernism we are left in the midst of the single greatest transformation of consciousness to take place since the human species emerged, certainly a transformation as significant as that which took place with the rise of the great civilizations. This experience of the great event which is the universe, of the great event which is the earth, and of the great event which is the human form of life, is an experience of such impact as to alter human consciousness on a scale associated with the classical revelation experiences of the past whereby the earlier cultural codings had been established.

The transformation to time-developmental consciousness can be considered a mutation moment in the earth–human order. A new paradigm or world view of what it is to be human has emerged, and that is why it is so exiting and painful and disruptive. One can consider this a mutation event of the entire order because even though the knowledge originally came out of a western cultural context, it is not related to any traditional culture. It is sustained on its own evidence and has attained a universal significance. The transformation can be understood as an advance in the control of energies. From the earliest control of animal muscle, we moved to exploiting wind and river power, to the use of steam, to the exploitation of the fire in petroleum, to control of the nuclear energies, and now to a control of the genetic orderings. These changes profoundly transformed the social fabric among humans and just as dramatically altered the bondedness between humans and the non-human world. It is probable that the industrial transformation with its movement to the cities, with its pervasive bureaucratization, with its massive shift away from the soil and the seasonal rhythms and into the factory and its machinery is the most extensive transformation of the human adventure. Even the transition out of the wilds and into a domesticated way of life does not rival modernity's claim as humanity's most disjunctive change.

Presently the human community is so involved in scientific and technological processes that we cannot withdraw even though the desirable achievements are now discovered to be inseparable from a multitude of undesirable effects. Marvellous advantages have accrued to human life through these instrumentalities along with enormous difficulties. Indeed, it is from the remarkable achievements of science and technology that many of our present difficulties arise. This can be seen in the population increase that has taken place throughout the world. This itself has led, at least temporarily, to further impoverishment and even to an impasse in our efforts to advance human welfare. With all of this taken into account, when we consider the deterioration of the biosphere of the earth along with the deterioration in many phases of human life in recent decades, serious questions arise as to the larger meaning of science and technology, and the manner in which they might function in the future if further deterioration of the human quality of life is to be avoided and improvement brought about.

Postmodern development   In my opening chapters, I located our present historical state as that of the terminal cenozoic stage within a larger arc of earth
history that has spanned the human and the pre-human. The appearance of
the human in the evolutionary flow of the earth's creative development has
been characterized by diverse forms of human participation within the earth's
processes. As we have just seen, our modern forms of human participation
with the earth have become problematic and dysfunctional. Our modern
human presence now appears to have disrupted our integral connection to the
larger earth processes. Our present systems of development have put us out of
phase with the larger evolutionary processes of the earth proper. Our present
terminal stage can be characterized as one of high entropy and dissipation.
Industrial exploitation has ravaged the planet. Thousands of poisons and toxic
substances are saturating the air, the water and the soil. The increasing harm
done to the natural world on a comprehensive scale is beginning to threaten
the human species itself.

We have said that at this time in the evolution of the planet the planetary
crisis is a consequence of our own limited awareness. The identification of
the person with the planet comes from a heightened awareness that one's
personal identity is intertwined with the planet and with the universe as a
totality. All of the major religions point to an intimate relationship between
the person and the cosmos. We are, thus, able to say that personal development is integrally related to planetary development. The integral connections
that we have had within the earth matrix in the past appear to have broken
and are fragmented. We must understand the precarious nature of the human
project at this point and, at the same time, take full responsibility for its
ultimate outcome. Our responsibilities must be taken into our conscious
awareness and followed through with the resolve that it is the fundamental
educational commitment for our time.

Integral human development

Integral human development allies the deepest development of the primordial self with the deep structure of the cosmos. It is an incredible realization
that you and I were present back there in the primordial fireball. There is a
type of biological remembering within our mother's womb that reminds us
that we have worn vestigial gills and tails and fins for hands. At this moment,
our very being is a presence of the past (Sheldrake 1988). We have within us
a deep wisdom and bondedness with our incredible evolutionary history and
a creativity within which we draw, from moment to moment, that has an
ingenuity that should astound and humble us.

As we have indicated, our recent past has witnessed an eclipse of a cosmological sense. In this context the development of a framework of value suffered

the limitations of the restricted world view that modernism stands for in the present. Ethics within this context were anthropomorphic. I believe that the cosmological dimensions of the universe story demand a new value synthesis which specifies an ethical coding consistent with the cosmological story. What is required, at this point, is an ethical approach that can work for the species as a whole. We need a series of guidelines for our reflections that can be held in common by humans everywhere, regardless of race, culture or societal status. How is this to be accomplished?

Within the context of the universe story, the good or moral action is that which enhances, amplifies or completes the development of the earth and universe towards differentiation, subjectivity and community. Activities which retard, obstruct or obliterate the differentiation, subjectivity and community are considered to be actions of questionable value. What can be seen in this orientation is that the meaning of moral action is not restricted to the human but encompasses all aspects of the earth community. Thus, the ethical is framed within a functional cosmology that issues from the larger universe and earth story. The cosmological task embedded in the process of *differentiation* is to articulate in the most developed sense who we are as persons and who we are as specific communities. We may, therefore, say that each person has a genius and destiny that must be expressed. Additionally, each community has a genius and destiny that must be given form. This destiny is an open destiny and is not pre-formed. The radical nature of differentiation is the creativity which brings with it the burden of being and becoming, different from everything else in the universe. We may add that to become oneself as a person or community is to become distinct, unique in different ways from all that exists in the present and all that has existed in the past or that will exist in the future. This means that what a person brings to any relationship can be given by no one else in the universe. The same can be said for communities. Each individual or community contributes a unique quality to every relationship it enters (Swimme and Berry 1992).

The ethical imperative of *subjectivity* has two tasks for its fulfilment. The first is to activate the full range of sentience proper to the human. Humans as a species enter the world dramatically incomplete. Our full development is completed through a lifetime of development. Development for humans means that human sensitivities are awakened and deepened through training so that we too can feel the universe. The second task is fulfilling the need for a more complete agency as accomplished through a deepening of our sensitivities. Complete agency means that through our development and fulfilment we become autonomous centres of agency. The development of this autonomy means that we as persons take ourselves seriously concerning our destinies as creators of the universe. We now can see that our evolution as a species has a very powerful effect. We are co-creators of the universe. The universe, at all times and in its full plenitude, can come into action as each particular person and only as such particular beings. We need to sink our hands into this power with an awareness of its meaning within the earth as a whole instead of relegating such power away or trivializing it or pretending that it does not exist (Swimme and Berry 1992).

Finally, *community* becomes an ethical imperative in the cosmological sense by our understanding that every human needs to become directly aware of our bonded relationships throughout the universe, especially in a direct way throughout our places of habitation. To discover that the realities of this bondedness sink into the shape of our central nervous systems, into the layered intelligence of our bodies – both the individual body and the ecosystem body – is to discover that all of the universe is bonded together in a deep mystery of communion. To enter into the relatedness does not mean to enter harmony. There are relationships formed out of disagreements, out of conflicts, out of fear. Nevertheless, within even difficult relationships, there is the capability for proceeding creatively. In the tension of difficulties and disagreements a creative advance can result. We need this ability for relating in times of disagreements as well as in times of harmony.

At the human level, this task of relatedness is a supreme challenge, for human society's enduring existence depends upon bonded face-to-face relationships. Much of civilization and of religion is primarily concerned with extending capacities for relationships. We need to develop our capabilities for entering relatedness throughout the range of human interaction, and for entering participatory relationships with the deep powers of the universe.

The present institutions of modernism have fostered a deeply truncated sense of the self that has caused great suffering, alienation and fragmentation in our century (Bellah 1985). Christopher Lasch (1978) characterizes this nihilist self-encapsulation as the 'minimal self'. What is more, the link between the minimal self and the mechanistic view of the world has very profound implications on how the natural world is experienced and acted upon from an educational perspective. From the mechanistic and individualistic world view, that creates nature as a mechanism, we ultimately see the subversion of the integral life community, supposedly for our own advantage. In the process we have torn apart the life system itself. Our technologies do not function in harmony with earth technologies. With chemicals we force the soil to produce beyond its natural rhythms. Having lost our ability to invoke natural forces, we seek by violence to impose mechanistic patterns on life processes. In consequence of such actions, we now live in a world of declining fertility, a wasted world, a world in which its purity and life-giving qualities have been dissipated. This dissipation that we now experience as the environmental crisis is more than a technological crisis at its deepest level. The position of individualism and the framing of the world from the 'minimal self' is a crisis of meaning encountered in the lost cosmological sense encountered at the end of the late cenozoic period. At a fundamental level, the defence of the environment is a defence of the cosmos, not solely a defence of scenery (Evernden 1985).

The primal matrix: the personal world as a relational totality

When we look carefully at the development of western social and political theory with its strong emphasis on the autonomous growth of individual monads, then it should not come as a surprise that our theories and practices designed to understand the personal world will be skewed towards a conception that bears the marks of the 'minimal self'. I have strongly argued in my own work on critical psychology (O'Sullivan 1984; 1990) that the personal world must be seen at its deepest level as a relational totality. For me the basic idea behind the person as a relational totality is that there is no sense of the person without the sense of the presence of community. Personal development is a complex process that involves the intricate dynamic relations of differentiation, subjectivity and communion.

To commence with a discussion of the development of the personal world and to embed it within the matrix of community, it is necessary to introduce the notion of reciprocity. My own work in this area draws inspiration from the philosopher John MacMurray (1957; 1961) who understands that the development of the person involves a type of reciprocity whereby the person is at once subject and object, encompassing both modes simultaneously.

We know, from recent research on infant development, that the infant is involved in a relational process with primary caretakers which gives the observer a sense of a form of joint intentionality that goes on between child and caretaker. When this process is successfully operating, the child's development seems to flourish. As persons, we seem to have a deep primordial need for reciprocal acknowledgement; in the absence of this aspect of deep sociability at an early vulnerable stage, there appears to be a breakdown in the development of the person that can be devastating. It would seem that humans are possessed of a compulsion to share their conscious understanding and emotions as intimately as possible. Intimacy here means a presence to one another at our deepest levels of subjectivity. It is clear that each species carries within it a deep coding of its responsibilities for the enhancement of the life processes of its own. Nevertheless, we are also very clearly aware that there is an inter-species awareness that from our very beginnings is opening us up to a wider world. This wider sense of connection with all of the powers of the world is a primary matrix for all of our subsequent development. I would characterize this as our original birthright or innocence where the powers of the universe stand poised to assist us on this wonderful journey that we call the gift of life. In the modern world we have limited our vision of the deep relational quality of all reality in what indigenous peoples call 'all my relations'. Our relations, although important within our species, have limited our appreciation to the sacredness of all life. Even though the human family, in its many manifestations, provides the initial primary matrix for the protection and development of human life, we are aware in what Chellis Glendinning (1995) calls the initial *primary* or *primal matrix* which embeds us both in depth and width in the wider context of both our planet and universe.

Stanislav Grof (1985) helps us in our understanding of this matrix with a map that traces a process of our development from our early perinatal history. In the early stages of development, Grof speaks of a perinatal matrix. At the very nascent stages of our infancy, the primary matrix provided by nurturing caretakers gives us a sense of belonging and security in the world which builds a basic trust and faith in the life process. The consciousness is an I-in-we consciousness. If all goes well during these early stages of birth and shortly thereafter, the lesson of this initiation is the discovery of a sense of belonging and connectedness that can be brought forward in ensuing development.

With the advent of the second stage of the matrix, there is potential for the development of a sense of personal integrity, centredness, capability; the potential for an I-consciousness. This is what I mean by the development of the personal world. The terrain of personal development harbours a need structure so that we grow and learn to function well, meet the demands of daily life, and participate in a full way in community life.

The final stage helps us to grow into a consciousness that allows us to draw vision and meaning from non-ordinary states of consciousness. It is a consciousness that Grof (1985) calls the transpersonal and he describes it as 'we are all one'. There is a unity of being where the self is world and the world is self. I will be calling this transpersonal level of consciousness the ecological self. It must be understood here that all of these states can and should be experienced at all levels of our development from early childhood to adulthood. For example, the reader should not be misled into thinking that Grof's last stage of the transpersonal is simply an adult stage or process. There is ample evidence that children often have a profound sense of the transpersonal. Indigenous cultures' presence to the natural world is grounded in a deep cosmological sense. The Omaha Blessing is a birth blessing which introduces the child to the cosmos. I had two occasions to witness Thomas Berry baptize a child with the invocation of the Omaha Prayer. His invocation was thus:

Hear ye Sun, Moon, Stars, all ye that move in the heavens,
I bid you hear me!

Into your midst has come a new life.
Consent ye I implore,
Make its path smooth, that it may reach the brow of the first hill.

Hear ye winds, Clouds, Rain, mist, all ye that move in the air,
I bid you hear me!
Into your midst has come a new life.
Make its path smooth that it may reach the brow of the second hill

Hear ye Hills, Valleys, Rivers, Lakes, Trees, Grasses, all ye of the earth,
I bid you hear me!
Into your midst has come a new life.
Make its path smooth that it may reach the brow of the third hill

Hear ye Birds, great and small that fly in the air,
Hear ye Animals, great and small, that dwell in the forest,
Hear ye Insects that creep among the grasses and the burrows on the ground,
I bid you hear me!
Into your midst has come a new life.
Make its path smooth, that it may reach the brow of the fourth hill.

Hear all ye of the heavens, all ye of the air, all ye of the earth,
I bid you hear me!
Into your midst has come a new life
Consent ye, consent ye all, I implore
Make its path smooth – then shall it travel beyond the four hills!

Trauma and violation: the disruption of the primal matrix

It is absolutely essential to understand that any sustained insult to the primary matrix in the process of growth and development can have devastating consequences for human growth. Disruption as a result of a breakdown in connection can result in trauma. The core experiences of psychological trauma are disempowerment and disconnection from others (Herman 1992). The deep scars that people endure as a result of the breakdown of the primary matrix are now being better understood in the study of what is called post-traumatic stress syndrome. Over the last two decades there has been detailed study and clinical research on victims of traumatic stress. The fragmentation and dis-connection in the primal matrix is a result of traumatic stress due to domestic violence and child abuse, combat debility, political terror and environmental devastation. Violation is violence under any of its many guises and we are now coming to understand the commonalities between rape survivors and combat veterans, between battered women and political prisoners, between the survivors of vast concentration camps created by tyrants who rule nations and the survivors of small hidden concentration camps created by tyrants at home (Herman 1992). We are now coming to understand that western civilizational history has created a profound disconnection with the natural world in all its manifestations beyond the human. As humans, we are now coming to understand how vital for our living is our connection with the natural world. The eco-feminist psychologist Chellis Glendinning gives us the sense of the scope and magnitude of the connection and the sense of homelessness that occurs with this historical loss of connection:

> Because we are creatures who were born to live in a vital participation with the natural world, the violation of this participation forms the basis of the *original trauma*. This is the systematic removal from our lives, from our previously assumed elliptical participation in the natural world – from the tendrils of earthly textures, the seasons of sun and stars, carrying our babies across rivers, hunting the sacred game, the power of the life force. It is a severance that in the western world was initiated slowly and subtly at first with domestication of plants and animals, grew in intensity with the emergence of large-scale civilizations, and has developed to pathological proportion with mass technological society – until today you and I can actually live for a week or a month without smelling a tree, witnessing the passage of the moon, or meeting an animal in the wild, much less knowing the spirits of these beings or fathoming the interconnections between their destinies and our own. Original trauma is the disorientation we experience, however consciously or unconsciously, because we do not live in a natural world. It is psychic displacement, the exile that is inherent in civilized life. It is our homelessness. (Glendinning 1995: 64)

The description of the trauma produced by a sense of homelessness that Glendinning talks about above cannot be ignored in our discussion of traumatic stress. We are re-awakening to the sense of loss that we have endured by being separated from the deeply nurturant matrix that the natural world offers to the human in its journey through life. A relationship of communion is an antidote to the encapsulated self of the postmodern human. This calls for an expansion of our present horizons on self-development to a broader ecological self.

Educating for a planetary consciousness: developing an ecological self

A relationship with ourselves and the world based on integrity through energetic affiliation rather than the erection of boundaries is a challenge to our postmodern encapsulated minimal self. Moving beyond the individualistic self or minimal self demands an expansive sense of self which we will identify as the ecological self. This *ecological self* integrates the basic dimensions of differentiation, subjectivity and communion. This ecological self is dynamically achieved through a process of identification. Thus, the ecological self is a process of identification. Warwick Fox (1990) suggests that there are three general kinds of bases for the experience of communality that may be referred to in ecological identification. These bases for identification are referred to as the *personal*, the *ontological*, and the *cosmological*.

Personally based identification refers to experiences of community with other entities that are brought about through the process of personal involvement with these entities. Personal identification refers not only to concrete entities such as friends, parents, relations, pets and so on, but also to more abstract entities such as schools, clubs, country, nation and continent. We refer to this process of identification as *personal* because we experience it as part of our identity and any assault upon their integrity is perceived as a personal assault upon ourselves (W. Fox 1990).

Personally based identification is contrasted to ontologically and cosmologically based identification by identifying the latter as *transpersonal*. Transpersonal relationships of identity are not primarily a function of the personal contacts or relationships of this or that person or institution. *Ontological identification* as transpersonal identification refers to experiences of communion and commonality 'with all that is that are brought about through deep seated realization of the fact that things just are'. Warwick Fox clarifies ontological identification in the following manner:

> The basic idea that I am attempting to communicate by referring to ontologically based identification is that the fact – the utterly astonishing fact – that things *are* impresses itself on some people in such a profound way that all that exists seems to stand out as foreground from a background of nonexistence, voidness, or emptiness – a background from which this foreground arises moment by moment. This sense of the specialness or privileged nature of all that exists means that 'the environment' or 'the world at large' is experienced not as mere backdrop against which our privileged egos and those entities with which they are most concerned play themselves out, but rather as just as much an expression of the manifesting of *Being* (i.e. of existence per se) as we ourselves are. We have perhaps all experienced this state of being, this sense of communality with all that is simply by virtue of the fact that it is, at certain moments. Things are! There is something rather than nothing! Amazing! (W. Fox 1990: 251)

This type of identification can be achieved by almost everyone on rare occasions but to have consistent and long-term ontological identification a path of rigorous spiritual development appears to be a necessary prerequisite. This type of identification sustains a deep identification with all that *is*. It involves a radical openness to all of existence and puts at a profound level of identification the more parochial concerns of personal identification.

A *cosmological identification* refers to experiences of communion and communality that arise from the deep-seated realization of the fact that we and all other manifestations of existence (i.e. differention) come into being from a single unfolding reality (W. Fox 1990). This type of realization or identification can be achieved through an empathic incorporation of mytho-logical, religious or scientific cosmologies. Teilhard de Chardin referred to this cosmic identification as an unending generative process:

> The farther and more deeply we penetrate into matter, by means of increas-ingly powerful methods, the more we are confounded by the interdependence of its parts. Each element of the cosmos is positively woven from all the others: from beneath itself by the mysterious phenomenon of 'composition,' which makes it subsistent through the apex of an organized whole; and from above through the influence of unities of a higher order which incorporate it and dominate it for its own ends. (de Chardin 1959: 256)

We have identified this cosmological orientation with the universe story. There are varying accounts of this deep-seated realization of the processes of the universe and our identification with the unfolding process. This rootedness in the entire cosmic process is obviously the source of enormous energies.

We can see this identification with the world views of most indigenous peoples, but also with Taoism as well as with the modern evolutionary perspectives of such figures as de Chardin (1959), Prigogine and Stengers (1984), or Jantsch (1984) to name a few. Most important for our times is the cosmological story whose source is in the findings of modern science. Evolu-tionary development is the great unifying theme of modern science. This conclusion is by no means a final statement on the universe story. Even with the strength of our present views of cosmic evolution we know that with time there will be a need for alteration and modifications in crucial respects. What we can prudently conclude, at this point, is a certain solidity in general directions even when some of the specifics are altered or modified and revised:

> We still have every reason to believe that the particular views that supersede these views will be entirely in conformity with the far more general idea that all entities in the universe are aspects of a single unfolding reality that has become increasingly differentiated over time. The justification for such confid-ence lies not only in the fact that *all* of the evidence that bears on the question across *all* scientific disciplines points in this general direction, but also in the fact that even the most radical scientific (i.e. empirically testable) challenges to our present scientific views also point in this general direction. (W. Fox 1990: 254)

What is ultimately at issue is not the evolutionary story but rather, the *mechanisms of evolution*. For example, what are the processes that underlie the increasing *differentiation* of the universe over time (W. Fox 1990; Sahtouris 1989)?

The picture of this cosmological identification that we have been describing brings with it an extraordinary historical demand for the human species. Our present difficulty is that we envisage the universe simply in its physical dimensions. We have lost our awareness that the universe has from the beginning been a psychic-spiritual as well as a material-physical reality. The entire course of the evolutionary process has been to enable the universe to find its expression in the blossoming of living forms and in the various modes of consciousness that are manifested throughout the earth. The earth is integral with itself throughout its entire extent in space and in the total sequence of its transformations in time. The high spiritual component has been there from the beginning as well as all those living forms that found expression at a later period. The present universe is the fireball in its explicated form, while the fireball is the present in its primordial form. The immense curvature of space holds all things together in an embrace that is sufficiently closed to provide structural integrity to the universe and yet sufficiently open to enable the universe to continue its unfolding. Within this context we need to articulate ourselves in a new appreciation of our cosmocentric identity. In ourselves and through our empirical observation the cosmos comes to itself in its supreme moment of self-reflection.

Besides this cosmic identity, the human as species deserves our special attention. We often speak of ourselves as individuals, as nations or cultures or ethnic groups. We talk about multinational projects or even global human organizations. But this is different from considering ourselves as species. Our problems are primarily problems of species. This is clear in every aspect of the human. There are indeed great difficulties in identifying just how to establish a viable context for a flourishing and sustainable human mode of being. Of one thing we can be sure, however; our own future is inseparable from the future of the larger life community which brought us into being and sustains us in every expression of our human quality of life; in our aesthetic and emotional sensitivities, in our intellectual perceptions, in our sense of the sacred as well as in our physical nourishment and our bodily healing.

Swimme and Berry (1992) offer us a cosmological context for survival, critique and vision for our historical moment. They venture the idea that our ethics begins where the universe begins, just as each of us began our existence when the universe began. Not only our physical shaping began with the origin of the universe; our spiritual shaping also began at this moment. So, too, the ethical formation of the universe. This ethical formation is governed by three basic principles: differentiation, subjectivity and communion.

Our present course is a violation of each of these three principles in their most primordial expression. Whereas the basic direction of the evolutionary process is towards constant differentiation within the order of the universe, our modern world is directed toward mono-cultures. This is the inherent direction of the machine and the entire industrial age. It requires a standardization, an invariant process of multiplication with no enrichment of meaning. In an acceptable ethical context we would recognize that the unique properties of each reality determine its absolute value both for the individual and for the community. These are fulfilled in each other. Violation of the individual is an assault on the community.

As a second ethical imperative derived from the cosmological process, we find that each individual is not only different from every other being in the universe, each individual also has its own inner articulation. Each being in its subjective depths carries the numinous mystery whence the universe emerges into being. This we might identify as the sacred depth of the individual.

As a third ethical imperative derived from the cosmological process, we find that the entire universe is bonded together in such a way that the presence of each individual is felt throughout the entire spatial and temporal range of the universe. This capacity for the bonding of the components of the universe with each other enables the vast variety of beings to come into existence in that gorgeous profusion that we observe about us.

The present ethical imperative is that this journey continues on into the future in the integrity of the unfolding life systems of the earth which presently are threatened in their survival. The great ethical failure of these times is our termination of this journey for so many of the most brilliant members of the life community. The horrendous fact of our times is that we are, as Norman Myers (1984) has indicated, in an extinction spasm that is likely to produce 'the greatest single setback' to life's abundance and diversity since the first flickerings of life almost 4 billion years ago. The labour and care and energy expended over some billions of years and untold billions of experiments to bring forth such a gorgeous earth is being negated within less than a century of what we consider as progress towards a better life in a better world. 'Wasteworld' and 'wonderworld' seem somehow to have exchanged places with each other.

The Council of All Beings: an educational ritual fostering ecological identity

The Council of All Beings refers to a particular ritual enactment and a set of group processes and practices which are designed to foster the sense of a wider personal identity which has been referred to as the 'ecological self'. Fostering this sense of identity through ritual has been the task of several deep ecologists and environmental activists in their work entitled *Thinking Like a Mountain: Towards a Council of All Beings* (Seed and Macy 1988). The educational value of this work is in its attempt to develop rituals that affirm the interconnectedness of the human and non-human world. The authors of this work point out that there are many ways of evoking the deep sense of identity referred to as the ecological self. Methods for inspiring the experience of ecological identity range from prayer, poetry, from wilderness vision quests to direct action in defence of the earth. The authors point out that we are in need of an 'affective education' when we are fostering ecological identity. This education must be grounded in the intentional wish to reunite with nature at deeper levels of evolutionary awareness. What follows is a brief description of the processes of ecological identity that the Council of All Beings seeks to foster with the wider biotic world beyond the human.

The opening of the processes of the Council involves engagement in a number of group exercises to help cultivate a consciousness of the human in the web of life. This is done by guided meditations on 'Evolutionary Remembering' and is followed by a period in a wooded area or wilderness setting in search of a non-human being (animal, plant, river, mountain) with which some connection is felt and which that person will represent at the Council. Each participant is asked to construct a mask or other representation of this being which will help the participants over the following days to learn to shed their exclusively human identification.

By mid-day the Council meeting commences. All of the participants learn that they are assembled to have a most sacred responsibility; to represent at the Council of All Beings, all of the species and all of the natural features of the earth. The participants are encouraged to understand that they are called together to consider the war being waged against us by the humans – the destruction of species life-support systems and landscapes and the threats to the very existence of the biosphere, and to consider what we may do about these things. Using guided meditations and ritual, the participants learn to move in and out of their humanness, to loosen up their sense of self by feeling the dust of stars flowing through their veins, by 'remembering' the evolutionary journey that 'They' have followed these 4.5 billion years of organic existence. Learning to let go of the culturally conditioned self and feel an interpenetration with all nature. There are in reality no boundaries. I *am* that. We *are* that.

When the evolutionary identification is completed, the Council convenes for the central despair ritual. Here the assembled beings call out to each other, and through each other to the whole earth, everything that they have learned of the threats to the earth and its component creatures. Expressions of sorrow, grief, despair and rage are invited.

Finally, the conclusion of the Council begins with preparatory exercises, rituals and guided meditations. When the Council convenes, an invitation is issued for some of those present to don their human identity and listen, on behalf of the humans, to the voice of the other 10 million species. They let the humans know how they feel about what is happening and how they feel about the whole human drama. Expressions of feelings are encouraged from all participants. Later, the participants reconvene as humans and ask the earth to empower them to represent, from this point on, the interests of the myriad species in their dealing with other humans.

This particular ritual is a limited example of how a sense of ecological identity could be fostered. It is an example of an adult learning process. I do not want the reader to be left with the impression that ecological selfhood is an educational task for adults only. We are very aware that children have a finely honed capability it identify with the 'web of life'. This makes the educational objective of 'ecological literacy' a lifelong process.

CHAPTER 8

Quality of Life Education: Transformative Ecozoic Vision

> Tell me, what is it you plan to do
> With your one wild and precious life?
>
> (Mary Oliver)

Our world, the place in which we find ourselves and where we play out the significant events of our lives, is sending us distress signals. We must concede that the planet which we inhabit is in trouble. It is difficult to go anywhere today and not be confronted by the wounding of our world and the tearing of the very fabric of life. The great challenge for us is to have the courage to embrace that world and bring it into our hearts. Our current problems are not susceptible to easy fixes and solutions. We, in the minority world (first world), must confront and come to terms with the quality of life that we have created for ourselves and also assume responsibility for how that manner of living has diminished the manner of living of countless peoples in the majority world and in our own. The bottom line, in the global market economy, is profit. The singular major goal is economic growth indexed in the gross national product (GNP). We have sold this dream of profit to our world by commodity fetishism. The western labour force has bought the notion of 'standard of living' but this is only a comparative phrase to tell you if your buying power has increased or decreased in wage potential. Standard of living does not add up to quality of life. Our economic market vision has left our whole culture with a crisis of meaning and a felt sense of homelessness. Michael Lerner (1996) maintains that we hunger more for meaning and purpose in life in the final analysis. Our cultural values, fixated on the market-place, have caught us up in a deep cynicism that makes us question whether there is any deeper meaning and higher purpose to life beyond material self-interest. The bottom line of all this materialism and glorification of self-interest is that we find ourselves in a world filled with mutual distrust and self-interest (Lerner 1996).

When people are asked to reflect seriously on their lives, it is surprising what they indicate is really important. Consumption is not an overriding priority. The preponderance of things that people name as meaningful to their lives are religious practice, conversation, family and community gatherings, theatre, music, dance, literature, sports, poetry, artistic and creative pursuits, education and appreciation of nature (Durning 1992). What is apparent is that a vast majority of people, even in our western consumer society, are dissatisfied and alienated from the cornucopia of commodities. This has ironically, in North America and elsewhere, led to an extended turn towards the political right and fascism. Michael Lerner (1996) warns that we will miss some important insights about the deep needs of people if we are dismissive in our understanding of the political right at this time. Neither he nor I condone the deeply xenophobic, sexist, racist and homophobic nature of this movement which is now very powerful. Nevertheless, a careful understanding of and reflection on the right's capturing the high ground of moral purpose may give us pause for reflection on the failure of more social democratic movements to inspire and move the popular imagination.

The political right has pulled off an incredible hat trick because it has been able to convince a broad populace that its programmes meet deep needs and fears at the same time. The political right has presented a programme to people that gives them a sense of caring and community that seems to be a truly deep-seated need. But the right has inculcated a value of caring that it sees accomplished only through a return to traditional patriarchal and church-dominated community. At the same time, it has wholly subscribed to the neo-liberal agenda of the free market economy which cancels out the politics of stable community at the level of everyday life (Giddens 1994).

From the framework of more a progressive politics and an open-ended sense of community, caring values need not be associated with repressive communities. This has not come about. The reason seems to be that when the social democratic solution is embedded in a framework of the competitive market and functioning as a restraint rather than an embodiment of a whole new way of living, the core values of market individualism eventually predominate over the caring values implied in social democratic programmes. Lerner (1996) concludes that the established categories of liberalism were inadequate to understand the rise of fascism in the 1920s and 1930s, and remain wanting in our understanding of the rise of right-wing movements throughout the advanced industrial world in the late 1990s. When Lerner reflects on progressive movements on the left, he sees similar inadequacies because the political left has ventured its most serious counter-positions to liberalism. He sees certain traits in common between these adversaries. He suggests that at moments of its greatest popularity the left has often attended to the meaning-dimension in its political activity, yet it never has incorporated into its theory an understanding of the legitimacy of the need for recognition or caring, much less the hunger for ethical or spiritual meaning.

In my introductory chapters, I have arrived at similar conclusions. In the discussion of the terminal stage of the cenozoic, a period of historical breakdown that we are now actively experiencing, I have noted that all received political traditions come up short in terms of dealing with the exigencies of our times. We need a new visionary politics that will certainly have to contain what Lerner (1996) calls a politics of hope and meaning. Although the politics of meaning must address the deepest needs of the human community, it will fall short if it does not embrace the larger earth community where humans are a part of a more complete system making up the fabric of life. We must hold our world in consort with the wider biotic community and enter that world in the most intimate manner possible. This is coming to terms with what Thomas Berry (1989) has identified in his eleventh principle.

We are in need of a transformative ecozoic vision. Our hearts must become one with the world and struggle for it as if it was part of our intimate selves. Today we must begin to see that our world has within it a deep interiority and subjectivity that allows us to say there is an *anima mundi.** The world is soulful and is a primal matrix for us to enter and grow into the life stream. The psychologist Mihaly Csikszentmihalyi has devoted over two decades to studying the conditions which make people's lives happy and fulfilling. One thing is clear from his extensive studies, money and consumption do not make the grade as a basic foundation for happy and fulfilled lives. His work is both groundbreaking and visionary in the area of 'quality of life' (Csikszentmihalyi 1990; 1993; 1997). Education for a quality of life is our way of growing into life with energy, vitality and joy; what Csikszentmihalyi identifies as 'flow'. Flow is a genuine state of consciousness that involves us in the very deeper recesses of concentration so focused that it amounts to absolute absorption. This type of absorption is a foundation for developing quality experiences in our lives (Csikszentmihalyi 1990). The fullest possible life is one that has a sense of human needs that honours differentiation, subjectivity and community both within the human community and extended to the very life of the earth and universe itself. Anthony Giddens refers to this orientation as 'life politics' (Giddens 1991; 1994). His 'life politics' orientation develops the issue of 'How should we live?' in a post-traditional order where the creation of morally justifiable forms of life will promote self-actualization in the context of global interdependence. It is to these types of concerns that we shall now turn.

---

* I am not using this term in the sense in which Jung and recent writers on the soul apply it. See, for example, Sardello (1995).

Human needs : a generative natural law conception

The idea of natural law is tied to the conception of an organized universe. The understanding of the concept of natural law comes after discernment of the regularity, the succession, the repetition of natural phenomena, the existence of cycles and the ability to make predictions on the basis of the existence of interrelations within the physical world. In western thought as early as Aristotle, we see that nature is treated as a source of justice even if besides nature there exist legal conceptions of justice. Natural law theories originated in ancient Greek philosophy. From the Renaissance on, they were used as an argument for liberal political doctrine. There is a resurgence of this line of thinking in contemporary thought (Runes 1955). For Aristotle, it is up to humans to discern by observation and by interrogating nature what is natural and what conforms to its order. Natural right consists precisely in finding that justice is in harmony with the natural order and therefore has an objective ground (Wiener 1973).

In western ethics, jurisprudence and political theory, some form of natural law and reasoning has been pursued as the foundation of a moral order. Although the concept has frequently been the source of fostering a sense of order based on hierarchical authority and has been used as a system to justify and make arbitrary arrangements seem as if they were natural (e.g. slavery is part of a natural order in Aristotle), we must not abandon it. We will consider a natural law perspective that is generative, dynamic and sensitive to evolutionary changes. We start this by considering the natural law perspective that is developed by Roberto Mangabeira Unger in his work *Knowledge and Politics* (1975). His position on a non-static natural law perspective is clear:

> It does not rely on the notion that mankind as a whole and each of its members has an essence or an understanding core that can somehow permeate history and biography. Instead, it starts out from the idea that the distinctive experience of personality is that of confronting a certain set of intelligible, interrelated problems that arise in one's dealings with nature, with others, and with onself. Insofar as both the problems and the ideal ways of responding to them are continuous in space and time, one may speak of a human nature and of a universal good. But continuity does not mean permanence. (Unger 1975: 215)

My orientation, similar to Unger above, takes a position of natural law that honours evolutionary processes, is open-ended and generative, and has a time-developmental historical understanding. We now move to the reason for following this line of thought.

My basic assumption in this chapter is that an education attuned to *quality of life* must be based on the foundation of authentic human needs. When we open up for consideration the terrain of human needs and contemplate just what they might be, we must also introduce the consideration that those needs are based in the deep interiority of our natures. Thomas Berry (1988; 1989) goes so far as to say that the deep structure of our needs is ultimately embedded in the wider processes of the earth and extend further to the universe itself. On this planet there has been a fantastic complex of genetic codes so interrelated that each depends upon all the others. The transgenetic cultural realm of the human enables our species to develop freely in ways that help us to form a unique identity in time and space. In addition, our cultural coding helps us to expand our species activities in language and imagination. This creative and imaginative process we call *human culture*. Cultural coding is a generative part of our nature; a nature that we have come to identify as second nature. The generative quality of the cultural coding is seen in the diversity of patterns that we encounter within a certain level of cultural development and is also seen in the historical evolutionary changes in human cultural stages that I have earlier identified as the Palaeolithic, the Neolithic, the classical civilizations, the modern scientific era, and the emergent ecozoic era.

At any given moment in time, every organism acts within a structure of limitations and possibilities. This is what I mean when we say we are subject to our natures. Part of our structure is also time-developmental. Within any given moment or period of time, the underlying structures of organisms and species have the imprint of habits from the past that allow natural habits to be formed by the organism's structure with its history. Rupert Sheldrake (1994) calls this presence of the past a morphogenic field. What Sheldrake is saying basically is that there are no pre-formed or final laws of nature. There is an open-ended and generative quality to the laws of nature as we now know them and as we come to know them. Thus, even though all organisms follow historical patterns of natural constraints and possibilities, they do so in an open system of evolution that allows both stability and creativity. But innovation is not arbitrary or capricious. Even within creative processes we see stabilities that are built in because of habits that have accumulated from the past. The more often a pattern of development is repeated, the more often it will be repeated again. Sheldrake postulates that the morphic fields are the means by which the habits of the species are built up, maintained and inherited. Sheldrake also offers a generative evolutionary theory of habit by saying that the whole evolutionary process, at all levels, involves an interplay of creativity and habit. He maintains that without creativity no new habits would come into being; thus nature would follow repetitive patterns and behave as if it were governed by non-evolutionary laws. Conversely, without the controlling influence of habit formation, creativity would be a chaotic process with nothing ever stabilized (Sheldrake 1994).

As I have maintained throughout this book, we are living in a period of human and earth history that is in a state of radical transformation. Some of the habitual patterns that we have inherited in the past have now become dysfunctional for our present circumstances. We are being driven, by necessity, to devise new patterns for living in order to survive in a manner that gives us a sustainable quality of life. I feel that we cannot deal with our present historical moment by surface responses to our difficulties. We are now becoming aware that our western scale of progress and development is not tuned to a human scale or, for that matter, the scale of the earth. Our task must be to deepen our understanding of development in a manner that takes the much wider spectrum of human needs into account.

Human scale development: a generative model of natural human needs

I am drawing heavily on the very creative model of human scale development offered by Manfred Max-Neef and Martin Hopenhayen (1989). The reader should understand that I am using this model not as a definitive conception of human needs. The model is being used in order to broaden and deepen the reader's understanding of the complexity of human needs and how human needs provide the basis for our understanding of quality of life. It must be understood, from the beginning of my discussion, that this model is more suggestive rather than a definitive or finalized treatment of human needs. Nevertheless, in offering a radically new conception of development, the authors of this model make plain that, in our present situation, we seem to be losing the capacity to dream. From my own perspective, I believe that the authors develop a very bold and imaginative conception of human needs which will serve as a heuristic for some of the ideas that I am trying to develop in this chapter. My sense of the importance of Max-Neef and Hopenhayen's (1989) work is based on how it complements my own conception of integral development. Their conception of development is focused and based on the satisfaction of fundamental human needs, on the generation of growing levels of self-reliance, on the construction of organic articulations of people with nature and technology, of global processes with local activity, of the personal with the social, of planning with autonomy, and of civil society with the state. Max-Neef and Hopenhayen maintain that the best development process will be one that allows for the greatest improvement in people's quality of life.

One of the assumptions of human scale development is that human needs must not be considered in isolation and that they are better looked at as a system where all human needs are interrelated and interactive. It is vitally important to understand that human needs in their integral system are not considered hierarchically organized. Needs satisfaction is, on the contrary, operating as simultaneities, complementarities and trade-offs. They have organized needs into two categories: existential and axiological in a matrix seen in Table 8.1. The matrix in Table 8.1 shows how the existential needs of Being, Having, Doing and Interacting relate to the axiological needs of Subsistence, Protection, Affection, Understanding, Participation, Idleness, Creation, Identity and Freedom. The authors make another important distinction between needs and satisfiers. They contend that food and shelter must not be seen as needs, but as satisfiers of the fundamental need for Subsistence. In a similar manner, education (both formal and informal), study, investigation, early stimulation and meditation are seen as satisfiers of the need for Understanding. Healing systems and preventive health systems can be classified as satisfiers of the need for Protection. Needs and satisfiers are not related to one another in a one-to-one correspondence. Thus a satisfier can contribute simultaneously to the satisfaction of different needs, and, conversely, a need may require various satisfiers in order to be met.

Two further postulates are offered in relation to the need–satisfier distinction. The first is that fundamental human needs are finite, few and classifiable. The second is that fundamental human needs are the same in all cultures and in all historical periods. We are a species. The changes that do take place, both over time and through cultures, are the ways and means by which needs are satisfied.

Each and every economic, political and social system adopts diverse methods for needs satisfaction. Identifying how needs are satisfied within a culture is a way to define the culture.

This model is quite subtle in dealing with the difficult issues of our time. A good example is given by Max-Neef and Hopenhayen (1989) in examining the complex phenomenon of world poverty. Their analysis broadens our understanding of this concept. Traditionally, the concept of poverty is limited to the difficulties of people who fall below a certain income threshold. Critiquing this conception as economistic, they suggest that poverty is not a singular; we are dealing with poverties. They make the statement that when any one of the fundamental human needs is not satisfied, we have a real state of human poverty. Some examples are poverty of subsistence (due to insufficient income, food, shelter), of protection (due to bad health systems, violence, arms race), of affection (due to authoritarianism, oppression, exploitive relations with the natural environments), of understanding (due to poor quality of education), of participation (due to marginalization and discrimination of women, children and minorities), of identity (due to imposition of alien values upon local and regional cultures, forced migration, political exile). Max-Neef and Hopenhayen maintain that each poverty generates pathologies. Their model deals with economic pathologies such as unemployment, external debt, hyperinflation, political pathologies such as fear at both individual and collective levels,

Table 8.1 Matrix of needs and satisfiers

Needs according to axiological categories	Needs according to existential categories			
	Being	Having	Doing	Interacting
Subsistence	Physical health, mental health, equilibrium, sense of humour, adaptability	Food, shelter, work	Feed, procreate, rest, work	Living environment, social setting
Protection	Care, adaptability, autonomy, equilibrium, solidarity	Insurance systems, savings, social security, health systems, rights, family, work	Cooperate, prevent, plan, take care of, cure, help	Living space, social environment, dwelling
Affection	Self-esteem, solidarity, respect, tolerance, generosity, receptiveness, passion, determination, sensuality, sense of humour	Friendships, family, partnerships, relationships with nature	Make love, caress, express emotions, share, take care of, cultivate, appreciate	Privacy, intimacy, home, spaces of togetherness
Understanding	Critical conscience, receptiveness, curiosity, astonishment, discipline, intuition, rationality	Literature, teachers, method, educational policies, communication policies	Investigate, study, experiment, educate, analyse, mediate	Settings of formative interaction, schools, universities, academies, groups, communities, family
Participation	Adaptability, receptiveness, solidarity, willingness, determination, dedication, respect, passion, sense of humour	Rights, responsibilities, duties, privileges, work	Become affiliated, co-operate, propose, share, dissent, obey, interact, agree on, express opinions	Settings of participative interaction, parties, associations, churches, communities, neighbourhoods, family

Idleness	Curiosity, receptiveness, imagination, recklessness, sense of humour, tranquility, sensuality	Games, spectacles, clubs, parties, peace of mind	Day-dream, brood, dream, recall old times, give way to fantasies, remember, relax, have fun, play	Privacy, intimacy, spaces of closeness, free time, surroundings, landscapes
Creation	Passion, determination, intuition, imagination, boldness, rationality, autonomy, inventiveness, curiosity	Abilities, skills, method, work	Work, invent, build, design, compose, interpret	Productive and feedback settings, workshops, cultural groups, audiences, spaces for expression, temporal freedom
Identity	Sense of belonging, consistency, differentiation, self-esteem, assertiveness	Symbols, language, religion, habits, customs, reference groups, sexuality, values, norms, historical memory, work	Commit oneself, integrate oneself, confront, decide on, get to know oneself, recognize oneself, actualize oneself, grow	Social rhythms, everyday settings, settings which one belongs to, maturation stages
Freedom	Autonomy, self-esteem, determination, passion, assertiveness, open-mindedness, boldness, rebelliousness, tolerance	Equal rights	Dissent, choose, be different from, run risks, develop awareness, commit oneself, disobey	Temporal/spatial plasticity

Note: The column of BEING registers *attributes*, personal or collective, that are expressed as nouns. The column of HAVING registers *institutions*, *norms*, *mechanisms*, *tools* (not in a material sense), *laws*, etc. that can be expressed in one or more words. The column of INTERACTING registers *locations* and *milieus* (as times and spaces). It stans for the Spanish *estar* or the german *befinden*, in the sense of time or space. Since there is no corresponding word in English, INTERACTING was chosen 'à faut de mieux'.

euphemisms (e.g. calling a ballistic missile a peacemaker) and violence, marginalization and exile.

The matrix of needs and satisfiers may serve as an exercise in self or cultural diagnosis. I propose to use this scale as a reflective diagnostic tool in assessing how our own culture is meeting the complexity of human needs.

Education for community and a sense of place

Because of the presence of subcultures even within an affluent society such as our own, I speak here of cultures of permanence because the topic must be dealt with differentially. When I refer to a culture of permanence, I am addressing an array of the fundamental human needs referred to in Table 8.1. Our society has progressively become alienating and rootless for the people who live in it. Because of the throw-away consumer economy, we seem to have become accustomed to a manner of living that has superficial values and puts consumption of products at the top of a value hierarchy. I have already established in Chapter 4 that consumer lifestyles are unfulfilling and seriously deficient in their ability to meet fundamental human needs. When I refer to the need for a culture of permanence, I am referring to a sense of continuity in one's environment where there are objects that have a sustained and lasting human value and there is a community that has a deep sense of location and place. On both accounts, modern affluent societies have cultivated the sense of impermanence by accenting an economy of products that are subject to planned obsolescence and a type of mobility that has the average North American moving at least ten times in a lifetime. Communities of this nature partially satisfy the need that we have for subsistence but this is complicated by our patterns of over-consumption which curtail our need for protection because we become prey to health diseases of affluence such as heart disease, stroke and hypertension. The alienated and anaemic quality of much of our community life today also frustrates our need for identity, especially for the social rhythms of everyday settings.

The need for a sense of community and place are particularly wanting in our culture. Wendell Berry (1978) maintains that our economy, governments, and educational systems do not run on the assumption that community has a value. As regards a sense of place, David Orr characterizes our culture as displaced; consuming a great deal of time and energy going somewhere else. The accelerated mobility of modern life brings us into contact with highways and airports where we spend countless hours of our life. Commenting on the quality of contemporary life, Orr (1992: 127) muses: 'Our lives are lived amidst the architectural expressions of displacement: the shopping mall, apartment, neon strip, freeway, glass office tower, and homogenized development – none of which encourage much sense of rootedness, responsibility, and belonging.'

Much of our immediate world is supplied from other places. Our toxic and radioactive wastes, garbage, sewage and industrial trash are shipped away from our immediate surroundings and, unknown to much of the population, consigned elsewhere.

As a result of globalization, rootlessness, transitoriness and dispossession are the fall-out of an increasing number of communities; people move to find better jobs, corporations move to find cheaper labour. Products for consumption move thousands of miles to reach global markets, fashion changes with each season, and neighbourhoods where people grew up shift within a generation. Our sense of belonging to a stable community and our security are lost in the shuffle of accelerated change and mobility. The result is the experience of a loss of connection to where we live, to people themselves and to the natural world that surrounds us (Nozick 1992). In our present economic situation of globalization, our sense of place is fractured as a result of a breakdown in communities all over the world. Marcia Nozick, in *No Place Like Home* (1992), articulates several factors that are bringing community life in Canada to crisis proportions. The incipient causes are economic de-industrialization, which is leaving thousands of people in small towns and in urban communities across the country unemployed due to plant closures; environmental degradation of crisis proportions, which is poisoning our local water supplies and the air we breathe in major cities, through industrial pollution, consumer waste and auto pollution; loss of local control over our communities, with major economic and political decisions made by higher levels of government or by companies whose head offices are elsewhere – by people who have no stake in the community except profit-taking or managing people; Social degradation and neglect of basic human needs, so that increasing numbers of people are marginalized, alienated, homeless, jobless, hungry and living in unsafe situations; erosion of local identity and cultural diversity as we conform to the homogenous values of the global village.

The depth of our need for a sense of place is akin to what other members of the natural world experience as a stable habitat. Although human beings appear to be incredibly flexible in their living arrangements, we nevertheless need a place to satisfy our needs for protection, affection, understanding, participation, idleness, creation, identity and freedom (see Table 8.1). In order to accomplish this today, there must be an alternative to unrestricted globalization which can help in the creation of a sense of community and place that can satisfy some of our fundamental needs that are being hampered by the present world economy.

Educational institutions at all levels must play a pivotal role in fostering a community's sense of place. This is accomplished by having, as part of the curriculum, studies of the 'bio-region'. Bio-regional study would encompass a study of the land, and a study of the history of the communities and peoples that have occupied the region. Education intended to cultivate a sense of history of an area enables people to have loyalties and commitment to the place of their dwelling.

In a time when the global economy can no longer be relied upon to provide the basic necessities of life, the cultivation of a sense of place has built within it a corrective to the vagaries of globalization. Educating for a sense of place has not only a history to give; it also has a history to make. In the latter context, locality education encourages each self-identified community to build in the educational goal of fostering an independent local economy capable of providing goods and services for the inhabitants of a locality.

Education for communities of diversity

Communities can have a sense of permanence and place and still lack an ingredient that is essential to the modern world. That ingredient is an interest in and tolerance for difference and diversity. One of the perennial problems that human communities have faced in the past, and still experience in the present, is a sense of solidarity with the community as an in-group while excluding and denigrating an out-group. The deep feelings involved in this process are seen in the hatred and paranoia that have plagued human history into the present time. One can mention Bosnia, Rwanda and Northern Ireland as examples of deep conflicts that set off hatred in groups and communities. Although the reasons for this inter-group and inter-racial hatred are complex and diverse, we know that it is a problem that knows no geographical, cultural or historical boundaries. In the latter part of the twentieth century, the violence arising from this type of hatred sometimes results in genocide. The pretensions of progress, in the twentieth century, are belied when we look at the violence perpetrated against peoples all over this planet. We see the fear of difference in xenophobia, racism, sexism, homophobia and religious fundamentalism. Frequently these -*isms* meld together but their final outcome is treating another group harshly on the basis of one difference or another. What can be seen, by the politics of exclusion, is a sense that the world would be better in one way or another if there was a convergence towards monoculture. Hitler's idea of the master race and the idea of ethnic cleansing are expressions of this. We know from the best scientific evidence that differences between peoples are not based on any biological superiority of one group over another. In an excellent anthology entitled *On Prejudice: A Global Perspective*, Daniela Gioseffi argues against a view of difference that assumes racial superiority:

> There is no primary physical or biological difference between Jew and German, African, European, or Asian, as all so-called races of humankind are inextricably mixed, stemming from the same genetic pool originating somewhere over

250,000 years ago in the heart of Africa. We are all born of the same natural creation. Without earth and without water in combination, in short, without *mud* from which all seeds and living creatures grow, there would be no life anywhere on Earth. This is, of course, not an 'Afrocentric' view, but biogenetic fact, having nothing to do with cultural values from any particular nation or with value judgments of any kind. It is ironic that neo-Nazi skinheads or the Klu Klux Klan defamers talk of 'mud people' as a pejorative term, since without the fertile mud of creation, no life could exist on Earth. (Gioseffi 1993: xi)

To follow up on this articulation of difference, we can look at the three principles of differentiation, subjectivity and communion as a reflective prism for looking at difference and diversity. Let us first consider a hypothetical closed community such as a dominantly white community with fundamental religious values. It is likely that a community of this nature will have a low tolerance for people of colour, exercise religious bigotry, and probably have a patriarchal structure that treats women in an oppressive manner. When a community lacks tolerance for differentiation within it, one finds oppressive hierarchical structures that lead to violence and bigotry. When hierarchical structures are present, there is a collapsed sense of the range of subjectivity that a community might have to offer. The dominant group has no ear for the richness of differences that are encoded in the subjective world of human beings who have unique senses of interiority. Subjectivity refers to the deep interiority of all beings. It can also be considered as that aspect of the human personality that is based in ultimate mystery. In the past this dimension has been called the soul. We are not only manifestly different; each human being has a deep intentionality which is enriched by its own history in the world. The infinite depths of all human beings of different races, sexes, sexual orientation, religion and so on demand a sense of awe and reverence. The rich texture of lives is lost in racial bigotry. We are now just beginning to appreciate how much was lost when the arrogance of our colonial heritage saw fit to destroy the incredible creativity and spirituality of indigenous cultures. A community that denigrates differentiation and is autistic to the deep inferiority of all beings (subjectivity) is lacking in creativity and usually deals with difference with both psychic and physical violence.

The example that I have given above is hypothetical. Nevertheless, it constitutes one of the many examples of intolerance and exclusion that we witness in the world today. In the global world towards which we are moving, there is an educational imperative for all members of the planet to enter communities of greater inclusion. Inclusion does not entail violation of boundaries. Inclusion means an openness to variety and difference with a sense of including all in a manner which attends to the uniqueness of each and every member. Thus, educating for an inclusive community is open to the fullest sense of differentiation and also to a sense of the deep mystery of each person when the principle of subjectivity is honoured. It is important to understand here that inclusive communities operate not on the basis of sameness but on the creativity of difference. Inclusion in today's world is not created in a vacuum. Most groups and communities present themselves at varying degrees of inclusion. Movement towards inclusion, in the sense that we are considering here, demands that we deal with inequities of power. This brings us to the road away from dominance and subordinance and to the issues of power equity and partnership in group and community life.

One of the perennial problems of community life is the presence of differences of power that lead to structures of oppression and domination. We can see oppression and domination both between and within human groupings. Structures of oppression and domination exist at all levels of human interaction and seem to be present in human history from its very beginning. Focusing on the history of colonialism and imperialism in our western historical past, we see that the culture of the West entered into other cultural heritages in a highly domineering and manipulative manner. Historically, the entry of western nations into Africa, Asia, the Far East and the Americas brought to these cultures conditions of violence and exploitation that go under the name of colonialism and imperialism. The deep arrogance of western culture had different manifestations depending on the colonial power and also on the peoples being colonized. Western cultural arrogance was manifested in the attitude that western culture was superior to all other cultures that it came into contact with. Although part of colonial domination was accomplished by physical force and power, there was also a psychic violence where the deep interiority of other peoples and cultures was violated. When I speak of deep interiority, I am referring to the principle of subjectivity. Western cultural heritage and religion allowed the West to consider other cultural heritages as heathen and inferior. What frequently happened is that in the process of denying the deep interiority and subjectivity of other cultures, our forebears arrived at the conclusion that other people were inferior and savage. This was tantamount to saying that another culture and its people were inhuman. The work of missionaries is a major sub-text of the colonial heritage. Not to underplay the sheer physical domination of western culture through force and intimidation, the psychic violation of other cultures is akin to soul murder. Thus the systems of colonialism and imperialism led us into a relationship with other peoples and communities that was based on physical and psychic force. This force was not only administered from the outside, it was also internalized from within. Colonialism led to internalized racism within the culture being dominated. This type of community synthesis is rooted on sets of human relations based on dominance and subordinance. The subordinant relation was internalized by the non-dominant culture. It must also be pointed out that there has always been resistance to this process and this has frequently been the basis for change that has led to some type of transformation of relations and even the overthrow of dominance. Two of the historically predominant forms of colonialism and its attendant racism have been towards the peoples of Africa and the indigenous peoples of the Americas and elsewhere. The outcome of these processes of dominance has led to slavery and genocide.

Colonialism has also been practised within western culture. The first major colonial journey of the British was to a neighbouring island, Ireland. The Anglo-Saxon culture of the British was markedly different to the culture of the Celtic people of Ireland. The British considered the Irish savages and they are referred to as such by the Queen's Historian in the reign of Elizabeth in the sixteenth century (Dawson 1956). This colonial heritage visited horrendous suffering on the Irish for centuries from which the Celtic people of this island are still recovering. Ireland was the British Empire's first colony and it is turning out, as seen in Northern Ireland, that it will be its last.

One of the mechanisms of dominance and subordinance goes under the name of 'divide and conquer'. Here the dominant group sets subordinates against one another. In Northern Ireland, the British transplanted a people of Protestant heritage into a predominantly Catholic population. They also favoured the Protestant group in terms of land use, social status and economic privilege. We can see the legacy of this in Northern Ireland where inter-group hatred and bigotry have been the lot of the descendants of British colonialism. Religious hatred covers over the complex psychic and economic factors that the British left in the wake of their colonial practices. Projection towards another group is a salient psychic factor in prejudice and racial hatred. The dynamics of projection operate at the level of nation as for individuals (Gioseffi 1993). Ireland was not a singular example of this type of colonial dominance. We see this in Asia, Africa and the Caribbean and wherever the British applied this principle.

It is interesting to note that the colonial history of western culture has certain ironic twists in the colonial–imperial drive that was played out historically. For example, in the Americas, the continent was divided up into North and South by the four major colonial powers of the fifteenth century. The British and French dominated the northern hemisphere and the Spanish Empire along with the Portuguese dominated the South. All of these western powers treated the indigenous peoples of the Americas as savages and subhuman and entered into incredibly oppressive relations of dominance and subordinance with these diverse first peoples. In their turn, in North America the British came to dominate the French and the northern hemisphere came to dominate the South.

It is important to understand, in giving these examples, the deep arrogance of our colonial tradition of domination. When we consider all of the peoples that have inhabited this earth, both in the past and in the present, we must understand that each and every person and group is the result of the creativity of billions of years of evolution. To have the cultural hubris to think that the creativity of the universe gave one group superiority over another is the result of an incredible inflation of one's own cultural gifts. We are coming to understand, at the end of the twentieth century, that the variety of cultures is the incredible expression of the deeper powers of differentiation, subjectivity and communion that the universe offers our species. The formidable educational challenge to think about and move towards is a 'world community' that honours the diversity of peoples in non-dominant and egalitarian ways. This is one of the major educational challenges facing the world today. What we should be striving for, at the planetary level of our species involvement, is a community that holds together without collapsing and obliterating human diversity. Thus our planetary community, within a human context, must hold simultaneously, and with creativity, the tensions of differentiation, subjectivity and communion. When these tensions are collapsed we have a drift towards monoculture and a loss of species creativity. We also have the ugly spectre of racism and cultural xenophobia. Under these conditions we are constantly plagued with the evil of genocide. At a less extreme level, we encounter the marginalization of peoples that has resulted in an increase in human rights violations, especially in those areas of the world that are subject to the economic exploitation of the West. For those people who are marginalized and subordinated, almost all basic human needs are lacking. For example, indigenous peoples all over the globe are the victims of human rights violations, that leave their needs for subsistence, protection, affection, understanding, participation, idleness, creation, identity and freedom unmet at all of the existential category levels (see Table 8.1).

When we turn to intra-group relations within communities, we have already seen in an earlier chapter that women all over this earth suffer at the hands of men under the dominance and subordinance structures of patriarchy. This type of dominance occurs in all cultures and races in the modern world, it is also operating over classes and ages. The structure of patriarchy operates globally. A planetary education must seek to resist and transform the institutions of patriarchy. Women all over the earth are subject to structures of patriarchal dominance and are the victims of pervasive male violence. At the same time, the structure of male violence operates differently in different cultures and also operates differently within the same societies. What we do know, from the literature on women discussed in previous chapters, is that gender roles leave women in subordinate positions within the structural conditions of patriarchy and these conditions of oppression operate globally. Patriarchal socialization shapes the consciousness of both men and women, not with uniform results among individuals, to be sure, but with an informing orientation. A pervasive message of subordinance goes out to women from a variety of sources, giving women the sense that they are not to be taken seriously. This happens in commerce, medicine and government to name a few institutions. Charlene Spretnak gives us a picture of some of the consequences of patriarchal dominance and subordinance for both sexes:

> Even within the delineations of patriarchally approved presentations of the female body, cultural messages tell her that she is inadequate – in need of bound feet or high heels, corsets, padded bras, dyed hair, and even plastic surgery. Depression, fear, self-loathing are common psychological themes for women raised under patriarchy. For men raised in such societies, the informing obsession is to be 'not women' – not emotionally invested in relationships, not 'vulnerable' through empathy, not weak in physicality (especially upper body strength), not docile. Autonomy is the goal, and there is a great pressure to distinguish onself from the pack. Life is often experienced as competitive, atomized, and alienating ... Rage, fear, and loneliness are common psychological themes for men raised under patriarchy; detachment from feelings is the acceptable coping strategy. (Spretnak 1991: 119–20)

As we can see above, the structures of dominance and subordinance that exist under patriarchy leave men at a level of emotional shallowness while the contribution of women is ignored and marginalized. The educational path out of patriarchal dominance towards more equitable relationships between men and women will open up new areas of diversity both for women and for men. Having said this, it must be understood that the issue of gender must be seen alongside other issues of discrimination, based on race, culture and sexual orientation. If this does not happen, these differences are put in competition with gender and each other. If we pay attention to gender discrimination without calling attention to racism, we can expect that racism or racist dominance is likely to occur. The same applies to sexual orientation; an area of difference to which we now turn.

We know historically and into the present that some people have wanted and created relationships of intimacy, sexual or not, with persons of their own sex, and other people have done it with people of the opposite sex, or with both sexes, in every culture and time from which we have any historical or anthropological records (Wishik and Pierce 1995). We also know that categories describing sexual diversity are used to oppress and to create dominance and subordinance. We can say with certainty that in western culture heterosexuality is the norm, with other forms of sexual orientation severely marginalized. Our own culture defines heterosexuality and homosexuality as polar opposites and there is a tendency to deny the existence of bisexuality or other sexual orientations or identities. We stigmatize homosexuality and bisexuality by attaching to them negative social, economic and religious consequences (Wishik and Pierce 1995). Compulsory heterosexuality forms the basic frame for our culture's sex/gender system and it has caused incredible social and individual damage to people whose sexual orientation puts them in the non-dominant position (e.g. gay, lesbian and people of bisexual orientations). Heterosexually dominant societies make it very difficult for individuals to accept any orientation and identity other than heterosexuality. Compulsive heterosexuality ascribes dominance to heterosexual people and subordinance to lesbian, gay males and bisexual people. It is sustained by a rigid hierarchy between heterosexuality and homosexuality and a denial of the existence of bisexuality. Here again, the issue of diversity becomes paramount. We are beginning to see a transition away from a dominance mode of compulsory heterosexuality. Our recent past has been characterized by an almost total denial of the existence of sexual diversity, or, when this existence was acknowledged, it was accompanied by negative judgements about non-heterosexual orientations. Today, we are beginning to accept that our world has within it different types of sexual orientation and a range of cultural lifestyles that allow the visible presence of gay men, lesbians and bisexual people to be part of a wider sense of community. To challenge compulsory heterosexism through education is to open people to a more inclusive sense of community in which various sexual orientations are accepted as part of a community's diversity.

To bring this section on diversity education to a close, I want to leave the reader with a point that has appeared many times in this work. Globalization of educational goals does not lead to a consciousness of a wider and diverse world. This is the incredible irony of the globalization process. What appears to happen in the advance towards globalization is the simultaneous development of a monoculture. What is sorely needed, in our present historical moment, is an education that counters the forces of monoculture and opens all of us to the richer planetary culture of diversity.

Education and the need for civic culture

Cultures of permanence with a sense of community and place are the basic empowering infrastructures for more extended involvement in wider communities of participation. In our globally integrated world today, it is not possible to restrict or curtail our involvement in worlds outside our immediate community. In spite of the importance of involvement and participation that appear to be necessary in our modern world, people and communities are alienated and disempowered from the many institutions that affect their world. There is a sense of disconnection from the political processes in so-called democratic societies that makes for disenfranchisement. We are no longer addressed as *citizens*. In a predominant culture of consumption we now answer to the name *consumer*. Lack of participation in the electoral processes of both local, regional and national politics is evident. In a country such as the United States, almost half the voting populace refrain from voting in national elections.

The intrusion of transnational business, at the level of local communities, has destabilized local people's sense of economic security. Transnational businesses move at the drop of a hat and have no further interest in those communities except for the bottom line of profit margins. The mass media, as I have said already, create a culture unto themelves. The saturation of mass media culture has led to a decline in the public life of communities.

The responses to globalization, bureaucratic government and media-driven community disempowerment are intermediary structures that bridge the local community to the larger global structures. We call these intermediary structures civil societies or cultures. The need for these intermediary structures is a response to the exigencies of our present global situation. The needs of an alert, conscious citizenry becomes clear as we assess our circumstances in the global world that we appear to be moving towards. The notion of citizen comes again to the fore. An alert citizenry is the ultimate check on the activities of politicians and commercial and financial institutions. Effective governance will depend on individuals exerting their rights and responsibilities, so as to monitor the activities of governments and apply pressure to ensure that the rule of international law is not violated. Good 'world citizens' will refuse to be influenced by the propaganda of governments or the media. They will be sensitive to the need to match consumerism with sustainable development, and to use their voting power to ensure that economic and financial policies reflect proper care of the world's resources.

The concept of the citizen reintroduces the idea of civil society. Civil society is not an idea of recent origin, but it appears to have re-emerged over the past twenty-five years as a useful concept to describe the autonomous space for citizen action, organization and theorization (Hall and O'Sullivan 1995). The domain of civil society covers an array of self-governing private organizations pursuing public purposes outside the formal apparatus of the state and not directly interested in economic profit. There is a worldwide organization called Civicus that has attempted to articulate the role and vision of these many thousands of organizations. The adult educator Budd Hall (1996) believes that civil society organizations can be divided into at least two streams. The first stream is identified as the sum total of local, national and regional forms of civil society structures whose tasks are to create ways to strengthen communication, coordination and reflection between the discrete organizations already existing. These include nurses, public health workers, social workers and teachers who make the numerous linkages with like-minded colleagues the world over. Added to the above, there is an entire new generation of civil society organizations created in both rich and poor countries during the 1970s and 1980s: the ubiquitous NGOs or non-governmental organizations.

The second stream of civil construction identified by Hall is represented in those organizations that have a specificity at the global level. These include the Nestlé milk boycott, the numerous environmental organizations such as Greenpeace and the World Wide Fund for Nature, women's organizations, peace groups, and a multitude of other groups that have arisen within spaces of world citizen action. For many of these organizations, no national or local identity can be necessarily attributed. They are frequently labelled INGOs or international non-governmental organizations (Hall 1996).

Both of these streams of civic culture serve numerous fundamental human needs. The differences between the many organizations will also dictate the types and patterns of human needs that are being met. When we refer back to Table 8.1, we can conclude that the needs of subsistence, protection, understanding, participation, identity and freedom are some of the core needs that are pursued by these organizations in their various ways of doing their work.

It is important to realize that civic culture organizations, more often than not, function independently of the organizations of transnational businesses as well as from governments and present a very different vision of the world. For example, when the economic summits of the G-7 meet there is another organization that is neither government nor business that meets alongside it. The alternative summit is called TOES (The Other Economic Summit) and is composed of NGOs from all around the world. It attempts to present an alternative economic view that opposes the mainstream views of globalization prevalent in the G-7. It is the meeting of many and diverse organizations spanning the ecological, feminist, majority world, human rights groups and so on. Perspectives on many of the sensitive problems that are ignored by mainstream economics are discussed.

The Earth Summit held in Brazil in 1992 was another case of two summits meeting next to one another. The main summit was organized around the themes of ecology and bio-diversity with the participation of all member nation-states in the UN. The alternative summit called the Global Forum had an incredible response from INGOs from all over the world. There were about 1,500 groups from about 163 countries. The events of the Global Forum consisted of meetings, workshops, debates, networking and seminars. The alternative Global Forum addressed physical, spiritual and political issues that were ignored in the Earth Summit. The International Forum concentrated on education and produced a Treaty on Environmental Education for Sustainable Societies and Global Responsibility. This treaty was developed by consensus by INGOs from five continents. They developed sixteen principles of environmental education that are equitable and sustainable. I quote them here because they represent the broad educational sympathies of this work and also provide a concrete illustration of a transformative educational vision.

1. Education is the right of all; we are all learners and educators.

2. Environmental education, whether formal, non-formal or informal, should be grounded in critical and innovative thinking in any place or time, promoting transformation and construction of society.

3. Environmental education is both individual and collective. It aims to develop local and global citizenship with respect for self-determination and the sovereignty of nations.

4. Environmental education is not neutral but is value-based. It is an act for social transformation.

5. Environmental education must involve a holistic approach and thus an inter-disciplinary focus in the relation between human beings, nature, and the universe.

6. Environmental education must stimulate solidarity, equality, and respect for human rights involving democratic strategies and an open climate of cultural exchange.

7. Environmental education should treat critical global issues, their causes and inter-relationships in a systemic approach and within their social and historical contexts. Fundamental issues in relation to development and the environment, such as population, health, peace, human rights, democracy, hunger, degradation of flora and fauna, should be perceived in this manner.

8. Environmental education must facilitate equal partnerships in the processes of decision-making at all levels and stages.

9. Environmental education must recover, recognize, respect, reflect, and utilize indigenous history and local cultures, as well as promote cultural, linguistic, and ecological diversity. This implies acknowledging the historical perspective of native peoples as a way to change ethnocentric approaches, as well as the encouragement of bilingual education.

10. Environmental education should empower all peoples and promote opportunities for grassroots democratic change and participation. This means that communities must regain control of their own destiny.

11. Environmental education values all different forms of knowledge. Knowledge is diverse, cumulative, and socially produced and should not be patented or monopolized.

12. Environmental education must be designed to enable people to manage conflicts in just and humane ways.

13. Environmental education must stimulate dialogue and cooperation among individuals and institutions in order to create new lifestyles which are based on meeting everyone's basic needs regardless of ethnic, gender, age, religion, class, physical or mental differences.

14. Environmental education requires a democratization of the mass media and its commitment to the interests of all sectors of society. Communication is an inalienable right and the mass media must be transformed into one of the main channels of education, not only by disseminating information on an egalitarian basis, but also through the exchange of means, values and experiences.

15. Environmental education must integrate knowledge, skills, values, attitudes and actions. It should convert every opportunity into an educational experience for sustainable societies.

16. Education must help develop an ethical awareness of all forms of life with which humans share this planet, respect all life cycles and impose limits on humans' exploitation of other life forms.

(*Environmental Education for Sustainable Societies and Global Responsibility* 1993)

It is important to note that these sixteen educational principles, presented by the International Forum at Rio, constitute an educational vision from grassroots organizations all over the world. It has a planetary consciousness that also calls for both human social justice and a sense of justice connected to the wider natural world. Within the principles there is an articulation of the need for diversity of knowledge that honours indigenous and local wisdoms. The aim of the Treaty on Environmental Education for Sustainable Societies and Global Responsibility is to elicit the commitment of peoples from all over the globe in a grassroots response that is an alternative to the competitive educational model of globalization. As such, this treaty shows how the presence of civic culture can forge a transformative vision of education that has at the forefront the needs of the planet and all of its peoples.

The empowering capacity of being a citizen in a wider civic culture serves many important fundamental human needs. If we look again at Table 8.1, we see that the axiological needs of Understanding, Participation, Creation, Identity and Freedom are met by participation in a civic culture. The existential needs interacting with the axiological cover the whole spectrum of Being, Having, Doing, Interacting. When these needs are being met, in their complex interaction there is a sense of participation that allows for empowered actors in consort with one another (i.e. solidarity). I believe that the basic resistance to the negative fall-out of transnational globalization comes from a highly empowered civic culture that operates at the global level.

Education and biocentric diversity: the human need for the diversity of the natural world

The disenchantment from the natural world that we have identified with the modern project in Chapters 2 and 3 has resulted in a dynamic process that has put human beings in an adversarial position to the natural world. We have, in the modern period, centred all our sense of value on the human historical project. We are currently experiencing a dynamic of shrinking from the world beyond the human, either through a belligerent distancing or by erecting a wall of indifference. This outcome has been one of the central components of the modern project. We now are beginning to understand the costs that this project of modernism entailed. The natural world beyond the human has become seriously degraded and we are now living in a clearly dysfunctional relationship with the natural world. Our sense of the natural world beyond the human is that it is an object to be manipulated and exploited for human designs. Thomas Berry (1988) speaks of the human as in a state of autism. He maintains that we have lost our sense of the awesome mystery surrounding us and we no longer understand the voices speaking to us from the surrounding world. The intensity of our scientific preoccupations coupled with our relentless commercial exploitation of the planet have left us in a state of insensitivity to the natural world in the deeper emotional, aesthetic, mythic and mystical communication. Just as autistic persons are enclosed in themselves so tightly that they cannot get out of themselves and nothing else can get in, so we are presently enclosed in our modern world and, as a society, we have lost our intimacy with the natural world. Modern education in industrial societies has been a journey away from intimacy into estrange-ment. We have been taught to see ourselves as separate and detached from the natural world. When we talk of our existence we speak of it as standing out from and separated from the universe and the natural world. This is the disenchantment that I spoke about in Chapter 3. Looked at from this per-spective, human consciousness is conscious in so far as it is seen as separated from the universe and the natural world. When we consider the western world view, we see the world outside our consciousness as silent and inert; dead matter to be manipulated and controlled at our fancy. The world outside human consciousness is an object to be used at our species' discretion and within the terms of our own needs and preferences. The only intimacy within this world view is human intimacy. Here we are locked into anthropocentrism. The only other voice besides our own is the human; all other aspects of the natural world are silent. Because we see the universe outside the human as having no voice, it follows that we have no capacity for intimacy with the natural world. We are not aware that we are living on the surface of things. This is part of the arrogance of western education. We look at cultures that profess an intimacy with the world outside human consciousness as primitive and underdeveloped. We see this clearly in the case of indigenous peoples whose intimacy with the natural world, and their closeness and reverence for the animal and plant world, are seen as retrograde within the modern temper. We in the modern western scientific tradition have failed to understand that we have a very limited capacity for communion with the world outside the human; we been trained to see only the human world as subjects.

What if the universe is a communion of subjects and not a collection of objects? This sense of communion with the natural world must now become fundamental to our educational experience (*Environmental Education for Sustainable Societies and Global Responsibility* 1993). We must move from an anthropocentric to a biocentric sense of reality and values. This begins in accepting the fact that the life community, the community of all living species, is superordinate in value and the primary concern of the human must be in the preservation and enhancement of this larger life community. When we consider that the universe is a communion of subjects and not a collection of objects we commence to hold as sacred the deep interiority of all aspects of being. As Charlene Spretnak (1991) puts it: 'humans are not the only subjects in the universe.' She indicates that it is within our sensibilities to envision the universe itself as a grand subject. A greater engagement with the natural world in terms of its deep subjectivity opens up a new sense of intimacy. When intimacy with the natural world is cultivated, we begin to see a differentiated consciousness to the world outside the human. Sensitivities to the animal and plant world open up a consciousness that brings about a sensitivity to the deeper rhythms of the biotic world. Humans now are able to enter a relationship with the natural world that honours the deep subjectivity and interiority of all aspects of reality. With this wider differentiated consciousness there is the expanded capacity to see all of reality as both different and a subjective presence. With this expanded sensitivity and awareness we commence to develop an inner poise that allows a deep relational insight into everything that we may experience in and around us.

We can say to conclude this section that a transformative vision of education should be built on the foundational processes of the universe: differentiation, subjectivity and communion. It allows a simultaneous articulation of both difference and the communal. The creativity of the community would be grounded in the awe and respect for the larger biotic community; the web of life (Spretnak 1991).

In conclusion, I shall complete this work by examining the core elements of a spirituality that sustains and nourishes the requisite *dream structure* for the transformative vision.

. . . .

Kindling the Fires of the Soul: Educating the Human Spirit in Our Time

The Great Liturgy. The newly developing ecological community needs a mystique that will provide the high exaltation appropriate to the existence of such a stupendous universe and such a glorious planet as that on which we live. This can be found in the renewal of human association with the great cosmic liturgy in the diurnal sequence of dawn and sunset as well as the great seasonal sequence, and the great hydrological cycles. This recalls to mind the earlier ritual celebrations of the classical period, although now these celebrations will take place within a new story of the universe and its emergence through evolutionary processes. (T. Berry 1989: 2)

> We shall not cease from exploration
> And the end of all our exploring
> Will be to arrive where we started
> And know the place for the first time
>
> (T.S. Eliot, *Four Quartets*)

I believe that any in-depth treatment of 'transformative education' must address the topic of spirituality and that educators must take on the concerns of the development of the spirit at a most fundamental level. Contemporary education suffers deeply by its eclipse of the spiritual dimension of our world and universe. Spirituality, in our times, has been seriously compromised by its identification with institutional religions.

Let me make it clear to the reader at the outset of the discussion of spirituality that I do not, for one moment, consider that spirituality is synonymous with institutional religion. Religion will not be extolled or demonized here. When I say that spirituality is not religion, I am stressing that spirituality is not the sole province of religion. Spirituality refers to the deeper resources of the human spirit and involves the non-physical, immaterial dimensions of our being; the energies, essences and part of us that existed before and will exist after the disintegration of the body. Religion attempts to institutionalize spirituality and in many instances this is done for the perpetuation of the institution rather than for the explicit welfare of the individual (Weil 1997).

I would take the position here that 'globalization' is becoming a religion. It is not a religion that cultivates the human spirit; in fact, it warps the human spirit by its egregious emphasis on material goods. What is happening in our time under the guise of 'globalization' is nothing less than soul murder. It is pervasive and appears to move at the speed of an aggressive cancer. The movement into 'globalization' of the world economy is most certainly a cancer of the human spirit. Simultaneously, because of our placement in the planetary order, as our souls degrade, we devastate the world of the spirit. We are beginning to see today, in some quarters, a sensitivity to the loss of soul in the world. The recent writings of Thomas Moore (1992; 1994) on the place of the soul in everyday life have received a wide audience in North America and elsewhere. Other writers addressing similar themes of the soul include James Hillman in *The Soul's Code* (1996) and Robert Sardello in *Facing the World with Soul* (1994) and *Love and the Soul* (1995). A more strenuous and rigorous treatment of the importance of the spiritual life in the modern world may be found in the numerous works of Ken Wilber. What I find compelling about Wilber's work, and this can be readily seen in his most recent work entitled *The Eye of the Spirit* (1997), is his integral treatment of spirituality that spans many disciplines and creates a landscape of concern that reopens the question of the centrality and ultimacy of the spirit in our modern world.

My own way of addressing the soul and spirit theme is through the prism of the three principles of differentiation, subjectivity and communion. In terms of differentiation, I submit to the reader that any discussion of spirituality today, within the context of education or otherwise, must honour the incredible richness and diversity of spiritual expression that are present within the human family. This richness is evident in the diverse expressions of the human spirit seen in many religions of the world. It is also manifest in the various expressions of spirituality outside institutional religions. It must be said emphatically, because of the trend towards monoculture in our time, that variety is the spice of life in this sphere. Religious fundamentalism, whether it be Christian, Judaic or Islamic, represents a failure of nerve in the operations of the human spirit. The desire for one religion, one culture, one world globalized economy is an aberration and foreclosure of the human spirit and, when the human spirit shuts down in this manner, we are truly in fields of danger. There are strong similarities in all forms of fundamentalism (Lerner 1996).

Diversity is one of the necessary ingredients of a healthy spirituality, yet it only touches the surface if we do not take into consideration the depth dimension of spirituality that is identified with the principle of subjectivity. I have spoken of this dimension under different guises throughout this book. In our present context, subjectivity represents that dimension of deep interiority that one identifies with the notion of the soul. I have spoken of the depth dimension of subjectivity in the context of interiority, autopoiesis, inscape. When we see things in their diversity we must also go below the surface of differences to appreciate the deep interiority of all creation. The eye is one organ that seems to pull us towards the deep interiority of all things. Looking into the eyes of some person or animal we are aware of the depth dimension of creation. We frequently refer to the organ of the eye as the window of the soul. And so it is. Experience for yourself the deep sense of mystery that is felt when looking into the eyes of a newborn child. Take a pet such as your dog, if you have the privilege to have one as a companion, and explore the deep mystery of things that are called forth in its gaze. The deeper significance of the development of a sense of the within of things, or 'inscape', allows us to ponder in greater depth the idea that we are a communion of subjects and not a collection of objects.

It is vitally important here for the reader to understand that when I use the term soul as subject, I am not thinking of a pre-formed reality or essence. There is a dynamism in my rendering which encompasses the autopoietic nature of subjectivity. Autopoiesis refers to the deep renewing qualities of all living structures that maintain and enhance the integrity of the structures of the life processes. It is this dimension of interiority that we sometimes refer to as the nourishment of the soul. In our own times we are virtually living in a famine situation as regards the nourishment of our souls. Recall, from Chapter 7 on integral development, how limited our contemporary consumer culture is in meeting our deepest needs.

Our subjective interiority does not develop in a vacuum. We know very clearly that the soul is nourished in community. The primary matrix that I spoke of in Chapter 7 points to the deep relational quality of all reality. We are persons not in our selves but in community. This deep relational quality of all of reality is referred to by indigenous peoples as 'all my relations'. Today it is absolutely necessary to understand that our spiritual development must be nurtured at both the macrophase and microphase of community. Our spirit is embedded in many levels of community. We are members of the universe community, the earth community, the animal community and the human community.

Our relation to the universe community involves us in the broadest context that the human spirit can understand. Thomas Berry (1988) speaks of the universe as a text without a context. We are members of the universe community that makes of us the stuff of stars. The universe is the primary sacred reality. In Thomas Berry's terms, we become sacred by our participation in the sacred dimension of the universe itself. All peoples, from time immemorial, have taken a vital interest in their relationship to the universe. The most wonderful myths have been spun by diverse peoples all over the earth celebrating our origin story within their understanding. The sense of the expansiveness of the universe is food for the soul. The awesome grandeur of it all leaves us both breathless and energized.

Before we are humans, we are earthlings. Our souls are nourished within the earth's matrix. It is a matrix that exhibits incredible variety and enormous grandeur. The earth's landscape is rich nourishment for the human spirit. Thomas Berry (personal communication, 1989) makes a parallel with the lunar landscape. He maintains that if we were moon creatures our souls would experience the desolation of the moon's landscape. Our planet has incredible variety and interiority which nourish the human spirit. When that matrix is soiled or made toxic it will have its concomitant effect on the development of the human spirit. To speak of the earth as our mother, as is common among native peoples, is not metaphor as such. It is truly appropriate to refer to the earth as our mother when we are speaking within an earth community context. The nurturance of the earth, as primal matrix for our species as well as many others, makes the choice of the term 'mother' apt and fitting. As earthlings, we are a species among species. The importance of this understanding cannot be understated. Swimme and Berry (1992) believe that we will never come to appreciate the full significance of human adjustment in this new biological era until we begin to think of the human as a species among species. We have thought about the human as nations, as cultures, as ethnic groups, as international organizations, even as the global human community; but none of these articulates the present human–earth issue so precisely as thinking about the human as a species among species.

This misunderstanding of our placement has had effects beyond the species level. Human influence in the industrial era has so upset the balance that the planet has gone into a burn-out phase that I have named the terminal cenozoic. The desolation of the human spirit that we are experiencing today is mirrored back to our souls by our own soiling of our primary matrix. What goes around comes around. Our western industrial view of the earth has been that the earth is a separated object from the human self that can be manipulated and exploited to suit our greed. This sense of the earth as object means that, as a historical people, we have ignored the wisdom of our ancestral heritage. In doing that, we have engendered a process of destruction of our habitat or matrix that has now reached perilous proportions. We have lost our spiritual connection to the earth and we are diminishing the growth of our spirit. Our western cultural horizon is destroying the spiritual dimension of our own lives and because of expansive globalization we are destroying the spiritual development of other peoples by intruding ourselves into their cultures and their lives. The historical cultural invasion into the lives of indigenous peoples, both historically and in the present, is a case in point. The incredible resilience of native peoples who are actively appropriating their traditions again gives us hope that the invasiveness can be set back on itself. To do this for ourselves today, we must follow the example of native peoples in their tenacity to preserve the integrity of their spirit world.

When we turn to the human community we can readily see how the matrix of community life can either enhance or detract from the growth of the spirit. We are now becoming fully aware of the importance of the primary matrix of the human community for the normal development of the spirit. When there is a violation of the primary matrix we find that the human spirit is severely compromised. The term schizophrenia in fact refers to the state of a broken spirit. In the Christian gospels, when you harm a child there is such a destruction to the order of things that even a compassionate Jesus would say that any human who would harm a child is worthy of having a millstone placed around the neck and being thrown into the sea. Knowing what we know today about the importance of the matrix of the human community for the development of the human spirit, it is incredible how our modern economic system violates some of our most vital human needs. Because our global economic system judges itself only in terms of profit, the compromise of the human spirit is totally ignored in its reckoning of accounts.

There is no place in the world economy governed by the profit motive for the cultivation and nourishment of the spiritual life. Leisure, contemplation and silence have no value in this system because none of these activities is governed by the motivation of profit. Peoples who attend to their spiritual life are seen as non-productive or underdeveloped. Our world economy places an emphasis only on material wants and needs, and there is no concern for the hunger that people have called the hunger of the spirit. From an educational point of view, our present state is in need of transformation. Our first and foremost task in life is to take hold of our spiritual destiny. These are not household words in education. Nevertheless, we are beginning to see a concern in education that opens on to considering education as a spiritual venture (Palmer 1993; R. Miller 1993; Moffett 1994). Here again, indigenous peoples are exemplary. One of the traditions of indigenous cultures is the 'vision quest'. Tom Brown Jr (1988: 4) crystallizes its importance: 'There is a world beyond our everyday physical, mental, and emotional experiences. It is a world beyond the five senses, and different than the realm of the imagination. It is a world of the unseen and eternal, the world of spirit and vision.'

In the vision quest, a person must take hold of a vision for his or her life that allows them to follow their vocation and destiny. May I say that the vision quest does not focus on economic destiny. With this in mind, we see how vital it is to have a community life that recognizes the importance of the growth of our spirits.

Diversities of spiritual expression

Within the human community, we have found in the past, and experience in the present, a diversity of expressions of human spirituality. It seems natural to the human in all ages and times to give expression to the sacred dimension of life. Though expressions of the sacred have differed dramatically, the fact of the presence of the sacred dimension in human life appears uncontested. We also acknowledge that our place in the universe exists within a time-developmental context. The sacred is also subject to this time-developmental context. We therefore should expect, in fact embrace, the view that the sacred dimension of life will have the colour and the diversity of the very unfolding creativity of the universe itself. This spirituality must also meet the unique needs of our present planetary conditions.

There is no spirituality today taken in itself that can pretend to be the full experience of the human spirit. Any pretensions along this line of thinking are both misguided and dangerous. The present escalation of diverse fundamentalisms is a case in point. We are in need of a spirituality whose scope and magnitude will open us up to the wonder and the joy of the universe. We are in need of a spirituality which has embedded within it a biocentric vision that keeps us vitally connected to the natural world and to the unfolding of the universe. We need an enchanted spirituality that awakens us to the awesome quality of our experience within this grand mystery that we have been born into. We need an embodied spirituality that connects our bodies to the deep mystery of things. We need a spirituality that expresses the multiple facets of the human (differentiation), the manifestation of our depth dimension of interiority (subjectivity), and a relational dimension that allows us to embed our lives into multiple expressions of community, opensing up into a deeper appreciation of the fact that we are participants in a grand planetary community. Matthew Fox gives us a sense of the awesome magnitude of creation and our place in it when he elaborates on the Lakota sense of the universe and their understanding of 'all my relations':

> Creation is all things and us. It is us in relationship with all things. 'All my relations,' the Lakota people pray whenever they smoke the sacred pipe or leave the sweatlodge. 'All our relations' implies all beings, all things, the ones we see and the ones we do not; the whirling galaxies and the wild suns, the black holes and the microorganisms, the trees and the stars, the fish and the whales, the wolves and the porpoises, the flowers and the rocks, the molten lava and the towering snow-capped mountains, the children we give birth to and their children, and theirs and theirs and theirs. The unemployed single mother and the university student, the campesino and the landowner, the frog in the pond and the snake in the grass, the colors of a bright sunny day and the utter darkness of a rain forest at night, the plumage of sparkling parrots

and the beat of an African drum, the kiva of the Hopi and the wonder of Chartres Cathedral, the excitement of New York City and the despair of an overcrowded prison are included as well. (M. Fox 1991: 7–8)

The very magnificence of creation calls forth a diversity of expressions for the celebration of this great mystery. It therefore should come as no surprise that people celebrate their existence in diverse forms over time and space. We know this to be true.

The diverse expressions of myths and stories resulted from and further enhanced the distinctive lifestyles whereby the various peoples of this earth related to each other, to the natural world about them, and to the numinous powers that provided their ultimate explanation for the emergence of the universe and for its patterns of activity. The differences in these myths and rituals reflect the diversity of life experience of the various peoples and the special features of the geographical area they inhabited. The myths and rituals gave meaning to their lives and evoked the psychic energy needed to confront the terrors inherent in the human condition (Swimme and Berry 1992). Swimme and Berry (1992) venture that the civilization process is an extension of the processes of natural selection constantly taking place not only within the human species but with the various tribal and civilizational divisions of the human. As the human community is constantly being selected out of the living systems of the planet, so too the civilizational structures are constantly being selected out of the great range of possibilities. We can, therefore, understand the multiple variety of expressions of spirituality that have existed over time and space. We should also not be surprised that within our current historical reality there are diversities that express the plentitude of the human spirit in our time. In marking some of these expressions, we have already noted that it is necessary to make a distinction between spirituality and religion. Although religion does not preclude spirituality, spirituality is not exhausted by religion. In our present period we have received the legacy of anthropocentric religions and science that have left us with rituals that do not address our relationship to the earth in its plenitude.

In our current historical situation, we are beginning to see forms of spirituality and their attendant rituals affirming the interconnectedness of the human and the non-human world. We are also seeing scientific openings that enhance a spirituality that connects us to the wider universe and its mysteries. *The Universe Story* by Brian Swimme and Thomas Berry (1992); Brian Swimme's *The Hidden Heart of the Cosmos* (1996); Rupert Sheldrake's *The Rebirth of Nature and God* (1994); Paul Davies's *God and the New Physics* (1984); Elisabet Sahtouris's *Gaia: The Human Journey from Chaos to Cosmos* (1989); Lynn Margulis's *Microcosmos* (1987); Carl Sagan's *Cosmos* (1980); and J. E. Lovelock's *The Ages of Gaia* (1988), are illustrative of this genre of interconnection.

Writers in the area of deep ecology are also attempting sets of rituals to inspire appreciation of the deep sense of interiority (subjectivity) of all things. Coming from perspectives well outside formal religions, deep ecologists such as John Seed and Joanna Macy, Pat Flemming, and Arne Naess (Seed and Macy 1988) have attempted to develop rituals for inspiring the experience of deep ecology ranging from prayer to poetry, from wilderness vision quests to direct action defence of the earth.

Eco-feminist writers are also paving a path of spirituality which resonates to the deep needs of both women and men. These writers include such authors as Susan Griffin (1978; 1995), Starhawk (1997), Riane Eisler (1988), Judith Plant (1989), Charlene Spretnak (1991) and others (Diamond and Ornstein 1990; La Chapelle 1988). Women's spirituality, in all its diversity, opens the door to a spirituality of embodiment, goddess spirituality and the recovery of a sense that the earth body and the human body are sacred in just proportions (Stone 1976; Eisler 1988; Starhawk 1979).

The spiritualites of the indigenous peoples of the Americas are just becoming to be appreciated after the onslaught of 500 years (Mander 1991; McGaa 1990; Storm 1972; Willoya 1962; Peterson 1990). Native people themselves, living in the contemporary world, are discovering and recovering their ancient wisdom as a corrective to the onslaught of the western psyche. The importance of this unique spirituality so attuned to the processes of the universe and the earth is also coming to be appreciated by non-native peoples who are trying to develop an earth-based spirituality. Native peoples proceed with both caution and generosity in sharing their ancient wisdom. Charlene Spretnak in her book *States of Grace: The Recovery of Meaning in the Postmodern Age* (1991), gives us a very clear sense of native spirituality and an authentic way for non-native people to relate to it:

> On our continent the Native American nations have maintained unbroken practices of earth-based spirituality for more than twenty-thousand years. Since contact with the European invaders, beginning five hundred years ago, native peoples' spiritual practices have often been targeted for eradication so that their cultural fabric might unravel and the Indians might become properly atomized team players in the modern world. Not only have hundreds of the natives maintained their spiritual practices against great odds over the centuries, but they are even willing to share some of their teachings with the dominant culture, believing it is not too late, even now, for all peoples to cultivate a loving awareness of the rest of the natural world and change our ways accordingly. Striving to repair modernity's severed connection from the rest of nature, longing to heal our deadening alienation, we can take inspiration from the ways of being that are artfully infused with sensitivity, humility, and love for the web of life. (Spretnak 1991: 89)

With this in mind, the historic event in September 1977, when the

Haudenosaunee presented a set of papers to the non-governmental organizations of the United Nations in Geneva, was significant. The Haudenosaunee
– known also as the Six Nations or Iroquois Confederacy – were once a
powerful people, living in the northeast portion of the North American
continent crossing the borders of what is now Canada and the United States.
The Haudenosaunee briefs were a response to a call within these non-governmental organizations to have indigenous peoples indicate the severity of the
oppressions of the 500 years after contact. The papers that were prepared
were given under the title *Basic Call to Consciousness* and they convey the point
of view of indigenous peoples; their sense that today human beings are
abusing one another, the planet we live on, and themselves. *The Basic Call to
Consciousness* clearly identifies western civilization as the very process of that
abuse of humanity and of nature. The perspective of the Basic Call is geological; the modern human is an infant, occupying a mere speck of time in
the vast spectrum of human experience. The Call is ultimately a call for
consciousness of the Sacred Web of Life in the Universe.

Although I have made a distinction between spirituality and religion, it
would be misleading the reader to suggest that they are mutually exclusive
categories. Religion appears to carry a two-edged sword in both spiritual and
public life. The main criticisms of organized religions are that they foster
uncreative social conservatism and stifle the life of the spirit. Although, in
many instances, this is the fact of the matter, it nevertheless is not *all* of the
matter. Although much of conventional religion is in the business of social
control, it must also be acknowledged that religious movements have also
been the focal point of social transformation and revolutionary vision. Guenter
Lewy, in his *Religion and Revolution* (1974), demonstrates quite conclusively
that religion can also be a force for revolutionary movements against oppressive authority. On the American continent, we have seen how a certain reading
of the Christian gospel opened the door to a religious spirit that focused on
liberation from oppression (Gutierrez 1973). The Sandinista revolution in
Nicaragua was embedded in Christian principles of liberation (M. Fox 1991).
We also see in North America a type of spirituality called 'creation spirituality'.
Matthew Fox has authored numerous books on creation spirituality that
combine Christian mysticism with contemporary struggles for social justice,
feminism, and environmentalism (1991; 1988; 1983). In Thomas Berry's
Befriending the Earth: A Theology of Reconciliation Between Humans and the Earth
(1991), we see a complementary horizon to Fox where a Christian Creation
spirituality is offered for consideration.

The work of Michael Lerner in *The Politics of Meaning* (1996) and *Jewish
Renewal: A Path to Healing and Transformation* (1994) is an attempt by a Jewish
scholar, psychotherapist and social activist to address the major issues that I
have dealt with in this book from the perspective of a believing and practising

orthodox Jew. In both his books, Lerner speaks to the major issues around globalization, ecology, racism, sexism and class structure. What is important in Lerner's work is not only the social issues that he addresses but also his venturing the importance of a spiritual basis for our lives. In addition, he speaks about Jewish religious renewal from the tradition of an orthodox Jew, with a disarming sincerity and commitment. Lerner opens a dimension of spirituality that links the prophetic dimensions of Judaism to a spirituality that addresses our present historical needs. His work also allows the non-Jewish reader like myself to see the rich resources that the Jewish tradition offers to our world. In the context of education, the recent works of Philip Wexler (1996) and Ann Adelson (1995) are also suggestive.

We in the West have been introduced to the eastern traditions of Islam (Said 1979), Hinduism and Buddhism. These traditions offer rich resources for meditation and contemplation. The work of my late friend Madan Handa, under the name of Maitreya, offers a sense of the sacred that starts within the inspiration of Hinduism but then opens up to perspectives beyond that tradition. Both Maitreya's (1988) and Sri Aurobindo's (McDermott 1987) work offer the reader a rich experience in the depth of the traditions of Hinduism and the ability of this orientation to address some of the major issues facing the modern world. We are also experiencing the incredible riches of the traditions of Buddhism in the life work of the Dalai Lama (1982; 1996), Thich Nhat Hanh (1992; 1994; 1996) and Joanna Macy (1983, 1989, 1991). Here again, there is both specificity and a universality that allow this rich tradition to address some of the major spiritual issues of our times. The continent of Africa also expresses the diversities of religious expression among its many peoples. Religion and spirituality have always been a major part of the daily lives of African peoples (Smart 1997). Traditional African cultures spiritualize their universe and endow the forces that threaten them with supernatural powers. The African scholar George Dei (1995b) points out that indigenous African ontologies express the essence of the relationship of the individual to the society and to the natural world.

It is important for us to understand here the deeper capabilities of all received religious traditions to renew themselves and to open up new avenues of vision for the development of the human spirit. It is really quite wonderful to behold a thinker from one spiritual tradition open up for consideration the depths of other traditions. For example, in *The Good Heart: A Buddhist Perspective on the Teachings of Jesus* (1996), we see his eminence the Dalai Lama explore and comment on well-known passages from each of the four Christian Gospels and make extraordinary correspondences between the narratives of the life of Jesus and the Buddha. In *Mystic and Zen Masters*, we see the reflections of a Christian monk on the richness of the eastern traditions of spirituality (Merton 1973). Basically, what this says is that we are at a point in history where differentiated traditions of spirituality are meeting each other and, without detracting from the uniqueness of a spiritual tradition, they are mutually deepening one another.

What we conclude here in relation to diversity and spiritual life is that the richness of the earth should be reflected in the rich offerings of diverse spiritual traditions. Without detracting from the integrity of any one tradition, we must understand that any retreat into a monoculture spirituality, as we see in the fundamentalisms today, will lead to very destructive consequences. As regards spiritualities in our world today, the operant direction is to 'let a thousand flowers grow'. As humans, we are moving into a highly differentiated world community that has the expectation of rich differentiation, a depth dimension of interiority and subjectivity never before imagined, and a community that opens us up into the deeper recesses of our universe story. The last thing we need is a failure of nerve, which is what I believe the emergence of fundamentalism represents.

Awe and mystery

The philosopher Gabriel Marcel once made the distinction between a problem and a mystery. A problem is a finite puzzle that exists to be solved, while a mystery is an infinitude that must be dwelt in without the fullness of answers. Another philosopher, Alfred North Whitehead, once said of philosophy that 'it begins in wonder and ends in wonder'. How many philosophers would make such a statement today? We live in a world that has trivialized wonder and we have ended up attempting to reinvent it in Disneyland or through 'virtual reality' (Mander 1991). The sense of awe that could be experienced by looking at the sky on a starry night is receding as we now regard the skies as a challenge to our industrial and military imagination. The western drive that propelled our exploitation of the planet now fuels our ambition to explore the stars and the further reaches of outer space. Nevertheless, we continue to return to the sacred and the sense of awe that the universe invites. We have, I believe, what Rudolf Otto (1969) calls a 'sense of the holy'. It is a sense of the numinous dimension of all reality. It is a sense that, when experienced, leaves us breathless. It is a sense that is frequently coupled with gratitude; a thankfulness for being a part of a great mystery.

This sense of wonder and awe seems to be part of our response to the real and is present from birth. We certainly see it in the gaze of the young and certainly in the young at heart. The sense of the numinous is present and activated at all levels. It is not confined to any one organ of the senses and it is activated in sight, sound, touch and all manner of sensing. In education we must let our sense of awe direct us in our understanding and we must resist being restricted by the shallowness of the market mentality. The expansive vision of our origin story is a corrective to the convergent monocultural vision of the global marketplace. The work of Swimme and Berry (1992) and Elisabet Sahtouris (1989) are just two examples that exemplify this direction. Brian Swimme, in *The Hidden Heart of the Cosmos (1996),* suggests that we bring some of the central discoveries that we have made about the cosmos to a meditative moment that expresses a single unifying concern. This concern is embodied in such questions as, What does it mean to exist, as a human, in this vast unfolding universe? What is our role here? What is our destiny?

This sense of destiny that comes from a deep meditation on the cosmos has been present to all peoples at all times. It has had a unique manifestation with the native peoples of the Americas. Thomas Berry (1988) observes that Indian peoples of the Americas have a special type of nature mysticism. Awareness of the numinous presence throughout the entire cosmic order establishes among these peoples one of the most integral forms of spirituality known to us. The grand vision of Black Elk is one of the most breathtaking visions of the cosmos and the human place in the circle of life. The incredible prophetic dimensions of this vision are astounding because it anticipates, at the beginning of this century, what is befalling us at the end of this century (Neihardt 1972).

The sense of awe that is evoked by the universe proper also has a unique resonance to the awesome beauty of the earth itself. We see this in a very compelling way in the reflections of the astronauts and cosmonauts who ventured into outer space. These men (they were almost all men) left the earth to journey into outer space as creatures of the cold war and they came back as creatures of the planet. The reflections of the astronauts about their journey into space moved from militarism to mysticism. The sense of awe evoked by the pristine beauty of the planet earth seemed to preclude a sense of nation-state consciousness. All seemed to be earth-identified creatures at the end of their incredible journeys (Kelley 1988). Two cases in point:

> The Earth at night looks even more magical than it does during the day. There is always a storm happening somewhere. Flashes of lightning sometimes cover up to a fourth of a continent. At first you see this as a natural disturbance, the eruption of splashes as a majestic spectacle. Aboard the spacecraft it's quiet. The peals of thunder cannot be heard, the gusts of wind cannot be felt, and it seems as if everything is calm, simply a play of light. All of a sudden, against your will you might imagine that the lightning comes not from a natural storm, but from the explosions of bombs. No. This must never occur. Let only the northern lights and lightning blaze above our precious jewel. (Vladimir Shatalov, USSR; cited in Kelley 1988: 36)

> You look out the window and you're looking back across blackness of space a quarter of a million miles away, looking back at the most beautiful star in the

heavens. You're not close enough to any other planets to see from pole to pole and across oceans and continents, and you can watch it turn and see there are no strings holding it up, and it's moving in a blackness that is almost beyond conception. (Eugene Cernan, USA; cited in Kelley 1988: 54)

We are now beginning to see some excellent writing that quickens our sense of the numinous quality of our planet. The works that I quote here are only a small illustration from a larger set of offerings that seem to mount daily. *The Blue Planet: A Celebration of the Earth* (1983) by Louise Young is no less than an earth history and life-story. In vibrant detail and beautiful prose, this author introduces the reader to revolutionary findings of geology that teach us that the earth is a dynamic, ever-evolving assembly of matter and energy. A wonderful introduction to earth science that moves the reader to a sense of the awesome nature of our beautiful planet. Don Gayton's *Landscapes of the Interior* (1996), a work of seventeen essays, explores the unique journey that plumbs the depths of the human connection with nature. Gayton's writings expose the reader to the unique mystique of the North American continent. The reader will also be impressed by Derrick Jensen's 'Listening to the Land' (1996). Jensen gathers conversations with environmentalists, theologians, Native Americans, psychologists, feminists, nature writers, ritualists, and explores with them their deeper understandings of the natural world. Finally, the most recent work of Paul Devereux, *Re-Visioning the Earth: A Guide to Opening the Healing Channels Between Mind and Nature* (1996), is a practical guide to using power and energy to heal ourselves emotionally, mentally and spiritually. At the bottom line, this work is awe-inspiring.

All of the works that I have quoted thus far are outside of the domain of professional educators. We will need to have cultivated, within an educational context, writers who express the importance of the sense of the numinous in education. Two contemporary North American educators come to mind. My colleague John Miller is an educator who is personally familiar with contemplative practices from both western and eastern cultures. In his book, *The Contemplative Practitioner* (1994), John Miller argues for the importance of a contemplative dimension in education. After reflecting on the work of David Schon, Miller ventures that education must have a contemplative dimension that is complementary to the process of reflection in education:

But is reflection enough? I would argue that there is an element that is necessary to good practice that is not included in the notion of reflection. Clearly we are talking about another level of experience that is beyond sense experience and even reflection. This third level adds to the holistic view of experience by connecting to being. This level, the level of the *contemplative practitioner*, is realized through various forms of contemplation such as meditation and myth. (J. Miller 1994)

Miller opens up an area of education that certainly goes against the grain of market exigencies. Meditation and the market are a poor mix.

In his recent work, *The Moral and Spiritual Crisis of Education* (1989), David Purpel argues that as educators we have specific responsibility for forging a broad educational belief system ever mindful of the problems involved in making any such effort as well as the problems inherent in not making such an attempt. The credo and goals are as follows:

1. *The examination and contemplation of the awe, wonder, and mystery of the universe.* Purpel notes that as educators we have a responsibility to examine the world and the universe that we inhabit and to share our reactions authentically and rationally; simultaneously we have a responsibility to be aware of and to share with our students the process of our observations. He states that we can and should confront this reality as a reflection of our comparative youth as a species in a universe that numbers its birthdays in the billions. Thus we are appropriately humble as any novice would be, maintaining, however, the confidence that over time we have come to know more and more, and perhaps at an accelerating rate. However paradoxically, our knowledge explosion has led to a deeper sense of the mystery of the most fundamental processes of origin and destiny. Educators perforce provide a basic context for their programme of studies, and as part of this context we need to establish the reality of the immense mystery that surrounds our existence of awesome complexity. This context is critical in that it locates us not only as interested observers of the mystery but as an aspect of the mystery as well. Thus, we have to establish from the beginning our ontological dimension (that we are people engaged in a process of defining our being). Moreover, this context helps to establish that such a process is an ongoing one, fraught with uncertainty and, hence, one that requires serious knowledge, reflection and research. Furthermore, it is a context that posits that, in such a process, we be ever mindful of the profundity of the task and the modesty of our progress. In this way we also catch a glimmer of our responsibilities – we are required to respond to our conditions, for if humans are to survive they must respond (Purpel 1989).

2. *The cultivation and nourishment of the process of meaning making.* As in our own context of the universe story, Purpel ventures that we are not simply a species concerned only with survival. More so, we are a species intent on creating systems of thought that explain our past and guide our present and future.

When educators examine these various thought systems, they confront the same type of diversity and complexity of cosmic explanations. In a parallel way, educators must also deal with the context of meaning within which educational activities are to be presented. The educational goal is not so much to teach a particular meaning system but rather to teach for the process of responding to that challenge. Educators must remind themselves and their students that any civilization or culture is a human construction, and it is a human responsibility to create or re-create culture; thus it is intellectually dishonest to encourage the notion that cultural institutions, values and beliefs are given. To a very significant degree, though certainly not responsible for the creation of our lives, we create our culture and our culture creates us. We live in a dialectical relationship with the mystery, with nature and with the culture. Therefore, in recognition of our important though limited role in the vast drama of existence, it is incumbent on us that we respond to our creative responsibilities.

Educators must help us all to see the nature of this creative process by sharpening our creative capacities and by exposing us to a variety of cultural creations. Not only do we need a culture that helps us to live, it must also help us to see the multiplicity and creativity of cultural creations in the tapestry we call life. The educational process is based on a very basic notion that the world makes sense and that we are involved in both determining and creating that sense. From almost the very beginning of their lives, people try to understand and control their world, and educational institutions must elaborate and nourish these impulses. This is not to say that educators should in any way try to encourage solipsism or self-indulgence. Rather, they should stress the collectively human basis of our culture, regarding subjectivity and imagination not so much as channelled into self-expression but as necessary to the impulse to create a life of moral significance (Purpel 1989: 114–15).

3. The cultivation and nourishment of the concept of oneness of nature and humanity, with the concurrent responsibility to strive for harmony, peace and justice. Within Purpel's credo, this conception of oneness and its cultivation is the personal affirmation of the mystery and gift of the grand story. The affirmation involves the acceptance of basic cosmological and moral principles. What is implied here is the basic acceptance of the belief that there is an ultimate sense in which we are essentially connected with each other, with nature and with the universe. In its most profound sense, this is the sine qua non of *cosmological identification*. Within this cosmological identification, we see an integral process that holds peace, harmony and social justice simultaneously. What is assumed here is a universe of harmony and meaning in which each individual human is inherently of worth, and that the dignity of all elements of the universe is significantly interrelated. Purpel maintains that harmony by its very definition demands justice and peace – dignity is indivisible. It is to be noted that Purpel does not fall into the trap of anthropomorphism. He makes note that:

> We must be mindful of our place in the universe and our relationship to nature, particularly in our responsibilities to preserve and enrich our environment. We must confront without hyperbole how we as a species have threatened not

only certain social institutions but the very existence of the planet as a living organism. Our struggle is to participate in the cosmic impulse for an ecology of natural, human, and universal joy, love and justice or, as we sometimes call it, harmony. Indeed, we see major and exciting possibilities emerging in this area in the emergence of the extraordinary consciousness-raising efforts represented in both the women's and ecological movements. Both of these broad movements have at their center a fundamental concern for intimacy and harmony, based on the recognition of our interdependence and our vision of wholeness. (Purpel 1989: 116)

4. *The cultivation, nourishment and the development of a cultural mythos that builds on a faith in the human capacity to participate in the creation of a world of justice, compassion, caring, love and joy.* Educators here again are in a posture of affirmation, not only of these moral principles but also of their 'sacred' quality. Purpel points out that educators can accept and act on moral principles of love, justice and compassion, and joy for all. At the same time it is important for all to accept the enormous difficulties inherent in the ways in which these terms are defined, experienced and implemented.

5. *The cultivation, nourishment and development of the ideals of community, compassion and interdependence within the traditions of democratic principles.* Purpel maintains that we as educators should celebrate this tradition, and as educators we should be mindful of the problems, difficulties and complexities that arise and will continue as a consequence of this moral orientation. There is surely no contradiction in affirming the broad principles and intentions of democracy and in being mindful of their problems. It is, in fact, the very spirit of democracy that allows, indeed encourages, continuous critical reflection and free inquiry by free people. We must also be ever mindful of considering the meaning of democratic institutions in the particular context of the social and political realities of specific historical moments. (Purpel 1989: 117–18)

6. *The cultivation, nourishment and development of attitudes of outrage and responsibility in the face of injustice and oppression.* Outrage at oppression is, however, an intelligent and rational response to a situation where our highest values are being violated. We must be wary when we pass off certain violations as minor or modest, as in an 'acceptable level' of unemployment casualties.

Purpel (1989) contends that these goals are such that they evoke assumptions, beliefs and values. In his view the values and attitudes represented in these goals are derived from dimensions of broad cultural consensus that might serve as a statement of our sense of the 'sacred', of our mythos and our platform of beliefs.

Eros

Audre Lorde, in her challenging essay *The Uses of the Erotic: The Erotic as Power* (1978), notes that the word erotic comes from the Greek word *eros* and is the personification of love in all its aspects. Her sense of the erotic is to speak of it as an assertion of the life-force; that creative energy empowered. This empowered energy comes to us in an embodied form. The connection of *eros* to passion is seen when it is understood that the erotic is not confined to sexual power; rather it is the moving force that propels every life-form from a state of mere potency to actuality. In 'The Passionate Life', Sam Keen (1994) locates *eros* as that life-force that moves birds to migrate or dandelions to spring. Our western world view puts us into an ambiguous and contradictory relationship with the deeper life-forces of *eros*. *Eros* is challenged in our culture and we have a history of separating spirit from our natural forms.

In Chapter 3, I made the point that the tenor of western thinking has led to a split between spirit and nature. Ralph Metzner (1993), in an excellent article on this subject, gives a historical sense of the build-up of this split:

> We have a deeply engrained belief that our spiritual life, our spiritual practices, must tend in the opposite direction than our nature. Spirit, we imagine, rises upward, into transcendent realms, whereas nature, which includes bodily sensations or feelings, sinks or draws us downward ... The deep-rooted pervasiveness of this spirit–nature dualism in European consciousness is such that it is hard for us to imagine how it could be otherwise ... Its disastrous consequences become clear when we reflect upon the fact that if we feel ourselves mentally and spiritually separate from our own nature (body, instincts, sensations, and so on) then this separation will be projected outward, so that we think of ourselves as separate from the great realm of nature, the Earth, all around us. Western culture – this great civilization of which we are so proud, in both its religious and humanist scientific world view – all have this dualism built into them. The material world is inert, insentient, and non-spiritual, and no kind of psychic or spiritual communication between humans and Earth or nature is possible according to this worldview. (Metzner 1993: 6)

The history of our culture is one of disembodiment. We have separated mind from matter, emotions from reason, body from spirit. It appears that patriarchal cultures have a long history of separating the body from the spirit (Spretnak 1978). Octavio Paz (1995) points out that Greek culture, well before Christianity, had a deep suspicion of the body in relation to carnal love. Plato considered the carnal embrace degenerate. Christian culture continued after the Greeks to reify the difference between the body and spirit, seeing them at war with one another. In our own period of history, our knowledge systems have also progressively brought us to a point of departure with nature that allows us to live in worlds of abstract disembodied realities (virtual reality).

As we tunnel into the deeper recesses of the mind, within virtual reality, we leave the natural world behind. We must ponder where this is leading us and to what end.

At the outset of our discussion, it is necessary to make a few initial distinctions in the relationship between spirit and matter. Ken Wilber (1995) makes an important distinction between three different world views on the relation between nature and spirit. The first world view is magical 'indissociation' where spirit is simply equated with nature (this-worldly). The second world view is that of mythic dissociation where nature and spirit are ontologically separate or divorced (other-worldly). The third is psychic mysticism where nature is a perfect expression of spirit (conjoined other-worldly and this-worldly).

Our western world view is most exemplified within the second world view of mythic dissociation. We have been trained to split our mind, body and spirit in this culture and this has been done through our religious training, scientific training and our educational institutions. The split is a given in our educational institutions of higher learning. bell hooks notes from the academy:

> Professors rarely speak of the place of eros or the erotic in our classrooms. Trained in the philosophical context of Western metaphysical dualism, many of us have accepted the notion that there is a split between the body and the mind. Believing this, individuals enter the classroom to teach as though only the mind is present, and not the body. To call attention to the body is to betray the legacy of repression and denial that has been handed down to us by our professional elders, who have usually been white and male. (hooks 1994: 191)

The whole trajectory of western culture is to create the nature/spirit split and to take us out of our senses (Berman 1989). People who write on the erotic frequently indicate from first-hand experience on how the split occurred in their lives. Alice Walker (1997) explains the split in her own life as a result of her exposure to patriarchal Christianity. In her recent book of essays on political activism, she explores her awareness, beginning in childhood, of the limitations of her received religion in its denigration of her most cherished instinctual, natural self; what she identifies as her pagan self. For women, there are frequent attempts to equate pornography and eroticism. Audre Lorde (1978) strenuously maintains that eroticism and pornography are diametrically opposed uses of the sexual. As opposed to pornography, the erotic reveals the deeply relational nature of embodiment. Lorde relates how the erotic functions for her at the deeply personal level. A long quote is warranted:

> The erotic functions for me in several ways, and the first is the power which comes from sharing deeply any pursuit with another person. The sharing of joy, whether physical, emotional, psychic or intellectual, forms the bridge

between the sharers which can be the basis for understanding much of what is not shared between them, and lessens the threat of their difference.

Another important way in which the erotic connection functions is the open and fearless underlining of my capacity for joy. In the way my body stretches to music and opens into response, hearkening to its deepest rhythms, so every level upon which I sense also opens to the erotically satisfying experience, whether it is dancing, building a bookcase, writing a poem, examining an idea.

That self-connection shared is a measure of the joy which I know myself to be capable of feeling, a reminder of my capacity for feeling. And that deep and irreplaceable knowledge of my capacity for joy comes to demand from all of my life that it be lived within the knowledge that such satisfaction is possible, and does not have to be called marriage, nor god, nor an afterlife.

This is one reason why the erotic is so feared, and so often relegated to the bedroom alone, when it is recognized at all. For once we begin to feel deeply all the aspects of our lives, we begin to demand from ourselves and from our lives' pursuits that they feel in accordance with that joy which we know ourselves to be capable of. Our erotic knowledge empowers us, becomes a lens through which we scrutinize all aspects of our existence, forcing ourselves to evaluate those aspects honestly in terms of their relative meaning within our lives. (Lorde 1978: 5).

Susan Griffin, in *The Eros of Everyday Life* (1995), takes the deep relational quality of eroticism and connects it to the community and the sacred. She also draws parallels on how ecology and social justice come together in light of the erotic:

There is an eros present in every meeting, and this is also sacred. One only has to listen inwardly to the histories and resonances of the word we use for religious experience. In Sanskrit the word *satsang* which translates into English as 'meeting' means 'godly gathering.' In the English language the word 'common' is linked through the word 'communicate' to 'communion' ... To exist in a state of communion is to be aware of the nature of existence. This is where ecology and social justice come together, with the knowledge that life is held in common. Whether we know it or not, we exist because we exchange, because we move the gift. And the knowledge of this is as crucial to the condition of the soul as its practice is to the body. (Griffin 1995: 150)

With the work of Susan Griffin (1978; 1995), Riane Eisler (1988), Octavio Paz (1995), Sam Keen (1994) and others, we are beginning to re-sacralize the erotic and that includes the most tender and passionate aspects of our sexuality. To do this there will, by the very necessity of the predominance of patriarchal male norms about sexuality, need to be a radical and fundamental revisioning of men's relationship to women. Male dominance is the operant norm in our culture. Within this patriarchal framework, women's bodies are not only not sacred, they are not their own. The deep desire for mutual pleasure is forfeited in this type of dominance relationship. Women's and men's bodies are not within this normative structure available for mutual pleasure. Instead, we see an attitude towards women's bodies that is invasive, manipulative and domineering. Instead of a relationship of mutual pleasure and delight, men relate to women in terms of power rather than pleasure. The confusion of male sexual violence with *eros* is a total misrepresentation of erotic passions. Rape is not an illustration of passion; it is rather an illustration of the misuse of power. Rape is a desecration pure and simple.

The deep pleasure that our bodies afford us in mutual embrace allows us to experience the deep joys that our existence affords us in spite of all the difficulties and sorrows of our lives. In celebrating the erotic, we do not discount the need for myth structures that take into account sorrow, pain and death as part of the cycles of nature and of life. Experience of the sacred in the erotic encounters of everyday life must be part of the celebration of our everyday existence. The theologian Carter Heyward makes this important parallel:

> As we come to experience as sacred, we begin to know ourselves as holy and to imagine ourselves sharing in the creation of one another and of our common well-being. As we recognize the faces of the Holy in the faces of our lovers and friends, as well as in our own, we begin to feel at ease in our body-selves – sensual, connected, and empowered. We become resources with one another of a wisdom and a pleasure in which heretofore we have not dared to believe. (Heyward 1989: 102)

We will have to develop origin stories that picture our coming into this world in delight and joy rather than in sorrow and sin. In contrast to images of our present culture of violence, Riane Eisler encourages the developing images spiritualizing the erotic, rather than eroticizing violence and domination. She says:

> Candles, music, flowers and wine – these we all know are the stuff of romance, of sex and of love. But candles, flowers, music, and wine are also the stuff of religious ritual, of our most sacred rites.
>
> Why is there a striking, though seldom noted, communality? Is it just accidental that *passion* is a word that we use for both sexual and mystical experiences? Or is there some long-forgotten but still powerful connection? Could it be the yearning of so many men and women for sex as something beautiful and magical is our long-repressed impulse toward a more spiritual, and at the same time more intensely passionate way of expressing sex and love? (Eisler 1995: 15).

Concerning these matters, we must realize that we are at a very significant cultural choice point or watershed in our times. Concurrently, I advocate that we come fully to our senses; there are cultural forces that are creating a new sense space called 'cyberspace'. This world does not connect to all of our senses but it invites us to a world different from the one that our senses have afforded us in their long evolutionary pattern. Instead of exploring reality, which is what the processes of evolution gave us our senses for, we can now create programmed realities in cyberspace. As with the area of genetic engineering, this mode of human presence takes on the character of the creator. Virtual reality is a human invention that invites us to witness the wonders of our mind in its encounter with the cyborg. But in the final analysis it is not the reality of the plentitude of our senses. Nevertheless, the virtual world holds out the promise that a world can be created from the richness of the natural world. This can be seen in the erotic world that the internet provides. Within the internet today, we are invited to a feast of pornographic fare never before so encompassing. The saturation of the internet with pornography, however, is merely an extension of our present systems of patriarchal domination. Sensuality in cyberspace carries with it the same systems of power dominance and dis-embodiment, and the same systems of disenfranchisement of women that our present culture encourages.

One therefore cannot expect that the joy of a full erotic life can be given to us in virtual reality. *Eros* must be enjoyed and celebrated relationally and bodily and with the full use of all our senses. Ritual is whole-body which engages the fullness of all our senses. Its deep relational pull expands the awareness of bodily presence into the wider life community. This expansion of the self is not the expansion of the mind, as in virtual reality. Rather, it is an expansion and intensification that is in part shaped by the experience of the ecstatic that accompanies the gift of ritual, awe. Also the appreciation of the erotic shapes new possibilities in a life increasingly understood to be relational and endlessly creative; limited only by human time and dynamics (Spretnak 1978).

Sanctuary and silence

Our modern world is overwhelmed with stimulation and hype. You can now watch television in many parts of the world for twenty-four hours a day. We are constantly inundated with advertising and sales pitches. Many of us find it difficult to be alone. Even though there is a deep relational quality to all of reality, this does not mitigate from a very fundamental reality of our lives. As much as humans need to be in relation, there is also a very deep need for silence. We all find it necessary to be alone and in silence (Storr 1988). We need sanctuaries where we can be in silence. By our market standards today, silence has no value. Silence is not productive. It does not enhance the gross national product. Silence does in some essential way enhance the quality of our lives. Looking back on the chapter on integral development, we see that the need for silence benefits some of our fundamental needs related to just being. Silence enables us to sanctify our lives. We are enabled in silence to come to a sense of the sacredness of our existence. We need to set off times and places to be in silence and alone. Places for silence are called sanctuaries. It is not for me to tell anyone either the time or place where silence is cultivated in their lives. All I wish to do here is to recognize how fundamentally important silence is in our lives and also acknowledge the need for a place set apart for its cultivation. Sanctuary is the soul's matrix.

Celebration

There is a day for every one of us in our existence where we become conscious and aware that we just *are*. We did not ask to be here, we did not choose to be here, we are just here. Some of us come into the world with the full use and potency of all of our senses, others do not. Some of us are born into affluence and plenty, others into poverty and want. We all come into existence with varieties of skin colour, different genders and different ethnicities. We all experience our lives in different locations of the world and in different class locations. We all experience our lives within the matrices of different world views. For all of our variety and difference we share one thing in common. We are all recipients of the *gift of life*. Although we will all experience pain and sorrow and probably in no apparent just proportion, we all feel at certain times in our life the joy of just existing. The gift of life is so precious that we go through great pains to continue our existence to see what life has in store for us around the next turn. We do not experience the joy of existence by ourselves. From the very beginning of our origins, we experience the joy of existence within the matrix of community life. The expression of the joy of existence is the very core of what we call celebration. Brian Swimme and Thomas Berry see 'celebration' at the very core of the universe itself. They indicate that if they were to choose a single expression for all of the universe it might be 'celebration':

> The awesome aspect of the universe is found in qualitatively different modes of expression throughout the entire cosmic order but especially on the planet Earth. There is no being that does not participate in this experience and mirror it forth in some way unique to itself and yet in a bonded relationship with the more comprehensive unity of the universe itself. Within this context of celebration we find ourselves, the human component of this celebratory community. Our own special role is to enable this entire community to reflect on and to celebrate itself and its deepest mystery in a special mode of conscious self-awareness. (Swimme and Berry 1992: 264)

Celebration must be accomplished at all levels of our conscious awareness.

From time immemorial the celebratory experience is consistently associated with the sense of the sacred. This sense of the numinous quality of all existence is seen in all cultural expressions of the sacred. The native peoples of the Americas celebrated their joy and gratitude in existence in their distinguished sense of participating in a single community with the entire range of beings in the natural world about them ('all my relations'). We see it in their ideas about the cosmos where all reality is seen within the 'circle of life'.

We find cause for celebration around significant core events such as the solstice, equinox, births, and wedding and funeral rituals that include a multiplicity of friends and relations. The loss of our sense of place in the cosmos and the corresponding loss of ritual concerning our participation in the great mystery of life are significant. The inability to express our sense of ecstasy and gratitude for the *gift of life* constitutes a loss of meaning about our vocation and place in the larger life processes. We live in an incredible time in earth history and we must capture the sense of our purpose through celebrating the fullness of our existence in both time and space. Celebration is an essential part of the ritual of existence. For creatures of the millennium, we must remind ourselves that we are about a great work. It is a joy to be part of this grandeur.

Bibliography

Abbey, Edward. 1982. *Down the River*. New York: Dutton.

Abram, David. 1996. *The Spell of the Sensuous*. New York: Vintage Books.

Adams, Henry. 1931 (1918). *The Education of Henry Adams*. New York: Random House-Modern Library.

Adelson, Ann. 1995. *Now What? Developing Our Future*. Ph D Dissertation. University of Toronto.

Apple, Michael. 1979. *Ideology and the Curriculum*. London: Routledge and Kegan Paul.

Aronowitz, Stanley and Henry Giroux. 1991. *Postmodern Education*. Minneapolis: University of Minnesota Press.

— 1993. *Education Still Under Siege*. Toronto: OISE Press.

Barnet, Richard. 1993. 'The End of Jobs.' *Harper's Magazine* (September): 18–24.

Barnet, R. and John Cavanagh. 1994. *Global Dreams: Imperial Corporations and the New World Order*. Toronto: Simon and Schuster.

Basic Call to Consciousness: Akwesasne Notes. 1978. Rooseveltown, NY: Mohawk Nation.

Bateson, Gregory. 1972. *Steps in an Ecology of Mind*. New York: Ballantine.

— 1980. *Mind in Nature: A Necessary Unity*. New York: Bantam.

Bellah, R. 1985. *Habits of the Heart*. New York: Harper and Row/Perennial Library.

Berman, Morris. 1981. *The Reenchantment of the World*. Ithaca, NY: Cornell University Press.

— 1989. *Coming to Our Senses: Body and Spirit in the Hidden History of the West*. New York: Bantam.

Bernanos, Georges. 1937. *Diary of a Country Priest*. New York: Macmillan.

Berry, Thomas. 1988. *The Dream of the Earth*. San Francisco: Sierra Club Books.

— 1989. 'Twelve Principles for Understanding the Universe and the Role of the Human in the Universe.' *Teilhard Perspective* 22. 1 (July): 1–3.

— 1991. *Befriending the Earth: A Theology of Reconciliation Between Humans and the Earth*. Mystic, CT: Twenty-Third Publications.

— 1993. 'A Moment of Grace: The Terminal Decade of the Twentieth Century.' Madan Handa Memorial Lecture, Toronto.

Berry, Wendell. 1978. *Home Economics*. San Francisco: North Point Press.

Bertell, Rosalie. 1985. *No Immediate Danger. Prognosis for a Radioactive Earth*. Toronto: Women's Educational Press.

Bhabha, Homi. 1990. 'The Other Question: Difference, Discrimination and the

Discourse of Colonialism.' In *Out There: Marginalization and Contemporary Culture*, ed. Russell Ferguson, Martha Gever, Trinh Minh-Ha and Cornell West. Cambridge, MA: MIT Press.

Bickmore, Kathy. 1997. 'Teaching Conflict Resolution.' *Theory Into Practice* 36. 1 (Winter): 3–10.

Bloom, Alan. 1987. *The Closing of the American Mind*. New York: Simon and Schuster.

Bohm, David. 1988. 'Postmodern Science in a Postmodern World.' In *The Reenchantment of Science: Postmodern Proposals*, ed. David Griffin. New York: State University of New York Press.

Bohm, David and David Peat. 1987. *Science, Order and Creativity*. Toronto: Bantam.

Bottomore, T. (ed.) 1983. *A Dictionary of Marxist Thought*. Cambridge, MA: Harvard University Press.

Bourdieu, T. and J. C. Passeron. 1977. *Reproduction in Education, Society and Culture*. Beverly Hills, CA: Sage Publications.

Bowers, C. A. 1993a. *Critical Essays on Education, Modernity, and the Recovery of the Ecological Imperative*. New York: Teachers' College/Colombia Press.

— 1993b. *Education, Cultural Myths, and the Ecological Crisis*. Albany, NY: State University of New York Press.

Bowles, Samuel and Herbert Gintis. 1976. *Schooling in Capitalist America*. New York: Basic Books.

Brenes-Castro, Abelardo. 1988. *Declaration of Human Responsibilities for Peace and Sustainable Development*. Costa Rica: University of Peace.

— (ed.). 1996. *Una Experiencia Pionera: Programa Cultura de Paz y Demoicracia en America Central*. Costa Rica: University of Peace.

Briggs, John and David Peat. 1989. *Turbulent Mirror: An Illustrated Guide to Chaos Theory and the Science of Wholeness*. New York: Harper and Row.

Brown, Lester R. et. al. (eds). 1988. *State of the World, 1988: A Worldwatch Institute Report on Progress Toward a Sustainable Society*. New York: W. W. Norton.

— 1990. *State of the World, 1990: A Worldwatch Institute Report on Progress Toward a Sustainable Society*. New York: W. W. Norton.

— 1991. *State of the World, 1991: A Worldwatch Institute Report on Progress Toward a Sustainable Society*. New York: W. W. Norton.

— 1996. *State of the World, 1996: A Worldwatch Institute Report on Progress Toward a Sustainable Society*. New York: W. W. Norton.

Brown Jr, Tom. 1988. *The Vision*. New York: Berkley Books.

Brundtland, H. 1987. *Our Common Future: The World Commission on Environment and Development*. Oxford: Oxford University Press.

Burger, Julian (ed.). 1990. *The Gaia Atlas of First Peoples*. New York: Anchor.

— 1993. 'An International Agenda.' In *State of the Peoples: A Global Human Rights Report on Societies in Danger*, ed. Marc Miller et al. Boston: Beacon Press.

Campbell, Joseph. 1988. *The Power of Myth*. New York: Doubleday.

Capra, Fritjof. 1983. *The Turning Point*. New York: Simon and Schuster.

Carson, Rachel. 1962. *Silent Spring*. Cambridge, MA: Riverside Press.

Chomsky, Noam. 1989a. *Necessary Illusions*. Montreal: CBC Publications.

— 1989b. *The Washington Connection and Third World Fascism*. Montreal: Black Rose Press.

— 1997. *Media Control: The Spiritual Achievement of Propaganda*. New York: Several Stories Press.

Clarke, Tony. 1997. *Silent Coup: Confronting the Big Business Takeover of Canada*. Toronto: James Lorimer and Co.

Clarke, Tony and Maude Barlow. 1997. *MAI: The Multilateral Agreement on Investment and the Threat to Canadian Sovereignty*. Toronto: Stoddart.

Clay, Jason. 1993. 'Looking back to go forward: Predicting and Preventing Human rights Violations'. In *State of the Peoples: A Global Human Rights Report on Societies in Danger*, ed. Marc Miller et al. Boston: Beacon Press.

Clover, Darlene, Shirley Follen and Budd Hall. 1998. *The Nature of Transformation: Environmental Adult and Popular Education*. Toronto: University of Toronto Press.

Cobb, Edith. 1977. *The Ecology of Imagination in Childhood*. New York: Colombia University Press.

Cockburn, Alexander. 1994. 'Beat The Devil.' *The Nation* 1, 3: 405.

Cohn, Carol. 1987. 'In the Rational World of Defense Intellectuals.' *Signs* 12, 4.

Collins, Michael. 1991. *Adult Education as Vocation: A Critical Role for the Adult Educator*. New York: Routledge.

— 1995. 'Critical Commentaries on the Role of Adult Educators.' In *In Defense of the Life World: Critical Perspectives on Adult Learning*, ed. Michael Welton. Albany, NY: SUNY Press.

Connell, Robert, D. Kessler, G. W. Dowsett and G. W. Ashenden. 1983. *Making the Difference: Schools, Families and Social Division*. Boston: George Allen and Unwin.

Cox, R. W. 1991. 'The Global Political Economy and Social Choice.' In *The New Era of Social Competition: State Policy and Market Power*, ed. D. Drache and M. Gertler. Montreal: McGill-Queens University Press.

Cremin, Lawrence. 1964. *The Transformation of The School*. New York: Vintage.

— 1976. *Traditions of American Education*. New York: Basic Books.

Csikszentmihali, Mihaly. 1990. *Flow: The Psychology of Optimal Experience*. New York: Harper Perennial.

— 1993. *The Evolving Self: A Psychology For The Third Millennium*. New York: Harper Perennial.

— 1997. *Finding Flow: The Psychology of Engagement with Everyday Life*. New York: Basic Books,

Cushman, Phillip. 1990. 'Why is the Self Empty: Toward a Historically Situated Psychology.' *American Psychologist* 45. 5: 599–610.

Dalai Lama. 1982. *Essence of Refined Gold*. Ithaca, NY: Snow Lion Publications.

— 1996. *The Good Heart: A Buddhist Perspective on the Teachings of Jesus*. Boston: Wisdom Publications.

Dale, Roger and Geoff Esland (eds). 1976. *Schooling and Capitalism: A Sociological Reader*. London: Routledge and Kegan Paul.

Daly, Herman E. 1973. *Toward a Steady-State Economy.* San Francisco: Freeman.

Daly, Herman E. and John Cobb. 1989. *For the Common Good: Redirecting the Economy Toward Community, the Environment, and a Sustainable Development.* Boston: Beacon Press.

Davies, Paul. 1984. *God and the New Physics.* London: Penguin Books.

Dawson, Christopher. 1956. *The Dynamics of World History.* New York: Sheed and Ward.

de Chardin, Teilhard. 1959. *The Phenomenon of Man.* New York: Harper Torchbacks.

Dei, George. 1994. 'Anti-Racist Education: Working Across Differences.' *Orbit* 25, 2.

— 1995a. *Drop Out or Push Out? The Dynamics of Black Students' Disengagement from School: A Report.* Toronto: Ontario Institute for Studies in Education.

— 1995b. 'Indigenous Knowledge as an Empowerment Tool.' In *Empowerment: Towards Sustainable Development,* ed. N. Singh and V. Titi. Toronto: Fernwood.

— 1996. *Anti-Racism Education: Theory and Practice.* Halifax, Nova Scotia: Fernwood.

de Lone, Richard. 1979. *Small Futures: Children, Inequality, and the Limits of Liberal Reform.* New York: Harcourt Brace Jovanovich.

Devall, Bill. 1988. *Simple in Means, Rich in Ends.* Salt Lake City: Peregrine Smith.

Devall, Bill and George Sessions. 1985. *Deep Ecology: Living as if Nature Mattered.* Salt Lake City: Peregrine Smith.

Devereux, Paul. 1996. *Re-Visioning the Earth: A Guide to Opening the Healing Channels Between Mind and Nature.* New York: Simon and Schuster.

Dewey, John. 1963. 'What Psychology Can Do For the Teacher.' In *John Dewey on Education: Selected Writings,* ed. R. Archambault. New York: Random House.

— 1966. *Democracy and Education.* New York: Free Press.

Dialogue: Newsletter of the University of Peace. 1996. San Jose, Costa Rica: Peace University.

Diamond, Irene and A. Ornstein. 1990. *Reweaving the World: The Emergence of Ecofeminism.* San Francisco: Sierra Club Books.

Dillard, Annie. 1974. *Pilgrim at Tinker Creek.* New York: Harper and Row.

— 1983. *Teaching a Stone to Talk: Expeditions and Encounters.* New York: Harper and Row.

Distress Signals. 1986. Video. Director, John Waler. National Film Board of Canada (17 December).

Durning, Alan. 1991. 'Asking How Much is Enough?' In *State of the World, 1991: A Worldwatch Institute Report on Progress Toward a Sustainable Society,* ed. Lester R. Brown et al. New York: W. W. Norton.

— 1992. *How Much is Enough: The Consumer Society and the Future of the Earth.* New York: W. W. Norton.

Dyson, Freeman. 1985. *Weapons and Hope.* New York: Harper Collophon.

Ehrlich, Paul R. and Anne H. Ehrlich. 1981. *Extinction: The Causes and Consequences of the Disappearance of Species.* New York: Random House.

Eiseley, Loren. 1960. *The Immense Journey.* New York: Random House.

— 1972. *The Unexpected Universe*. New York: Harcourt Brace Jovanovich.

— 1978. *The Star Thrower*. New York: Times Books.

Eisler, Riane. 1988. *The Chalice and the Blade: Our History, Our Future*. San Francisco: Harper and Row.

— 1995. *Sacred Pleasure: Sex, Myth, and the Politics of the Body*. San Francisco. Harper San Francisco.

Eisler, Riane and David Loye. 1990. *The Partnership Way*. San Francisco: Harper and Row.

Ekins, Paul Hillman. 1992. *The Gaia Atlas of Green Economics*. Toronto: Anchor Books.

Eliade, Mircea. 1959. *Cosmos and History: The Myth of the Eternal Return*. New York: Harper Torchbooks.

Eliot, T. S. 1969. *The Complete Poems and Plays of T. S. Eliot*. London: Faber and Faber.

Ellul, Jaques. 1964. *The Technological Society*. New York: Vintage/Random House.

Environmental Education for Sustainable Societies and Global Responsibility. 1993. Environmental Education Treaty. Brazil.

Epp-Tiessen, Ester. 1990. 'Project Ploughshares.' Working Paper. Waterloo, Ontario.

Evereet-Green, Robert. 1997. 'Arts, Not IBM, Makes Kids Smarter.' *Toronto Star* (17 November).

Evernden, Neil. 1985. *The Natural Alien*. Toronto: University of Toronto Press.

Ewen, Stuart. 1976. *Captains of Consciousness: Advertising and the Social Roots of the Consumer Culture*. New York: McGraw Hill.

Fiske, John. 1978. *Reading Television*. London: Methuen.

Foley, Griff. 1993. *Adult Education and Capitalist Reorganization*. Sydney, Australia: University of Technology.

Fox, Matthew. 1983. *Original Blessing: A Primer in Creation Spirituality*. Santa Fe: Bear and Co.

— 1988. *The Coming of the Cosmic Christ*. San Francisco: Harper and Row.

— 1991. *Creation Spirituality*. San Francisco: Harper San Francisco.

Fox, Stephen. 1981. *John Muir and His Legacy: The American Conservation Movement*. Boston: Little, Brown.

Fox, Warwick. 1990. *Toward Transpersonal Ecology*. Boston: Shambhala.

Freire, Paolo. 1970. *The Pedagogy of the Oppressed*. New York: Seabury Press.

French, Marilyn. 1992. *The War Against Women*. Toronto: Summit.

Frye, Marilyn. 1983. *The Politics of Reality*. Freedom, CA: Crossing Press.

Galtung, Johann. 1982. *Environment, Development, and Military Activity*. Oslo: Universitetsforlaget.

Gare, Arran. 1995. *Postmodernism and the Environmental Crisis*. New York: Routledge.

Gayton, Don (ed.). 1996. *Landscapes of the Interior: Re-Explorations of Nature and the Human Spirit*. Gabriola Island, BC: New Society Publishers.

Georgescu-Roegen, Nicholas. 1971. *The Entrophy Law and the Economic Process.* Cambridge, MA: Harvard University Press.

Gerbner, George. 1970. 'Cultural Indicators: The Case of Violence in Televison Drama.' *Annals of the American Association of Political and Social Science* 338, 23.

Giddens, Anthony. 1990. *The Consequences of Modernity.* Stanford, CA: Stanford University Press.

— 1991. *Modernity and Self Identity: Self and Society in the Late Modern Age.* Stanford, CA: Standford University Press.

— 1994. *Beyond Left and Right: The Future of Radical Politics.* Stanford, CA: Stanford University Press.

Gimbutas, Marija. 1974. *The Gods and Goddesses of Old Europe, 7000 to 3500 B.C.: Myths, Legends, and Cult Images.* London and Berkeley, CA: Thames and Hudson and University of California Press.

Ginsberg, Morris. 1973. 'Progress in the Modern Era.' In *Dictionary of the History of Ideas,* ed. Philip Wiener. New York: Charles Scribner and Sons: 633–50.

Gioseffi, Daniela (ed.) 1993. *On Prejudice: A Global Perspective.* New York: Anchor Books.

Glendinning, Chellis. 1995. *My Name is Chellis and I'm Recovering from Western Civilization.* Boston: Shambhala.

Goldson, Rose. 1977. *The Show and Tell Machine.* New York: Delta.

Gourevitch, Phillip. 1995. 'Rwanda: A Case of Genocide.' *New Yorker* (March): 41–84.

Gramsci, Antonio. 1971. *Selections from Prison Notebooks.* New York: International Publishers.

Grant, George. 1983. *Modernity and Responsibility.* Toronto: University of Toronto Press.

Graveline, Fyre Jean. 1998. *Circle Works: Transforming Eurocentric Consciousness.* Halifax, Nova Scotia: Fernwood.

Griffin, David (ed.). 1988a. *The Reenchantment of Science: Postmodern Proposals.* New York: SUNY Press.

— (ed.). 1988b. *Spirituality and Society: Postmodern Visions.* New York: SUNY Press.

— (ed.). 1990. *Sacred Interconnections.* Albany, NY: State University of New York Press.

Griffin, Susan. 1978. *Woman and Nature: The Roaring Inside Her.* New York: Harper and Row.

— 1995. *The Eros of Everyday Life.* New York: Doubleday.

Grof, Stanislav. 1985. *Beyond the Brain.* Albany, NY: State University of New York Press.

Gutierrez, G. 1973. *A Theology of Liberation.* Marynoll, NY: Orbis Books.

Hall, Budd. 1996. 'Adult Education, Globalization and the Development of Global Civil Society.' World Congress of Comparative Education.

Hall, Budd and Edmund V. O'Sullivan. 1995. 'Transformative Learning: Contexts and Practices.' In *Empowerment: Toward Sustainable Development,* ed. N. Singh and V. Titi. Toronto: Fernwood.

Handa, Madan. 1982. *Manifesto for a Peaceful World Order: A Gandhian Perspective.* Toronto: Cosmic Way Publications.

Haraway, Donna. 1991. *Simians, Cyborgs and Women: The Reinvention of Nature.* New York: Routledge.

Harman, Willis. 1988. *Global Mind Change: The Promise of the Last Years of the Twentieth Century.* Indianapolis: Knowledge Systems Inc.

Hart, Mechhthild. 1995. 'Working and Education for Life.' In *Defense of the Life World: Critical Perspectives on Adult Learning,* ed. Michael Welton. Albany, NY: SUNY Press.

Henderson, Hazel. 1992. *Creating Alternative Futures.* Boston: Perigtine Books.

Herman, Edward and Noam Chomsky. 1988. *Manufacturing of Consent.* New York: Pantheon Books.

Herman, Judith. 1992. *Trauma and Recovery: The Aftermath of Violence from Domestic Abuse and Political Terror.* New York: Basic Books.

Heyward, Carter. 1989. *Touching Our Strength.* San Francisco: Harper.

Hillman, James. 1996. *The Soul's Code: In Search of Character and Calling.* New York: Random House.

Hofstadter, Richard. 1955. *Social Darwinism in American Thought.* New York: George Braziller.

Holland, Joe and Peter Henriot. 1984. *Social Analysis: Linking Faith and Social Justice.* Washington, DC: Orbis.

hooks, bell. 1994. *Teaching to Transgress.* New York: Routledge.

Hopkins, Gerard Manley. 1959. *The Journals and Papers of Gerard Manley Hopkins.* Toronto: Oxford University Press.

Hurtig, M. 1991. *The Betrayal of Canada.* Toronto: Stoddart.

Hutchins, Robert Maynard. 1959. *A General Introduction to the Great Books and to a Liberal Education.* Toronto: Encyclopaedia Britannica.

Hutchinson, David. 1998. *Growing Up Greed.* New York: Teachers College Press.

Isla, Ana. 1996. 'Downplaying Ecological Stress: Debt-for-Nature Swaps.' Unpublished MS. Toronto.

Jantsch, Erich. 1984. *The Self-Organizing Universe: Scientific and Human Implications of the Emerging Paradigm of Evolution.* New York: Pergamon Press.

Jensen, Derrick. 1996. 'Listening to the Land.' In *Landscapes of the Interior: Re-Explorations of Nature and the Human Spirit,* ed. Don Gayton. Gabriola Island, British Colombia: New Society Publishers.

Kaplan, Robert D. 1994. 'The Coming of Anarchy.' *Atlantic Monthly* (February): 44–76.

Katz, Michael. 1968. *The Irony of Early School Reform.* Cambridge, MA: Harvard University Press.

Kaufman, Michael. 1997. 'Working with Young Men to End Sexism.' *Orbit* 28, 1: 14–17.

Keen, Sam. 1994. *Hymns to an Unknown God.* New York: Bantam.

Kelley, Kevin (ed.). 1988. *The Home Planet.* Don Mills, Ontario: Addison-Wesley.

Kennedy, Paul. 1993. *Preparing for the Twenty-First Century*. New York: Harper.

Knowles, Malcolm. 1986. *Using Learning Contracts: Pratical Approaches to Individualizing and Structuring Learning*. San Francisco: Josey-Bass.

Knudston, Peter and David Suzuki. 1992. *The Wisdom of Elders*. Toronto: Stoddart.

Korten, D. 1991. 'People Centered Development: An Alternative for a World in Crisis.' People Centered Development Forum, Manilla, Philippines.

— *When Corporations Rule the World*. 1995. West Hartford, CT: Kumarian Press.

Kothari, Rajni. 1988. *Transformation and Survival: In Search of Humane World Order*. Delhi: Ajanta Publications.

Kropotkin, P. 1895. *Mutual Aid*. Brighton: Horizon Press.

La Chapelle, Dolores. 1988. *Sacred Land, Sacred Sex, Rapture of the Deep: Concerning Deep Ecology and Celebrating Life*. Silverton, CO: Fine Hill Arts.

Larkin, June. 1997. 'Confronting Sexual Harassment in Schools.' *Orbit* 28, 1.

Lasch, Christopher. 1978. *The Culture of Narcissism*. New York: W. W. Norton.

— 1989. 'Progress: The Last Superstition.' *Tikkun* 4, 3 (May\June): 27–30.

Latouche, Serge. 1993. *In the Wake of the Affluent Society: An Exploration of Post-Development*. London: Zed Books.

Leopold, Aldo. 1949. *A Sand County Almanac*. New York: Oxford University Press.

Lerner, Michael. 1994. *Jewish Renewal: A Path to Healing and Transformation*. New York: Grosset/Putnam.

— 1996. *The Politics of Meaning*. Reading, MA: Addison-Wesley,

Lewy, Guenter. 1974. *Religion and Revolution*. New York: Oxford University Press.

Lifton, Robert Jay. 1993. *The Protean Self*. New York: Basic Books.

Livingstone, David (ed.). 1987. *Critical Pedagogy and Cultural Power*. South Hadley, MA: Bergin and Garvey.

Lopez, Barry Holstun. 1986. *Arctic Dreams*. New York: Charles Scribner and Sons.

Lorde, Audre. 1978. *The Uses of the Erotic: The Erotic as Power*. New York: Out and Out Books.

— 1990. 'Age, Race, Class, and Sex: Women Redefining Difference.' In *Out There: Marginalization and Contemporary Culture*, ed. Russell Ferguson, Martha Gever, Trinh Minh-Ha and Cornell West. Cambridge, MA: MIT Press.

Lovelock, James E. 1979. *Gaia: A New Look at Life on Earth*. New York: Oxford University Press.

— 1987. *Gaia: A Model for Planetary and Cellular Survival*. Boston, MA: Lindisfarne Press.

— 1988. *The Ages of Gaia: A Biography of our Living Earth*. Boston, MA: Lindisfarne Press.

Lynn, Marion and Eimear O'Neill. 1995. 'Families, Power, and Violence.' In *Canadian Families: Diversity, Conflict, and Change*, ed. Ann Duffy and Mancy Mandell. Toronto: Harcourt Brace: 271–305.

Lyons, Thomas and Edmund V. O'Sullivan. (1992). 'Educating for a Global Perspective.' *Orbit* 1.

McDermott, R. (ed.). 1987. *The Essential Aurobindo*. Rochester, VT: Inner Tradition/Lindisfarne Press.

McGaa, Ed Eagle Man. 1990. *Mother Earth Spirituality: Native American Paths to Healing Ourselves and Our World*. San Francisco: Harper San Francisco.

McKibben, Bill. 1989. *The End of Nature*. New York: Random House.

MacMurray, John. 1957. *The Self as Agent*. London: Faber and Faber.

— *Persons in Relation*. 1961. London: Faber and Faber.

McPhail, Thomas. 1981. *Electronic Colonialism*. Beverly Hills, CA: Sage Publications.

Macy, Joanna. 1983. *Despair and Power in the Nuclear Age*. Philadelphia: New Society Publishers.

— 1989. 'Awakening to the Ecological Self.' In *Healing the Wounds*, ed. Judith Plant. Toronto: Between the Lines.

— 1991. *World as Lover, World as Self*. Berkeley, CA: Parallax Press.

Maitreya. 1988. *The Gospel of Peace*. Toronto: Universal Way Publications.

Mander, Jerry. 1991. *In the Absence of the Sacred: The Failure of Technology and the Survival of Indian Nations*. San Francisco: Sierra Club Books.

Mander, Jerry and Edward Goldsmith. 1996. *The Case Against the Global Economy*. San Francisco: Sierra Club Books.

Margulis, Lynn. 1987. *Microcosmos: Four Billion Years of Evolution from Our Microbial Ancestors*. London: George Allen and Unwin.

Margulis, Lynn and Karlene Schwartz. 1982. *Five Kingdoms: An Illustrated Guide to the Phyla of Life on Earth*. San Francisco: Freeman.

Mason, Mike. 1997. *Development and Disorder: A History of the Third World Since 1945*. Toronto: Between the Lines.

Max-Neef, Manfred E. A. and Martin Hopenhayen. 1989. 'Another Development: Human Scale Development.' *Development Dialogue* 1: 17–61.

Meizerow, Jack. 1995. 'Transformation Theory of Adult Learning.' In *Defense of the Life World: Critical Perspectives on Adult Learning*, ed. Michael Welton. Albany, NY: SUNY Press.

Menzies, Heather. 1989. *Fast Forward: How Technology is Changing Your Life*. Toronto: Macmillan of Canada.

Merchant, Carolyn. 1980. *The Death of Nature: Women, Ecology, and the Scientific Revolution*. New York: Harper and Row.

— 1995. *Earthcare*. New York: Routledge.

Merton, Thomas. 1967. *Mystics and Zen Masters*. New York: Delta Books.

— 1973. *The Asian journals of Thomas Merton*. New York: New Directions Publication.

Metzner, Ralph. 1993. 'The Split Between Spirit and Nature in European Consciousness.' *Trumpeter* 10, 1.

Mies, Maria. 1986. *Patriarchy and Accumulation on a World Scale: Women in the International Division of Labor*. London: Zed Books.

Mies, Maria and Vandana Shiva. 1993. *Ecofeminism*. Halifax, Nova Scotia: Fernwood.

Milbrath, Lester, W. 1989. *Envisioning a Sustainable Society: Learning Our Way Out*. Albany, NY: State University of New York Press.

Miles, Angela. 1996. *Integrative Feminisms: Building Global Visions*. New York: Routledge.

Miller, John. 1994. *The Contemplative Practitioner.* Toronto: OISE Press.

— 1996. *The Holistic Curriculum: Revised and Expanded Edition.* Toronto: OISE Press.

Miller, R. (ed.). 1993. *The Renewal of Meaning in Education.* Brandon, VT: Holistic Education Press.

Mitter, Swasti. 1986. *Common Fate Common Bond: Women in the Global Economy.* London: Pluto Press.

Mische, Patricia. 1989. 'Ecological Security in an Interdependent World'. *Breakthrough: A Publication of Global Education Associates* 1 (4) Summer–Fall.

Moffett, J. 1994. *The Universal Schoolhouse.* San Francisco: Josey-Bass.

Montessori, Maria. 1973. *The Education of the Human Potential.* Madras, India: Kalakshetra Publications.

Moore, Thomas. 1992. *Care of the Soul.* New York: HarperCollins.

— 1994. *Soul Mates: Honoring the Mysteries of Love and Relationship.* New York: HarperCollins.

Mumford, Lewis. 1961. *The City in History: Its Origins, Its Transformations, and Its Prospects.* New York: Harcourt, Brace, and World.

Myers, Norman (ed.). 1984. *Gaia: An Atlas of Planet Management.* Garden City, NY: Anchor/Doubleday.

Neihardt, John G. 1972. *Black Elk Speaks: Being the Life Story of a Holy Man of the Oglala Sioux.* New York: Washington Square Press.

Neisser, Ulric. 1967. *Cognitive Psychology.* New York: Appleton Century Crofts.

Nelson, Joyce. 1989. *Sultans of Sleaze.* Toronto: Between the Lines.

New Internationalist. 1990. 'The Poor Step Up Trade Wars'. 294 (February).

— 1991. 'Test Tube Coup: Biotechs Global Takeover'. 217 (March).

— 1992. 230 (April).

— 1997. 'Gene dream'. 293 (August).

Noble, David. 1977. *America by Design: Science, Technology, and the Rise of Corporate Capitalism.* New York: Oxford University Press.

— 1992. *A World Without Women: The Christian Clerical Culture of Western Science.* New York: Oxford University Press.

Nozick, Marcia. 1992. *No Place Like Home.* Ottawa: Canadian Council of Social Development.

Oliver, Donald W. and Kathleen Waldron Gershman. 1989. *Education, Modernity and Fractured Meaning: Toward a Process Theory of Teaching and Learning.* Albany, NY: State University of New York Press.

Oliver, Mary. 1992. *New and Selected Poems.* Boston: Beacon Press.

O'Neill, Eimear. 1998. 'From Global Economies to Local Cuts: Globalization and Structural Change in Our Own Backyard.' In *Confronting the Cuts: A Sourcebook for Women in Ontario*, ed. L. Ricciutelli, J. Larkin and E. O'Neill. Toronto: Inanna Publications and Education Inc.: 3–11.

Ornstein, Robert and Paul Ehrlich. 1989. *New World New Mind.* New York: Simon and Schuster.

Orr, David, W. 1992. *Ecological Literacy: Education and the Transition to a Postmodern World.* Albany, NY: State University of New York Press.

Ortega y Gasset, José. 1957. *The Revolt of the Masses*. New York, W. W. Norton.

O'Sullivan, Edmund. 1980. 'Can Values Be Taught?' In *Moral Development and Socialization*, ed. E. Turiel. Boston: Allyn and Bacon.

— 1983. 'Computers, Culture and Educational Futures: A Critical Appraisal.' *Interchange* 4, 3 (Winter): 17–26.

— 1984. *Critical Psychology: An Interpretation of the Personal World*. New York: Plenum Press.

— 1985. 'Computers, Culture and Educational Futures: A Meditation on Mindstorms.' *Interchange* 16, 3 (Fall): 1–18.

— 1990. *Critical Psychology and Critical Pedagogy*. New York. Bergin and Garvey.

Otto, Rudolph. 1969. *The Idea of the Holy*. New York: Oxford University Press.

Palmer, Parker. 1993. *To Know as We are Known*. San Francisco: Harper and Row.

Paz, Octavio. 1995. *The Double Flame: Love and Eroticism*. New York: Harcourt Brace and Co.

Peterson, Scott. 1990. *Native American Prophesies: Examining the History, Wisdom and Startling Predictions of Visionary Native Americans*. New York: Paragon House.

Phillips, Charles. 1957. *The Development of Education in Canada*. Toronto: W. J. Gage and Co.

Pierce, Carol Wagner. 1994. *A Male/Female Continuum: Paths to Colleagueship*. Lacona, NH: New Dynamics Publications.

Pike, Graham and David Selby. 1988. *Global Teacher, Global Learner*. Toronto: Hodder and Stoughton.

Plant, Judith (ed.). 1989. *Healing the Wounds*. Toronto: Between the Lines.

Postel, Sandra. 1992. 'Denial in a Decisive Decade.' In *State of the World, 1992: A Worldwatch Institute Report on Progress Toward a Sustainable Society*, ed. Lester R. Brown et al. New York: W. W. Norton.

Prigogine, Ilya and Isabelle Stengers. 1984. *Order Out of Chaos: Man's New Dialogue with Nature*. New York: Bantam.

The Progress of Nations. 1997. New York: UNICEF.

Purpel, David. 1989. *The Moral and Spiritual Crisis in Education: A Curriculum for Justice and Compassion in Education*. Grangy, MA: Bergin and Garvey.

Quarter, Jack. 1992. *Canada's Social Economy*. Toronto: James Lorimer and Co.

Quarter, Jack, and Fred Matthews. 1987. 'Back to the Basics.' In *Critical Pedagogy and Cultural Power*, ed. David Livingstone. Massachusetts: Bergin and Garvey: 99–119.

Ransom, David. 1992. 'Green Justice.' *New Internationalist* 30 (April).

Reed, Carole Ann. 1994. 'The Omission of Anti-Semitism in Anti-Racism.' *Canadian Woman Studies/les cahiers de la femme* 14, 2 (Spring): 68–71.

Regehr, E. 1996. 'Weapons and war: Arms trade control as conflict resolution'. *Project Ploughshares Monitor* (September).

Renner, Michael. 1991. 'Assessing the Military's War on the Environment.' In *State of the World, 1991 A Worldwatch Institute Report on Progress Toward a Sustainable Society*, ed. Lester R. Brown. New York: W. W. Norton.

Rifkin, Jeremy. 1981. *Entropy.* New York: Viking.

— 1991. *Biosphere Politics: A New Consciousness for a New Century.* New York: Crown.

— 1995. *The End of Work.* New York: Jeremy Tarcher/Putnam Books,

Rifkin, Jeremy and Nicanor Perlas. 1983. *Algeny.* New York: Viking.

Roberts, W. Bacher. 1993. *Get a Life: A Green Cure For Canada's Economic Blues.* Toronto: Get A Life Publishing House.

Roman, Leslie and Linda Eyre (eds). 1997. *Dangerous Territories: Struggles for Difference and Equality.* London: Routledge.

Rosen, Edward. 1973. 'Cosmology from Antiquity to 1850.' In *Dictionary of the History of Ideas,* ed. Philip Wiener. New York: Charles Scribner and Sons.

Ross, Rupert. 1996. *Returning to the Teachings.* Toronto: Penguin Books.

Roszak, T. 1978. *Person/Plant: The Creative Disintegration of Industrial Society.* Garden City, NY: Doubleday.

Rowledge, D. and L. Keeth. 1991. 'We've Gotta Have It: Economic Growth as an Addiction.' *Environment network News:* 3–5.

Runes, D. 1955. *The Dictionary of Philosophy.* New Jersey: Littlefield Adams.

Russell, Peter. 1983. *The Global Brain.* Los Angeles: J. P. Tarcher.

Ryan, J. C. 1992. 'Conserving Biological Diversity.' In *State of the World, 1992. A Worldwatch Institute Report on Progress Toward a Sustainable Society,* ed. Lester R. Brown. New York: W. W. Norton.

Sachs, Wolfgang. 1992. 'Development.' *New Internationalist* 202.

Sagan, Carl. 1980. *Cosmos.* New York: Random House.

Sahtouris, Elisabet. 1989. *Gaia: The Human Journey from Chaos to Cosmos.* New York: Pocket Books Collophon.

Said, Edward. 1979. *Orientalism.* New York: Vintage Books.

— *Culture and Imperialism.* 1993. New York: Alfred A. Knopf.

Sale, Kirkpatrick. 1980. *Human Scale.* New York: Coward McCann and Geohegan.

— 1985. *Dwellers in the Land: The Bioregional Vision.* San Francisco: Sierra Club Books.

Sardello, Robert. 1994. *Facing the World with Soul: The Reimagination of Modern Life.* New York: HarperCollins.

— 1995. *Love and the Soul: Creating a Future for Earth.* New York: HarperCollins.

Schaef, A. 1987. *When Society Becomes Addict.* San Francisco: Harper and Row.

Schorer, Mark. 1946. *William Blake: The Politics of Vision.* New York: Vintage Books.

Schiller, Herbert. 1983. *The World Crisis and the New Information Technologies.* San Diego: Paper.

Schweickart, Russell. 1988. Preface. In *The Home Planet,* ed. Kevin Kelley. Don Mills, Ontario: Addison-Wesley.

Seager, Joni. 1993. *Earth Follies: Coming to Feminist Terms with the Global Environmental Crisis.* New York: Routledge.

— 1995. *The New State of the Earth Atlas,* 2nd edn. New York: Touchstone.

Seed, John and Joanna Macy. 1988. *Thinking Like a Mountain: Towards a Council of All Beings.* Philadelphia: New Society Publishers.

Selby, D. 1995. *Earthkind: A Teachers' Handbook on Humane Education*. Stoke-on Trent: Trentum.

Sheldrake, Rupert. 1988. *The Presence of The Past: Morphic Resonance and the Habits of Nature*. New York: Times Books.

— 1994. *The Rebirth of Nature and God*. Rochester, VT: Park Street Press.

Shiva, Vandana. 1989. *Staying Alive: Women, Ecology and Development*. London: Zed Books.

— 1992. 'Global Bullies: Tread Gently on the Earth.' *New Internationalist* (April).

— 1995. *Monocultures of the Mind: Perspectives on Biodiversity and Biotechnology*. London: Zed Books.

Sioui, George. 1992. *Amerindian Autohistory: An Essay on the Foundation of a Social Ethic*. Montreal: McGill University Press.

Smart, N. 1997. *Dimensions of the Sacred*. London: Fontana.

Smith, Huston. 1992. *Forgotten Truth: The Common Vision of the World's Religions*. New York: Harper.

Smith, James. 1993 'Foreword.' *New Internationalist* 308.

Spretnak, Charlene. 1978. *The Spiritual Dimension of Green Politics*. Santa Fe: Bear and Co.

— 1991. *States of Grace: The Recovery of Meaning in the Postmodern Age*. San Francisco: Harper and Row.

Starhawk. 1979. *The Spiral Dance: A Rebirth of the Ancient Religion of the Great Goddess*. San Francisco: Harper and Row.

— 1997. *The Pagan Book of Living and Dying*. San Francisco: Harper San Francisco.

Stone, Merlin. 1976. *When God Was a Woman*. New York: Harvest.

Storm, Hyemeyohsts. 1972. *Seven Arrows*. New York: Ballantine.

Storr, Anthony. 1988. *Solitude*. London: Fontana.

Suzuki, David and Peter Knudston. 1988. *Genethics: The Ethics of Engineering Life*. Toronto: Stoddart.

Swimme, Brian. 1984. *The Universe is a Green Dragon: A Cosmic Creation Story*. Santa Fe, NM: Bear and Co.

— 1996. *The Hidden Heart of the Cosmos*. Marynoll, New York: Orbis Books.

Swimme, Brian and Thomas Berry. 1992. *The Universe Story: An Autobiography from Planet Earth*. San Francisco: Harper and Row.

Taylor, Charles. 1991. *The Malaise of Modernity*. Toronto: Anansi.

'Test Tube Coup: Biotech's Global Takeover.' 1991. *New Internationalist* 217 (March).

Thich Nhat Hanh. 1992. *Touching Peace: Practicing the Art of Mindful Living*. Berkeley, CA: Parallax Press.

— 1994. *A Joyful Path: Community Transformation and Peace*. Berkeley, CA: Parallax Press.

— 1996. *Breathe! You Are Alive*. Berkeley, CA: Parallax Press.

Thomas, Lewis. 1975. *The Lives of a Cell: Notes of a Biology Watcher*. New York: Bantam.

Trend, David *Crisis of meaning in Culture + Education*

— 1980. *The Medusa and the Snail: More Notes of a Biology Watcher.* New York: Bantam.

— 1984. *Late Night Thoughts on Listening to Mahler's Ninth Symphony.* New York: Bantam.

Thompson, William Irvin. 1987. *Gaia: A Way of Knowing.* Barrington, MA: Lindisfarne Press.

Tough, Alan. 1981. *Learning Without a Teacher.* Toronto: OISE Press.

Toulmin, Stephen. 1985. *The Return to Cosmology.* Berkeley, CA: University of California Press.

Turk, Jim. 1992. 'Training is the Answer'. In *Training for What? Labour Perspectives on Job Training,* ed. Nancy Jackson. Toronto: Our Schools/Ourselves Foundation.

Turner, Frederick. 1980. *Beyond Geography: The Western Spirit Against the Wilderness.* New York: Viking Press.

Unger, Roberto Mangabeira. 1975. *Knowledge and Politics.* New York: Free Press.

Wackernagel, M. and W. Rees. 1996. *Our Ecological Footprint: Reducing Human Impact on the Earth.* Gabriola Island, BC: New Society Publishers.

Walker, Alice. 1997. *Anything We Love Can be Saved: A Writer's Activism.* New York: Random House.

Wangoola, Paul and Frank Youngman. 1996. *Towards A Transformative Political Economy of Adult Education.* De Kalb, IL: Northern Illinois Press.

Waring, Marilyn. 1988. *If Women Counted: A New Feminist Economics.* San Francisco: Harper and Row.

Weber, Max. 1958. *The Spirit of Capitalism and the Protestant Ethic.* New York: Charles Scribner and Sons.

Weil, Andrew. 1997. *8 Weeks to Optimum Health.* New York: Alfred A. Knopf.

Welton, M. 1995. 'In Defense of the Lifeworld.' In *Defense of the Life World: Critical Perspectives on Adult Learning,* ed. Michael Welton. Albany, NY: SUNY Press.

Wexler, Philip. 1996. *Holy Sparks: Social Theory, Education and Religion.* Toronto: Canadian Scholar Press.

Wiener, Philip (ed.). 1973. *Dictionary of the History of Ideas.* New York: Charles Scribner and Sons.

Wilber, Ken. 1995. *Sex, Ecology, Spirituality: The Spirit of Evolution.* Boston: Shambhala.

— 1996. *A Brief History of Everything.* Boston: Shambhala.

— 1997. *The Eye of the Spirit: An Integral Vision for a World Gone Slightly Mad.* Boston: Shambhala.

Williams, Raymond. 1976. *Key Words: A Vocabulary of Culture and Society.* London: Fontana.

Willoya, William. 1962. *Warriors of the Rainbow: Strange and Prophetic Dreams of the Indian Peoples.* Happy Camp, CA: Naturegraph Publishers.

Wishik, Heather and Carol Pierce. 1995. *Sexual Orientation and Identity.* Lacona, NH: New Dynamics.

Wolf, E. C. 1988. 'Avoiding a Mass Extinction of Species.' In *State of the World,*

1988: A Worldwatch Institute Report on Progress Toward a Sustainable Society, eds Lester R. Brown et al. New York: W. W. Norton.

Wolf, Sandra. 1994. *Engendering Equity: Transforming Curriculum.* Toronto: Ministry of Education of Ontario.

World Guide 1997/1998: Alternative Reference to Countries of the Planet. 1997. World of Women, Instituto Del Tercer Mundo.

Worster, Donald. 1977. *Nature's Economy: A History of Ecological Ideas.* Cambridge: Cambridge University Press.

Wynne, Edward. 1987. 'Managing Effective Schools: The Moral Element.' In *Educational Policy for Effective Schools,* ed. Mark Holmes. Toronto: OISE Press.

Yeats, William Butler. 1983. 'The Second Coming.' In *Modern Poetry,* ed. Maynard Mack. New York: New American Library.

Young, Louise. 1983. *The Blue Planet: A Celebration of the Earth.* New York: New American Library.

Zarate, Jose. 1994 'Racism and Indigeneous Education.' *Orbit* 25, 2.

Index

Nietscmann, Bernard, 147
non-governmental organizations, 253–4
non-violence, 135, 147, 161, 173
Northern Ireland, 149–50, 172, 246, 249
Nozick, Marcia, 118; *No Place Like Home*, 245
nuclear industry, and 'omnicide', 141
'nuclear priesthood', 142
nuclear waste, 140
nuclear weapons, 135, 140, 141, 142

Odyssey project, Northern Ireland, 174
Oliver, Mary, 235
Omaha Blessing, 226–7
O'Neill, Eimear, 36–7
organicity, 30, 95, 99
Ornstein, Robert, 199
Orr, David, 202, 244
O'Sullivan, Edmund: *Critical Psychology and Critical Pedagogy*, 63; *Critical Psychology: An Interpretation of the Personal World*, 63
Otto, Rudolf, 269
outrage at oppression, 274
ozone layer, depletion of, 17, 19

paradigm, notion of, 8
patriarchy, 29, 128, 133, 134–5, 137, 138–40, 141, 144–7, 160, 164, 165, 5172, 173, 175, 250, 251, 277; and relation to modern science, 86–90; interpretations of, 136
Paz, Octavio, 275, 277
peace education, 133–76; in Northern Ireland, 173–5
Perlas, Nicanor, 91, 113, 114, 115
Piaget, Jean, 50, 211
Pierce, Carole, 165
Pike, Graham, 65
planetary consciousness, 19, 180, 181–3, 194, 201, 202, 207, 256; educating for, 228–32
planned obsolescence, 15–16
Plant, Judith, 266
Plato, 80, 180, 275; *The Republic*, 79
pollution, 18, 157, 191, 222; by armed forces, 139, 140
post-modern education, 28–31
post-traumatic stress syndrome, 227
Postel, Sandra, 17, 131
postmodernity, 1, 3, 28, 45, 66, 100, 181, 197, 222; reconstructive, 182
poverty, 20, 21, 25, 58, 110, 119, 140, 158, 161, 170, 221; complexity of, 241; definition of, 109

Prigogine, Ilya, 181, 209, 230
primal matrix, 225–7, 261; disruption of, 227–8
privilege, 133, 134; emancipation from, 130; global, 128, 131, 157; location of, 133–4; male, 164, 165; northern, 47, 129; white, 162
progress, 40, 49, 50, 52, 107; notion of, 104–7; symbolism of, 126
progressive technozoic current, 47, 49–54
Ptolemy: cosmology of, 81, 82, 86; theory of epicycles, 80
Purpel, David, *The Moral and Spiritual Crisis of Education*, 272–4

quality of life, education for *see* education, for quality of life

race, 34, 37, 160; hierarchies of, 8
racism, 133, 134, 147–55, 162, 163, 246, 248, 251; environmental, 153–5; of British colonialism, 150–1; stereotypes, 151; systemic, 148–51
rainforests, 170; destruction of, 33, 140
Ransom, David, 157
rape, 26, 144, 278
rationalism, critique of, 57, 64
rationality, 28, 51; decontextualized, 143
Reagan, Ronald, 52, 105, 142
Reed, Carole Ann, 149
relatedness, 224, 261
religion, 97, 222, 224, 259–60, 267; hatred within, 249
Renner, Michael, 140
Rifkin, Jeremy: and Nicanor Perlas, *Algeny*, 91, 113, 114, 115; *Biosphere Politics*, 118, 194–5; *The End of Work*, 167–8
rightwing parties, 100, 236
romanticism, 56, 57, 65
Russell, Peter, *The Global Brain*, 213
Ryan, John, 170

Sachs, Wolfgang, 108, 109
sacred: earth as, 68; location of, 60
sacred dimension, 23, 261, 264, 269, 274, 277, 278, 281
Sagan, Carl, *Cosmos*, 72, 188, 189, 265
Sahtouris, Elisabet, *Gaia: The Human Journey from Chaos to Cosmos*, 73, 184, 265, 270
Said, Edward, 8, 107, 151, 163
Said, Homi Bhabha, 151